"*The repackaging of classics is a tried and trusted winner, but Tim Coates has come up with something entirely original: the repackaging of history. His* **uncovered editions** *collect papers from the archive of The Stationery Office into verbatim narratives, so, for instance, in* UFOs in the House of Lords *we get a hilarious recreation, directly from Hansard, of a nutty debate that took place in 1979 … This is inspired publishing, not only archivally valuable but capable of bringing the past back to life without the usual filter of academic or biographer.*" **Guardian**

"The Irish Uprising *is a little treasure of a book and anyone with an interest in Irish history will really enjoy it. Its structure is extremely unusual as it is compiled from historic official reports published by the British government from 1914 to 1920 … For anyone studying this period of history* The Irish Uprising *is a must as the correspondence and accounts within it are extremely illuminating and the subtle nuances of meaning can be teased out of the terms and phrasing to be more revelatory than the actual words themselves.*" **Irish Press, Belfast**

"*Voyeurs of all ages will enjoy the original text of the Denning report on Profumo. It is infinitely superior to the film version of the scandal, containing such gems as: 'One night I was invited to a dinner party at the home of a very, very rich man. After I arrived, I discovered it was rather an unusual dinner party. All the guests had taken off their clothes … The most intriguing person was a man with a black mask over his face. At first I thought this was a party gimmick. But the truth was that this man is so well known and holds such a responsible position that he did not want to be associated with anything improper.'*" **Times Higher Education Supplement**

"*Very good to read … insight into important things … inexorably moving … If you want to read about the Titanic, you won't read a better thing … a revelation.*" **Open Book, BBC Radio 4**

"*Congratulations to The Stationery Office for unearthing and reissuing such an enjoyable vignette*" [*on Wilfrid Blunt's Egyptian Garden*] **The Spectator**

uncovered editions
www.uncovered-editions.co.uk

Series editor: Tim Coates
Managing editor: Michele Staple

Other titles in the series

The Amritsar Massacre: General Dyer in the Punjab, 1919
Attack on Pearl Harbor, 1941
Bloody Sunday, 1972: Lord Widgery's Report
The Boer War: Ladysmith and Mafeking, 1900
British Battles of World War I, 1914–15
The British Invasion of Tibet: Colonel Younghusband, 1904
Defeat at Gallipoli: the Dardanelles Commission Part II, 1915–16
D Day to VE Day: General Eisenhower's Report, 1944–45
Escape from Germany, 1939–45
Florence Nightingale and the Crimea, 1854–55
The Irish Uprising, 1914–21
John Profumo and Christine Keeler, 1963
The Judgment of Nuremberg, 1946
King Guezo of Dahomey, 1850–52
Letters of Henry VIII, 1526–29
Lord Kitchener and Winston Churchill: the Dardanelles Commission Part I, 1914–15
The Loss of the Titanic, 1912
R.101: the Airship Disaster, 1930
Rillington Place, 1949
The Russian Revolution, 1917
The Siege of Kars, 1855
The Siege of the Peking Embassy, 1900
The Strange Story of Adolf Beck
Tragedy at Bethnal Green
Travels in Mongolia, 1902
UFOs in the House of Lords, 1979
War in the Falklands, 1982
War 1914: Punishing the Serbs
War 1939: Dealing with Adolf Hitler
Wilfrid Blunt's Egyptian Garden: Fox-hunting in Cairo

Other compendium titles in the *uncovered editions* series

The World War I Collection
The World War II Collection
Tragic Journeys

Forthcoming titles

The Assassination of John F Kennedy, 1963
The Cuban Missile Crisis, 1962
The Great Train Robbery, 1963
Mr Hosie's Journey to Tibet, 1904
St Valentine's Day Massacre, 1929
Trials of Oscar Wilde
UFOs in the US, 1947

uncovered editions

THE
SIEGE
COLLECTION

∘◦⋈◦∘

THE SIEGE OF KARS, 1855

THE BOER WAR: LADYSMITH AND MAFEKING, 1900

THE SIEGE OF THE PEKING
EMBASSY, 1900

London: The Stationery Office

Applications for reproduction should be made in writing to
The Stationery Office Limited, St Crispins, Duke Street, Norwich NR3 1PD.

ISBN 0 11 702464 3

The Siege of Kars, 1855 was first published in 1856 as *Papers relative to Military Affairs in Asiatic Turkey, and the Defence and Capitulation of Kars.*
© Crown copyright
Also available separately, ISBN 0117024546, © The Stationery Office 2000.

The Boer War: Ladysmith and Mafeking, 1900 was first published by HMSO as Cd. 457 and 458 (1901), and Cd. 463, 968 and 987 (1902).
© Crown copyright
Also available separately, ISBN 0117024082, © The Stationery Office 1999.

The Siege of the Peking Embassy, 1900 was first published by HMSO as Cd 257 (1900) and Cd 442 (1901).
© Crown copyright
Also available separately, ISBN 0117024562, © The Stationery Office 2000.

A CIP catalogue record for this book is available from the British Library.

Cover photograph © Public Record Office.
All maps produced by Sandra Lockwood of Artworks Design, Norwich.

Typeset by J&L Composition Ltd, Filey, North Yorkshire.
Printed in the United Kingdom by The Stationery Office, London.
TJ4246 C30 8/01 652726 19585

CONTENTS

About the series

Uncovered editions are historic official papers which have not previously been available in a popular form, and have been chosen for the quality of their story-telling. Some subjects are familiar, but others are less well known. Each is a moment in history.

About the series editor, Tim Coates

Tim Coates studied at University College, Oxford and at the University of Stirling. After working in the theatre for a number of years, he took up bookselling and became managing director, firstly of Sherratt and Hughes bookshops, and then of Waterstone's. He is known for his support for foreign literature, particularly from the Czech Republic. The idea for *uncovered editions* came while searching through the bookshelves of his late father-in-law, Air Commodore Patrick Cave, OBE. He is married to Bridget Cave, has two sons, and lives in London.

Tim Coates welcomes views and ideas on the *uncovered editions* series. He can be e-mailed at tim.coates@theso.co.uk

THE SIEGE OF KARS, 1855

DESPATCHES RELATIVE TO THE DEFENCE AND CAPITULATION OF KARS

CONTENTS

SELECTED GLOSSARY

acquirement	experience
admission	consent
advices	official intelligence
agio	exchange rate fee
approbation	approval
arabas	country carts
assigned	referred to
bar	bank at the mouth of a river or harbour
barbette	platform for heavy guns
Bashi-Bozouk	member of the notoriously brutal Turkish Irregulars of the 19th century
breastworks	hastily constructed fieldworks
cantonment	temporary military quarters
casus belli	justified by war
chaussée	route
Circassia	region in the northwest Russian Caucasus, on the Black Sea
circumjacent	surrounding
condign	worthy
conducing	leading
culvert	arched channel for carrying water under a road
drachm	dram
dragoman	interpreter or professional guide
driblet	trickle
échelon	formation of troops, in parallel divisions
embrasure	opening in a wall for a cannon
épaulement	sidework of a battery or fieldwork
equinoctial	equal day and night
estafette	military courier or express
exactions	oppressive demands
firman	decree
grape	shot that shatters
Horse	Cavalry
imposts	taxes
insalubrity	unhealthy conditions
invest	lay siege to
Koordistan	Kurdistan

Koords	Kurds
league	1.376 modern English miles
magazines	storehouses
malversation	corrupt administration
mudir	governor of village or canton
Muharem	the first month of the Muslim year
Mussulman	Muslim
nowise	in no way
Pasha	a title for a high-ranking member of the Turkish Army
piastre	unit of currency in former Middle East; piece of eight
picquet	picket
Porte, the	Turkish imperial government (after the Sublime Porte: the chief office of the Ottoman government at Constantinople
prefer	present (charges)
prevision	foresight, prediction
proximate	approximate
Ramazan	Ramadan
rencontre	encounter
redif	militia
redoubt	fieldwork enclosed on all sides
rescript	edict, decree
Roumelia	former Turkish province in the Balkans
sanguinary	bloody
Seraskier	the Turkish Minister for War
Seraskierat	Turkish war office at Constantinople
signal	remarkable, significant
specie	coined money
Therapia	village north of Constantinople
treat with	negotiate
tumbril	two-wheeled military cart
vali	governor of a Turkish province
vaunting	boastful
victualling	feeding
vidette	mounted sentry

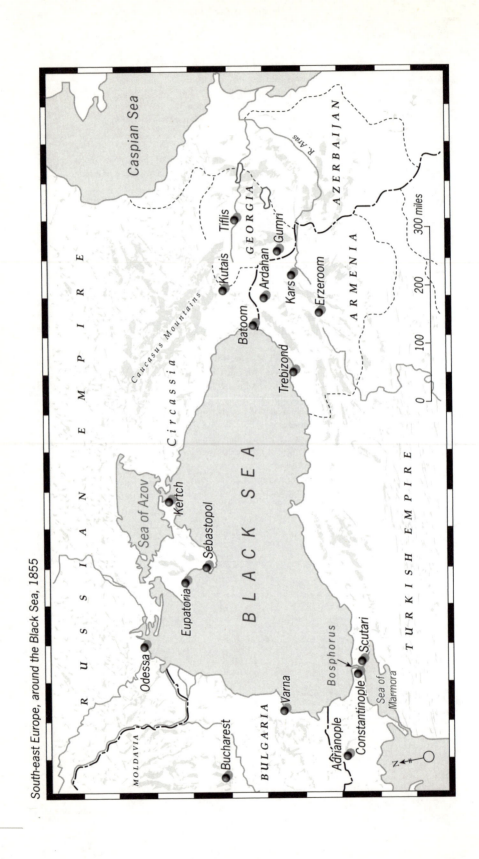

South-east Europe, around the Black Sea, 1855

In June 1855, while the British were fighting alongside the French and the Turkish armies against the Russians in the Crimean War (1854–56), a little-known but serious siege in the eastern corner of Turkey was begun. It was to endure for five months, exacting a terrible toll on the inhabitants and military garrison of that besieged city. That city was Kars, a fortress set within the mountains of the Caucasus, and close to the border of the Russian and Turkish empires.

The causes of the Crimean War were complex, but one of its main purposes, as far as the British and French were concerned, was to stop the expansion of the Russian Empire in the region of the Black Sea. To this end, the British were giving assistance to the Turkish army by "lending out" their experienced officers to lead garrisons and train soldiers. This often led to a clash of cultures, which is evident in the despatches that follow. The ways and methods of the Turkish army were not those with which a British officer was familiar.

In reading the despatches that tell the story of the siege of Kars, it is helpful to know that Lord Stratford de Redcliffe was the British ambassador in the Turkish capital of Constantinople, and James Brant was the British consul in Erzeroom, one of the nearest cities to Kars. Stratford de Redcliffe's main pre-occupation was the support of the British army before Sebastopol, with the innumerable problems of supply and medical care that had arisen. Sebastopol in fact fell to the Allies in September 1855, while the siege of Kars was in its third month.

In London, the Earl of Clarendon was the Secretary of State for Foreign Affairs and Lord Panmure was the Secretary of State for War in the administration of Lord Palmerston, which was formed in February 1855. The central character, however, was General William Fenwick Williams (1800–83), a British soldier who was appointed British Military Commissioner with the Turkish Army in Asia in 1854. When news reached him of an impending attack on Kars by the Russian army, he hastened to Kars forthwith, arriving in June 1855, and began organising the garrison there. Vassif Pasha was the commander of the Turkish garrison in Kars, who was to be advised by General Williams.

The selected despatches begin in May 1855, and have been arranged in date order. The reader should be aware that there was often considerable delay between the sending and receiving of correspondence.

The siege of Kars, 1855

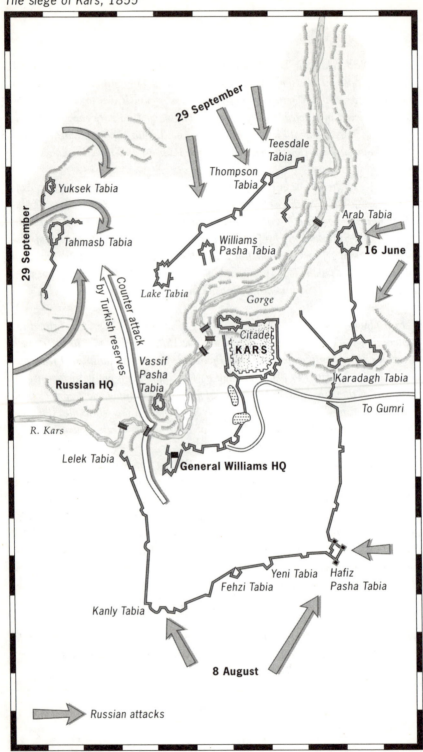

- Yuksek Tabia
- Teesdale Tabia
- 29 September
- Thompson Tabia
- Tahmasb Tabia
- 29 September
- Williams Pasha Tabia
- Arab Tabia
- 16 June
- Lake Tabia
- Gorge
- Counter attack by Turkish reserves
- Citadel
- **KARS**
- Vassif Pasha Tabia
- **Russian HQ**
- Karadagh Tabia
- *R. Kars*
- To Gumri
- Lelek Tabia
- **General Williams HQ**
- Hafiz Pasha Tabia
- Yeni Tabia
- Fehzi Tabia
- Kanly Tabia
- **8 August**
- Russian attacks

MAY TO JUNE 1855

Brigadier-General Williams to the Earl of Clarendon (received June 25)
Erzeroom, May 29, 1855

My Lord,

Since I had the honour to address your Lordship on the affairs of the army of Kars, I have exerted every effort to send forward provisions to its head-quarters, and to the detachments at Toprak-Kaleh. More than 4,000 mules and horses have been dispatched through my sole exertions, independent of those in the Government employ, and now that the peasants have sown their corn and barley, the arabas of the country will be at the disposal of the Government. I have also sent eight siege-guns to Kars, to add to those now in position there.

I received last night a communication from Colonel Lake, stating that a large Russian force, consisting of 28,000 Infantry, 7,500 Cavalry, and 64 pieces of Artillery, was assembled round Gumri, and that the Mushir [Vassif Pasha] had received information of the intention of the enemy to attack Kars. We have in that entrenched camp 13,900 Infantry, 1,500 Cavalry, 1,500 Artillerymen, and 42 field-pieces.

The Mushir has, therefore, sent for the troops under Mehmet Pasha, at Moossul, to come to Erzeroom, and has also directed Mustafa Pasha to quit Diarbekir and proceed to the same destination. His Excellency has also sent to Constantinople for troops. The Mushir acquiesced in my views respecting the Ramazan fast, and the garrison is consequently enabled to labour in the fortifications, as well as to keep a vigilant look-out at night.

All the forts commanding Erzeroom being armed, they were inaugurated yesterday. Mehmed Pasha, the newly arrived Vali, at my request, sent about 3,000 armed Mussulman citizens into them during the ceremony, and

I hope that in the event of an attack these men will render material assistance to the slender detachments of regular troops now stationed in them.

Major Teesdale is still encamped with the workmen at the passes leading into this plain from that of Hassan-Kaleh, and after the departure of the next post I shall rejoin the Mushir, or at an earlier day if the enemy move from their cantonment around Gumri. I have also heard from Major Olpherts (27th instant), at Toprak-Kaleh. He was using all his efforts to give me information, and keep me in communication with Veli Pasha, and also reports the march of Russian troops towards Gumri.

W. F. WILLIAMS

Brigadier-General Williams to the Earl of Clarendon (received June 25)
Pass of Dévéboyonou,
near Erzeroom, June 3, 1855

(Extract)

I left Erzeroom yesterday, *en route* for Kars, which place the enemy has announced, in an order of the day, his intention to attack. The Mushir had sent for all the good troops, Cavalry, Infantry, and Artillery, of the Toprak-Kaleh detachment, which would have thrown that road, from Erivan to Erzeroom, open. I however begged his Excellency to countermand this order, and all is again as it should be on the Byazid route.

If the Russians leave Georgia to attack Kars, it would show that our spies and travellers have underrated their strength, or that they find no succour coming to us either from Trezibond or Batoom; be this as it may, I have now four months' provisions in that garrison, and I trust the Central Government and the Allies will soon prove to this remnant of an army that it is not absolutely forgotten by them.

Liva Mustafa Pasha was tried last week for drunkenness and cowardice in the battle of Injé-Dereh. A Colonel and two Majors are also compromised; and I hope this example will prove salutary at the present moment, when the enemy menace, and the timid indulge in fear of the Russians, as well as distrust in the Government who has so cruelly neglected them.

Brigadier-General Williams to the Earl of Clarendon (received July 11)
Kars, June 9, 1855

My Lord,

On the day after I addressed your Lordship from Dévéboyonou, I received from Colonel Lake the confirmation of the intention of the Russians to attack this place in great force. I also got a confidential message from the Mushir proposing to abandon Kars and defend Erzeroom. I instantly wrote back to Colonel Lake to beg the Mushir to act with the utmost vigour, and pressed on and reached Kars the day before yesterday, where I have used every endeavour to instil energy into the mind of the Mushir, and I likewise abstained from remonstrating with his Excellency on his strange proposition to abandon a place which we had been at such trouble to provision and fortify, thinking, as

I do, that he feels the weight of the false step he was about to take, and is willing to act upon my suggestions.

With this impression, I have been occupied all day in stationing the troops in the various batteries, in arming and supplying those batteries with ammunition, and in addressing to each regiment words of encouragement and hope. The enemy, in force about 30,000 men of all arms, accompanied by a train and vast supplies necessary for a siege, is within four hours of us, and will, most probably, attack us tomorrow.

I have advised the Mushir to write to Mustafa Pasha, of Batoom, for 5,000 to be directed on Ardahan, and to Veli Pasha, of Toprak-Kaleh, to prepare for an instant march when he shall have received orders for it. This is all I can do in our isolated and neglected state, and I am happy to say that our garrison appears in good spirits, and promises me to do its duty.

W. F. WILLIAMS

Lord Stratford de Redcliffe to M. Pisani
British Embassy, June 13, 1855

Sir,

I learn from Brigadier-General Williams that the Russians appeared, when he wrote, to be meditating an attack on the army at Kars, and I fear we shall have to deplore the little or tardy attention paid to my earnest and repeated requisitions for supplies and reinforcements. Even now, at the eleventh hour, it is most desirable that all which it is in the power of the Government to do in these respects, should be done without a moment's delay. According to my last advices from General Williams, money was greatly wanted, and he presses the demand most earnestly upon me. See Fuad Pasha and the Seraskier without delay, and urge them to send off as large a sum as they can possibly spare, while they are preparing whatever may yet be forwarded in point of men and supplies. The case does really seem to be very urgent.

I learn from our Consul at Trebizond, that the Russians had made an attack on Choorooksoo, and been repulsed with loss after a sharp engagement. Has the Porte any news of this?

Now that Circassia is cleared of the Russians, why should not the old idea of uniting the army at Batoom with that of Kars be acted upon in the present emergency? Suggest this impressively. I am assured that Batoom may be held with a very small force, supposing it to have works sufficient to be relied on; but of this I am no judge.

STRATFORD DE REDCLIFFE

Brigadier-General Williams to the Earl of Clarendon (received July 11)
Kars, June 15, 1855

My Lord,

Since I last had the honour to address your Lordship our entrenchments have been materially strengthened by connecting the redoubts on the heights behind the town by an épaulement, and by closing the gorges of those on the plain in front of the town. I refer your Lordship to the sketch of these works which I had the honour to forward from Erzeroom. Since Colonel Lake arrived in Kars he has shown great skill and industry in improving the defective and hastily thrown up works of last year. In the labour consequent on these efforts the troops have evinced the greatest zeal and good humour, and I can with truth assure your Lordship that I never saw works executed with greater rapidity nor in a neater manner than by our Infantry, whose discipline has been most carefully attended to by Captain Thompson.

I have entrusted the defensive works on the heights behind Kars to Major Teesdale, and those on the Karadagh to Captain Thompson; on these officers devolve the safety of the outposts by night, as well as their various duties by day: Colonel Lake taking upon himself the outposts and pickets of the works on the plain, and also occasional visits to the advanced posts, which have been placed under Baron de Schwartzenburg.

Yesterday Colonel Lake, accompanied by Dr Sandwith, who interpreted for him, was attacked at the advanced posts, those posts having been incautiously pushed forward before he arrived on the ground; the Colonel's party retired with the loss of nine men killed.

The enemy's army has been encamped since its arrival in this vicinity at the villages of Zaïm and Akché-Kalla, at the distance of three and four hours respectively; his detachments have penetrated to Ardahan, from whence ours had been withdrawn, destroyed some entrenchments erected last year, and purchased corn; the enemy has also made an incursion into Childir, and, indeed, is master of the country lying between this and the Russian frontier as far west as he chooses to push his foraging parties.

Yesterday a large force detached by the enemy to seize Ardahan returned to camp at Zaïm, and the spies report an immediate attack on our entrenchments. Their numbers have now assumed a more probable form, and I believe 30,000 of all arms, including Irregulars, to be about the truth.

W. F. WILLIAMS

Brigadier-General Williams to the Earl of Clarendon (received July 11)

Kars, June 17, 1855

My Lord,

Circumstances leading me to believe that Mehmed Pasha, the newly appointed Governor of Erzeroom, was treating with indifference the urgent demands of the Mushir for the levying of Irregular Horse, and for the forwarding of provisions to this garrison, I addressed a letter to his Excellency, a copy of which I beg to enclose for your Lordship's information. I have also written to the Chief of Agara, Sherif Bey, begging him to levy as many native Riflemen as possible, and march them on Kars.

I have also taken advantage of the good disposition evinced by the Mussulman inhabitants of this town, to enrol 800 of them, and they are now at their stations with the regular troops.

W. F. WILLIAMS

Enclosure

Brigadier-General Williams to Mehmed Pasha

Kars, June 13, 1855

Excellency,

You are well aware that we are very short of provisions in this garrison, and that, although we have a good supply of grain at Yenikeuy (a village 50 miles off on the road to Erzeroom), it is not in our power, under the present circumstances, to send either arabas or pack-horses to bring it this way. It has therefore been considered necessary, after due consultation, to give his Excellency Sirra Pasha full powers to make such arrangements at Yenikeuy, Erzeroom, and other places, as he may deem fitting for providing, without loss of time, this garrison with provisions, and he has been furnished with letters to the different authorities to that effect.

This army owes its present straitened circumstances in great measure to the weakness and neglect of your Excellency's predecessor, and I myself witnessed whilst in Erzeroom a marked want of activity on the part of the members of the Civil Council; but I doubt not that you, who have shown yourself a zealous officer of the State, will in this respect display more activity even than you have done as heretofore, and I hope that by doing your utmost to supply the wants of this army, you will thus afford me an opportunity of giving a favourable report of your conduct to my Government. In the meantime, I feel it my duty to tell your Excellency that since your arrival in Erzeroom not a single araba of grain has reached here from your quarter, and I earnestly beg your Excellency not to lose sight of this most important branch of the service, and also to be good enough to afford Sirra Pasha every assistance in your power.

I have seen today two despatches written by your Excellency in reply to the Mushir's request for Bashi-Bozouks, by which you make it out impossible to collect any Bashi-Bozouks at all in your vast province! I sincerely regret to have to bring to the knowledge of my Government this apparent and evident disinclination on the part of your Excellency to act up to the duties imposed on you as Civil Governor, at a time, too, when, menaced as we are by the enemy, we require the presence of a vast body of Irregular Horse to keep open our communications with our central magazines.

I advise your Excellency as a friend to consider the dangerous position in which such a refusal on your part would inevitably place this army.

W. F. WILLIAMS

Brigadier-General Williams to the Earl of Clarendon (received July 11)

Kars, June 17, 1855

My Lord,

Yesterday, being the feast of the Baïram, I fully anticipated an attack, and the troops were consequently held in readiness throughout the preceding night, and stood to their arms before daylight.

Our advanced posts were driven in soon after daylight, and the Russian army appeared on the height about half-past 6 o'clock: its advanced guard consisted of three regiments of Regular Cossacks, supported by Artillery and rockets. The main body of Infantry marched in three columns, flanked by three regiments of Dragoons and supported by six batteries of eight guns each. In the rear appeared a strong column of Reserve Infantry, then the waggons carrying, as I have since heard, three days' provision. The whole force could not have been less than 25,000.

Nothing could be more perfect than the handling of the enemy's army as it advanced upon the front of our entrenchments, formed by the line of works called Arab Tabia, Karadagh, and Hafiz Pasha Tabia, and facing the Gumri road. Our Cavalry pickets and Bashi-Bozouks retired, skirmishing with the Regular Cossacks, until within 1,000 yards of our lines, when the enemy's Cavalry made a desperate rush, supported by its reserves of skirmishers, and also by a Rocket troop, to enter the camp with our outnumbered Cavalry under Baron Schwartzenburg; but they were instantly checked by the Artillery from Arab Tabia, Karadagh, and Hafiz Pasha Tabia; they then fell back upon the main body of the Russian army, which retired in the same order in which it had advanced; and after halting for a few minutes finally disappeared over the hills, and has resumed its old camping-ground at Zaïm and Akché-Kalla.

As the enemy carried off their dead we could not ascertain their loss, but it is estimated from 100 to 150; ours amounted to 6 killed and 8 wounded.

The spirit of the Turkish troops was excellent, evincing, as they did, as much readiness in the defence as they had shown in the construction of their épaulements. If the enemy had attempted to carry his original intention into execution he would, I confidently believe, have met with signal disaster.

The precautions which I have recommended the Mushir to take are in nowise slackened, and we are now preparing for an attack of the heights in the rear of the city. The labour of the officers of my staff has been incessant, and I have to record my thanks to Colonel Lake, to Major Teesdale, and Captain Thompson, and to Dr Sandwith, as well as to Messrs Churchill and Zohrab, the secretaries and interpreters, whose duties are equally arduous and fatiguing.

W. F. WILLIAMS

Brigadier-General Williams to the Earl of Clarendon (received July 11)
Kars, June 19, 1855

My Lord,

I have the honour to inform your Lordship that the enemy yesterday at daylight broke up his camps at Zaïm and Akché-Kalla, and made a flank march round our entrenched camp, and is now in great force (30,000) within an hour's march of the weakest part of our position, which he may attack at any moment.

Veli Pasha has also the enemy before him. He has been ordered to defend himself if attacked, but if the enemy's force is small, he is directed on Kupri-Keuy to defend Erzeroom.

Unfortunately we have no Irregular Cavalry either with this or the Toprak-Kaleh force. I have frequently represented to Her Majesty's Ambassador the incompetency of Ismail Pasha, the late Governor-General of Erzeroom, whose duty it was to levy this essential force; unfortunately I have received no answer to these representations, beyond a bare acknowledgment of my despatches.

The enemy has already partially interrupted our communications with Erzeroom, but I hope this despatch will reach its destination.

W. F. WILLIAMS

Brigadier-General Williams to the Earl of Clarendon (received July 18)
Kars, June 23, 1855

My Lord,

The Mushir has this moment informed me that, in consequence of the enemy having intercepted the direct communications with Erzeroom, he should send off, in an hour, a courier by an indirect route. I must, therefore, in as few words as possible, detail the events which have occurred since I informed your Lordship, on the 19th instant, that the Russian army under General Mouravieff had, by a flank march, established itself opposite our entrenched camp, at a distance of three miles.

The rain has been so heavy and incessant as to prevent the enemy from any attempt to attack our lines, but he has pushed forward large bodies of Cavalry, supported by guns, burnt the surrounding villages, and destroyed one of our small depôts of grain at Chiplaklee, eight hours on the Erzeroom Road, and probably thinking that our entrenchments are too formidable to take by a *coup de main*, he has sent to Gumri for eight heavy guns belonging to that fortress, which are now on their way to his camp.

The duties of our garrison have been most trying, in consequence of the torrents of rain, but the spirit of the troops is good.

I urgently recommend the immediate landing of troops at Trebizond, and, if the season will admit of it, strong demonstrations from Redoute-Kaleh.

W. F. WILLIAMS

Brigadier-General Williams to the Earl of Clarendon (received July 26)
Kars, June 27, 1855

My Lord,

The continued rains which I reported to your Lordship in my last despatch, prevented any movement on the part of the enemy till yesterday morning, when twenty-two battalions of Infantry and a large force of Cavalry and Artillery advanced on our lines; their right division being directed on Hafiz Pasha Tabia, and their left on Kanly Tabia; this being the weakest face of our defences. Every disposition on our part was made to receive the attack, and the spirit of the Turkish troops was firm and soldierlike; but the enemy having advanced more cautiously than he did on the former occasion, halted without the range of our guns, and, having remained long enough to make the most minute reconnaissance, retired to his camp after keeping us under arms eight hours.

The damage done by the rain to our entrenchments had previously been carefully repaired, and we have taken advantage of the inactivity of the enemy today to add considerably to the interior lines of defence.

The Russian army being master of the surrounding country, plunders it daily, and supplies itself with fuel by unroofing the houses of the Mussulman villages, but spares those inhabited by the Armenians.

I regret to inform your Lordship that the mail bags brought to Erzeroom by the English Tatar from Constantinople, and forwarded by the Consul, fell into the enemy's hands, so we are ignorant of what has recently taken place in Europe or the Crimea. General Mouravieff politely sent back all such private letters as were barren of public or political news.

W. F. WILLIAMS

Brigadier-General Williams to the Earl of Clarendon (received July 26)

Kars, June 28, 1855

My Lord,

The Russian army quitted its camp before Kars this morning at daylight, and has marched three hours to the south-east, more effectually, I presume, to interrupt our communication with Erzeroom. The command of land transport enjoyed by the enemy is enormous, and their convoys are admirably arranged; our garrison, on the contrary, has not funds to procure arabas or country carts, even supposing that the surrounding country possessed them: we must, therefore, hold this place till the last moment, whilst the enemy is master of all without the reach of our guns; moreover, the troops, who have conducted themselves so well since General Mouravieff appeared before Kars, are 23, 27, and 28 months in arrears of pay.

The Mushir has just received a despatch by his Aide-de-camp, Feky Bey, from Mehemet Pasha, the newly appointed Seraskier, to the effect that no assistance could be expected from Constantinople, but that he would write to Mustafa Pasha, of Batoom, to send us up 5,000 men, whereas that General has recently written to me to say that he had only 3,772 regular troops, and was pressed by the enemy. The Seraskier further promises to send 15,000 purses and 500 artillerymen, from the Dardanelles, and two battalions of Infantry and four squadrons of Cavalry are the only troops which he can spare from Diarbekir and Aleppo.

To this state has the apathy and indifference of the authorities at the capital reduced its Asiatic provinces.

W. F. WILLIAMS

Brigadier-General Williams to the Earl of Clarendon (received July 26)
Kars, June 30, 1855

My Lord,

The enemy yesterday detached a large force, consisting of Infantry, Cavalry, and Artillery, towards the pass leading to Yenikeuy, where we have magazines of wheat and barley. The true object of this movement cannot yet be ascertained; but the Mushir has written to Veli Pasha, who is now encamped at Kupri-Keuy and covers Erzeroom, to be on his guard, and in the event of the advance of the enemy in force, to retire to the first Erzeroom entrenchments of Déveboyonou, and thence into the redoubts which command that city. Tahir Pasha, who recently came here to assist in the defence of Kars, goes off tonight to Erzeroom, where his experience in the management of Artillery, and his knowledge of English, will be of great value.

I trust that the authorities of Constantinople will see the necessity of sending succour to Asia, both by way of Trebizond and Batoom. We have not enough Regular Infantry to effectively man our lines, our Cavalry cannot compete for a moment with that of the enemy, and in the Land Transport Department we are deficient; the fact, moreover, of our having supplies at Yenikeuny is to be attributed to the imbecility and indifference of Ismail Pasha, the late Governor-General of Erzeroom, who was repeatedly begged by me to forward those supplies on to Kars instead of unloading them at that distant depôt.

W. F. WILLIAMS

Lord Stratford de Redcliffe to the Earl of Clarendon (received July 11)
Constantinople, June 30, 1855

My Lord,

The meeting which I had previously announced to your Lordship, took place this morning at the Grand Vizier's house on the Bosphorus. In addition to his Highness, the Seraskier and Fuad Pasha were present. I was accompanied by Brigadier-General Mansfield.

We found that the Porte had received advices from Vassif Pasha, brought by an officer who had left Kars about eleven days before. Despatches from General Williams also came to hand at the moment we were entering into conference. Their latest date was the 19th instant.

It appears from both sources, that the Russians, advancing from Gumri with an amount of force varying from 20,000 to 30,000, had presented themselves before Kars; that a partial engagement of Cavalry had taken place, followed two days later by an attack, which had been repulsed, on the part of the enemy, and that the town was threatened with a siege.

I collected from the Turkish officer, that when he left the scene of action, rain was falling in torrents, the waters of the river were out, and the Russians had no choice but to encamp. It appears, from the English statements, that the defences of the fortress were deemed to be of considerable strength, that the place was provisioned for a month, and that the Turkish army may be estimated at 18,000 men.

It was clear, to all present, that whether the Russians besieged or turned Kars, the Turkish army required an effort to be made for its relief with all practicable dispatch, and that of three possible modes of acting for that purpose, the only one likely to prove effective was an expedition by Kutais into Georgia. To send reinforcements by Trebizond would be at best a palliative. To establish an entrenched camp at Redoute-Kaleh, would, at this unhealthy season, be equivalent to consigning the troops to destruction.

The real question was, whether a force, numerically sufficient, and in all respects effective, could be collected in time at Kutais to make an excursion into Georgia and threaten the communications of the Russian army, placing it indeed between two hostile forces should the Turkish army still be in a condition to take the field.

It was for the Turkish Ministers to solve this problem, and they proposed that the expeditionary force should be composed of 12,000 men from Batoom and the neighbouring stations; of the troops made over to General Vivian, and estimated at 10,000 of all arms; of General Beatson's Irregular Cavalry, of 10,000 men to be detached from the army in Bulgaria as the complement of the Turkish Contingent; of 5,000 more derived from the same source; of an Egyptian regiment of horse now here, and of another regiment expected from Tunis. To these the Seraskier proposed to add 2,000 Albanians by way of riflemen. These several forces completed, according to the figures, would present a total of 44,400 men, not perhaps to be reckoned with prudence at more than 36,000 effective.

Admitting the urgency of the case, and the consequent necessity of incurring a certain degree of hazard, I called attention to the importance of not exposing the Turkish Contingent, or General Beatson's Horse, prematurely, to a trial beyond their strength. It was accordingly understood that supposing the expedition to be resolved upon, neither of these corps would be required to embark for Redoute-Kaleh until the preparations were completed in other respects; and it is to be hoped that the interval thus gained for their benefit would suffice to secure their efficiency. I took, moreover, the liberty of remarking that the proposed expedition, besides being prepared with secrecy and sanctioned by superior authority, must finally depend for its adoption on our available means of providing it with all the requisite appliances. This indispensable field of inquiry might be investigated with advantage by General Vivian, the Seraskier Pasha, and Brigadier-General Mansfield, who, indeed, have undertaken to meet tomorrow for that purpose.

The Turkish Ministers having expressed their readiness to entrust the direction of the expedition, should it eventually take place, to a British Commander, and to accept General Vivian in that capacity, subject, of course, to the approval of Her Majesty's Government, I lost no time after our separation, in communicating personally with that officer, and putting him in possession of all that had passed on the subject of our discussion.

It only remains for me at present to refer your Lordship to the accompanying memorandum, for which I am indebted to General Mansfield. It contains information resulting from inquiries addressed to the Seraskier and his colleagues on several matters, from which it is most desirable, with a view to our ultimate success, that all uncertainty should, as far as possible, be removed.

STRATFORD DE REDCLIFFE

Enclosure

Information obtained from the Seraskier with reference to the proposal of the Porte to relieve the Army of Kars by an operation from Redoute-Kaleh towards Tiflis

Questions having been put to the Seraskier, the following information was obtained:

1. The country in the neighbourhood of Redoute-Kaleh is declared to be low and marshy.
2. A sufficient supply of grain for the maintenance of an army without the importation of corn cannot be found. The country from the coast to Kutais cannot supply the necessary magazines.
3. Ships engaged in the supply of the army would seek Batoom for safe anchorage. Redoute-Kaleh is impracticable except for boats of small draught.
4. The exact distance from Redoute-Kaleh to Kutais is eighteen hours or about fifty English miles.
5. There is no coast road practicable for guns from Batoom.
6. The River Rhion is navigable by boats as far as Kutais. The necessary boats can be sent from Trebizond.
7. The streams which run into the Rhion below Kutais are not of any significance, and are not serious obstacles to the advance of an army.
8. The population of Kutais is about 10,000, rather under than over that number.
9. The climate of Kutais is more healthy than that of the coast. It is, therefore, more prudent to throw the troops forward, after their disembarkation, as quickly as possible.
10. Labourers can be secured in the country to assist the engineers in forming an entrenched camp at Redoute-Kaleh.
11. The population in the region referred to is indifferently disposed towards the Turkish Government, since the fatal affairs of last year. It would be very difficult to attract recruits to the ranks independently of raising the country on a grand scale by acting on the Chiefs.
12. The force at Batoom and in its neighbourhood is 15,000 strong, of whom 12,000 effective men can be spared for the expedition.

13. Of these 700 or 800 men are Artillerymen. There are 30 or 32 field-guns quite ready, besides some guns of position.

14. It is also said that means of land transport for the 12,000 men at Batoom are actually available.

15. It is declared that the Russians have constructed a *chaussée* [route] from Tiflis to Redoute-Kaleh, the commerce on that line having been always much favoured by them.

16. The Porte would depend upon the British and French Admirals for assistance in transporting the troops to Redoute-Kaleh. But many steamers and transports may be spared from the transport fleet engaged in supplying Omer Pasha. Besides that, the Porte is prepared to buy other transports for this purpose.

17. The Porte proposes to give the command of the army, which, when concentrated, will exceed 43,000 men of all arms, to Lieutenant-General Vivian, now in command of the Turkish Contingent. The latter would form a division of the force.

18. The details of the force cannot, however, be analysed and decided on, till a decision is made that the design shall be put into execution.

19. There are some officers attached to the Seraskier who possess a considerable local knowledge of the country alluded to, and would be placed at the disposal of Lieutenant-General Vivian.

20. The force will be composed as follows:

Vivian's Contingent	20,000
Beatson's★	3,000
Batoom Garrison	12,000
Albanians	2,000
To be drawn from Bulgaria	5,000
Regiment of Egyptian Regular Cavalry	800
Tunis Horse	600
Total	43,400

W. R. MANSFIELD
Brigadier-General

★3,000 men are raised. The force to be levied by Major-General Beatson, when completed, will be 4,000.

JULY 1855

Lord Stratford de Redcliffe to the Earl of Clarendon (received July 11)
Therapia, July 1, 1855

My Lord,

Agreeably to what I stated in my preceding despatch, Lieutenant-General Vivian and Brigadier-General Mansfield waited this morning on the Seraskier at his Excellency's office in town. Fuad Pasha attended at the request of the Seraskier; M. Pisani was also present.

Enclosed herewith for your Lordship's information is a memorandum containing General Mansfield's notes of what took place on that occasion. The statement promised by General Vivian can hardly reach me before tomorrow, and perhaps not in time to be forwarded by the messenger.

Your Lordship will do me the honour to bear in mind that the proposed diversion at Redoute-Kaleh originated with the Porte; that recognising the urgency of the case I have endeavoured to obviate such manifest objections as the premature employment of the Turkish Contingent, and the exposure of troops to a climate which, at this season of the year, has been characterised as pestilential on the coast of Circassia; and that I lean entirely on military opinions as to the means of eventually carrying out the proposed expedition.

I propose at the same time to reserve the approval of Her Majesty's Government, and to afford the Commanders-in-chief an opportunity of declaring their opinions.

I have to add, in conclusion, that an entrenched position at Redoute-Kaleh will probably be found indispensable as a point of retreat in case of any signal reverse; and, with a view to future questions, it may be desirable to have it clearly understood that the Turkish Contingent is to be regarded in the light of a British force, composing the principal part of the expeditionary army.

STRATFORD DE REDCLIFFE

Enclosure

Memorandum of interview between the Seraskier, Fuad Pasha, Lieutenant-General Vivian, and Brigadier-General Mansfield, on the 30th of June, 1855

The Seraskier, before the arrival of Fuad Pasha, spoke of the affairs of the Turkish Contingent under the command of Lieutenant-General Vivian. That force has now actually in camp 8,500 men, two battalions having joined this very day. The remaining 1,500 men necessary to complete the first half of the Contingent are in Constantinople ready, and will be sent to the camp forthwith.

The second half of the Contingent to be assembled at Varna. If the plan discussed at the house of Aali Pasha is decided on, the orders for them to assemble at Varna to be immediately sent. If there is no such object, the Seraskier considers a further reference must be in the first instance made to Omer Pasha, who would take offence if a large portion of the troops in Bulgaria were drafted away without his consent: but in case of the project being decided on to form an army to operate towards Georgia, of course that such a reference might be put aside, considering the urgency of the matter. Supposing the order to be sent without delay to Bulgaria, 10,000 men could be assembled and ready to be transferred to the officers deputed by General Vivian at Varna in 15 days.

On being asked what steps could be taken to form a depôt in case of the Contingent being sent on service, he replied that it was not the Turkish custom to form depôts; that the Porte raised about 18,000 or 20,000 recruits a year, who were immediately sent to the different battalions.

On the matter of arms, he declared that he was ready to supply the Contingent with 15,000 percussion muskets immediately, although he trusted that the Minié guns sent for from England by General Vivian would soon make their appearance. The percussion muskets are now in the arsenal, and there is plenty of ammunition.

Fuad Pasha having arrived, General Vivian desired that his Excellency would have the goodness to explain exactly the views of the Turkish Government on the subject of an expedition to the coast, in which it was proposed to employ him.

Fuad Pasha then, at great length, went over all the matters which had been brought forward before his Excellency Lord Stratford de Redcliffe, the day before.

He explained the situation of the army of Kars, and that it was proposed to relieve that army by a powerful diversion. That this diversion could be best made, indeed, only made, from Redoute-Kaleh, or some place in its vicinity, for the landing of troops and the establishment of a basis of operations. That troops so landing should be thrown in advance as quickly as possibly on

Kutais, and operate towards Tiflis, where it is considered the real objects of a war against Russia by the allies may be best obtained. That by such a grand operation the best chance for the army of Kars is secured, whereas by any other mode means would be frittered away, without result, either immediate or ultimate, to the good of the cause. That if the project is not adopted from want of means they must have recourse to those measures in which they have no confidence. General Vivian replied that he should like to know what means were disposable for so great a plan.

Fuad Pasha answered that, in the first place, there was of the Contingent now ready, actually at Buyukdere	10,000
That part of the Contingent to be immediately assembled in Bulgaria	10,000
To be drawn in addition from the garrisons in Bulgaria, and attached to the British Contingent in camp	5,000
Beatson's Horse	3,000
Albanian Light Troops	2,000
Garrison at Batoom and in the neighbourhood	12,000
One regiment of Egyptian Regular Cavalry	800
A body of Cavalry expected immediately from Tunis	600
Total	43,400

It was proposed to give the command of their army to General Vivian himself. On being pressed as to the means of transport inland, Fuad Pasha declared that the plans once fairly decided on, every effort would be made to furnish all the means of whatever description.

General Vivian said that he begged that he might not be misunderstood. That he put himself out of the question; but that it was one thing to throw an army on a coast, and another to feed and move it. That it was necessary for him to have exact details on this matter, on which success depends altogether. Further, that he quite admitted the justice of the reasoning addressed to him, which seemed to vouch for the necessity of employing his Contingent, that there was a State necessity against which he, as a military officer, had nothing to say. But that while he admitted this he must inform the Porte that the employment of the Contingent was premature, and, as is self-evident, cannot but interfere with the arrangements and organisation he has so much at heart.

Important, however, as these considerations are, that it is his business to carry out the orders, as far as lies in his power, of the Government under which he is acting, and that his only desire is to do that as effectually as may be, according to the injunctions he may receive from Her Majesty's Ambassador. But that putting all personal considerations on one side, they cannot be too careful in arranging the necessary matters of detail, sea and land transport, provisioning and victualling, ammunition, payment, etc.

To this Fuad Effendi agreed, and proposed that General Vivian should sketch out on paper what he considered indispensable to enable this project to be carried out. That the officers of the Porte would then be able to judge whether they had the necessary means; but that there ought to be no delay. General Vivian promised to send such a document the next day, and expressed his gratitude for the high honour which had been conferred on him.

W. R. MANSFIELD

Major Olpherts to Lord Stratford de Redcliffe

Erzeroom, July 2, 1855

(Extract)

I think it my duty to acquaint your Lordship with the state of affairs in this quarter up to the latest moment, lest the communications which you receive from General Williams be interrupted by the Russians, who were yesterday in force on the direct road between this and Kars, at the village of Chiplaklee, and whose advanced posts towards Erzeroom had reached Yenikeuy, a village situated on the Soghanli-Dagh range—the principal natural barrier to their rapid progress into the heart of Armenia.

I saw General Williams at Kars, on Friday evening, but only for a few minutes (having ridden in on my own responsibility), as the enemy were then moving towards Chiplaklee, and the General required my immediate return to the force under his Excellency Veli Pasha, at Kupri-Keuy. I have been with the Pasha's Division since the middle of May last, at Euch-Kelissa, on the Byazid frontier. We withdrew from this position when Kars was attacked, to our present one at Kupri-Keuy, covering Erzeroom about 25 miles behind us.

At Kars all were well, and no immediate danger apprehended for the safety of its garrison, but the intentions of the enemy are not yet apparent; their late move to the Soghanli-Dagh Passes, while it still more isolates Kars, threatens Erzeroom. I beg, therefore, most respectfully to suggest to your Excellency the necessity of urging upon the Porte the dispatch of reinforcements to Trebizond.

I write this from the house of Mr Consul Brant, to whose care, I beg, my Lord, you will kindly send any reply with which your Lordship may be pleased to favour me. My proper headquarters are with his Excellency Veli Pasha, at Kupri-Keuy. I have explained to the three Pashas in camp, and to the Pashas of the Medjlis here, my views and procedure in addressing your Excellency, and they have assured me that a similar communication has been made by them to his Excellency the Seraskier, so that I hope not a day may be lost, for the foe are all but at the very gates of this capital.

Consul Brant to Lord Stratford de Redcliffe
Erzeroom, July 3, 1855

My Lord,

I have the honour to inform your Excellency that I received a letter from Kars, dated 26th instant. The Russians took the post from hence, conveying the letters brought by Mazloom Tatar. General Mouravieff politely forwarded to Kars those which contained no news, and no allusions to the war; but he kept back the despatches, the newspapers, and private letters which contained news.

At 6 a.m. on the 26th, General Williams and his staff were roused by an alarm given of the advance of the Russian army. It bore down on Kars in two columns, one approaching by the Gumri road, and the other directly in the face of Kars; they halted their army at about a mile and a half or two miles from the Turkish works. At 10.30 p.m., they fired one gun, and retired to their camp. The force is said to have consisted of about twenty-two battalions.

General Williams desired the writer to tell me, in case his despatches should not reach in time for the post of the 3rd of July, to communicate the above intelligence.

His Excellency Hafiz Pasha of Trebizond is preparing a large force of Bashi-Bozouks; from the haste with which they are collected and the classes which are to contribute to swell up the number, I should think the real efficiency of the reinforcement will be small. Better to have 10,000 European soldiers than such hordes of undisciplined men.

If 10,000 good troops were quickly landed at Trebizond, and brought up here by rapid marches, easing the men by loading their knapsacks and other traps on horses, they could arrive here easily in ten days from Trebizond; such a force would suffice for defence, and other reinforcements could follow more leisurely.

Veli Pasha's division is at eleven hours' distance from hence, on the Kars road, waiting orders what direction to take, with Infantry, Cavalry, Artillery, and Bashi-Bozouks. I am told there may be about 8,000 men; but the numbers of each I am not able to state.

I send this by a return messenger from Trebizond.

Jas. Brant

Lord Stratford de Redcliffe to the Earl of Clarendon (received July 16)
Therapia, July 5, 1855

My Lord,

No information, as far as I know, has reached Constantinople respecting the state of affairs at Kars. My latest despatch from General Williams was dated on the 19th ultimo. The correspondence which I forwarded to your Lordship has, no doubt, stated the same particulars which were conveyed to me.

Enclosed herewith, in copy, is the last despatch which I have addressed to Her Majesty's Commissioner. It distresses me greatly that I am unable to hold out any more immediate prospects of relief.

STRATFORD DE REDCLIFFE

Enclosure

Lord Stratford de Redcliffe to Brigadier-General Williams

Therapia, June 22, 1855

Sir,

I have the honour to acknowledge the receipt of your several despatches to the 19th ultimo; and while I express my concern at the danger to which the Turkish army at Kars appears to be exposed, I cannot but admire the spirit with which you were prepared to meet the enemy.

I have never ceased to recommend that reinforcements and supplies should be sent to Vassif Pasha; and I hope you are persuaded that the shortcomings of the late Seraskier are as much condemned by me as by you.

I am now engaged in concerting measures for the relief of the Turkish forces in Kars and Erzeroom; but if anything efficient can be accomplished, it must be, I fear, more or less a waste of time; and we trust that, whether the enemy stop to besiege Kars, or mask it and push on to Erzeroom, the Turkish Commander will be able, with your support, to maintain a firm position.

STRATFORD DE REDCLIFFE

Brigadier-General Williams to the Earl of Clarendon (received July 26)

Kars, July 7, 1855

My Lord,

The force detached by the Russian General on the 29th ultimo in the direction of Yenikeuy, which I have already had the honour of communicating to your Lordship, consisted of 15 battalions of Infantry, 40 guns, and three regiments of Cavalry; and, as I anticipated, he destroyed our magazines of biscuit, wheat, and barley, which contained, at least, two months' supply for our garrison. The remainder of the enemy's army comprised an equal force with that of the expeditionary column, and was posted in a most commanding position, only assailable at one point, and that by a long *détour*, and out of our power to disturb, without risking the ultimate fate of our garrison.

The position occupied by Veli Pasha at Kupri-Keuy, and the fortifications recently constructed at Erzeroom, no doubt, prevented the Russian General from hazarding an attack in that direction; for his numerous and excellent Cavalry, and overpowering field artillery (80 guns), render him master of everything out of the reach of our cannon.

Yesterday the enemy returned to the camp before Kars, and his reunited forces are ready either to assault or to more closely invest us, by cutting off our only remaining communication with Erzeroom *via* Olti.

W. F. WILLIAMS

Vice-Consul Stevens to Lord Stratford de Redcliffe
Trebizond, July 9, 1855

My Lord,
I have the honour to report that our Pasha left for Erzeroom yesterday with 300 artillerymen and 20 field-pieces. A large force of Irregulars, which may reach the sum of 10,000, is now assembling, and will march today for the same place.

FRA. I. STEVENS

Lord Stratford de Redcliffe to the Earl of Clarendon (received July 23)
Therapia, July 12, 1855

My Lord,
Conceiving that your Lordship must feel anxious to obtain as much information as possible respecting the present state of the army at Kars, I do myself the honour to enclose herewith an extract of a private letter from Erzeroom, communicated to me by a private hand, and derived from what I consider to be a reliable and well-informed source.

STRATFORD DE REDCLIFFE

Enclosure

Extract from a letter dated Erzeroom, June 26, 1855
Our letters from Kars are dated the 23rd. The Russians were then in their camp almost swamped by the rain. They sent out their horsemen, and they have full liberty to do so as they please, for the Turks have no mounted men to oppose them. They came to Chiplaklee, one station beyond Yenikeuy [villages on the road between Kars and Erzeroom] and there they destroyed some grain, and retired to their camp. They sent to Gumri for eight heavy guns to play on Kars; they stuck in the mud near Arpatchai, but horses and men were sent to get them out and bring them to their camp. It is about an hour from Kars, and the tents can be seen and counted; but they are spread over a wide space, probably to make the army appear larger; they have ascertained that their force is 24,000, among which a large proportion of Cavalry, a great part irregular. The Turkish troops are in high spirits, and the townspeople full of courage and alacrity; about 1,000 have been supplied with arms, at their own request, and come to their post on the least alarm without being sent for. The Russians will never take Kars but by a regular siege, and those within have no fears while they have ammunition; nevertheless it was indispensable to send up succours.

Lord Stratford de Redcliffe to the Earl of Clarendon (received July 23)
Therapia, July 12, 1855

My Lord,
The extreme importance of obtaining correct data before the expedition proposed for the relief of the Turkish army at Kars be finally submitted to Her Majesty's Government, produces an unavoidable delay in the progress

and preparation of the plan. The Turkish Government has decided on sending confidential officers to examine the localities at Trebizond, Batoom, and
Redoute-Kaleh, with a view to forming a more correct idea of their
resources and difficulties. I hope that General Vivian and Sir Edmund Lyons
will pursue the same course, and that an officer from each service will be
sent in a suitable vessel to obtain the requisite information on the coast. I
have already applied to General Vivian and Rear-Admiral Grey for the purpose, and I shall avail myself of the earliest opportunity to make a similar
application to Admiral Sir Edmund Lyons.

I abstain from troubling your Lordship with particulars until I can sub-
mit the complete result of the present inquiries to Her Majesty's
Government. The general nature and object of the plan entertained by the
Porte, and promoted as a matter of eventual execution by Her Majesty's
Embassy, has been explained to your Lordship in my preceding despatches.

STRATFORD DE REDCLIFFE

Lieutenant-Colonel Simmons to Lieutenant-General Simpson

Camp near Kamara, July 12, 1855

Sir,

Omer Pasha sent to you yesterday a note in which he proposed that he
should go with the 25,000 men he had brought from Eupatoria to make a
diversion in favour of the garrison of Kars and the Ottoman army in Asia.

Since sending that note he has received a communication from the
Government at Constantinople in which he is entreated to consider what
can be done to save the interests of Turkey in Asia.

The Government inform him that if Kars should fall there is no force to
prevent the Russians marching directly upon Constantinople, and it is probable that success on the part of the Russians would decide the Persians to
take arms against the allies.

The Porte have proposed to General Vivian to take the Turkish
Contingent there, and both Lord Stratford and General Vivian have
expressed their willingness that it should go.

Omer Pasha, however, thinks that there will be great risk in sending
them there, as the men are not yet acquainted with their officers; the officers
do not speak their language, and consequently cannot command them in the
field, and the Contingent, although it might form a garrison, cannot yet be
in a condition to march into the interior. The force of the Contingent also
is small to make the contemplated operation.

Omer Pasha also thinks that possessing, as he does, the confidence of the
Turks, and being well known in Asia, where he has made several campaigns,
he is more likely to gain the sympathies and assistance of the inhabitants in
provisioning, in gaining information, etc., than strangers who do not know
the language or country.

Under these circumstances, Omer Pasha thinks that it will be decidedly
advisable, in the interest of the common cause, that the Contingent should

be assembled at Shumla, as proposed by him, where it could be organised and made ready for the field by next spring; that he should take the whole of his force hence, and from Kertch, with Cavalry from Eupatoria, and, if necessary, an additional number of men from Bulgaria, and make the operation himself.

By threatening the communications of the Russians with Georgia, they will be obliged to abandon the siege of Kars; and the winter ensuing, all operations would be suspended until the spring of 1856, and time will thus be gained to form an army in Asia sufficient to protect the Turkish dominions on that side, which Omer Pasha confidently thinks he could do by his influence and knowledge of the country.

Omer Pasha has requested me to submit these considerations to you previous to the conference which he has requested General Pélissier to assemble.

J. L. A. SIMMONS

The Earl of Clarendon to Lord Stratford de Redcliffe
Foreign Office, July 13, 1855

My Lord,
The plan proposed by the Porte for the relief of the Turkish army at Kars, as sketched out in your Excellency's despatches of the 30th of June and 1st instant, has been attentively considered by Her Majesty's Government; and I have to state to your Excellency that it appears to be objectionable for the following reasons:

It would be in the greatest degree imprudent to throw on an unwholesome coast, without means of land transport, without any certainty of provision, without an assured communication with the rear, without an accurate knowledge of the country to be traversed, or the strength of the enemy to be encountered, and with the probability of a hostile population, 40,000 men, hurriedly collected from various quarters, imperfectly disciplined, doubtfully armed and equipped, and as yet unorganised, and to expose them at once to all the hazards and difficulties of a campaign against a Russian army. They would fall ill between Redoute-Kaleh and Kutais, and be defeated between Kutais and Tiflis. Moreover, the fragments to be united for the purpose of composing this army are so scattered about, that the crisis, if it is to take place, would be over long before it could reach the scene of action.

Her Majesty's Government are of the opinion that the wiser course would be to send reinforcements to the rear of the Turkish army, instead of sending an expedition to the rear of the Russian army. The reinforcements might go to Trebizond, and be directed from thence upon Erzeroom. The distance from Trebizond to Erzeroom is less than from Redoute-Kaleh to Tiflis, and the march is through a friendly instead of through a hostile country; and at Erzeroom the army would meet supporting friends instead of opposing enemies, and supplies instead of famine.

If the army at Kars cannot maintain that position against the Russians, it should fall back upon Erzeroom, and the whole Turkish force should be concentrated there. If the Russians are to be defeated, it will be easier to defeat them by the whole force collected, than by divided portions of that force; and a defeat would be the more decisive, the further it took place within the Turkish frontier.

Trebizond is a port where supplies of all kinds might be landed; and Her Majesty's Government believe that it is a healthy place, and that Erzeroom is so likewise.

Such an arrangement as that which I have described would give time for collecting and organising the various detached corps of which the proposed army of 40,000 men is to be composed; and Her Majesty's Government entirely concur in Lieutenant-General Vivian's opinion that an army thrown on a coast without means of transport and supplies, is doomed to destruction.

CLARENDON

The Earl of Clarendon to Lord Stratford de Redcliffe
Foreign Office, July 14, 1855

(Telegraphic)

The plan for reinforcing the army at Kars, contained in your despatches of the 30th June and 1st instant, is disapproved. The reasons will be sent by the messenger today against employing the Turkish Contingent until it is fit for service.

Trebizond ought to be the base of operations, and if the Turkish army of Kars and Erzeroom cannot hold out at the latter place against the Russians, it might fall back on Trebizond, where it would easily be reinforced.

Lord Panmure to Lieutenant-General Vivian
War Department, July 14, 1855

Sir,

I transmit herewith, for your information, a copy of a despatch [dated July 13, 1855] which the Earl of Clarendon has addressed by the present opportunity to Her Majesty's Ambassador at Constantinople, on the subject of the plan proposed by the Porte for the relief of the Turkish army at Kars, and I have to acquaint you that I entirely concur in all that is said in that despatch as to the objectionable character of the plan proposed by the Porte.

I place such full reliance on your professional ability that I feel no anxiety lest you should undertake any expedition of a nature so wild and ill-digested as that contemplated by the Porte.

Whilst it is your duty to give every aid in your power, not simply as commanding the Contingent, but as a British officer enjoying the confidence of Her Majesty's Government, to our allies the Turks, it is at the same time necessary that you should be cautious in not risking the honour of the British name and your own reputation by undertaking military operations for which proper bases have not been laid down, communications opened, supplies arranged, and transport provided.

A *coup de main* by means of suddenly throwing an army on the coast to threaten, or even to attack an enemy's stronghold, is one thing; but a deliberate expedition to invade an enemy's country, and on his own territory to make war upon him, is quite another.

In the first case, something may be hazarded; but in the other, every preparation must precede action.

Moreover, from all the information which has reached me, I have every reason to believe the army of Batoom to be in a deplorable state. I know the Contingent to be scarcely organised; of the Bulgarian troops you can have no knowledge, and I presume that Beatson's Horse are as little reduced to control and discipline as your own troops. In short, I am assured that it would be madness to attempt to succour Brigadier-General Williams in this way. It is too late to regret the policy which has left that gallant officer and his army exposed to such straits; but it would only be opening the way to fresh failure to follow out such schemes as have been proposed for the purpose of relieving him. You must, as I have no doubt you feel, lose no time in getting your force into order for service, which will be sure to await you somewhere, as soon as you are ready for it; but organisation is as necessary for an army as endurance and valour, and without the former the latter qualities are utterly unavailing.

PANMURE

Brigadier-General Williams to the Earl of Clarendon (received August 8)
Kars, July 14, 1855

My Lord,
Since the date of my last despatch of the 7th instant, we have diligently worked at an interior line of entrenchments on the town side, as the enemy's camp remained stationary on the hills in that direction.

On the 12th instant General Mouravieff marched three hours to the south, and encamped at the village of Boyouk-Tikmeh, leaving eight battalions, two batteries, and a regiment of cavalry to observe our garrison. I at once conceived his object to be that of attacking the southern heights above Kars, which form the key of our defences, and by the crowning of which Kars was taken in 1828. We consequently began to entrench those eminences, and the enemy made minute reconnaissances of them on the 11th and 12th instant.

Yesterday, the whole Russian army marched towards them, and the force left by the enemy on the heights in our front moved up close to Kanly Tabia to engage our attention; but we were, nevertheless, enabled by our central position so to reinforce the menaced heights, that General Mouravieff, after some hours of close reconnaissance, retired to his camp. As this visit was made with his entire army, I presume he would have assailed us if he had found such a step desirable to his future operations.

The enemy remains quiet today, but our new redoubts on those hills are pressed forward with vigour, and, indeed, enthusiasm by the troops.

I have just heard that the Russian General expects reinforcements from Byazid *via* Gumri, and that those troops, recently expelled from the garrisons of the coast of Circassia, are also marching into the interior of Georgia, and may take part in the future operations against Asia Minor.

W. F. WILLIAMS

The Earl of Clarendon to Brigadier-General Williams

Foreign Office, July 18, 1855

Sir,

I have great pleasure in conveying to you the cordial approbation of Her Majesty's Government for the untiring zeal and energy which you have displayed in collecting supplies, in keeping up the spirit of the Turkish army, and in placing Kars in such a state of defence that the first attack of the Russians was a signal failure.

Her Majesty's Government do not doubt that you will perservere in the same course, notwithstanding the great difficulties of every kind against which you have to contend, and they trust that your exertions will meet with the success which they so well deserve.

The Earl of Clarendon to Lord Stratford de Redcliffe

Foreign Office, July 19, 1855

(Extract)

I have received your Excellency's despatch of the 6th of July, reporting that most of the articles required have been sent to the army at Kars by the Porte, and I have to state to you the Her Majesty's Government fear that the succour will arrive too late.

Brigadier-General Williams to the Earl of Clarendon (received August 20)

Kars, July 21, 1855

My Lord,

From the date of my last despatch on the 14th up to the present time, the Russian army has remained in the camps occupied by it prior to the third demonstration made by General Mouravieff against our entrenched positions. His powerful Cavalry, however, has not been inactive, having blocked up the roads leading from this to Erzeroom, *via* Olti, and also the one to Ardahan, by which we received our scanty supply of barley. Fortunately we have in store nearly three months' supplies of biscuit, flour, and wheat; we therefore may hope to be relieved before this amount of food is consumed. Any reinforcements sent by the Turks, from whatever quarter they may be, must come with convoys of provisions; otherwise, such accessories of force would amount to positive loss to the chances we now feel of holding out until the allied Governments, by wise combinations and sufficient forces, can oblige the Russian army to retire into Georgia.

There is a report in circulation relative to the Russian troops recently expelled from the forts in the Black Sea which causes us anxiety, namely, that several battalions of them have reached Tiflis; it is, however, added "in great disorder"; but such is the discipline of the Russian army, that these bands may soon be reorganised and added to General Mouravieff's forces now before us.

The Russian General has now minutely and closely observed our positions. As he marched round us, we have anticipated his arrival at the menaced point, by adding to and increasing the strength of our defences, at which the Turkish Infantry work with cheerfulness and surprising tact and intelligence.

W. F. WILLIAMS

Lord Stratford de Redcliffe to the Earl of Clarendon (received August 1)

Therapia, July 23, 1855

(Extract)

Omer Pasha is still here. He has been most graciously received, and also most generously rewarded by the Sultan, who has conferred a considerable grant of land upon him. I need not add that he is on excellent terms with His Majesty's Ministers, and particularly with the Seraskier Pasha. His Highness, accompanied by the last-mentioned Minister, called upon me yesterday. He is expected to leave on his return to the Crimea in four or five days.

With respect to the dangers which threaten Turkey from the side of Kars, he proposes to add 25,000 men to the 10,000 or 12,000 at Batoom; to place himself at their head, and to make an incursion towards Georgia, starting from Redoute-Kaleh, and turning Kutais to good account.

This idea was debated last night in a Council at the Grand Vizier's, and the result of the deliberations, as communicated to the Embassy through M. Pisani, was, that the troops to be employed in the above-mentioned manner under the command of Omer, should be taken from Eupatoria to the amount of 20,000, and from Bulgaria to the amount of 5,000, and that the Contingent, with its numbers completed, should occupy the vacant space at Eupatoria. By way of alternative, it is proposed that if the above-mentioned plan be deemed objectionable, it might be so far modified as to take only 10,000 men from the Crimea, and 15,000 from Bulgaria, including those destined to form part of the Contingent.

The Council professes itself ready to listen to any other suggestion proceeding from the two Embassies, in case that neither one nor the other of the preceding plans should be accepted.

I must confine myself, from want of time, to a statement of these leading points. My personal impression is that Eupatoria would be an advantageous position for the more complete organisation of the Contingent; that the absence of Omer Pasha from before Sebastopol, supposing the troops to remain there under a suitable commander, would be free from the objections lying against any serious diminution of their numbers, and that it might even be productive of some beneficial results.

I propose to communicate on the whole subject freely with my French colleague, and, after advising the Porte to the best of our judgment, to refer to the Commanders-in-chief, and to report again to your Lordship. It is, of course to be understood that my course of opinion is guided by a knowledge of your Lordship's objection to a premature employment of General Vivian's corps.

Brigadier-General Williams to the Earl of Clarendon (received August 24)

Kars, July 28, 1855

My Lord,

The enemy still occupies the camps indicated in my despatch of the 21st instant; but having learned from spies that General Mouravieff intended to move the bulk of his army from Boyouk-Tikmeh to Komansoor, a village only an hour's march to the south-east of our camp entrenchments, every effort has been made to strengthen them, and by four days' cheerful but incessant labour, the Infantry has completed five rows of *trous de loups* round the redoubts and breastworks, extending 6,000 yards; these conical holes, three feet in diameter and three feet deep, add much to our power of resistance.

The enemy's powerful Cavalry still block up the roads leading to Erzeroom and Ardahan, and destroy the growing crops; his Transport Department, as I have already informed your Lordship, is enormous; yesterday a convoy of 5,000 waggons passed towards their great camp, protected by every possible combination on the part of the enemy.

I beg to bring under your Lordship's notice the state of the clothing of this army, and to suggest that immediate steps be taken by the authorities at Constantinople to prepare and forward, without delay, the winter supply, including fezes, cloaks, shoes, and boots; and I also trust that money may be sent to Erzeroom, with orders to Tahir Pasha to cause large supplies of biscuit to be baked, and, above all, a land-carriage (consisting of camels and arabas) to be organised, this army being totally deficient of such an indispensable necessity.

W. F. WILLIAMS

Lord Stratford de Redcliffe to the Earl of Clarendon (received August 8)

Therapia, July 30, 1855

(Extract)

The unfavourable judgment passed by Her Majesty's Government on the plans which have been lately under discussion, with a view to the relief of the Sultan's army at Kars, has naturally increased the Porte's embarrassment. It was my duty to make it known to the Turkish Ministers, not only as an opinion, but, with respect to General Vivian's Contingent, as a veto. A most serious dilemma is the immediate result. Her Majesty's Government not only withhold the Contingent, but express a decided preference for the alternative of sending reinforcements to Erzeroom by the way of Trebizond. This opinion is not adopted by the Porte, or indeed by any official or personal authority here. The Seraskier, Omer Pasha, General Guyon, and our own officers, as far as I have means of knowing, agree with the Porte and the French Embassy in preferring a diversion on the side of Redoute-Kaleh, as offering better chances of success, supposing, of course, that the necessary means of transport supply and other indispensable wants can be sufficiently provided. France is at the same time decidedly adverse to any diminution of force in the Crimea; and Omer Pasha, ready to place himself at the head of an Asiatic expedition, requires for that purpose a part of the troops now there.

Such being the present state of the case, I am precluded from contributing to the Porte's extrication from its difficulties, otherwise than by countenancing some new location of the Contingent, which, without exposing the corps to a premature trial, might enable a force of the same amount to be detached for service elsewhere.

No final decision has yet been taken by the Porte. My colleague the French Ambassador has written for General Pélissier's opinion, and Omer Pasha is still in attendance on his Government.

Meanwhile the advices from Kars are not encouraging, and time of precious value is unavoidably wasted in doubt and uncertainty.

AUGUST 1855

The Earl of Clarendon to Lord Cowley

Foreign Office, August 1, 1855

My Lord,

I transmit to your Excellency herewith a copy of a despatch [Lord Stratford de Redcliffe to the Earl of Clarendon, dated July 23, 1855] from Viscount Stratford de Redcliffe, respecting the suggestions made by Omer Pasha during his visit to Constantinople, for the relief of the Turkish army at Kars; and with reference to that passage in which his Excellency states that the result of the deliberations of the Divan was, that the troops to be employed in the manner suggested by Omer Pasha, and under his command, should be taken from Eupatoria to the amount of 20,000 men, and from Bulgaria to the amount of 5,000, and that the British Contingent, with its numbers completed, should occupy the vacant space at Eupatoria. I have to state to your Excellency that Her Majesty's Government are favourably disposed to this proposition, and they hope that the Government of the Emperor will concur in it.

CLARENDON

Lord Cowley to the Earl of Clarendon

Paris, August 2, 1855, 2.15 p.m.

(Telegraphic)

Count Walewski foresees objections to the proposal contained in your despatch of yesterday.

He will submit it, however, to the Emperor, and hopes to give me His Majesty's answer on Saturday.

Lord Stratford de Redcliffe to the Earl of Clarendon (received August 16)

Therapia, August 2, 1855

My Lord,

The closing words of your Lordship's despatch of the 19th ultimo are, I apprehend, but too likely to be realised. Whatever supplies have been forwarded to the army at Kars since it became known at Constantinople that the Russians had advanced on that side may reach Erzeroom, but have only a slender chance of going beyond. I would observe at the same time that, little as the Turkish authorities have done themselves credit by their treatment of the army, they hardly deserve the imputation which is conveyed by the preceding words of your Lordship's despatch. Tardy and incomplete as their measures were, notwithstanding the frequent remonstrances and earnest recommendations of Her Majesty's Embassy, attention, to a certain degree, had been paid to the wants of the army, and my correspondence bears witness to much that was done, even under the perverse administration of Riza Pasha, towards the supply of those wants. It is a mistake to attribute the deficiency to a wilful neglect of the Asiatic troops. The troops in Europe were naturally the first object of the Porte's solicitude, and those troops enjoyed the advantage of being commanded by Omer Pasha. But they also experienced, in a less degree, the effects of a bad administrative system, not less corrupt in the military than other departments, and above all of inadequate finances and an exhausted Treasury. I never can forget that when a portion of Omer Pasha's army entered Bucharest on the retreat of the Russians, a regiment of the Sultan's Guards was described by Mr Colquhoun as marching with bare feet over roads covered with snow.

STRATFORD DE REDCLIFFE

The Earl of Clarendon to Lord Cowley

Foreign Office, August 3, 1855

(Extract)

Her Majesty's Government have learnt with regret by your Excellency's telegraphic despatch of yesterday that Count Walewski does not concur with them in the opinion that Omer Pasha and a portion of the army under his command might be sent to Asia to effect a diversion for the relief of Kars and the adjoining country, now menaced by the Russian forces under General Mouravieff, while their place in the Crimea might be filled up by the Turco-British Contingent under Lieutenant-General Vivian.

Her Majesty's Government, however, consider the relief of the Turkish troops in Asia of such vital importance, that they cannot abstain from laying before the Government of the Emperor the various arguments by which they consider the plan recommended by them may be supported.

It is plain that without assistance the whole Turkish force in Asia must be destroyed or captured. The force at Kars is surrounded, and even if able to defend its position against assault, which may be doubted, it must surrender when its provisions are exhausted, and that will happen in a few weeks.

The immediate result would be that 13,000 Turkish troops would become prisoners of war, and a strong position be occupied by the Russians.

But, moreover, Kars taken, Erzeroom must share the like fate, and the whole of the neighbouring country would be in the hands of the Russians, while the season would be too far advanced for military operations to drive them out of it.

If, on the other hand, the allies do not take Sebastopol before the winter, the Russians, by occupying Asia Minor, will have a considerable advantage over the allies, and as the Russians have nothing to do on the Danube, and are free from apprehension anywhere to the north of the Danube, they can send into Georgia, and thence into Asia Minor, a force of considerable magnitude. This would be striking a serious blow to the Turkish Empire, and one the effects of which it would be difficult to remedy. If, on the other hand, Omer Pasha were to go to Redoute-Kaleh or Erzeroom with a sufficient force, the Russians would be driven back, or forced to retire.

Omer Pasha's knowledge of Asiatic Turkey would give him advantages in carrying on war there which no other Commander can possess, while in the Crimea his presence is comparatively of no value.

Her Majesty's Government indeed feel doubtful whether, if the Turkish Government should desire to avail itself of Omer Pasha's special qualification for service in Asia, any just objections could be made to the Porte's utilising in that quarter the services of one who has proved himself to be so able a Commander, and who has succeeded in organising an efficient army at a moment when some of the most important provinces of the Turkish Empire are invaded by the enemy, and where a considerable Turkish force is in danger of being made prisoners of war.

Her Majesty's Government would doubt whether it was wise, even if they felt sure that they had the right to do so, to object to the adoption by the Porte of such a course, especially as the transfer of the Contingent under Lieutenant-General Vivian either to Balaklava or to Eupatoria, whichever might be deemed best, would fill up, or nearly so, the void occasioned by the removal of Omer Pasha and a portion of his force to Asia Minor, and the reinforcements sent to Lieutenant-General Vivian and to the British and French armies would add still further to the aggregate force of the allied armies in the Crimea.

Her Majesty's Government wish that your Excellency should submit these observations without delay to the French Government, in the hope that they may be induced to take a different view of the question from that which they have hitherto entertained, and may enable your Excellency to convey to Viscount Stratford de Redcliffe by the messenger of tomorrow, while a similar communication is made to M. de Thouvenel by the French Government, authority to recommend the Porte to adopt the course of detaching Omer Pasha and an adequate portion of his army to Asia Minor, so that by this means the only resource which now remains for averting from the Turkish army in Asia the great disaster which there is too much reason to apprehend is impending over it, may at all events not be left untried.

Kars, August 3, 1855

My Lord,

On the 31st ultimo General Mouravieff broke up his camp at Boyouk-Tikmeh, and stationed 15 battalions of Infantry, 1 regiment of Dragoons, 2 regiments of Cossacks, 500 Irregular Cavalry, and 40 guns, in a defensible position at Komansoor, about one hour to the south of us. With the remaining half of his army, the Russian General again moved towards the mountain-pass of Soghanli-Dagh, on the Erzeroom road. I observed his camp-fires yesterday at daybreak, from the heights above Kars, distant eight hours from us, but none were visible this morning.

Veli Pasha has been informed of this movement on the part of the enemy, and I have also written to Major Olpherts on the subject. If we are to credit the reports brought in by our spies, General Mouravieff meditates an advance upon Erzeroom, but I believe his object to be the devastation of the country, and more especially the destruction of the growing crops, in which barbarous measures the army now in our front is daily occupied.

We steadily add to the strength of our field-works, and yesterday we seized the cattle of the surrounding villages, to prevent their falling into the hands of the enemy, and to add to the chance of our holding out till relieved by the allies.

We are enabled to procure small sums of money from merchants, by giving favourable exchanges for sovereigns on the Erzeroom Military Defterdar, but I regret to state that he has so far forgotten his duty, as to refuse the payment of those bills, for which, I trust, he will be called to account by the Seraskier. It is thus that the Turks will upset every combination and chance of success for a few piastres of agio, whilst they themselves hesitate not to rob by wholesale.

The most active civil functionary in this camp is Kiarami Effendi, who is worthy of any reward which the Mushir may apply for, and I beg to recommend him to the good offices of your Lordship.

The spirits and disposition of the troops are excellent. We have still nearly two months' provision, except barley, which has failed us, our carriage communications with Erzeroom being entirely cut off.

W. F. WILLIAMS

Paris, August 4, 1855, 3.15 p.m.

(Telegraphic)

The French Government will not oppose the projected expedition to Asia Minor, under Omer Pasha, provided that the numbers of the Turkish Contingent before Sebastopol are not diminished.

The Earl of Clarendon to Lord Stratford de Redcliffe

Foreign Office, August 4, 1855

(Extract)

My despatch to Lord Cowley of yesterday's date contains a full statement of the grounds on which Her Majesty's Government consider such a movement under Omer Pasha advisable, and I have received this afternoon from his Excellency the telegraphic message which I enclose [see above], announcing that the French Government will not oppose the desired expedition.

Immediately on receipt of this message, I sent to your Excellency a despatch in the following terms:

> August 4. Omer Pasha can go to relieve Kars, provided he does not diminish the Turkish troops before Sebastopol, or disturb the garrison of Yenikale.
>
> Desire Vivian to hold himself in readiness to go to Eupatoria with his Turkish Contingent.

Consul Brant to the Earl of Clarendon (received August 29)

Erzeroom, August 7, 1855

My Lord,

I have the honour to enclose the copies of four despatches I addressed to his Excellency the Viscount Stratford de Redcliffe. I might have condensed them, but I preferred giving things in detail, that your Lordship might the better judge of the total incompetency of the Turkish officers to command military operations.

General Williams is now beleaguered in Kars, and must be starved out, if succours are not sent. The country around Kars has no resources left, and they have nothing to hope for but from strong reinforcements. It is, I confess, beyond my comprehension, how the Russians have been allowed, without control, to ravage the country; it will bring on a famine I expect, or else unheard-of dearness of food, and it would be difficult to estimate the immense loss of property which has been already incurred, and the still greater which may be anticipated.

JAS. BRANT

Enclosure 1

Consul Brant to Lord Stratford de Redcliffe

Erzeroom, August 3, 1855

My Lord,

I have the honour to report to your Excellency that yesterday, late in the evening, a report was spread that the Russians had reached Kupri-Keuy, and that the force under Veli Pasha was in full retreat on Erzeroom. I did not give credit to this rumour, as we hear so many similar every day; but near 11 o'clock at night, Hafiz Pasha called at my house, and when I heard of his being at the door, I went down: he was on horseback, and accompanied by a guard; he took me aside and told me that credible information had come that the Russians were actually at Kupri-Keuy, but he did not appear to know with certainty that Veli Pasha had retreated before them.

At past midnight the Defterdar sent me a letter informing me that Veli Pasha's force was on its retreat towards Erzeroom, and inviting me to attend a Council to be held next morning. I went, hoping to ascertain the real state of matters; but I found none of the Military Pashas there, but only the members of the Civil Medjlis, the Musteshar, the two Defterdars, Civil and Military, the Armenian Bishop, and some of the chiefs of the trading community. The Austrian Consul was already there, and the French soon joined the Assembly. No individual took the lead; no one seemed to know the object of the meeting; and a great deal of desultory conversation took place, which tended to no result, except the issue of an order that no families should quit the city, to prevent alarm spreading, and likewise an order to send some Bashi-Bozouks to occupy a by-pass, leading from the Plain of Passin into that of Erzeroom, which had not been fortified or noticed. I remarked that this was not a Military Council, and that such questions belonged to the General commanding, and should be proposed to the Council of War. It did not seem to be clear who was the commanding officer, and nobody knew exactly whither all the Military Pashas had gone to, nor on what errand.

On leaving me last night Hafiz Pasha went up to the forts and arranged for manning the guns, and mounting others, as well as placing Bashi-Bozouks in the redoubts. This morning several large guns were mounted in the forts. I left the Council without having learned anything to be depended on with regard to the Russians; but the French Consul, who had been at a village on the Plain of Passin, the day before, hearing of the Russian force being at Kupri-Keuy, came into town, and found the roads so choked with flying men, women, and children, mixed up with Bashi-Bozouks, as to render them almost impassable. All the villages were abandoned, the cattle left at the mercy of the Koords, who were driving them off, and then burning the houses. The evil of this will be very serious, even if it goes no further, the loss immense, and the replacing of so much food very difficult; and it is the more to be regretted, as very little foresight and attention to the army of Asia might have obviated the misery, the desolation, and the loss of property which must ensue.

The Division of Veli Pasha, increased by the garrison here, and reinforcements, though small, which have been gradually joining, should render the Turkish force, well commanded and occupying a strong position, as it now does, on the Pass of the Dévéboyonou, one hour and a half from the city, quite capable of making a successful resistance to the Russian invading force, which is variously represented at from 12,000 to 17,000 men of all arms, the most, I should say, Irregulars. There are hordes of Bashi-Bozouks here, who behave as usual—cowardly towards the enemy, cruelly towards their friends, and who, useless as they are, eat up the country, and cost what would support a small, useful, regular force, which might do real service in the field, and that the Bashi-Bozouks never did and never will do.

JAS. BRANT

Enclosure 2

Consul Brant to Lord Stratford de Redcliffe

Erzeroom, August 4, 1855

My Lord,

I have the honour to report to your Excellency, that today all the Pashas have been out at the camp at the Dévéboyonou.

There were innumerable reports as to the movements of the Russians, but it appears that they have not advanced, but are encamped at the village of Hassan-Kaleh, at a distance of about three leagues [4 miles] from the entrenched position of the Turkish force on the Dévéboyonou.

In the evening at about 6 o'clock, Hafiz Pasha came into town; and having made my preparations and hired horses, I addressed him a note, requesting an escort for my family, which I thought it prudent to remove under the circumstances. He expressed regret that I had come to such a determination, as it would spread alarm in the city, but he promised to call the next day and arrange the matter.

Another object I had in view was to learn some particulars of the relative forces of the Russians and Turks, and the probable result of the advance of the former; but his room was so crowded with persons, that my dragoman could not speak a word to him privately, but he only learned generally that the Russian force was estimated at between 800 to 1,200 men, with twelve or sixteen guns, while Hafiz Pasha reckoned the whole Turkish force at the entrenched position, in the redoubts around the town, and in the city, at about 20,000 or 25,000, if not 30,000 men of all arms, but mostly Bashi-Bozouks.

My dragoman also heard that Hafiz Pasha was of opinion that the Russians should be attacked, as he considered it disgraceful to allow them the complete possession of the plain with an inferior force, and that in consequence of his difference of opinion from the other Pashas, he had retired from the camp. He inferred from the Pasha's expressions that he was disgusted with the Commanders of the army.

I received this morning a note from Major Olpherts, from the Turkish camp. He said their positions could not be forced in front, and could not be taken unless by surprise, or by being outflanked. He thought the Russian force could not exceed 8,000 men, with ten or fourteen guns, as reported; and unless it was reinforced from Kars, there was no danger.

The Major does not allude to there being confusion or disorder in the camp, though I heard that it existed.

JAS. BRANT

Enclosure 3

Consul Brant to Lord Stratford de Redcliffe

Erzeroom, August 6, 1855

(Extract)

I have the honour to inform your Excellency, that yesterday several of the Pashas came from the camp to attend a Council, which was attended by a great many of the principal Turks.

After its breaking up, Hafiz Pasha called on me on his way to the camp. He would scarcely wait to allow me time to ask a question. He wished me to defer the departure of my family, in order not to alarm the public; but as I pressed for a guard, remarking that women and children could but add to the confusion, he promised one should be ready for this morning. I told him that I had myself no intention to depart until the last moment.

He complained that his Bashi-Bozouks were unprovided with tents, and exposed to the heat of the sun by day, and the cold air by night, and were falling sick and deserting. They were allowed but a small loaf of bad bread. Their conduct inspires a great alarm in the town, and all the shops are closed. The Pasha said he must go to the camp to speak a word of encouragement to his men, or they would all desert.

The French Consul yesterday morning received advices from the camp, which not being explicit or encouraging, he proposed riding out to ascertain the real state of matters. Towards evening he returned: the Russian camp was in the same position it was at first, and the troops had not made any movement.

At the camp everything was in the greatest state of confusion; guns, shot, and ammunition in distant places; no preparations made for a defence; no knowledge of the extent of the enemy's force; and no one seemed employed to any useful purpose. In short, it appeared to the Consul, that were the Russians to have made an attack, scarce any attempt at resistance would have been made. He estimated the Turkish force at from 8,000 to 10,000—about 6,000 Infantry, Cavalry, and Artillery, and the rest Bashi-Bozouks. This, I think, from all I can learn, is about correct. There are nearly 40 good guns.

Veli Pasha commands the regular troops; Mehmed Pasha, our Vali, all the Bashi-Bozouks, except the Trebizond and Lazistan, which are under Hafiz Pasha. There seems to be great jealousy and want of cordial understanding amongst the Commanders, none of whom seem to possess the requisite qualities of judgment, military knowledge, and courage.

The Bashi-Bozouks go out to camp and come in when they think proper, and are apparently under no sort of control.

In the evening Hafiz Pasha came into town, and sent me a message to beg I would not quit in the morning, as the Russians had retreated, and we should confer together on the subject on the morrow. It had been observed that the Russians had moved their tents in the afternoon, but as it is their custom, this was not supposed to indicate any movement of consequence;

but the Mudir of Hassan-Kaleh sent word to the camp that the Russians had gone to Kupri-Keuy. The motive of this retreat is unknown as yet.

Enclosure 4

Consul Brant to Lord Stratford de Redcliffe

Erzeroom, August 7, 1855

My Lord,

I have the honour to report to your Excellency that the Russians have retreated on the Kars road, having razed the earthworks at Kupri-Keuy, for which purpose they took with them 200 Armenians from Hassan-Kaleh; and they further took 100 araba-loads of grain from Government stores.

Everything that I have stated in my three last despatches has been fully confirmed by trustworthy persons, but I have not spoken with sufficient severity of the imbecile and cowardly conduct of the Pashas; they would undoubtedly have run away if they had been attacked, although, with the number of guns they had, their position, if tolerably well defended, could not have been forced by an enemy treble the numbers of the Russians. It is pretty certain they had not above 8,000 men in all, with 10 guns. The conduct as well of the Pashas as of the Laz, destroys all confidence in the safety of the town; if attacked, it will probably, in such case, be plundered both by the defenders and the enemy; and I have thought it prudent to remove my family to Trebizond.

JAS. BRANT

Brigadier-General Williams to the Earl of Clarendon (received September 19)

Kars, August 10, 1855

My Lord,

I had the honour, on the 3rd instant, of acquainting your Lordship with the movement of General Mouravieff towards Erzeroom, and I have since learned that prior to that advance, the Russian General had received a reinforcement of a regiment of Infantry from Georgia, making up a total of 33 battalions of Infantry. The force he left to observe us consisted of 18 battalions of Infantry, three regiments of Cavalry, and 54 guns. As neither our numbers (which I abstain from stating) nor our organisation could hold out a chance of success in any attack upon such an army as now observes us, I have advised the Mushir still further to strengthen his entrenchments, and this counsel his Excellency has steadily carried out, through the zealous superintendence of Colonel Lake.

During the absence of the Russian Commander-in-chief, the General in command of the corps of observation has kept our garrison on the alert, more especially his Cavalry, which, from its superior numbers and discipline, is master of the neighbourhood. But on the 8th instant, the enemy, losing sight of his usual precautions, advanced with large masses of Infantry, Cavalry, and Artillery, to within gun-shot of the Kanly Tabia, on the south-east angle of our entrenched camp, when a well-directed fire from the guns of that redoubt obliged him to retire with the loss of several officers and many men.

With regard to the movements of General Mouravieff, I learn through a verbal message from Veli Pasha, sent by an orderly dragoon from the close vicinity of the Déveboyonou, that he had executed his instructions by falling back from Kupri-Keuy on that Pass, which I had selected, and in part fortified, before I left Erzeroom; but I am still ignorant of what has subsequently taken place between the two armies in that neighbourhood, although a week has elapsed since the arrival of the orderly dragoon above alluded to. If, however, we can believe a man who has just reached Kars from the Soghanli-Dagh, and who assures me that General Mouravieff's corps d'armée was camped last night on this side of that mountain-pass, and consequently in the Plain of Kars, I must draw the gratifying conclusion, that he has found Veli Pasha's position, joined to the fortifications of Erzeroom, too strong to molest without losses which he was not prepared to risk.

Be this as it may, I trust the allies will, by a prompt diversion in Georgia, oblige General Mouravieff to retire; otherwise nothing can save Kars from falling into his hands. We are now on two-thirds of our ration of bread, and the cattle seized from the villages will not supply animal food for anything like the period named in my last despatch. The horses of the Cavalry and Artillery begin to feel the want of barley, and will soon be unfit for service.

W. F. WILLIAMS

Lord Stratford de Redcliffe to the Earl of Clarendon (received August 24)
Therapia, August 12, 1855

My Lord,

From the conversation which I held this morning with Omer Pasha, and also from what passed at my interview, as mentioned elsewhere, with the Ottoman Secretary of State, I conclude that the Porte is firmly resolved on attempting to relieve the army at Kars, by a diversion from some point of the coast near, if not exactly at, Redoute-Kaleh.

Your Lordship is already apprised of the grounds on which opinions are entertained in favour of that plan. The Ottoman Commander-in-chief is fully convinced that any attempt to operate by the way of Trebizond and Erzeroom would prove abortive. Besides the want of time and difficulties occasioned by the badness of the road, his Highness argues that on no military calculation could he reckon upon being able to meet on equal terms the Russian army now engaged in besieging Kars, and advancing on Erzeroom.

The Porte is to hold a Council this afternoon, and Omer Pasha is to be present at its deliberations. The decision, whatever it may be, at its close, will be communicated to the two Embassies, and the principle of abstaining from any mode of action calculated to impede or discourage the general operations of the alliance appeared to meet with the full admission [consent] of Fuad Pasha.

STRATFORD DE REDCLIFFE

Consul Brant to the Earl of Clarendon (received September 3)
Erzeroom, August 13, 1855

My Lord,

I have the honour to enclose a copy of a despatch I this day addressed to Her Majesty's Ambassador at the Porte.

It is painful for me to repeat so often the same disgusting tale of incompetency in the Governors and Chiefs, of venality, corruption, and cowardice in all classes; but I conceive I should not be doing my duty were I to shrink from exposing these things, in order that your Lordship may form a true estimate of the difficulties to be encountered in remedying these crying evils.

There should be here a General like General Williams, with sufficient authority to keep the Turkish Pashas to their duty, otherwise they will never do it, in defending their country. Although there are troops here wasting their time in perfect idleness, yet bands of Koords are allowed to complete the ruin of the poor inhabitants of the Plain of Passin, which the Russians only partially effected.

Our Vali, Mehmed Pasha, is in the camp with a number of irregular soldiers, and witnessing the terrified inhabitants flying from the Koords who had driven them from their homes, does nothing to protect them, nor to avert the dreadful calamities inflicted on them by their fellow subjects.

I have often represented how useless these Koords were as subjects to the Sultan, and how dangerous in time of war with Russia, yet but very partial and ineffectual attempts have been made to keep them under control; and now they are entirely freed from it, they prove themselves worse foes to their Sovereign than the armies of a nation with whom he is at open war.

JAS. BRANT

Enclosure

Consul Brant to Lord Stratford de Redcliffe
Erzeroom, August 13, 1855

(Extract)

I have the honour to report to your Excellency that the Russian force which invaded Hassan-Kaleh, after retiring, divided itself, one portion taking the road to Kars, the other retracing its steps to Toprak-Kaleh. The Turkish army retains its position at the Dévéboyonou, waiting, it is said, orders from the Mushir at Kars, although there has been a talk of its resuming its position at Kupri-Keuy, leaving the defences of the Dévéboyonou to the Bashi-Bozouk. Every day, nay every hour, shows that the military officers of rank are worse than incompetent. There is no union amongst them; each asserting his right to command, and intriguing against the others, to the detriment of discipline and efficiency, and to the ruin of the Sultan's cause; and yet the resources for defence are immense—sufficient, if well employed, to resist General Mouravieff's whole army; but the capacity is wanting: every officer is trying to appropriate to himself power for the sake of securing a good share of plunder, and instead of considering how he can best serve his country, thinks only of serving his own selfish purposes.

The Bashi-Bozouks commit, as usual, every kind of excess, and desert in crowds; they are the terror of the inhabitants, and more dreaded than the Russians. Provisions are getting scarce, and increasing in price; disease is spreading amongst an ill-fed, ill-sheltered, and reckless crowd of lawless men, who are brought hither by compulsion, and have neither the courage nor the inclination to fight in the cause of the Sultan, and who destroy the resources of the country as they pass and repass through it. There must have arrived up to this time near 30,000, and I should estimate that the force remaining can scarce amount to 10,000; it is said that a further number of 15,000 will soon arrive.

Reports are continually spread of attacks on Kars, successfully repulsed, countenanced by, if not originating with, the military authorities; so that one doubts everything one hears. This is a system with the Turks, but what it can tend to but distrust and discouragement, it would be difficult to imagine.

When I ascertained that the retreat of the Russians was a reality and not a feint, I deferred the removal of my family to avoid the great expense, inconvenience, and danger.

Brigadier-General Williams to the Earl of Clarendon (received September 10)
Kars, August 15, 1855

(Extract)

By the last messenger I had the honour to inform your Lordship of the report brought in as to the return of General Mouravieff to the plain of Kars; I am now enabled to confirm this intelligence, and to state that the united Russian army is encamped in front of the key to our entrenched position, to the defences of which we have added and still continue to add.

A messenger yesterday reached us from Veli Pasha from the fortified position of the Pass of Dévéboyonou near Erzeroom, from which it appears that General Mouravieff retired without attempting to force it; and I have reason to believe that Hafiz Pasha made, in the meantime, every effort to put the new forts around Erzeroom in a proper state of defence.

The demonstration which the enemy recently made against Kanly Tabia, of which I had the honour to acquaint your Lordship by the last messenger, cost them a general officer, a Colonel, five Captains, and 220 sub-officers and men. We witnessed from the heights the funeral of an officer of high rank, and the preparations for burying their dead. The fire of our Artillery was most creditable, obliging that of the enemy to retire after firing four rounds.

General Mouravieff's army now before us, consists of 28 battalions of Infantry, 6,000 Cavalry, and 76 guns; 5 battalions, with Irregular Horse and 4 guns, must be added to this force—they are employed in escorting the convoys from Gumri. The enemy's Cavalry is now so stationed on the Erzeroom roads as to cut off every source of information or supply.

P.S. A peasant, well acquainted with the country, will endeavour to take this despatch over the mountains.

The Earl of Clarendon to Lord Stratford de Redcliffe
Foreign Office, August 16, 1855

My Lord,

With reference to your Excellency's despatch of the 2nd instant, respecting supplies to the army of Kars, I have to inform you that Her Majesty's Government have much reason to doubt whether the supplies which Riza Pasha informed you he had forwarded to the army at Kars ever reached their destination, or ever left Constantinople.

CLARENDON

Lieutenant-Colonel Simmons to the Earl of Clarendon (received August 29)
Constantinople, August 20, 1855

My Lord,

I have to inform your Lordship that an aide-de-camp of the Seraskier arrived last evening from Kars, which he left about fifteen days since, having taken his departure by night, and carefully avoiding in his route the most fre-quented roads. He was not the bearer of despatches, as it appeared dangerous to entrust him with written documents, for fear of his falling into the enemy's hands.

He reports that, at the time of his departure, the stores within the town of Kars did not contain more than sufficient provisions for the garrison for one month, or five weeks at the outside, and that they were not well pro-vided with ammunition. This, however, does not appear to be of much consequence, as General Mouravieff had proclaimed to his army, which, by the reinforcements it has received, is stated now to number about 50,000 men, to reduce the town of Kars by starvation, and to capture the garrison without firing a shot.

It is evident that his proceedings correspond with this announcement, for the Russians have not opened trenches against the town, and merely con-tent themselves with a strict blockade.

They have caused the inhabitants to remove everything in the shape of provisions throughout a district within a radius of eight hours (28 miles) round Kars as a centre.

The Russians had advanced, and shown themselves within ten miles of Erzeroom, the Turks not being in sufficient force to oppose them at Kupri-Keuy, about 30 miles from Erzeroom, where they had thrown up some entrenchments to cover the town. The Russians, however, had since fallen back again towards Kars.

The force at Erzeroom consists of 6,000 Regular troops, and 12,000 Irregular, but many of these latter are leaving and dispersing.

I learned the above from Omer Pasha this morning, and from his con-versation it is evident that the Porte are deeply impressed with the deplorable state of affairs in Asia, and are almost in despair at the apparent certainty of losing, towards the end of this month or early in September, the garrison of Kars, 16,000 men, with nearly 200 pieces of artillery, of which about 70 are field guns.

It would appear, from the Pasha's observations, that they attribute this approaching disaster primarily to the mismanagement and neglect of affairs by the late Government, and look upon Reshid and Riza Pashas as especially culpable.

It would appear also that they are very much grieved and disappointed at the time which has been lost in endeavouring to recover their position, and save the garrison of Kars, and that the Cabinets of Paris and London, as well as the military authorities in the Crimea, have not considered the subject in that serious aspect in which it presents itself to the Porte, but have objected to the propositions which have hitherto been made with a view to retrieving their position and preventing the disaster.

Omer Pasha has authorised me to state as his opinion, that he feels satisfied that the effect will be very shortly felt, probably within a few weeks, by the advance of the enemy's cavalry, which is very numerous, and by a prohibition which he will impose upon the inhabitants to prevent all articles of provision from being brought to Trebizond, Samsoon, and Sinope, for exportation for the use of the allies.

Some of the Koords, it appears, have already joined the Russians, and probably a decisive success at Kars will take effect on the Persians.

The result will be that a great part of the Asiatic dominions of the Porte, with its resources in men, money, and provisions, will be lost for a time at least to the Turks.

The loss of revenue will be most seriously felt by the Turks in the prosecution of the war; and Omer Pasha appears to think that there may even be difficulty in keeping the soldiers of the army of Roumelia together, as they have been in great measure recruited in Asia, and hearing that their country is open to the Russians, without any force, however small, to oppose their progress through it, they will naturally, if not sent, seek to desert, with the hope of saving their families from the hands of the enemy.

The whole of these considerations, which press with great weight on the Porte, cause Omer Pasha more than ever to desire to make a decided movement with the least possible loss of time, with the troops, according to the proposition which I forwarded to your Lordship in my despatch of the 16th instant.

For this reason he hopes to obtain the assistance of France and England for the conveyance of his troops and for provisioning his army; for he says that without it the Turks alone cannot perform the operation within a reasonable time, and therefore the small force, 6,000 men, in Erzeroom, will be dispersed, making, with the garrison of Kars, a loss of 22,000 men to the common cause, besides a numerous artillery.

From the turn affairs have taken, he appears to consider it questionable where the point of disembarkation should be, but must leave its determination to the development of events and to the movements which the Russians may hereafter decide on making.

J. L. A. SIMMONS

Brigadier-General Williams to the Earl of Clarendon (received September 19)
Kars, August 21, 1855

(Extract)

Since I had the honour to address your Lordship on the 15th instant, the enemy's Infantry and Artillery have remained in the camp they then occupied. The Cavalry, supported by Horse Artillery and rockets, however, has taken a strong hill-position to the north-west, about an hour's march from our lines, and assisted by his numerous Irregular Horse, cuts off all communications with Erzeroom, *via* Olti, with Ardahan, or indeed any other place from whence we could draw supplies of any kind.

A convoy of 3,000 arabas, or country carts, and 2,000 camels, is now in sight coming from Gumri. Battering guns, drawn by bullocks, accompany this convoy. I have, therefore, requested Colonel Lake to convert the barbette battery of Kanly Tabia into one with embrasures, and to take such measures for strengthening the armament of this and other works as the occasion requires.

The weather is oppressively hot, yet the troops are in excellent health; the hospital list amounting to 289.

Should Her Majesty's Government and its allies determine on making Trebizond the base of future operations against Georgia, I still trust that an immediate and powerful demonstration will be made by a Turkish army from Redoute-Kaleh; and for the present defence of Erzeroom, I would beg strongly to urge the landing of a division of General Vivian's force at Trebizond, and a rapid advance upon Erzeroom, so as to ensure the retention of that important fortified post in the hands of the allies, even if this division of the Contingent found itself unable to succour us.

Brigadier-General Williams to the Earl of Clarendon (received October 1)
Kars, August 25, 1855

My Lord,

The Russian Cavalry, which now amounts to 8,000, has so narrowed the circle from which we cut our forage and scanty supply of barley in the ear, that detailed orders will be forwarded by this courier to Tahir Pasha, the Chief of the Military Medjlis of Erzeroom, and also to Mehmed Pasha, the Governor-General of the Province, to endeavour to throw convoys (however small) of barley into Kars. Directions will also accompany these orders with regard to the storing of the harvest now reaping in and around the city of Erzeroom.

I am sorry to inform your Lordship that great apathy reigns at Erzeroom from the highest functionary to the lowest; every Pasha and Bey who has been charged with missions from this camp to that city has, in his turn, disappeared from the scene—a scene from which all of high rank are glad to escape. I therefore trust that, through your Lordship's representations, they may receive from the Porte the most stringent orders to execute the directions forwarded to them by the Mushir.

We have just heard that one of the detachments of Infantry and Cavalry (under Coblian Ali Bey) which so harass us, has marched towards Ahkiska, which place is menaced by an incursion of Irregulars, by order of Mustafa Pasha of Batoom. This will convince your Lordship that a serious demonstration from Redoute-Kaleh would cause the immediate departure of at least a large corps of General Mouravieff's army, whose camps remain where they were when I last had the honour to address your Lordship. A portion of the Irregular Riflemen of Lazistan recently evinced a mutinous spirit, and when caught in the act of pillage by Major Teesdale, drew their weapons upon him. By my insistence the Mushir caused them to be flogged and imprisoned; their rifles and other arms were destroyed in presence of their comrades; and this prompt punishment has completely restored order.

By means of numerous and well-paid spies, the enemy has been able to obtain all the information he desired. I, two days ago, induced the Mushir to try and execute a Mussulman, on whom were found the proofs of his guilt, and the inhabitants of the town expressed great satisfaction at his fate. Another Mussulman is also under sentence, and will be hanged. The Mushir has also proclaimed his determination to shoot all deserters who may again fall into our hands.

In thus taking every precaution against treachery, we cheerfully persevere, in the hope that our long and painful blockade may yet terminate favourably; for the enemy, thus far, does not seem inclined to enter on a more active course towards us.

W. F. WILLIAMS

Lieutenant-Colonel Simmons to the Earl of Clarendon (received September 5)
Constantinople, August 26, 1855

My Lord,
I have to inform your Lordship that Omer Pasha has stated to me that he will not be able to leave Constantinople for five or six days, as he is occupied in making the necessary arrangements for the expedition to Asia, and his presence here is absolutely required to complete them.

I yesterday was present at a meeting at the Capudan Pasha's, at which the Seraskier and Omer Pasha were present, and when the necessary orders were given for carrying the following arrangements into execution:

According to the calculations then made, the Turkish sailing fleet, consisting of six ships, are capable of carrying, at one time, 5,950 men, or 1,360 horses. The steamers belonging to the Government, seven in number, of which three have been recently purchased, with five others which the Government have either hired or are in the point of hiring, are capable of carrying at one time 10,450 men or 2,060 horses.

Orders were therefore given for these ships, the greater part of which have already proceeded to Sizopolis or Varna, to embark three batteries of Artillery with *matériel* and horses complete, and to fill up entirely with baggage horses, which will proceed at once, the sailing vessels towed by steamers to Batoom.

They will then return and load entirely with Infantry.

Omer Pasha hopes thus to land 15,000 men and 3,420 horses in Asia in two trips of the Turkish fleet alone, the operation occupying from three weeks to a month, or for each voyage from ten days to a fortnight. This calculation, however, may differ very much from the reality, if the weather should prove to be tempestuous, and prevent the sailing ships from being towed.

The baggage horses and artillery being landed, the Pasha hopes that, so soon as the Infantry arrive, he will be able at once to advance with the troops already there, so as to take them out of the unhealthy climate of the coast, and to make some slight demonstration before the arrival of the rest of his troops from the Crimea.

The pontoon train and remainder of the baggage horses will follow according as the means of transport are found.

Omer Pasha is most desirous that assistance should be given by the allies in conveying the troops and their *matériel* from before Sebastopol, and baggage horses from Sizopolis; and he considers the most practicable way in which this could be done, would be by allowing the English fleet to convey the troops on from before Sebastopol to Asia, after having conveyed the Contingent to Balaklava to replace them.

The Pasha intends himself to go to the coast of Asia to examine the positions and obtain information before the first ships can arrive and disembark their freights.

J. L. A. SIMMONS

SEPTEMBER 1855

Brigadier-General Williams to the Earl of Clarendon (received October 1)
Kars, September 1, 1855

My Lord,

Since I addressed your Lordship on the 25th ultimo, the enemy's Cavalry has received a reinforcement of 2,000 men, and presses, if possible, still more closely on our picquets and advanced posts, where a daily struggle takes place for forage, which has, for several days, failed to supply our wants; a large portion, therefore, of our attenuated Cavalry horses has been sent from the camp, in order to seek subsistence beyond the mountains, and out of the reach of the enemy's Cavalry, which cannot be estimated at less than 10,000. General Mouravieff, with his Infantry and Artillery, occupies the same positions which he held when I last wrote.

It is with the utmost difficulty that either horse or foot messengers escape the vigilance of the enemy, and I abstain from entering into details which might fall into their hands. The garrison preserves its health, notwithstanding the great difference of temperature between day and night; its spirit, I am happy to add, is excellent.

W. F. WILLIAMS

Consul Brant to the Earl of Clarendon (received October 1)
Erzeroom, September 4, 1855

My Lord,

I have the honour to enclose a copy of a despatch I addressed to Viscount Stratford de Redcliffe, yesterday, regarding Kars.

The avowal of Tahir Pasha, that he has not under him a single officer of courage or enterprise, is a lamentable proof, if such were wanting, of the total inefficiency of the Turkish officers. I much fear that General Williams is in a very precarious position, and that the provisions of the garrison will not hold out while succours are coming. Something might have been done before this. The failure in preserving Kars is not merely the defeat of a small force—it is the loss of an immense number of guns, ammunition, and stores of all kinds, which it would take a serious amount of money, and no small exertions, to replace; and besides that, the works made at Kars and here would render both places almost impregnable in the hands of the Russians, and it would demand a summer's campaign, and 50,000 good troops, to recover what 10,000 men, sent up now, might have saved.

I cannot conceive how the Turkish Government can have been so apathetic; it must have been long since informed of the danger of delay, and so small an effort was needed to prevent so terrible a calamity as the loss of Kars and Erzeroom. If Omer Pasha be quick in his movements, he may yet be in time, but delay is fraught with imminent danger; and I shall be very anxious until I hear of the landing of an adequate force at Redoute-Kaleh, as Kars, by that event alone, might, I hope, be saved.

JAS. BRANT

Enclosure

Consul Brant to Lord Stratford de Redcliffe

Erzeroom, September 3, 1855

My Lord,

I received a letter from Kars of the 25th August, in which General Williams begged me to urge Tahir Pasha to do something for their relief, observing that a regiment of Cavalry having gone from Kars and passed the Russian posts, it might return, each horseman bringing in two bags of barley. I waited on Tahir Pasha, and he promised that he would leave nothing undone to relieve the garrison.

At Olti, about half-way, there are stores of everything, but the Commander there, Aali Pasha, is credulous and timid, and is prevented from making attempts to throw in supplies by exaggerated reports he hears of the danger of the undertaking and the certainty of failure. Tahir Pasha observed that Aali Pasha, by his timidity, paralyses those under him who have more energy than himself, and he begged me to represent to General Williams that there is not a single officer amongst all the forces out of Kars who has spirit or enterprise enough to make an attempt at introducing relief, though he were promised promotion for success, as I had suggested.

Tahir Pasha said that he would go himself to Olti and see what he could do, and Major Stuart and Captain Cameron expressed their wish to accompany him, and do their best to assist in an attempt to get into Kars with a body of Cavalry carrying barley.

There are three regiments now outside Kars, reckoning about 1,200 men, beside some Irregular Horse, so that by a successful effort a considerable supply might be introduced, and I should expect that such a body would be too strong to be stopped by any outposts it might encounter, if the trial were made secretly and by the least frequented paths.

General Williams dare not express himself clearly as to his exact position in regard to the stock of provisions, but from what he does say and from what I have heard from other quarters, I much fear that they are beginning to run very short, and that if such efficient succours as would oblige the Russians to retreat do not speedily arrive, or supplies cannot be introduced, it will not be possible to hold out until the snow obliges the enemy to retire.

Omer Pasha was reported to be about to land immediately at Redoute-Kaleh with 30,000 troops, but I yesterday heard that he would not embark from Constantinople before the 1st Muharem, I believe ten days hence; and when matters begin once to be deferred, there is no saying how often they may be again postponed, while every minute's delay may bring on the catastrophe which is sought to be prevented.

I would therefore represent to your Excellency the necessity of stimulating the Turkish Government to hasten forward succours, for if Kars be taken, Erzeroom must of course fall, and the losses these events would occasion the Turkish Government are such as would be beyond its power to repair, and, besides, an enormous sacrifice of blood and treasure, a very large army, and a year's campaign, would be required to recover the two cities, which in the hands of Russia might become impregnable.

Jas. Brant

Consul Brant to the Earl of Clarendon (received October 1)
Erzeroom, September 4, 1855

My Lord,

I have the honour to report to your Lordship that a person who arrived from Kars later than the post, states that on the 29th August the Russians made a double attack on Kars: one a feint, at the Veli Pasha Tabia, with four battalions, a few guns, and some Bashi-Bozouks; the other, a serious one, with their whole force on the Kanly Tabia.

The first was repulsed by a sortie of some Turkish troops, and the other by the Artillery, which did great execution on the assailants with grape. On their retreat, in confusion, they were followed up by some Turkish Cavalry and Bashi-Bozouks to the edge of their camp.

More is not known, and possibly the account may be an exaggeration, if not an invention.

The military authorities, however, credit the fact of an attack having been made and repulsed.

Jas. Brant

Consul Brant to the Earl of Clarendon (received October 1)

Erzeroom, September 5, 1855

(Extract)

I have the honour to enclose a memorandum, dated the 1st instant, from General Williams, of which he desired me to forward your Lordship a copy. It arrived this evening at sunset.

Enclosure

Memorandum

Kars, September 1, 1855

The most is made of our provisions; the soldier is reduced to half-allowances of bread and meat, or rice butter; sometimes 100 drachms of biscuit instead of bread; nothing besides. No money. Mussulman population (3,000 rifles) will soon be reduced to starvation. Armenians are ordered to quit the town tomorrow. No barley; scarcely any forage. Cavalry reduced to walking skeletons, and sent out of garrison; Artillery horses soon the same. How will the field-pieces be moved after that?

The apathy of superior officers is quite distressing. We can hold out two months more. What is being done for the relief of this army?

W. F. WILLIAMS

Lord Stratford de Redcliffe to the Earl of Clarendon (received September 19)

Therapia, September 6, 1855

My Lord,

In consequence of your Lordship's continued persuasion, as expressed in your despatch of the 16th ultimo, that no part of the supplies destined for the Turkish forces at Kars ever reached that army, if even they ever left Constantinople, I have repeated my enquiries, and the result is the following statement, made by the person whom I principally employed, and who is officially responsible for the correctness of his statements: "I have ascertained that every article demanded by the Commander-in-chief and General Williams, was duly transmitted." My informant was allowed to inspect the official registers. The Seraskier at the same time thinks it possible that the supplies may not have gone beyond Erzeroom, whither the winter clothing, which was lately applied for, is now being conveyed. The arrival of a reinforcement of Artillerymen in that city has given much satisfaction.

When I saw the Seraskier two days ago, I urged him to send a supply of provisions, if possible, for the army at Kars. He assured me that it would be impossible for the convoy to reach its destination.

STRATFORD DE REDCLIFFE

The Earl of Clarendon to Lieutenant-Colonel Simmons

Foreign Office, September 7, 1855

Sir,

The account of the arrangements proposed by Omer Pasha for the relief of the army in Asia, which is contained in your despatch of the 26th ultimo, is inconsistent with subsequent statements which have reached Her Majesty's Government.

In your despatch you report that Omer Pasha reckons upon taking a portion of the Turkish troops from before Sebastopol and replacing them by General Vivian's Contingent. But it appears by a despatch of a later date from General Simpson, that Omer Pasha has given it as his opinion that General Vivian's Contingent would not be fit to take up a position before Sebastopol until next spring; and in consequence of that opinion, and by reason of General Simpson's protest against having the Contingent sent to him, which protest was founded upon Omer Pasha's opinion, Her Majesty's Government have determined that the Contingent shall not go to join the army before Sebastopol.

CLARENDON

Brigadier-General Williams to the Earl of Clarendon (received October 8)

Kars, September 7, 1855

My Lord,

I had the honour of addressing your Lordship on the 1st instant; on the following night we succeeded in getting 1,500 of our starving horses out of the camp and over the mountains, in spite of the blockading Cavalry. We have not yet heard how many of our horses and men fell into the enemy's hands, but from the reports of spies I should think about 150 of all kinds were captured.

The execution of two spies has, in a great measure, broken up the party within our camp which gave the enemy information.

A dangerous amount of desertion took place on the nights of the 4th and 5th instant, but having shot an Infantry and an Artillery deserter, the mischief was arrested. The town and army now know that no spy or deserter shall escape his doom if taken.

We work without cessation on our entrenchments, and, although on short rations, hope to hold out until relieved, and in the meantime confidently look forward to repulse the enemy if he should assault our works.

We have been obliged to destroy many of our Cavalry horses today, in consequence of want of forage for them.

W. F. WILLIAMS

Brigadier-General Williams to the Earl of Clarendon (received October 25)

Kars, September 10, 1855

(Extract)

The Mushir proposes to endeavour to get tonight a messenger through the enemy's videttes; and I avail myself of the opportunity to inform your

Lordship that the Russian army and its detachments occupy the positions they did on the 7th. Their Cavalry are now employed in setting fire to the dry grass on which we endeavour to feed our horses, and for which daily skirmishes take place (up to within the range of our long guns).

The weather has become cold, and snow fell on the surrounding hills on the night of the 8th; but after the equinoctial gales we may have two months sufficiently moderate to admit of military operations. I therefore continue the work of adding to our defences. "Trous de loups" have been made round our entrenchments on the heights, which extend more than a mile from Veli Pasha Tabia to the English Tabias; in the meantime the interior line of the town has not been neglected.

In spite of the military executions I informed your Lordship of in my last despatch, desertion to a serious extent occurred last night; I therefore advised the Mushir to disband the regiment of Redif, from which all these desertions have taken place, to put the officers on half-pay, and to distribute the men amongst the companies of the other corps. The sentence was executed this morning, to the astonishment of the officers and soldiers of this unworthy regiment; and I trust we have now struck at the root of the evil, for the general disposition of the garrison is admirable.

Consul Brant to the Earl of Clarendon (received October 8)
Erzeroom, September 11, 1855

My Lord,

I have the honour to enclose a copy of a despatch I this day addressed to his Excellency the Viscount Stratford de Redcliffe regarding the position of Kars, and the measures adopted for its relief. I consider them incomplete unless a force be sent up direct to Kars by Trebizond and Erzeroom. I would not wish to throw discouragement on the result of the expedition under Omer Pasha, but I cannot divest my mind of great anxiety as to its result from the effects of the climate, and the nature of the country it will have to traverse in its advance on Tiflis—a country of swamps, woods, and rivers, and of small resources for provisioning an army; possessed by an active enemy like the Russians, I conceive the only chance of success against Tiflis (the safety of the army depends on its success) consists in a rapid march through the country. If the proceedings of Omer Pasha be dilatory, he will lose half his men by sickness and privations, and will effect nothing.

In my opinion a much safer plan would have been to have sent even a smaller force by this route. The expedition has been too long delayed, and by this delay its success has been imperilled. I hope most sincerely that my prevision may prove incorrect; everything depends on the activity and energy of Omer Pasha, and the support he may receive from his own Government. If the latter be not greater than my experience leads me to anticipate, I can feel no confidence in a favourable result, and I cannot help thinking that 10,000 European troops, with 3,000 or 4,000 Cavalry, sent to Kars a month ago by this route, would have effected more than the present expedition, even if it proves as large and as complete as it is reported to be.

JAS. BRANT

Consul Brant to Lord Stratford de Redcliffe
Erzeroom, September 11, 1855

My Lord,

I have the honour to inform your Excellency that I received a visit from Saleh Bey, a Miralai of Cavalry, who has just arrived from Kars. He is going on to Constantinople, to represent on the part of the Mushir the dangerous predicament in which the garrison stands, unless immediate and direct succours be sent for its relief. He says that Omer Pasha's army will require a month or more before it can move from the coast, and General Mouravieff may not find it necessary to retire from before Kars for some weeks, and then possibly he will take only his best troops, leaving a sufficient force to maintain the blockade. Now although this force may be small, and the troops not very choice, it will answer the purpose, for the Turkish garrison cannot move a step beyond the entrenchments, because it has no Cavalry, and may be said to be without Artillery, the horses being so reduced in condition that they cannot drag the guns. Thus, while there be any force before Kars, supplied with guns and Cavalry, the garrison cannot venture to issue from its works. The stock of provisions is so small that it will not last until the period arrives when the snow will oblige the enemy to retire to their winter-quarters; so that if succours be not sent up to Kars by Trebizond, without a moment's delay, the garrison may be forced to abandon the place, with the guns and ammunition, and to seek its safety in retreat at any risk.

This is exactly what Saleh Bey stated, and which a letter I saw from Baron Schwartzenburg confirms.

It may happen that General Mouravieff may think it hazardous to leave a small force before the place, not knowing exactly the resources of the garrison, or he may think it necessary to concentrate all his forces to meet the advance of Omer Pasha; still it would be most imprudent to risk the capture of Kars on a matter of opinion as to what General Mouravieff may decide on doing, and therefore the only safe course is to send up to Kars, by way of Trebizond, a sufficient force to oblige the Russians to retire. It might be considered presumptuous in me to say authoritatively what force would suffice, but if I might venture to express an opinion, I should say that 10,000 Infantry and 3,000 to 4,000 Cavalry, all good troops, would effect the purpose. There are guns enough here already. I cannot help feeling that were the troops European the purpose would be effected with more ease and certainty.

The relief of Kars is a matter of too great importance to be treated with indifference or apathy, for besides its being due to its gallant defenders to rescue them from their dangerous position, the loss of the fortress with its guns would seriously increase the difficulties of a future campaign.

I would therefore presume to press on your Excellency the necessity of inducing the Porte to send up, without a moment's delay, a force to relieve Kars, quite independent of Omer Pasha's army. From the usual mode of proceeding of the Turkish Government, it may be apprehended that having dispatched Omer Pasha with a large force, it may consider that it has done all that is required; but if the first effort be not followed up by other prompt and energetic measures, the expedition may prove only an additional disaster, and Kars may still fall.

JAS. BRANT

Brigadier-General Williams to the Earl of Clarendon (received October 25)
Kars, September 14, 1855

My Lord,

Having learnt that the Bashi-Bozouks of Lazistan, now in garrison at Erzeroom, had committed many acts of violence towards the townspeople, I have written by this estafette to Tahir Pasha, the Chief of the Military Medjlis of that city, to enjoin him to repress, with the utmost promptitude and severity, any future similar acts.

From my more recent despatches your Lordship will have perceived that desertion is the great evil against which we have to contend. In spite of the example exhibited to the troops in the disbanding of the regiment of Redif, as detailed in my despatch of the 10th instant, we had no less than six desertions yesterday; fortunately we recaptured two of them; they proved to be men of the corps in question. They were tried by a Council of War, and instantly shot. On their trial they denounced the parties (inhabitants of Kars) who had instigated them to this act of treason, and furnished them with peasants' clothes to enable them to effect their purpose. Three of these men were seized in a house where the musket of one of the prisoners who suffered yesterday was found, together with the clothes and appointments of seven more deserters. There can be little doubt that these wretches are in communication with the enemy, as proclamations were found on the last-captured spy, offering any deserters free passage through the Russian posts to their homes.

A Council of War has tried and condemned these men, who will be hanged today in the market-place; and the appointments of the seven deserters who have escaped by their agency will be exhibited on the gallows, as a further proof of their guilt.

Your Lordship will learn with pleasure that, up to this moment, no Christian subject of the Sultan has betrayed us, all those who have so justly forfeited their lives being Mussulmans.

With regard to the movements of the enemy, it is impossible for us to obtain any information, except through their deserters. By the deposition of two of them, it would appear that General Mouravieff quitted his camp on the night of the 10th instant, and marched with from twelve to seven battalions in the direction of the Soghanli-Dagh, or Mountain Pass on the Erzeroom road: whether this be for the purpose of attacking Penek and Olti (where the

Russian General may suppose that we have collected supplies), or in order to gather the harvest in other districts, cannot, as yet at least, be ascertained; but I have written to Tahir Pasha, at Erzeroom, on the subject, and urged him to procure all the grain within a certain radius round that city.

The health and spirit of our troops are most satisfactory; on the part of the enemy, on the contrary, I believe much sickness to exist.

W. F. WILLIAMS

Lord Stratford de Redcliffe to the Earl of Clarendon (received September 26)
Therapia, September 15, 1855

(Extract)

Anxious, as in duty bound, to co-operate to the utmost of my power towards the relief of the Sultan's army at Kars, I wrote more than two months ago to Her Majesty's Consul at Bagdad, requesting that he would employ his good offices, in order, if possible, to produce that kind of reliable understanding between the Pasha of the province and the discontented tribes in his vicinity, as might warrant his Excellency in sending a portion of the regular troops at his disposal, if not to Kars, at least in that direction.

The suggestion was little better than a forlorn hope, and Captain Jones's answer reached me only yesterday. I learn from its contents that he sees great objections to the proposed interference, for reasons which he has stated with much frankness, and, as it would seem, with an adequate knowledge of the subject.

Brigadier-General Williams to the Earl of Clarendon (received October 25)
Kars, September 19, 1855

My Lord,

I have the honour to enclose, for your Lordship's information, the copy of a despatch which I have this day addressed to his Excellency the Viscount Stratford de Redcliffe.

W. F. WILLIAMS

Enclosure

Brigadier-General Williams to Lord Stratford de Redcliffe
Kars, September 19, 1855

My Lord,

I have the honour to acknowledge the receipt of your Excellency's despatch of the 21st ultimo, conveying intelligence which, it is needless for me to assure your Lordship, afforded pleasure and imparted hope to all within these entrenchments.

The large force detached from the Russian Army, which I informed your Lordship was operating in the neighbourhood of the Soghanli-Dagh, was seen by my foot-messenger about eight days ago marching in the direction of Penjrood in Geuleh, where Haji Ali Pasha and several other officers who had recently left Kars, were stationed, for the purpose of pasturing the Cavalry and Artillery horses which accompanied them, and for seizing a favourable opportunity to get barley into our camp.

Haji Ali Pasha, with his attendants, having incautiously ventured too far from these detachments, was taken prisoner, and is now in the Russian camp, opposite our entrenchments.

This is the second Pasha who has been taken in this manner, Bahlool Pasha, the hereditary Chief of Byazid, having fallen into the enemy's hands near Euch-Kelissa about two months ago. I should state to your Lordship that by Prince Paskiewitch's official reports on the last war, this very Bahlool Pasha allowed himself to be taken prisoner in Byazid, and whilst in the enemy's hands exerted himself as an active partisan in their favour by intriguing with and rendering neutral several of the Sultan's Koordish subjects.

The similarity of the game played and playing by this man forces me to bring him to your Excellency's notice; the more so, as several of the Koordish bands of Horse under Veli Pasha during the recent unsuccessful operations of the Russian General-in-chief against Erzeroom, disbanded and fled to their homes without firing a shot.

Another very serious coincidence is the conduct of the principal Mussulman inhabitants of Erzeroom during the late panic. There is no doubt that they would have negotiated with the enemy if the forts around the city had not restrained them, and prevented an attack from the Russian army. I can only conclude that, as in 1829, Russian gold was ready at hand to effect its work.

The Christian notables and their flock alone (under their Bishop) showed true loyalty, and I have thanked them, through his Reverence, in the name of the British Government.

Two officers have particularly distinguished themselves since the enemy's army sat down before Kars—Colonel Kadri Bey, of the 2nd Regiment of Anatolia, and Colonel Kadri Bey, of the 6th Regiment of Arabistan. I have consulted with the Mushir, and received his permission to bring the names of these officers to the notice of your Lordship, in order that your influence might be instrumental in obtaining for them the rank of Liva or Brigadier-General.

W. F. WILLIAMS

The Earl of Clarendon to Brigadier-General Williams
Foreign Office, September 20, 1855

Sir,

I enclose for your information a copy of a despatch from Viscount Stratford de Redcliffe [dated September 6, 1855], respecting the steps taken to forward supplies for the use of the army at Kars.

CLARENDON

Lord Stratford de Redcliffe to the Earl of Clarendon (received October 1)

Therapia, September 20, 1855

My Lord,

On the receipt of the last despatches from Kars and Erzeroom, urging the increased necessity of immediate relief, I addressed a fresh remonstrance, accompanied with strong suggestions, to the Porte, upon that subject.

A copy of my letter, duplicate of which was sent to the Seraskier, is enclosed herewith for your Lordship's information.

STRATFORD DE REDCLIFFE

Enclosure

Lord Stratford de Redcliffe to Fuad Pasha

(Translation)

Therapia, September 18, 1855

Sir,

I have just received despatches from Kars and Erzeroom, and I think it my duty to direct your most serious attention to a part of their contents without loss of time.

There is a report that fifteen days ago an attack of the Russians was repulsed by the garrison of Kars; but as your Excellency has received no confirmation of this report, I may be at least permitted to doubt its correctness. What we know for certain is ominous of evil. The army and the garrison begin to feel strongly the effect of their isolation. The provisions are so much diminished, that it has been judged necessary to put the troops on half rations. The horses are attenuated by famine—part of the Cavalry had been obliged to be sent at any risk to the other side of the mountains. The Russians, on the contrary, are reinforcing that arm, and threaten to cut off even the most secret means of communication. In spite of these difficulties, it is of the greatest urgency that no means should be neglected of introducing provisions into the town. Success is not impossible, and the object to be gained is worth the risk. Unhappily the agents, both civil and military, upon whom rests the immediate responsibility, have not up to this time evinced that energy and resolution which circumstances so critical demand. For this reason I address the Porte, through the medium of your Excellency, so that the necessary orders may forthwith be sent from here, and that a vigorous impulse may be given to the authorities at Erzeroom. The delays which have retarded the expedition of Omer Pasha give additional importance to the duties to be performed on the side of Erzeroom.

It wants but five weeks to the winter of that country, and every possible effort ought to be made to provide the troops with the means of prolonging their resistance during that painful interval.

STRATFORD DE REDCLIFFE

Lord Stratford de Redcliffe to the Earl of Clarendon (received October 8)
Therapia, September 26, 1855

My Lord,

In answer to my inquiries at the Porte, I am assured that nothing further has been received from Omer Pasha; that the passage of troops and the conveyance of provisions are in progress, though slowly, in consequence of the limited command of transport for those purposes.

It is impossible not to apprehend that the many changes of plan, the exigencies of our operations at Sebastopol, and heavy demands on the transport service, concur to diminish the hope of relieving Kars.

In reply to my earnest solicitations that a peremptory order should be immediately sent to the commanders at or near Erzeroom to attempt the introduction of provisions into Kars at every risk, I am assured by the Seraskier that orders to that effect are already on the road.

Advices from General Williams to the 7th are not expressive of despair; but the accounts delivered orally at the Porte by an aide-de-camp, dispatched from Kars by Vassif Pasha, represent the danger from want of provisions as very urgent, and I grieve to add that the Turkish Ministers conceive it impracticable to afford any relief in that respect, although it appears that of 1,500 Horse sent out from Kars, only 150, or, according to the Turkish version, 300 and an officer were intercepted by the enemy.

STRATFORD DE REDCLIFFE

Brigadier-General Williams to the Earl of Clarendon (received October 25)
Kars, September 28, 1855

My Lord,

The measures which I detailed in my last despatch have, I am happy to inform your Lordship, entirely put a stop to desertion and conspiracy.

The glorious news of the destruction of Sebastopol and of the Russian fleet reached us four days ago; two royal salutes were fired on the occasion, and the details of these events were read to the troops and the men of Kars, who have throughout our long struggle evinced equal activity and determination. The spirit which reigns within our entrenchments is excellent.

The Mushir has received late news from Omer Pasha, whose army was rapidly concentrating on the Choorooksoo, and who intended to begin his operations against Georgia without a moment's unnecessary delay.

I regret to inform your Lordship that cholera appeared amongst us on the 26th instant; the enemy, I hear and believe, has suffered severely; his camp being so close to us, and on the banks of the Kars-tchai, the river, as usual in these countries, has conveyed the disease to us. Dr Sandwith has taken all necessary measures to prevent the spreading of the evil.

The enemy sent off yesterday about 3,000 loaded arabas or carts to Gumri, and last night lanterns were seen along that road, which, coupled with the displacement of several hospital tents in the great camp, lead me to anticipate a move on the part of the Russian General.

If I can credit the reports of peasants brought in at various times within the last ten days, the enemy has detached (during the night and unperceived by us) a force of 8,000 men towards Ahkiska. This intelligence, however, requires confirmation. Be this as it may, stringent orders will go today to the military and civil authorities of Erzeroom to prepare provisions and land carriage for instant transmission to this garrison, in the event of a retrograde movement on the part of the enemy.

W. F. WILLIAMS

Brigadier-General Williams to the Earl of Clarendon
(received October 25)

Kars, September 29, 1855

My Lord,

I have now the honour to inform your Lordship that General Mouravieff, with the bulk of his army, at daybreak this morning attacked our entrenched position on the heights above Kars and on the opposite side of the river. The battle lasted, without a moment's intermission, for nearly seven hours, when the enemy was driven off in the greatest disorder, with the loss of 2,500 dead and nearly double that number of wounded, who were for the most part carried off by the retreating enemy. Upwards of 4,000 muskets were left on the field.

Your Lordship can, without a description on my part, imagine the determination of the assailants and the undaunted courage of the troops who defended the position for so many hours.

The Mushir will doubtlessly at a future moment bring before his Government the conduct of those officers who have distinguished themselves on this day, a day so glorious for the Turkish arms.

On my part I have great gratification in acquainting your Lordship with the gallant conduct of Lieutenant-Colonel Lake, Major Teesdale, and Captain Thompson, who rendered the most important service in defending the redoubts of Veli Pasha Tabia, Tahmasb Tabia, and Arab Tabia. I beg to recommend these officers to your Lordship's protection.

I beg also to name my Secretary, Mr Churchill, an Attaché of Her Majesty's Mission in Persia; he directed the fire of a battery throughout the action, and caused the enemy great loss.

I also beg to draw your Lordship's attention to the gallant bearing of Messrs Zohrab and Rennisson, who as interpreters to Lieutenant-Colonel Lake and Major Teesdale rendered very effective service. Dr Sandwith has been most active and efficient in the management of the ambulances and in the hospital arrangements.

We are now employed in the burial of the dead, and I will have the honour by the next messenger of detailing the movements of this eventful day.

Our loss was about 700 killed and wounded.

W. F. WILLIAMS

Brigadier-General Williams to the Earl of Clarendon (received October 29)

Kars, September 30, 1855

My Lord,

We could not get the messenger out of the lines last night. Today we have repaired our breastworks, filled the tumbrils and replenished the pouches of the Infantry, so that everything, as well as everybody, is ready for the Russians, should they wish to try their fortunes once more.

We have collected, and are now burying the enemy's dead, at least 3,000; round the scenes of especial strife, and in all the camps, they have been firing volleys over those they took away, and who were slain at some distance by round shot; the number of wounded cannot be less than 4,000. If we had only possessed a few hundred Cavalry we should have utterly destroyed their army: their loss in officers has been enormous, and they behaved splendidly; three were killed on the platform of the gun in Tackmas Tabia, which at that moment was worked by Major Teesdale, who then sprang out and led two charges with the bayonet; the Turks fought like heroes, Colonel Lake retook the English Tabias, with the bayonet, too; and Colonel Thompson crushed them with his guns from Arab Tabia.

Such was the deadly fire of our Riflemen (Regular Chasseurs) that 800 dead bodies now lie in front of an épaulement defended by 400 of that arm. I am so fatigued that I can scarcely hold my pen, but I am sure your Lordship will pardon the scrawl. I leave it, as well as my despatch, open for the perusal of the Ambassador.

W. F. WILLIAMS

OCTOBER 1855

The Earl of Clarendon to Lord Stratford de Redcliffe
Foreign Office, October 3, 1855

My Lord,

Her Majesty's Government approve of the representation which you made to the Porte, urging the necessity of immediate steps for the relief of Kars, as conveyed in your note to Fuad Pasha, of which a copy is enclosed in your despatch of the 20th ultimo.

CLARENDON

Brigadier-General Williams to the Earl of Clarendon (received November 8)
Kars, October 3, 1855

(Extract)

I had the honour to announce to your Lordship on the evening of the 29th ultimo the glorious victory gained on the morning of that day by the Sultan's troops on the heights above Kars over the Russian army commanded by General Mouravieff, and I now beg to furnish your Lordship with the principal incidents of that sanguinary battle.

Your Lordship will perhaps recollect that in my despatch of the 28th June, I stated that the Russian General, after his second demonstration against the southern face of our entrenchments, which is flanked by Hafiz Pasha Tabia and Kanly Tabia, marched south, and established his camp at Boyouk-Tikmeh, a village situated about four miles from Kars. Knowing that General Mouravieff served in the army which took Kars in 1828, I conceived his last manœuvre to be preparatory either to a reconnaissance or an attack upon the heights of Tahmasb, from whence the Russians successfully pushed their approaches in the year above cited.

Whilst, therefore, the enemy's columns were in march towards Boyouk-Tikmeh, I visited those heights with Lieutenant-Colonel Lake, and, after studying the ground, decided upon the nature of the works to be thrown up; these were planned and executed by Lieutenant-Colonel Lake with great skill and energy. I enclose, for your Lordship's information, a plan made by that officer of the town and its neighbouring heights, which are situated on the opposite side of the river of the Kars-tchai, over which three temporary bridges had been thrown to keep up our communications.

Your Lordship will observe that whilst our camp and magazines in the town were rendered as safe as circumstances would allow, the hills above Kars commanded all, and were therefore the keys of our position.

The entrenchments of Tahmasb being those nearest the enemy's camp, demanded the greatest vigilance from all entrusted in their defence. General Kmety, a gallant Hungarian officer, commanded the division which occupied this eminence; he was assisted by Major-General Hussein Pasha, and my Aide-de-camp, Major Teesdale, who has acted as Chief of the Staff.

Throughout the investment, which has now lasted four months, the troops in all the redoubts and entrenchments have kept a vigilant look-out during the night, and, at their appointed stations, stood to their arms long before daybreak.

In my despatch of the 29th ultimo I informed your Lordship of the arrival of the news of the fall of Sebastopol, and of the landing of Omer Pasha at Batoom. I also acquainted your Lordship with the fact that the Russian General was engaged in sending off immense trains of heavy baggage into Georgia, and showing every indication of a speedy retreat. This in nowise threw us off our guard, and Lieutenant-Colonel Lake was directed to strengthen many points in our extensive and undermanned lines; and amongst other works, the Tabia bearing my name was constructed.

At four o'clock on the eventful morning of the 29th, the enemy's columns were reporting to be advancing on the Tahmasb front. They were three in number, supported by 24 guns; the first or right column being directed on Tahmasb Tabia, the second on Yuksek Tabia, and the third on the breastwork called Rennisson Lines. As soon as the first gun announced the approach of the enemy, the reserves were put under arms in a central position, from which succours could be dispatched either to Tahmasb or the English lines.

The mist and imperfect light of the dawning day induced the enemy to believe that he was about to surprise us; he advanced with his usual steadiness and intrepidity, but on getting within range, he was saluted with a crushing fire of artillery from all points of the line; this unexpected reception, however, only drew forth loud hurrahs from the Russian Infantry as it rushed up the hill on the redoubts and breastworks. These works poured forth a fire of musketry and rifles which told with fearful effect on the close columns of attack, more especially on the left one, which being opposed by a battalion of 450 Chasseurs, armed with Minié rifles, was, after long and desperate fighting, completely broken and sent headlong down the hill, leaving 850 dead on the field, besides those carried off by their comrades.

The central column precipitated itself on the redoubts of Tahmasb and Yuksek Tabias, where desperate fighting occurred and lasted for several hours, the enemy being repulsed in all his attempts to enter the closed redoubts, which mutually flanked each other with their artillery and musketry, and made terrible havoc in the ranks of the assailants; and it was here that Generals Kmety and Hussein Pasha, together with Major Teesdale, so conspicuously displayed their courage and conduct. Lieutenant-General Kerim Pasha also repaired to the scene of desperate strife to encourage the troops, and was wounded in the shoulder, and had two horses killed under him.

The right column of the Russian Infantry, supported by a battery, eventually turned the left flank of the entrenched wing of the Tahmasb defences, and whilst the Russian battery opened on the rear of the closed redoubt at its salient angle, their Infantry penetrated considerably behind our position.

Observing the commencement of this movement, and anticipating its consequences, Lieutenant Colonel Lake, who had taken the direction of affairs in the English Tabias, was instructed to send a battalion from Fort Lake to the assistance of the defenders of Tahmasb, and at the same time two battalions of the Reserves were moved across the flying bridge, and upon the rocky height of Laz Teppè Tabia. These three reinforcing columns met each other at that point, and, being hidden from the enemy by the rocky nature of the ground, confronted him at a most opportune moment; they deployed, opened their fire, which stopped, and soon drove back, the enemy's reserves, which were then vigorously charged with the bayonet at the same moment when General Kmety and Major Teesdale issued from the redoubts at Tahmasb and charged the assailants. The whole of that portion of the enemy's Infantry and Artillery now broke, and fled down the heights under a murderous fire of musketry. This occurred at half-past 11, after a combat of seven hours.

In this part of the field the enemy had, including his reserves, 22 battalions of Infantry, a large force of Dragoons and Cossacks, together with 32 guns.

Whilst this struggle which I have attempted to describe was occurring at Tahmasb, a most severe combat was going on at the eastern portion of the line called the English Tabias.

About half-past 5 o'clock a.m. a Russian column, consisting of eight battalions of Infantry, three regiments of Cavalry, and 16 guns, advanced from the valley of Tchakmak, and assaulted those small redoubts, which, after as stout a resistance as their unavoidably feeble garrisons could oppose, fell into their hands, together with the connecting breastworks defended by townsmen and mountaineers from Lazistan, whose clannish flags, according to their custom, were planted before them on the épaulements, and, consequently, fell into the enemy's hands; but before the firing had begun in this portion of the field, Captain Thompson had received orders to send a battalion of Infantry from each of the heights of Karadagh and Arab Tabia to reinforce the English lines. This reinforcement descended the deep gully through which flows the Kars river, passed a bridge recently thrown across it, and ascended the opposite precipitous bank by a zig-zag path which led into the line of works named by the Turks Ingliz Tabias—the English batteries. Their arrival was as opportune as that of the reserves directed towards Tahmasb, which I have had the honour to describe in the former part of this despatch; these battalions, joined to those directed by Lieutenant-Colonel Lake, gallantly attacked and drove the Russians out of the redoubts at the point of the bayonet, after the artillery of the enemy had been driven from those lines by the cross fire directed from Fort Lake, and from Arab Tabia and Karadagh by Captain Thompson. This officer deserves my best thanks for having seized a favourable moment to remove a heavy gun from the eastern to the western extremity of Karadagh, and with it inflicted severe loss on the enemy.

After the Russian Infantry were driven from the English redoubts, the whole of their attacking force of Cavalry, Artillery, and Infantry retreated with precipitation, plied with round shot from all the batteries bearing on their columns. During their temporary success, however, the enemy captured two of our light guns, which the mortality amongst our horses, from famine, prevented our withdrawing from their advanced positions. He also carried off his wounded and many of his dead; yet he left 363 of the latter within and in front of these entrenchments; and his retreat occurred at least an hour before the assailants of Tahmasb were put to flight.

During this combat, which lasted nearly seven hours, the Turkish Infantry, as well as Artillery, fought with the most determined courage; and when it is recollected that they had worked on their entrenchments, and guarded them by night, throughout a period extending to nearly four months—when it is borne in mind that they were ill-clothed, and received less than half a ration of bread—that they have remained without pay for 29 months, I think your Lordship will admit that they have proved themselves worthy of the admiration of Europe, and established an undoubted claim to be placed amongst the most distinguished of its troops.

With regard to the enemy, as long as there was a chance of success he persevered with undaunted courage, and the Russian officers displayed the greatest gallantry. Their loss was immense; they left on the field more than 5,000 dead, which it took the Turkish Infantry four days to bury. Their wounded and prisoners, in our possession, amounts to 160, whilst those who were carried off are said to be upwards of 7,000.

As the garrison was afflicted with cholera, and I was apprehensive of a great increase of the malady should this melancholy duty of the burial of the dead be not pushed forward with every possible vigour by our fatigued and jaded soldiers, I daily visited the scene of strife to encourage them in their almost endless task; and I can assure your Lordship that the whole battlefield presented a scene which is more easy to conceive than to describe, being literally covered with the enemy's dead and dying.

The Turkish dead and wounded were removed on the night of the battle. The dead numbered 362, the wounded 631. The townspeople, who also fought with spirit, lost 101 men.

His Excellency the Mushir has reported to his Government those officers who particularly distinguished themselves—a difficult task in an army which has shown such desperate valour throughout the unusual period of seven hours of uninterrupted combat.

The Earl of Clarendon to Lord Stratford de Redcliffe
Foreign Office, October 4, 1855

My Lord,

Brigadier-General Williams has reported to me that great apathy exists amongst the Turkish functionaries at Erzeroom, and that every Pasha and Bey who has been charged with missions from the camp at Kars to Erzeroom, has disappeared from the scene of operations.

I have to state to your Excellency, with reference to these facts, that urgent instructions should be sent by the Porte to the authorities at Erzeroom, directing them to execute the instructions forwarded to them by the Mushir.

CLARENDON

The Earl of Clarendon to Brigadier-General Williams
Foreign Office, October 4, 1855

Sir,

I have to state to you that Her Majesty's Government entirely approve your proceedings, as reported in your despatch of the 25th of August.

I have instructed Her Majesty's Ambassador at Constantinople to urge the Porte to send instructions to the authorities at Erzeroom in the sense suggested by you in that despatch.

CLARENDON

Consul Brant to the Earl of Clarendon (received October 25)
Erzeroom, October 5, 1855

(Extract)

I am anxious not to detain the messenger who carries your Lordship the news of the brilliant repulse of the Russian army in its attack on Kars. I am sure your Lordship will appreciate the services of General Williams and his small band of heroes who have achieved so much under every possible discouragement, and in spite of so much apathy, incapacity, and jealousy on the part of the Turkish military commanders.

Kars was still as closely invested as ever, and it is impossible to say when the Russian General may think fit to retire, though I imagine he will scarce be bold enough to try another assault.

It is a subject of sincere congratulation that the loss on the side of the Turks was so small, and especially so that every European remained unharmed.

Brigadier-General Williams to the Earl of Clarendon (received November 8)

Kars, October 12, 1855

My Lord,

Notwithstanding the severe defeat experienced by the enemy, he still block-ades us closely, and the erection of huts in his camp this morning shows that he intends to continue this course.

He knows that all our Cavalry horses and the great majority of the Artillery horses are dead of starvation, and that we cannot take the field; he is also aware that cholera inflicts severe losses on us, which are aggravated by the difficulty we have of burying the horses.

Under these circumstances, I address these few lines to your Lordship, with a hope that such representations may be instantly made to General Omer, to act with vigour and decision against Georgia; otherwise, in spite of our brilliant victory, we must ultimately fall into the enemy's hands.

W. F. WILLIAMS

Lord Stratford de Redcliffe to the Earl of Clarendon (received October 25)

Therapia, October 15, 1855

My Lord,

Immediately on receipt of despatches from Kars announcing the repulse of the Russians with circumstances so highly honourable to all within the walls of that fortress, and more particularly to Brigadier-General Williams, and the British officers and others serving under him, I wrote to congratulate the Porte on so glorious and seasonable a success, expressing a hope that justice would be done to our gallant countrymen by a suitable expression of the Sultan's approval.

I am happy to say that the Turkish Ministers show every disposition to meet my wishes, and to obtain the Sultan's consent to an adequate demon-stration in favour of those to whom the victory, under Providence, is principally due.

Copies of the correspondence which passed on the occasion are enclosed herewith for your Lordship's information. Fuad Pasha's letter to me, and my communication to him, crossed each other on the way.

A letter of the 30th ultimo, from Kars, received at Erzeroom, and trans-mitted in substance to the French Embassy, affirms that the Russian forces, after their defeat, had retired within their cantonments.

STRATFORD DE REDCLIFFE

Enclosure 1

Fuad Pasha to Lord Stratford de Redcliffe

(Translation)

October 13, 1855

Sir,

An official report from the General Commandant at Kars, dated 29th of September, announces to us the following news:

The Russians attacked Kars on that day, and the combat lasted eight hours, and during the contest, which was hard fought in the extreme, the enemy entered several times into some of the batteries, from which he was driven back with considerable loss: after displaying unheard-of efforts, the Russians were forced to yield before the courage of our brave soldiers, and to retire completely routed. Besides the dead and wounded carried off during the action, they have left in the trenches and all round the place 4,000 dead, 100 prisoners, and 1 piece of artillery. Our loss is between 700 and 800, amongst whom we have to deplore the death of several superior officers. This magnificent affair covers the besieged army with glory, and adds another laurel to the success of the alliance. The Russians were preparing to retreat, with the intention of raising the siege.

In hastening to bring to the knowledge of your Excellency this welcome news, I avail, etc.

FUAD

P.S. Vassif Pasha makes very honourable mention of General Williams, and congratulates himself on the loyal assistance which that General has given him.

Enclosure 2

Lord Stratford de Redcliffe to Fuad Pasha

(Translation)

October 13, 1855

Sir,

In acknowledging the receipt of the letter in which your Excellency has been so good as to communicate to me the welcome news which you have just received from Kars, I have a real pleasure in reiterating the congratulations which I had already expressed when transmitting through M. Pisani the information of the same import which had reached me from General Williams. The brilliant success obtained over the enemy by the Ottoman army is the more worthy of public rejoicing, as being the result of the loyal and patriotic sentiments which have inspired that army with the determination to dare and suffer everything in a most critical position.

All the allies have just cause to pride themselves upon the victorious bravery which the Imperial troops and the inhabitants of Kars have shown during a deadly conflict of seven hours' duration, and I learn with pleasure from your Excellency, that Vassif Pasha, in his report of the event, has not forgotten how much the brave General Williams and the other officers of my country have contributed to the triumph of his arms both on the ever-memorable 29th of September, and also from the commencement of the siege, and even before the approach of the Russian battalions.

I doubt not that the Government of His Majesty the Sultan will cause the public to participate in the joy which it experiences upon this happy occasion, and I should be too much flattered at the opportunity of adding my feeble tribute to the general manifestations of rejoicing.

STRATFORD DE REDCLIFFE

Consul Brant to the Earl of Clarendon (received November 8)
Erzeroom, October 16, 1855

(Extract)

I have the honour to enclose copy of a despatch I addressed to his Excellency Viscount Stratford de Redcliffe, when forwarding General Williams' despatch. I sincerely hope his Excellency will induce the Porte, as well to hasten Omer Pasha's movements, as to send troops up hither, and if great expedition be not employed, they may reach too late.

I am greatly disappointed that, notwithstanding the arrival of Omer Pasha in Georgia, and the terrible defeat of the Russian army on the 29th September, General Mouravieff has not withdrawn within the Georgian frontier, and I can only attribute this to his conviction that Omer Pasha will not march on Tiflis this winter, and the certainty that the Kars army cannot molest his, because it has no horses for its Artillery and no Cavalry, and therefore must of necessity remain within its entrenchments.

Enclosure

Consul Brant to Lord Stratford de Redcliffe
Erzeroom, October 16, 1855

(Extract)

I have the honour to enclose a despatch sent to me by General Williams to be forwarded to your Excellency, and I hope no time may be lost in relieving the Kars army.

I had hoped that the signal defeat the Russian army met with would have caused its immediate retreat; but it would appear that General Mouravieff still hopes to starve out the garrison.

I learn from the coast that Omer Pasha's army reaches so tardily that there is little chance of its being able to move in advance this winter.

Kars, October 19, 1855

My Lord,

The enclosed letters, addressed to his Excellency Omer Pasha, will show your Lordship that I took the earliest opportunity of entering into communication with that general officer, but although Batoom, the base of his operations, is but four days' journey from Kars, not a word has been heard, either by the mouth of one of his aides-de-camp, or otherwise, subsequently to the message which I have had the honour to inform your Lordship Omer Pasha sent by one of Vassif Pasha's officers. We are, therefore, totally in the dark with regard to the movements of the relieving army.

I have, on two occasions, had the honour of laying before your Lordship the state of our affairs here, and it is therefore needless for me to say that we will hold out against famine, and resist any future attack of the enemy to the last.

I regret to state that desertion has again commenced, and with it, military executions, for I am determined that no deserter who again falls into our hands shall escape the punishment due to his infamy.

The enemy annoys us much by night alerts, but the spirit of the garrison is admirable, and I am happy to acquaint your Lordship that there has been a sensible decrease of cholera since I last had the honour of writing.

W. F. WILLIAMS

Enclosure 1

Brigadier-General Williams to Omer Pasha

(Translation)

Kars, October 2, 1855

Excellency,

Major Mahmood Effendi being about to leave tonight, with despatches from the Mushir of this army, I hasten to seize the opportunity of offering to your Excellency, as Generalissimo of the troops of His Majesty the Sultan, my congratulations upon the glorious victory obtained by this army over the Russians upon the 29th of last month.

His Excellency the Mushir will give you a detailed account of the events of that memorable day. I shall confine myself to observing that the interment of the Russians left dead on the field of battle is continued this morning. More than 4,000 have been already buried. Consequently the losses of General Mouravieff cannot be less than 8,000 men, probably still more, for the number of wounded who escaped from the field of battle on the side of the Russian camp was enormous.

A large convoy of waggons is proceeding at this moment, by the mountain-road opposite, towards Gumri; but the future alone can make known to us the ulterior intentions of the Russian General.

W. F. WILLIAMS

Enclosure 2

Brigadier-General Williams to Omer Pasha

(Translation)

Kars, October 10, 1855

Highness,

His Excellency the Mushir intending to send you an express tonight, I take advantage of the opportunity to inform you that the enemy, after having sent off many of his wounded and much of his baggage to Gumri, remains in the position which he occupied previous to the assault, and that even at this moment a convoy (supposed to be of provisions) is in sight coming from the Russian frontier.

This would seem to indicate that General Mouravieff contemplates the continuation of the blockade to which we have now been subjected for more than four months.

Your Highness knows, without doubt, the fact that nearly all our horses, both of the Cavalry and the Artillery, exist no longer, in consequence of the utter want of forage.

W. F. WILLIAMS

Lord Stratford de Redcliffe to the Earl of Clarendon (received November 1)

Therapia, October 21, 1855

My Lord,

I have the honour to transmit herewith copies of my latest despatches to Her Majesty's Commissioner at Kars. I take this opportunity to supply an omission which has occurred in my despatch of the 15th instant, and to forward copies of an instruction which I addressed to M. Pisani the moment I heard of the victory of Kars, and of his report in reply to it.

STRATFORD DE REDCLIFFE

Enclosure 1

Lord Stratford de Redcliffe to Brigadier-General Williams

Therapia, October 19, 1855

Sir,

I cannot better convey to you the impressions produced, not only on this Embassy, but on the Turkish Government, and indeed on the whole population of Constantinople not devoted to Russia, than by forwarding to you, as I have the honour to do herewith, the correspondence which passed between myself and the Ottoman Secretary of State on the arrival of your despatch of the 29th ultimo, and of those addressed at the same time by Vassif Pasha to the Porte.

I beg to offer both to you and the officers under your command, as well as to the Turkish Commander-in-chief, my cordial congratulations.

I am authorised by the Turkish Ministers to inform you that an officer will be sent on purpose by the Sultan, as soon as circumstances admit of it, to present to you and other officers of Kars those marks of high distinction which His Majesty is in the habit of conferring on such occasions.

STRATFORD DE REDCLIFFE

Enclosure 2

Lord Stratford de Redcliffe to Brigadier-General Williams

Therapia, October 19, 1855

Sir,

Referring to what you state in your despatch of the 19th ultimo respecting Bahlool Pasha, I have brought the circumstances you mention to the knowledge of the Grand Vizier, and I trust that proper attention will be paid to the suspicious conduct of that individual.

I am happy to meet your wishes, in so far as it depends upon me, with respect to the two Colonels whom you have recommended in the same despatch.

STRATFORD DE REDCLIFFE

Enclosure 3

Lord Stratford de Redcliffe to M. E. Pisani

Therapia, October 12, 1855

Dear Sir,

I wish you to wait on the Grand Vizier tomorrow, and to offer my hearty congratulations on the brilliant success which has been obtained under such trying circumstances by the Sultan's army at Kars. It appears that the Russians attacked that place with the greater part of their forces on the 29th ultimo, and that, after seven hours' hard fighting, they were compelled to submit in disorder with a loss of 2,500 killed, twice that number in wounded, and 4,000 muskets left on the field. Later accounts state that they had actually retreated, or were preparing to retreat, from before the place. I presume that the Porte has received advices of the same purport from Vassif Pasha.

Orders have been sent to prepare convoys of ammunition and provisions at Erzeroom with a view to the supply of Kars at the earliest possible moment, and I trust that whatever the Porte can possibly do to second the preparations will be done without delay.

So important and glorious a repulse of powerful and well-commanded enemies reflects the highest honour on all concerned, and I have no doubt that His Majesty the Sultan will hasten to encourage the survivors by a signal demonstration of his approval and favour.

With respect to the British officers who have had so large a share in the fatigues, privations, and dangers of the siege, I am convinced that the Porte, of her own accord, will make the acknowledgments due to them. I venture to hope that an officer will be sent direct from the Sultan with His Majesty's gracious acceptance of their services, and such honourable rewards as the occasion appears to require. It will afford me the highest satisfaction to be made the channel of some assurance to this effect.

Read this instruction to the Grand Vizier and to Fuad Pasha.

STRATFORD DE REDCLIFFE

Enclosure 4

M. E. Pisani to Lord Stratford de Redcliffe

Yenikeuy, October 13, 1855

My Lord,

I have the honour to report that having read and explained to the Grand Vizier and Fuad Pasha the whole of your Excellency's instructions to me of yesterday's date, respecting the intelligence from Kars, and directing me to offer your hearty congratulations on the brilliant success which has been obtained by the Sultan's army etc. I am requested by the Ministers to thank your Excellency for your friendly and kind congratulations, and to inform you that, as soon as Vassif Pasha's despatches reached the Porte, his Highness lost no time in laying them before the Sultan, accompanied with a report containing suggestions as to the advisability of encouraging the services by a signal demonstration of his Imperial approval and favour: and your Excellency may be assured, added he, that the British officers who so highly contributed to the success of the glorious repulse of the common enemy, will not be forgotten, and their services duly acknowledged.

The Grand Vizier, therefore, authorises your Excellency to give them assurances to this effect. With reference to ammunition and provisions to be sent from Erzeroom for the supply of Kars, the Grand Vizier said that the aide-de camp who brought Vassif Pasha's despatches states that a convoy of 10,000 horses were ready to start with the necessary supplies.

You may depend, observed his Highness, that the Porte, under the management of a Seraskier like Mehmed Rushdi, cannot fail to do its duty, and give satisfaction.

Vassif Pasha praises very highly the services and courage displayed by the inhabitants on this occasion, and recommends that they should be handsomely rewarded. The Porte's intention appears to be, if sanctioned by the Sultan, to exempt them for three years from all direct and indirect taxes.

ET. PISANI

Brigadier-General Williams to the Earl of Clarendon (received November 29)
Kars, October 23, 1855

My Lord,
Our courier has been for the four last nights unable to pass the enemy's videttes; he will try again tonight, and I avail myself of the opportunity to state that we heard yesterday of the expedition to Erzeroom, under Selim Pasha, and that I have requested Mr Brant to see that General on his arrival in Erzeroom, and to urge on him my hope that he will use the most energetic means to succour this garrison.

All our horses are dead of starvation, and we have not carriage for a load of ammunition, if we are ultimately obliged to abandon Kars. The garrison has been without animal food for more than a fortnight.

W. F. WILLIAMS

Lord Stratford de Redcliffe to the Earl of Clarendon (received November 7)
Therapia, October 24, 1855

My Lord,
Enclosed herewith, for your Lordship's information, is a translated copy of the Sultan's rescript, acknowledging the brilliant successes obtained by the garrison and inhabitants of Kars, more particularly in their repulse of the Russians on the 29th ultimo.

Your Lordship will be glad to observe that the services of General Williams are pointedly acknowledged, by the Sultan's declared intention of sending him the decoration of the Order of Medjidiyé and a sabre of honour.

The British officers serving under General Williams will, no doubt, be severally distinguished, according to their ranks, as soon as their names are sent in by the Commander-in-chief.

It is the Sultan's intention to grant the inhabitants of Kars an exemption from taxes and conscription from the present period till the end of three years after the conclusion of peace.

STRATFORD DE REDCLIFFE

Enclosure

Firman to the Army at Kars

(Translation)
To the Commander of my army in Anatolia, Mehmed Vassif Pasha etc.

Be it known to you on receipt of this Imperial rescript, you, the above lauded Vizier, that I felicitate you, and together with you, the Feriks, the Emirs, the Zabits, and all the valorous soldiers, on the complete success which has at this time crowned your arms. You have held Kars during four months against an enemy three times your strength; you have displayed the greatest qualities of the soldier in your steadiness, the maintenance of discipline, and in supporting privations, and have all proved yourselves to be endowed with courage.

This quality, moreover, as evinced by you on the 17th of Mouharem, in your resistance to the enemy's attack, is a great subject of glorification to our country and to our race, and it will merit the approbation of the whole world.

You have proved yourselves to be the worthy companions and brothers-in-arms of the brave allies who acquired glorious triumphs in the Crimea, and of the valorous men whose names are illustrated by the siege of Silistria. From the Commander to the private soldier, you have all, as well as the auxiliary Commanders and officers in the service of our army, given full proof of your courage and devotion, and have gained a triumph which will illustrate a great page in the history of the present war, together with your own names. Your services are deserving of my Royal acknowledgment, and you are, all of you, the objects of my constant good wishes.

Those who have laid down their lives in the cause of their country and their race, will ever hold a place in my benevolent recollection. The orphans which they have left I will consider as my own children, and they shall all of them receive proofs of my Royal and special benefaction. All those who have taken a part in this victory shall, in appreciation of their services, receive the honorific medal which I have ordered to be forthwith prepared.

The honour of rewarding the special services of the Commander and superior officers is reflected on the whole army. You, personally, have evinced zeal and ability, as well in commanding the troops as in defending (the place) and conducing to the present triumphant result; and you report that the illustrious Feriks etc., Kerim Pasha, and Williams Pasha, and the Mirliva Pasha, gave especial proofs of devotion and valour. I have, therefore, conferred upon you a sabre enriched with diamonds; upon Kerim and Williams Pashas, the second class of my Imperial order of the Medjidiyé, together with a sabre; and, as a special favour to the Mirliva Pashas and other Emirs and Zabits, to reward those who have given proof of worth and valour, I have ordered to be transmitted to you a set of the distinctive classes of my Imperial order of the Medjidiyé, as well as of the honorific military orders. I appreciate fully the zeal and courage displayed by all the inhabitants of Kars, and the recompense due to them is treated of elsewhere.

The service rendered by you all is deserving of praise and approbation, and in mark of my favour, as well as in grateful appreciation of those services, I have caused the present Imperial rescript to be given from my Royal Divan, and to be sent to you decorated with my sovereign hand.

On receipt of this illustrious decree, you will widely proclaim my Royal pleasure and my satisfaction to all my Emirs, Zabits, and soldiers of the army; and you will use all your endeavours that they should so continue to conduct themselves, in conformity to my Royal wishes, and with their faithful duty, in supporting with devotion and courage the cause of the Empire, so as to increase the Royal favour which I entertain on their behalf.

Be it thus known unto you; and place full reliance on the Imperial cypher.

Given in the middle of the month of Sefer the propitious, in the year 1272.

The Earl of Clarendon to Lord Stratford de Redcliffe

Foreign Office, October 26, 1855

My Lord,

With reference to your Excellency's despatch of the 15th instant, I have to inform you that Her Majesty's Government approve of the note which you addressed to Fuad Effendi on the 13th of October, respecting the victory of the 29th ultimo over the Russians at Kars.

CLARENDON

The Earl of Clarendon to Lord Stratford de Redcliffe

Foreign Office, October 26, 1855

My Lord,

I have received from Brigadier-General Williams a copy of a despatch which he addressed to your Excellency on the 19th ultimo, respecting the fidelity and loyalty to the Sultan of the Christians at Kars; and I have to express to you the hope of Her Majesty's Government that you have brought to the knowledge of the Porte, and have recommended for some favourable notice, the good conduct of those Christian subjects of the Sultan, not one of whom appears to have deserted.

CLARENDON

Lord Stratford de Redcliffe to the Earl of Clarendon (received November 8)

Therapia, October 29, 1855

My Lord,

I have the honour to forward to your Lordship, herewith, in translation, a copy of the firman by which the Sultan has expressed his sense of the services rendered by the inhabitants of Kars in the late repulse of the Russians from that town.

STRATFORD DE REDCLIFFE

Enclosure

Firman to the inhabitants of Kars

(Translation)

Mehemed Vassif Pasha, Commander of my forces in Asia Minor etc., and Ismail Pasha, Mouteserif of the Sanjak of Kars etc.

Be it known to you, on receipt of this Imperial rescript, that since the beginning of the present war the people of Kars have evinced a good spirit of zeal and devotion. They have thus, from the time that the place was beleaguered by the enemy, shared all the sufferings and the valour of my soldiers. When the enemy assaulted Kars on the 17th of Mouharem, the inhabitants, more particularly, joined my troops with one accord, and devoted their lives to the service of their country. They are co-actors in a triumph that will be recorded in history, and their services are highly appreciated by my Royal person. I shall not only remember them ever with affectionate wishes, but in recompense for their glorious deed, the inhabitants of Kars proper shall, during the war, and for three years after the war, be free from all imposts. Moreover, as they have by this means rendered the military service due by them, the conscription will be dispensed with in favour of the inhabitants of Kars proper during the above period. Those who have distinguished themselves during the war shall be rewarded with nishans, according to their services.

Such is my Imperial will. I have ordered that this exalted rescript, decorated with my Royal hand, should be issued from the Royal Divan, to be proclaimed in evidence of my favour towards the people of Kars.

It is now transmitted to you, the above lauded Mushir and Mouteserif; and you will cause it to be read before the assembly of the whole people; and you will make every one feel how highly my Imperial Majesty appreciates the services rendered by them. You will then cause the same to be inscribed on the records of the Mekhemeh to the glorification of the descendants of all the inhabitants. Hasten to carry out the injunctions of my Royal pleasure.

Be it thus known unto you, and put full credence in the Imperial cypher.

Given in the middle of the propitious month of Sefer, in the year 1272.

Brigadier-General Williams to the Earl of Clarendon (received November 29)
Kars, October 31, 1855

My Lord,

In my despatch of the 3rd instant, in which I had the honour to detail the movements of the battle on the heights of Kars, I omitted to state that the enemy in his retreat left a tumbril on the field.

I have now great pleasure in stating for your Lordship's information that immediately after the battle his Excellency the Mushir, in virtue of the authority with which he is invested by the Sultan, conferred the second class of the Imperial Order of the Medjidiyé on Lieutenant-Colonel Lake for his distinguished services on that day; on Major Teesdale, Captain Thompson, Mr Churchill, and Dr Sandwith, the third class of that Order; and on Messrs Zohrab and Rennisson he bestowed the fourth class.

As these decorations were received in view of the position which their courage and conduct so materially assisted in defending, I trust that your Lordship will obtain Her Majesty's gracious permission to accept and wear them.

His Excellency the Mushir has also named Colonel Lake a General of Brigade in the Turkish army, Major Teesdale a Lieutenant-Colonel, and Captain Thompson a Major in that army; and his Excellency assures me that he has written for the confirmation of those ranks so honourably won by the officers in question.

W. F. WILLIAMS

NOVEMBER 1855

The Earl of Clarendon to Lord Stratford de Redcliffe

Foreign Office, November 1, 1855

My Lord,

I have to state to your Excellency that Her Majesty's Government approve of the correspondence of which copies are enclosed in your despatch of the 21st ultimo, and having reference to the late victory at Kars.

The mode of rewarding the inhabitants of Kars for their good conduct on this occasion, and which the Porte seems, from M. Pisani's report, to be disposed to adopt, namely, that of exempting them from taxation for three years, appears very judicious and likely to stimulate the people of other places to similar exertions.

CLARENDON

The Earl of Clarendon to Brigadier-General Williams

Foreign Office, November 2, 1855

Sir,

I have received your despatch of the 29th of September last, announcing that General Mouravieff, with the bulk of his army, had at daybreak that morning attacked your entrenched position on the heights above Kars, and on the opposite side of the river, and that after an engagement which lasted nearly seven hours, the enemy was driven off in the greatest disorder and with considerable loss.

I beg to congratulate you upon this brilliant and important victory, which reflects the highest credit upon the garrison of Kars.

It is my agreeable duty to convey to you, and to the British officers under your command, the cordial approbation of the Queen and of Her

Majesty's Government, for the energy, the perseverance, and the valour with which, for many months, and under circumstances of extraordinary difficulty, you have laboured with Lieutenant-Colonel Lake, Major Teesdale, and Captain Thompson, together with Mr Churchill and Dr Sandwith, to sustain the spirit and discipline of the Turkish troops, and to place the defences of Kars in a state to resist successfully the attack of the Russian army.

I shall not fail to recommend these officers to the Queen for the rewards due to their gallantry.

CLARENDON

The Earl of Clarendon to Lord Stratford de Redcliffe
Foreign Office, November 3, 1855

My Lord,
I enclose, for your Excellency's information, a copy of a despatch [dated November 2, 1855] which I have addressed to Brigadier-General Williams, conveying to him and to the British officers under his command the cordial approbation of the Queen and of Her Majesty's Government of their conduct during the operations at Kars.

CLARENDON

Lord Stratford de Redcliffe to the Earl of Clarendon (received November 19)
Therapia, November 4, 1855

(Extract)
In addition to the Sultan's approval of the conduct of his army at Kars, His Majesty's principal Ministers have addressed a letter of congratulation and thanks to the defenders of that fortress; a translation of the letter in question is enclosed herewith for your Lordship's information.

Enclosure

Address from the Porte to the defenders of Kars
The signal victory which you have gained by the grace of God, and under the auspices of His Majesty the Sultan, is an event which will fill a bright page in history. The courage and valour displayed on this occasion by your Excellency, the officers and soldiers of the Sultan's army under your command, and by the inhabitants of Kars, are deserving of universal praise. They have been duly appreciated by His Imperial Majesty, who has graciously extended his Royal favour towards yourself, the army under your command, and the people of Kars, in reward of the brilliant service rendered by them.

The sufferings undergone by the Imperial forces beleaguered in Kars have troubled the sleep and repose of all of us, and we have never ceased to pray for their safety and success. We were conscious of the zeal and intrepidity which animated your Excellency, and of the infinite mercy of God, and found consolation in this reflection. On the other hand, we worked day and night in devising means to oblige the enemy to raise the siege, and the joyful tidings of this victory has infused new life into us. Such a service rendered to our gracious Master is a glory to the state and to the nation, and His Majesty has permitted that we likewise, as companions, should offer our thanks and congratulations to our brethren, who have been made worthy of so great a victory. We, therefore, from the bottom of our hearts, offer our warm thanks and congratulations to your Excellency, and all the officers and troops of the army, our brothers; and by that you will convey the same to all of them, with our prayers for their prosperity and salvation.

Consul Brant to the Earl of Clarendon *(received December 6)*

Erzeroom, November 11, 1855

(Extract)

I have the honour to transmit your Lordship a message from the Mushir at Kars to his Excellency Selim Pasha, received yesterday afternoon, which General Williams desired me to communicate to your Lordship, as well as to Viscount Stratford de Redcliffe and Sir James Simpson:

> Our affairs are desperate. Let Selim Pasha's force, with that of Veli Pasha, excepting those intended to garrison the forts of Erzeroom, march upon Kars immediately. Let Mehmet Pasha seize and put at the disposal of the Military Pashas the whole land-carriage of the country. If Selim Pasha has not arrived, let Tahir Pasha send him an express instantly with this message.

I invited Tahir Pasha to come to my house, which he politely did, and there met Majors Stuart and Peel, and Captain Cameron; and after consultation it was agreed that his Excellency should at once visit the Mushir, and urge him to hasten the departure of his force. Early this morning all the British officers waited on the Mushir, who promised, that on the 13th he would march to Kupri-Keuy, and that his further movements would be guided by those of the Russian Byazid Division. The Mushir will have with him a force of about 5,000 Infantry, 2,000 Cavalry (Regulars 1,500, and 500 Irregulars), with 24 guns. His inclination seemed to be to give battle to the Russian Division, which being only 3,000 strong with 6 small guns, his Excellency hoped to defeat, and afterwards to march on Kars. I must say that Selim Pasha has been very dilatory since his arrival, and seemed little disposed to advance at all until the troops promised him by the Seraskier should have arrived; but Major Stuart has, after much persuasion, brought him to his present resolution, as the necessity of the Kars garrison admitted of no delay, and the arrival of the promised troops seems very remote and uncertain, as they have not yet reached Trebizond. I hope the Mushir will follow up his present resolve, and if he will be guided by Major Stuart, I trust a diversion will be made to enable provisions to be introduced to Kars, by the Russians concentrating their troops so as to be prepared for a threatened attack of the army of Selim Pasha.

Consul Brant to the Earl of Clarendon (received December 6)
Erzeroom, November 12, 1855

My Lord,
Yesterday afternoon I received from Kars a despatch from General Williams, who directed me to send a copy to your Lordship, to Viscount Stratford de Redcliffe, and to Sir James Simpson:

Kars, October 3, 1855

I have told the English officers to join Selim and Veli Pashas in their advance. The enemy came today with 12 battalions and 2 batteries, and 500 carts, to destroy the village of Shorak, and carry off the wood of the houses. He was driven out by our Artillery with loss; he set fire to it, and withdrew. Urge on the relieving army, and also increase activity in sending troops from Constantinople. The enemy has struck his tents, and hutted his army.

The village of Shorak was under the Tahmasb Tabia, and the danger of the enemy's attempt, and his want of wood, either for firing or for sheltering his troops, may be guessed by the large force employed. The troops expected to join Selim Pasha are very slow in their movements, although the Mushir declares he has notice of their embarkation at Constantinople from the Seraskier Pasha; no information of their arrival at Trebizond has been received. The Russians hutting their troops, indicates the severe cold in tents, and, possibly, either their wish to be prepared for a hasty retreat, or their determination to remain where they are for a longer period. It would be difficult to divine their true motive, but I would fain hope it may not be the last; for if so, the garrison will eventually be forced to yield to famine.

The season has singularly favoured the Russians, by the snow and bad weather coming so late this year, but I think it cannot be delayed under any circumstances beyond the end of this month.

JAMES BRANT

Lord Stratford de Redcliffe to the Earl of Clarendon (received November 29)
Therapia, November 19, 1855

My Lord,
I avail myself of today's messenger to forward to your Lordship the substance of a despatch from Brigadier-General Williams dated the 6th instant.

A previous despatch from the same officer dated the 23rd ultimo, and received only two days ago, was immediately communicated by my direction to the Turkish Ministers, who assert that Selim Pasha is authorised to attempt the relief of Kars. Supposing the instructions to have reached him, he is probably acting at this moment in obedience to their tenor.

STRATFORD DE REDCLIFFE

Enclosure

Consul Brant to Lord Stratford de Redcliffe

Erzeroom, November 6, 1855

My Lord,

I have the honour to inform your Excellency that I received this morning a despatch from General Williams, the contents of which he desired me to communicate to your Excellency.

The General says: "I have on my shoulders the management of the starving population, as well as that of the army. I take from the rich, and give to the poor, but am now obliged to issue corn from the public stores. I hope Omer Pasha is at least acting like a brave and resolute man. The enemy showed his diminished army yesterday, 16 battalions from 400 to 500 each, 3 regiments of Dragoons, 3 of Cossacks, and 40 guns."

JAMES BRANT

Major Simmons to the Earl of Clarendon (received December 18)

Camp on the Sieva, November 19, 1855

(Extract)

I have to inform your Lordship that the army broke up from Zugdidi on the 15th instant, on which day the communications were opened between the advanced guard at Chopi and Redoute-Kaleh, where Omer Pasha has formed depôts for provisioning the troops. The distance from Redoute-Kaleh to Chopi is about 18 miles, along a road in great measure macadamised, and, consequently, the provisioning of the troops will be much facilitated.

The advanced guard is now at Senaki on the Tikour, the main body being at the village of Taklit (marked Seklami on the map) on the River Sieva. The army is now detained whilst provisions are being brought up from Redoute-Kaleh, and a dêpot formed here, the distance from the sea being about 30 miles.

As soon as this depôt shall be formed, probably in two days, Omer Pasha proposes collecting his army which is now écheloned along the road from the Tikour to Zugdidi, and then moving on again *en masse*.

The troops have been écheloned in this manner to facilitate their provisioning. In the meantime a reconnaissance has been pushed on to the Tkeniss Zkhal which separates Mingrelia from Immeritia; and it appears that the Russians have entirely evacuated this province. In their retreat they have destroyed all the bridges, and even large culverts on the road; they have abandoned several positions temporarily fortified, and especially the position of this camp, where there is a strong entrenchment which was thrown up last year, covering a large extent of ground and naturally of great strength.

In it were enclosed temporary barracks and a depôt of provisions. Both have been destroyed by fire, as also have a range of temporary barracks at

Chopi, and considerable magazines and stores at Cheta, and at Senaki on the Tikour.

In fact, the farther the Turkish army penetrates the country, the more evident it is that the Russians have miscalculated their powers of resistance; and the results of the success of the 6th instant become more apparent. Their losses on that occasion must have been great, and may be moderately estimated at from 1,600 to 1,800 killed and wounded.

I am happy to inform your Lordship that the very strict measures taken by Omer Pasha to prevent pillage have met with great success. The Abassians, who at first caused so much fear to the inhabitants of Mingrelia, and had commenced committing great havoc amongst them, stealing even children, have been sent back into their own country, some of them after receiving severe chastisement from the Turkish military authorities. The few Circassians that remain are held in check; and as to the troops themselves, I do not think, although they have generally found the villages deserted, the whole army have plundered to the value of ten pounds, and to that extent only in articles of consumption. The result is, that as the army advances in the country the villages are less deserted; and I do not despair of the army even deriving some little benefit from the resources of the country: these, however, are not numerous, and will be confined to hay and Indian corn for the horses, and a small supply of meat with some few bât-horses [pack-horses]. The country, however, as the army proceeds to the eastward, improves and becomes more cultivated.

I have to inform your Lordship that, according to reports received, the Russians in retiring have burnt their gun-boat flotilla on the Rhion. In fact, everything appears to indicate now their inability to resist for any length of time on this side of Kutais. It is not improbable, however, that in order to gain time for the removal of their sick and stores, they may oppose the passage of the Tkeniss-Zkal.

I would further observe to your Lordship that this army, which numbers in all about 40,000 men, will require strong available reinforcements, if they are to maintain their position at or in front of Kutais, against the Russian army, after it shall be reinforced by Mouravieff's army from before Kars.

The Turkish General, as his army is at present disposed, has not much more than 20,000 men to meet the enemy in an advanced position.

He has been able to make no use of the force of 10,000 men which formed the army of Batoom, under Mustafa Pasha, before the diversion in favour of the army of Kars was in contemplation, that force being very much disorganised by mismanagement and weakened by disease. Some little has been done to re-establish it, and probably 6,000 men may be counted upon from it in the spring. The remainder of Omer Pasha's army consists of 16,000 men from before Sebastopol, and 15,000 men from Roumelia, strong detachments of whom it has been necessary to leave to protect the magazines at Soukoum-Kaleh and Tchimshera, to hold Zugdidi and to maintain the communications of the army, so that when the army reaches Kutais it will not much exceed 20,000 men.

If, as has been reported, General Mouravieff has broken up from before Kars, and is on the march to reinforce General Mukrainsky, in Immeritia, the Russian General will have the superiority of force, and it may be expected that the Turkish forces, unaided, will not be able to maintain their position. This union, however, of the Russian forces cannot be expected to take place before the spring.

With reference to the measures to be taken for carrying on the war next spring, I feel convinced that as the results which have hitherto been obtained here are to be attributed to the presence of the troops which Her Majesty's and the French Governments consented to being brought from before Sebastopol, so they can only be maintained and brought to a more successful issue by forming a considerable corps of reserve from the Turkish troops which have already served in Roumelia or the Crimea, under the command of Omer Pasha.

Consul Brant to the Earl of Clarendon (received December 14)

Erzeroom, November 20, 1855

My Lord,

I have the honour to enclose a copy of a despatch which I addressed yesterday to his Excellency the Viscount Stratford de Redcliffe.

Major Stuart and myself have done all we could to urge Selim Pasha to advance, but I fear he is too timid, and wants only a pretext to delay here.

The Kars garrison is in imminent danger, and I am really afraid it must surrender. I am apprehensive Omer Pasha will not advance rapidly enough, and General Mouravieff seems determined to hold out as long as possible. The season favours him signally.

I am in a great state of anxiety, for bravery and skill will soon be unavailing, and they cannot stand out against famine.

JAMES BRANT

Enclosure

Consul Brant to Lord Stratford de Redcliffe

Erzeroom, November 19, 1855

(Extract)

I have the honour to inform your Excellency that a peasant from Kars brought me today a few lines from General Williams of the 12th.

The General evidently seems to be in the belief that Selim Pasha has received the troops promised, of whose arrival at Trebizond, however, we have heard nothing, and his Excellency has requested both Major Stuart and myself to entreat your Excellency to hasten their expedition. A Colonel arrived with a long letter from his Excellency Vassif Pasha to Selim Pasha. The precise contents of this letter I do not know, but the object was to urge on his Excellency to the relief of the garrison. Selim Pasha inspected his troops yesterday, and they mustered between 5,000 and 6,000 Infantry: most of the Cavalry were on duty at the outposts; they will amount to nearly 2,000, chiefly Regulars, and besides these, they could collect 1,500 to 2,000 Bashi-Bozouks, if not more. The troops are in good health, well armed and clothed, and have lately received four months' pay, and I have no hesitation in saying that such a force under an active and brave General could relieve Kars; but I have seen enough of Selim Pasha to have discovered that he is neither active nor energetic, nor brave; and I have long feared that he would not advance. He has a new excuse for delay every day; today it was, that he must wait a change of weather: it is much finer than we had any reason to expect at this season, beautifully clear, though a little cold at night, and I can only say that as finer weather cannot be expected before next summer, it is evident his Excellency will not leave Erzeroom. Selim is superior in rank to Vassif Pasha, and will not therefore obey his orders. The former's character was well known from his conduct in the command of the Choorooksoo army, which by neglect he allowed to perish, and yet in circumstances which demand immediate action, a slow and indolent Mushir like him is sent up. It really makes me fear that the Seraskier has no wish or intention of saving from destruction General Williams and his little band of heroes. I would therefore once more earnestly entreat your Excellency to see that a General of character be sent up, with at least a few good troops, with positive orders that they must arrive here in 20 or 25 days, and that every assistance the country can furnish, be afforded to effect this.

If a proper man be not at hand, the Porte had better avail of the services of General Cannon and his staff, who are at Trebizond; but should the General be sent, your Excellency must insist that he have the absolute and uncontrolled command of this division, and that not one hour be lost in coming to a decision. The Russians cannot have many troops before Kars, I should think not more than 12,000, and they are discouraged, and have no heart to fight; but in the camp it is said that General Mouravieff is of so obstinate a character, that he will never abandon the siege, even though he should risk his own life, and the destruction of his whole army, by a desperate assault, or by frost or famine. He has put his troops into huts which are well constructed and having plenty of firewood, they can stand the frost for some time yet, and too long, alas! for the safety of the garrison of Kars, which in the last extremity can do nothing but surrender; for without Cavalry, and without horses for their guns, they could never, I imagine, cut their way through the enemy, who is still superior in numbers, taking into account his numerous Cavalry and Artillery.

Omer Pasha is too slow in his movements to hope anything from him. About twelve days ago, his Excellency was still on the coast, and although he had gained a victory, I suppose he will require time before he can resume his advance.

I ask your Excellency, is the Kars army to be allowed to perish? Is nothing to be done to relieve it? For all that the Porte has lately done, is quite insufficient for the purpose. I before pointed out that Omer Pasha's army should have been directed on Kars by way of Erzeroom, and not on Georgia, and had that been done Kars might long since have been saved. I now fear it must surrender, and to confer honours on its gallant defenders, while they be left to perish is a cruel mockery, and an indelible disgrace to the Turkish Government, as well as to those of the allied Powers.

The Earl of Clarendon to Lord Stratford de Redcliffe

Foreign Office, November 21, 1855

My Lord,

With reference to your Excellency's despatch of the 4th instant, I have to state to you that Her Majesty's Government concur with your Excellency as to the character of the letter which the Sultan's Ministers have addressed to the defenders of Kars.

The neglected garrison of Kars will at least have the satisfaction of knowing that their sufferings troubled the sleep and repose of the Turkish Ministers, who, in default of all ordinary measures of relief, never ceased to pray for their safety and success.

CLARENDON

Consul Brant to the Earl of Clarendon (received December 21)

Erzeroom, November 24, 1855

(Extract)

I have the honour to inform your Lordship that messenger after messenger has reached me for several days past from General Williams, pressing for succours. I have received short notes from him of the 12th, 13th, and 16th, all to this purport.

Today a despatch came in, of which, by General Williams' desire, I have the honour to send to your Lordship a copy; I experienced the most painful feelings on perusing its contents. That after so gallant a defence, Kars should fall into the hands of a thrice-beaten enemy, on account of the apathy of the Porte and the cowardice and imbecility of Selim Pasha, is intolerably distressing; but the consolatory feeling remains that, however disgrace may attach to those parties whose duty it was to have prevented this melancholy termination of so glorious a struggle, the brave garrison, and the inimitable director of its energies and operations, will to the last maintain their character for valour, skill, foresight, and every soldierly virtue, and that while noble deeds are appreciated, the defence of Kars will stand prominent among the achievements of a war unsurpassed by any other in acts of daring gallantry.

Major Stuart has repeatedly waited on Selim Pasha and has in urgent terms entreated him to advance to the relief of Kars; the Major has done so again today, but met with the same coolness and refusal. His Excellency will neither attempt the relief of the place, nor will he advance to cover the retreat of the garrison, and refuses even to send a strong detachment of Cavalry towards Kars, which the Major and his officers offered to accompany in the hope of rendering assistance to the retiring army.

Selim Pasha now pretends that he fears danger to Erzeroom from the Byazid division and talks of advancing to attack it, but this is a mere pretext to cover his cowardice. I fear there is nothing to be done to help this neglected army: a retreat without Cavalry or Artillery in face of an enemy who commands a large number of both, seems inevitable, and I tremble for the result.

Omer Pasha is too distant and seems too slow in his movements to hope anything from him; and hence all relief is denied: the garrison therefore has nothing to depend upon but its own bravery, and the unflinching resolution, the consummate prudence and skill of its gallant Commander and his heroic band of European officers. Had Selim Pasha not been sent up hither something might have been effected. Veli Pasha would have probably not attempted more than Selim Pasha himself, but if the command had been given to Tahir Pasha, which, without the presence of Selim Pasha, it was in the power of Vassif Pasha to have ordered, I think relief could have been got into Kars. But as soon as Selim Pasha arrived, all control over the troops here was taken out of Vassif Pasha's hands.

The reputation of Selim Pasha might have led to the anticipation of what has happened; he was so well known as wanting in military knowledge and courage, as well as in administrative talent, that the Seraskier Pasha who named him should be made responsible for the incapacity of his protégé, and Selim Pasha should not be allowed to escape the punishment due to his cowardice and heartless conduct.

Enclosure

Brigadier-General Williams to Consul Brant

Kars, November 19, 1855

Tell Lords Clarendon and Redcliffe that the Russian army is hutted now and takes no notice of either Omer or Selim Pashas. They cannot have acted as they ought to have done. We divide our bread with the starving townspeople. No animal food for seven weeks. I kill horses in my stable secretly, and send the meat to the hospital, which is now very crowded. We can hold out, and try to retreat over the mountains *via* Olti. Have provisions sent in that direction, before the 18th day after this date. We shall carry three days' biscuit with us.

Lord Stratford de Redcliffe to the Earl of Clarendon (received December 6)

Therapia, November 26, 1855

My Lord,

The day before yesterday I received despatches from Kars, Erzeroom, and Trebizond. The substance of them in every essential point is contained in the accompanying abstract. I lost no time in bringing them to the knowledge of the Turkish Ministers. My instruction to M. Pisani is enclosed herewith. I requested General Mansfield also to lend his assistance. The result of his conversation with the Seraskier Pasha is contained in a report of which copy is transmitted herewith for your Lordship's information. An extract of M. Pisani's report is added.

Your Lordship will observe with satisfaction that Omer Pasha's movements are more promising than the accounts from Trebizond allowed me to suppose.

Your Lordship will also take note of what fell from the Turkish Ministers respecting Colonel Stein and Mustafa Pasha.

I had already applied to Admiral Grey for means of transport, and he had undertaken to embark 1,200 or 1,400 troops for Trebizond, and five companies at the Dardanelles, but the horse transports are all employed for our own Cavalry.

I hasten now to resume my application in favour of the Egyptian Infantry at Eupatoria, and I have sent Lord Napier to propose to M. Thouvenel that we should join in placing a large advance from the Loan Fund at the immediate disposal of the Turkish Government under proper securities as to its application.

The difficulties of which the Seraskier made mention to General Mansfield appear to have resulted from the slowness of the preliminary communications announced by the Porte as preparatory to the meeting of the Commission.

STRATFORD DE REDCLIFFE

Enclosure 1

Lord Stratford de Redcliffe to M. E. Pisani

Therapia, November 24, 1855

Sir,

I send you herewith an abstract of news from Kars, Erzeroom, and Trebizond.

You will lose no time in communicating the contents to Fuad Pasha, the Grand Vizier, and the Seraskier, and you will repeat yet once more my urgent demand that whatever it is possible to do to afford an additional chance for the delivery of Kars and its brave garrison, should be attempted without a moment's delay. Express at the same time the regret which I feel at the apparent inefficiency of Omer Pasha's movements, at his neglecting to communicate by Batoom with Kars, at the confidence which he has placed in Ferhad Pasha, and at his continued toleration of Mustafa Pasha.

You will earnestly implore the Turkish Ministers to do whatever may still depend upon those to remedy these crying evils.

I hope that Admiral Grey has been able to comply with the Seraskier's request for transport. You had better communicate with that officer, and ascertain the result of my application to him.

STRATFORD DE REDCLIFFE

P.S. I write to General Mansfield that he may afford you the advantage of his advice and co-operation.

Enclosure 2

Abstract of news from Kars, Erzeroom, and Trebizond

Therapia, November 24, 1855

News from Kars to November 3rd; from Erzeroom to November 12th; from Trebizond to November 17th.

Kars: Russians with 12 battalions, 2 batteries, and 500 carts, had tried to destroy the village of Shorak, for the sake of the wood. They were driven off by the artillery from Tahmasb Tabia, but burnt the village first. The Russians were hutting their troops. Weather favourable to them. Garrison of Kars in great distress. Earnest demands for an advance from Erzeroom, and reinforcements from Constantinople.

Erzeroom: Complaints of the slowness of troops expected from Constantinople, and of Selim Pasha.

Kars: Vassif Pasha writes—"Our affairs are desperate." Forces of Selim Pasha and Veli Pasha, excepting garrisons, ordered to march for Kars, with all the land carriage of the country.

Erzeroom: The Mushir had promised the British officers, who urged him to move with 5,000 Infantry and 2,000 Cavalry, and 24 guns, against the Russian division of 3,000, and 6 guns, to give battle, produce a concentration in forces and get provisions into Kars.

Kars: Loud complaints of not having heard from Omer Pasha for many weeks, though four days takes a foot messenger from Batoom.

Ferhad Pasha has written these words to Kerim Pasha—"On Vassif Pasha will fall all the disgrace of Williams Pasha's acts."

Trebizond: Omer Pasha had found Zugdidi strongly fortified, and was in consequence marching towards Redoute-Kaleh. The Russians had carried off 3,000 head of sheep from Mustafa Pasha's division, and attacked a Circassian village, massacring the inhabitants.

Enclosure 3

Extracts from M. E. Pisani's reports

Pera, November 25, 1855

In pursuance of your Excellency's instruction of yesterday's date, I lost no time in communicating to Fuad Pasha, the Grand Vizier, and the Seraskier Pasha, the "abstract of news" from Kars, Erzeroom, and Trebizond, and have the honour to report the result of my interview with those Ministers.

With reference to the intelligence contained in the abstract enclosed in your Excellency's instruction, both the Porte and the Seraskier received similar accounts, with the exception, however, of the last paragraph caught from the letters from Trebizond.

The foot messenger who brought the letters from Kars says that the Russian troops had made up their minds to abandon the siege of Kars, when they received intelligence from an Armenian inhabitant of the place that the Turks had hardly fifteen days' provisions; the Russian General thought it worth his while to continue the siege. Meanwhile the traitor, said the messenger, was summarily tried and hanged.

In a council which was held the night before last at the Grand Vizier's residence, it was decided that 8,000 men out of the 12,000 forming the Egyptian division at present at Eupatoria, will be forthwith embarked for Trebizond on their way to Erzeroom; and the Porte wishes to ascertain whether the British Admiral Commanding-in-chief can spare one or two steamers to keep them in conveying a portion of the said division to its destination. A similar application will also be made to the French Embassy.

All this, said his Highness and Excellency, requires money for its execution. The Treasury is much embarrassed, and unless 100,000 purses or 50,000,000 piastres are paid them on account, out of the loan, every operation must be stopped. Omer Pasha demands money, Vassif Pasha likewise, and the Commander at Eupatoria. Besides, the grain merchants and others refuse to give provisions unless they be paid ready money. Under these circumstances, both the Grand Vizier and Fuad Pasha urgently beg of your Excellency to be so good as to take their demand into due consideration, and issue orders to the proper quarter.

The Seraskier Pasha told me that he wrote to Omer Pasha some time back about Ferhad Pasha and that he will write to him again. His Excellency himself is not at all pleased with that man. As to Mustafa Pasha he thinks it proper to inform you, that before Omer Pasha's arrival at Redoute-Kaleh, Mustafa Pasha had applied and obtained leave to go for a change of air to Trebizond, where he had already gone; and subsequently he was to come to Constantinople, when Omer Pasha sent one of his aides-de-camp with a letter ordering Mustafa Pasha to join him. He obeyed the order against his inclination. At all events the Seraskier will endeavour to persuade Omer Pasha to send him to Constantinople. M. Thouvenel also made representations against Mustafa Pasha's remaining there.

Enclosure 4

Brigadier-General Mansfield to Lord Stratford de Redcliffe
Pera, November 25, 1855

My Lord,

On the receipt of your Excellency's note of yesterday with its enclosure, I called on M. Pisani, and arranged to accompany him to the Seraskier this morning at an early hour.

We found his Excellency very unwell, but able to attend to business. He had received intelligence regarding the state of things similar to that communicated to your Excellency. He exonerated Omer Pasha from blame and explained his position; the account of his Excellency differing essentially from what has been conveyed to your Excellency in that respect. On the 17th instant Omer Pasha's first division marched on Zugdidi. It was to be followed by a second one immediately. According to the report of Ahmed Pasha, the Admiral on the coast, to the Captain Pasha, the Generalissimo was now actually established at that place. This report was actually a day or two later than the last news from Omer Pasha. The latter had sent a squadron of Cavalry to Redoute-Kaleh from Zugdidi. This probably accounts for the report that he was marching on that road, whereas only a partial movement or reconnaissance had taken place.

Hassan Pasha had marched from Redoute-Kaleh with three or four battalions on the road towards Kutais, and had occupied the entrenchments three hours distant from that place, so long held by the enemy and now found to be evacuated, in consequence of the flank movement of Omer Pasha from Soukoum-Kaleh on Zugdidi.

At the same time Mustafa Pasha had left Batoom and had actually reached Ozurgheti by the date of the last report. Thus there are now three columns, that of Omer Pasha at Zugdidi, that of Hassan Pasha from Redoute-Kaleh, and that of Mustafa Pasha from Batoom, executing a movement of concentration on Kutais.

Omer Pasha has written urgently, requiring that every available transport horse shall be sent to him. Upon the arrival of such animals depends his ability to move forward strongly. The report of Ahmed Pasha is confirmed by that of the Captain of the steamer which arrived yesterday.

A Council of Ministers sat last night.

Full powers have in consequence been sent to Selim Pasha, the Mushir at Erzeroom, to do whatever can be achieved for the relief of Kars.

There are now at Constantinople, ready to sail to Trebizond, 850 riflemen and 120 gunners. These men embark tomorrow in an English steamer hired by the Seraskier for the purpose at 250,000 piastres, as that to be furnished by Admiral Grey will not be ready till Thursday the 29th instant. In the last 25 days, including the above-mentioned men, reinforcements to the amount of 4,000 men will have sailed from Trebizond, to be pushed on at once to strengthen Selim Pasha, who received a fortnight ago stringent orders to attack the Russians posted at Yenikeuy on the road to Kars.

In short, everything has been done that is possible with the means at hand. The old soldiers have all been taken away from the guard-houses at Constantinople and sent towards the seat of war, their places being filled up by recruits.

Marshal Pélissier having proposed that the Turkish troops should be sent from Eupatoria to Varna to winter, the Government of the Sultan had determined to send from thence 8,000 Egyptian Regulars to Trebizond, this being the first occasion in which they have been permitted to touch the army at Eupatoria. They entreat assistance to enable this most necessary movement to be carried out immediately. Every day is of the most urgent consequence.

After it has been effected, they calculate that the force under Selim Pasha will be not less than 25,000 men, composed as follows: 10,000 men at Erzeroom, 6,000 at Trebizond, 8,000 Egyptian, and 3,000 Bashi-Bozouks.

A short time ago the Russians were preparing to evacuate their positions round Kars, but the Seraskier fears they have received information from parties inside. An Armenian had been discovered in the fact of sending an emissary to the enemy with a message to the effect that the garrison had not 14 days' provisions left. The two men had been hanged.

The inhabitants had made an offer to Vassif Pasha to sally out and attack the Russians with 4,000 of the regular troops. This spirited offer had not been immediately accepted, as it was thought better to wait for a combination with Selim Pasha. The distance from Batoom to Kars cannot be effected by a foot passenger in four days. It is 56 hours.

In conclusion, his Excellency turned round to me and said that I was as well aware as he of the continuous exertion made to help the garrison by him, but that from the first we had been agreed on the necessity of a large and well-combined effort. That Omer Pasha had been delayed by causes over which, unfortunately, he could not exercise control. It was an affair of the Alliance. It had all along been understood that such measures as it was in their power to take without the army which had been detained in the Crimea, would not suffice for the object in view: still they had persevered, as in duty bound. His Excellency then proceeded to tell me, with much force, that the Turks were absolutely debarred from executing what was necessary for the prosecution of the campaign, by the delay in giving them the advantage of the Loan.

The grain, to the amount of 1,000,000 kilos, brought by him for the service of the army, was not forwarded to the coast because they could not pay for it.

The Commander of an army at Eupatoria, numbering 35,000 men, had only 300,000 piastres in his chest. When the large reinforcements arrived at Trebizond, there would not be a piastre to buy the animals and supplies needed for their movement.

His Excellency then declared that he had written to the Grand Vizier, that if money were not forthcoming from that source, in a week from this date, he would resign his office.

To this I did not make any reply, but I would earnestly suggest to your Excellency that if means be not taken immediately to supply the military chest of the Turkish Government, it is actually impossible for them to carry on forward movements, or even to keep their troops together.

Perhaps it might be expedient to let them have a sum in advance at once, although the Commissioners may not have terminated their labours; otherwise counsel is unavailing, and the prosecution of the campaign an impossibility. I must entreat your Excellency's pardon for hazarding this suggestion, but I am convinced that in it alone lies the chance of relieving the garrison of Kars, and of ultimate success wherever the Turkish army is concerned.

W. R. MANSFIELD

P.S. I have omitted to mention that his Excellency expressed his belief that the number of Russians in the immediate neighbourhood of Kars does not now exceed 12,000 men.

W. R. M.

Consul Brant to the Earl of Clarendon (received December 21)
Erzeroom, November 27, 1855

(Extract)

I yesterday received a note from General Williams of the 17th, and Major Stuart one of the 21st, both inquiring about Selim Pasha's movements.

The General does not appear to have received any of my notes, and still hopes for relief. Vassif Pasha has also written to Selim Pasha, urging him to make haste. Intelligence has reached Selim Pasha, that 2,000 men had landed at Trebizond, and were hastening on, and on their arrival he promised Major Stuart that he would advance, but pretexts for delay will not be wanting until he will declare it too late. The conduct of Selim Pasha would justify the suspicion that he was sent here expressly to prevent timely succours from reaching Kars and not to press on relief. Such at any rate has been the result of his every action.

It is reported that General Mouravieff has detached some part of his force towards Ahkiska, to strengthen the army which is to oppose Omer Pasha; if this be confirmed, the retreat of the Kars army may be more easily effected and I hope prove less disastrous than it otherwise would have been, and possibly General Mouravieff may be satisfied with the capture of Kars, and be prudent enough to respect the despair of the army whose valour has already cost him so dear, and thus may leave it unmolested in its retreat.

General Williams desires me to abstain from sending him any letters, as they are sure to fall into the enemy's hands.

Snow fell for the first time at Kars on the 21st instant, but the Russian troops are comfortably hutted, and give no indication of an inclination to retire.

Consul Brant to the Earl of Clarendon (received December 21)

Erzeroom, November 27, 1855

My Lord,

I have the painful duty to announce to your Lordship the surrender of Kars. It was brought this moment by General Kmety.

When General Williams learnt on the 23rd, by a communication from me, that Selim Pasha would not advance, he saw that all hope had vanished. The soldiers were dying by 100 a day of famine. They were mere skeletons and were incapable of fighting or flying. The women brought their children to the General's house for food, and there they left them, and the city was strewed with dead and dying. Under these circumstances the General called together all the Pashas, and asked them if they thought their soldiers could resist longer, or could possibly retreat; they all declared either an impossibility. The next day, General Williams sent Major Teesdale, at 2 p.m. to General Mouravieff's camp, to ask him to appoint an hour the following day for an interview, to treat for a surrender. At sunset, Major Teesdale had not returned, and General Kmety and General Kolman left with a guard of Koords to cut their way through the Russian patrols. They passed several and at last were stopped by one, and separated, and it was after 24 hours that they rejoined each other, and in three days and nights they reached this in safety. General Kmety does not know more than above stated as to terms, but he says the garrison being in so distressed a state, it must submit to any conditions General Mouravieff chose to dictate.

I am hurried to save [catch] the post, but tomorrow will send off an express messenger with such further particulars as I can learn.

JAMES BRANT

Consul Brant to the Earl of Clarendon (received December 27)

Erzeroom, November 28, 1855

(Extract)

I had the honour yesterday evening to address your Lordship a few hasty lines, to inform you that Kars had offered to capitulate.

General Kmety had then just arrived from thence, having, with General Kolman, escaped the Russian patrols. He was charged by Brigadier-General Sir William Williams to communicate to me the fall of Kars, and the sad events which preceded it. Late on the 22nd a foot messenger reached him with a packet from me. This was the first he had received since that which conveyed the news of the fall of Sebastopol, several weeks before. The General kept its contents secret for 24 hours. He then called in from his out-stations General Kmety, and told him how little hope my communication held out of assistance from Selim Pasha; and seeing that famine, which had already filled the hospitals with sick, was beginning to produce a serious mortality among the troops—about 80 having died that day—and their bread being reduced to a few days, he declared he could see no possibility of holding out any longer, and he proposed next morning assembling the Pashas, to consider their position. Early on the morning of the 24th all the Pashas assembled, and their actual situation, with their prospects, was clearly laid before them by the General, who asked them whether a prolonged defence was possible, or whether the troops could or would attempt a retreat. Both questions were answered in the negative by every Pasha declaring the men, with few exceptions, were not in a physical or moral condition to march or fight. The General then proposed that he should request an interview of General Mouravieff for the next day, to treat for terms, which being thankfully acceded to, at about half-past 2 p.m. of the 24th, Major Teesdale was dispatched with the message to the Russian camp.

When the decision to retreat was adopted, Generals Kmety and Kolman requested General Williams to accept their resignation, and to allow them to make their way through the Russian patrols. They had been condemned to death by the Austrian Government, for the part they had taken in the Hungarian War of Independence, and they expected that, if made prisoners they should be delivered up by the Russians to their Government, and their fate would be in such case certain. General Williams promised to do all in his power to make special conditions for them, but as their swords had now become useless, they entreated permission to retire, to which the General consented, after thanking them in the warmest and most feeling terms for their gallantry and good service.

Major Teesdale had not returned by nightfall from the Russian camp, and Generals Kmety and Kolman, wishing to profit of an hour of darkness before the rising of the moon, to glide by the Russian patrols unmolested, took their leave of their companions in arms, and accompanied by five brave and trusty Koords, hired as an escort, quitted the famine-stricken city. The party by their knowledge of the modes of challenging the Russian patrols, passed close by two unmolested, but a third recognised them, and they were obliged to disperse over the hills, and met again 24 hours afterwards at a place of rendezvous fixed on, and from thence they came hither without further rencontre, after riding uninterruptedly for three days and nights. General Kmety says that the position of the garrison and city was such that any conditions, however hard, must be accepted. Human nature could neither resist longer nor endure more. Scarcely 1,000 men of the whole garrison were in a state to use their weapons, and not many more could have sustained a march pursued by an enemy. Had a retreat been attempted very few would have survived it; those who escaped the arms of the enemy would have died of exhaustion. The women crowded round the General's house with their starving children crying for food, and throwing down their little ones at his gate, would not depart but with food. Himself, whom it had been their delight to salute and recognise as he passed they no longer noticed kindly, but hurried by with an ominous half-averted scowl; the same look was perceived in the soldiers; and how must this have lacerated a breast which always overflowed with tenderness towards suffering humanity.

Lieutenant-Colonel Lake was suffering from gout, brought on by night patrolling and fatigue in the trenches; Mr Zohrab was laid up with typhus, but was recovering; the other officers were well. Nothing is yet known as to the conditions of the surrender; probably a few days will inform us.

General Kmety says that Sir William Williams had received the information of the honour conferred on him by Her Majesty, and that when he congratulated him, Sir William thanked him in a few words and with a faint smile; his mind was then overwhelmed by painful feelings, and occupied by the impending calamity, and he could scarce feel pleasure even at the honour received.

Brigadier-General Williams to the Earl of Clarendon (received January 6, 1856)
Russian Camp near Kars, November 29, 1855

My Lord,

From the various despatches in cypher which I have addressed to your Lordship through Mr Brant, the intelligence which I have now the misfortune to announce must have been expected by your Lordship.

I had received direct promises of succour from Selim Pasha; and Omer Pasha's operations, until I knew that his movements were directed towards Soukoum-Kaleh, had buoyed me up in my determination to hold out to the last moment; this intelligence from the Generalissimo reached me on the 24th instant, by the same post which brought me positive news, from Mr Brant, of the indisposition or inability of Selim Pasha to advance further than Kupri-Keuy.

We had, up to that date, suffered from cold, want of sufficient clothing, and starvation, without a murmur escaping from the troops. They fell dead at their posts, in their tents, and throughout the camp, as brave men should who cling to their duty through the slightest glimmering of hope of saving a place entrusted to their custody. From the day of their glorious victory, on the 29th September, they had not tasted animal food, and their nourishment consisted of two-fifths of a ration of bread and the roots of grass, which they had scarcely strength to dig for; yet night and day they stood to their arms, their wasted frames showing the fearful effects of starvation, but their sparkling eyes telling me what they would do were the enemy again to attack them.

We had now lost nearly 2,000 men by starvation, and the townspeople also suffered, and would have died by hundreds if I had not divided the bread of the soldiers amongst those who had bravely fought by their side. I therefore begged the Mushir to call a council of war, which, on being told that we had only six days' rations, came unanimously to the conclusion that nothing was left to us but a capitulation; and that the debility of the men, and total want of Cavalry, Field Artillery, and ammunition mules, rendered any attempt to retreat impossible.

The Mushir then deputed me to treat with General Mouravieff, and I consequently waited on his Excellency on the 25th instant. He at first seemed determined to make prisoners of all who defended the place, but as the Redif, or Militia, and the townspeople formed a large portion of the Infantry, I made a successful appeal to his humanity, which, coupled with the obvious measure of destroying our artillery and stores, to which we should have had recourse previous to an unconditional surrender, brought about the Convention which I have now the honour to enclose for your Lordship's information, without the expression of unavailing regret.

I have only to add that the stipulations were carried into effect yesterday; that myself, my officers, and the regular troops composing the last garrison, amounting to 8,000 of all arms, are prisoners of war, and that the Irregulars, numbering 6,000, have marched towards their respective homes.

I and my officers are to march for Tiflis tomorrow, there to await the decision of the Emperor as to the place of our abode in Russia.

W. F. WILLIAMS

Enclosure

Précis of the Convention between General Mouravieff and Major-General Sir William Williams, relative to the surrender of Kars

1. The fortress of Kars shall be delivered up intact.
2. The garrison of Kars, with the Turkish Commander-in-chief, shall march out with the honours of war, and become prisoners. The officers, in consideration of their gallant defence of the place, shall retain their swords.
3. The private property of the whole garrison shall be respected.
4. The Redifs (militia), Bashi-Bozouks and Laz, shall be allowed to return to their homes.
5. The non-combatants, such as medical officers, scribes, and hospital attendants, shall be allowed to return to their homes.
6. General Williams shall be allowed the privilege of making a list of certain Hungarian and other European officers, to enable them to return to their homes.
7. The persons mentioned in Articles 4, 5, and 6, are in honour bound not to serve against Russia during the present war.
8. The inhabitants of Kars will be protected, in their persons and property.
9. The public buildings and the monuments of the town will be respected.

November 27, 1855

DECEMBER 1855

General Williams to the Earl of Clarendon (received January, 1856)

Gumri, December 2, 1855

(Extract)

I have arrived thus far on my long journey, receiving, at every step, the kindest offices of, I may say, every officer in the Russian army, from the highest to the lowest.

Lord Stratford de Redcliffe to the Earl of Clarendon (received December 14)

Therapia, December 3, 1855

(Extract)

Intelligence from Kars, of necessity brief and secret, continues to augur ill for the fate of the gallant army beleaguered in that fortress. The latest accounts are from Mr Brant, who has sent them on to your Lordship. His despatch of the 20th ultimo reached me the night before last, and I lost not an instant in sending instructions to General Mansfield and M. Pisani. At this late hour nothing can possibly be attempted otherwise than in the spirit of a forlorn hope, but I am anxious that no stone should be left unturned on our side that may afford a chance of relief. I have been careful to bring the conduct of Selim Pasha under the notice of the Porte, and especially under that of his responsible chief, the Seraskier; suggesting at the same time the advantage which might be derived from sending a British officer, if not to take the command of the Turkish forces at Erzeroom, at least to advise with some degree of authority.

Enclosed herewith in copy is General Mansfield's report of his discussion with the Seraskier. I have nothing to add, except that Admiral Grey affords at my request all the assistance in his power for the transport of Turkish troops to Trebizond.

Enclosure

Brigadier-General Mansfield to Lord Stratford de Redcliffe

Pera, December 2, 1855

(Extract)

I have the honour to return Mr Brant's despatch, and to inform your Excellency that, in company with M. Etienne Pisani, I this morning visited the Seraskier Pasha. A conversation ensued in accordance with your Excellency's instructions.

His Excellency observed that by this time three out of four battalions of Infantry, sent from hence to reinforce Selim Pasha at Erzeroom, must have arrived. He is, consequently, now at the head of about 13,500 men. After the Council sat, of which your Excellency was informed in my despatch of the 25th ultimo, an order was sent to Selim Pasha in the name of the Sultan, to run all hazards for the relief of Kars. That order will reach him tomorrow. Till the arrival of the reinforcement above alluded to, Selim Pasha was deterred from moving, on account of the presence of a moveable Russian corps of observation on the Byazid road, consisting of from 5,000 to 6,000 men. The Pasha could not, with regard to that corps, leave Erzeroom altogether without troops.

His Excellency did not understand why the garrison of Kars did not attempt a sortie.

Mr Brant was in error in supposing Selim Pasha would not obey Vassif Pasha, on account of the former being the senior in rank. The reverse is the case; besides that, Vassif Pasha has been nominated Commander-in-chief of all the troops in the country where the operations are going on. Selim Pasha is a brave energetic man, and possessed of much experience. He commanded a division in the Egyptian campaign, when Sir Charles Napier was successful, and has been in several general actions. He is not a man who has been educated in a school, but his practical knowledge is considerable; the Seraskier is in the act of sending to his assistance on his staff, Mouhlip Pasha, alias Stourdja, of Wallachia, who distinguished himself much on the Danube and is highly educated.

Three steamers, two British and one Turkish, have gone to Eupatoria to ship Egyptians for Trebizond. As soon as Admiral Grey reported another to be ready, which his Excellency expected immediately, it would proceed on the same day.

In conclusion, his Excellency assured me that the minutes of the last Council had been sent to Selim Pasha, with an injunction to spare no exertion, and that he could not be held responsible if his army were lost in the attempt to help the garrison of Kars.

Major Stuart to the Earl of Clarendon (received January 1, 1856)

Erzeroom, December 5, 1855

(Extract)

Referring to my letter of the 28th ultimo, I have the honour to inform you that intelligence has since been received which confirms the fact of the surrender of Kars.

The latest accounts from that place are to the 27th ultimo, on which day the terms of capitulation were signed; on the 28th the Russians were to march in; and General Williams, Colonel Lake, Major Teesdale, and Captain Thompson, were to proceed under escort to Tiflis.

Mr Churchill, Secretary to General Williams, was, at his own request, permitted to accompany him.

It would appear that General Mouravieff evinced on this occasion all the consideration that was due to the brave garrison with which he had to deal; with the exception of General Williams and the Mushir, all the officers were allowed to retain their swords. The non-combatants were not included among prisoners. The Redif troops, numbering about 9,000, were dismissed to their homes; but the Nizam, between 4,000 and 5,000 strong, were to be sent to Georgia.

A special stipulation was also agreed to, that liberty should be granted to such persons as General Williams should think fit to name. The General peremptorily insisted upon this point, his object being to provide for the safety of those European officers in the Turkish army who were serving with him: among those who received the benefit of it was Baron Schwartzenburg; he arrived here on the 3rd instant, and from him I have obtained the foregoing particulars. He also mentioned that the last ration was drawn from the stores before he left; but immediately after the capitulation was signed, 200 horses laden with provisions were sent by Mouravieff into the town.

I have not yet heard from General Williams; but he sent word to say he would write from Gumri.

The Earl of Clarendon to Lord Stratford de Redcliffe

Foreign Office, December 7, 1855

My Lord,

I have received your Excellency's despatch of the 26th of November, and I have to inform you in reply that Her Majesty's Government entirely approve the steps which you have taken with a view to the relief of Kars.

CLARENDON

Lord Stratford de Redcliffe to the Earl of Clarendon (received December 9)

Therapia, December 8, 1855, 1.30 a.m.

(Telegraph)

I learn with the deepest concern by despatches of the 27th November, just received from Her Majesty's Consul at Erzeroom, that Vassif Pasha and

General Williams have been reduced by a painful necessity to despair of saving Kars from the enemy. Mr Brant has not stated, nor indeed does he appear to have known, what conditions, if any, had been settled.

Major Teesdale had been sent on the 23rd to propose an interview with General Mouravieff for the purpose of treating for a surrender. That officer not having returned at sunset, General Kmety and General Kolman were sent to force their way through the Russian patrols, and finally in three days reached Erzeroom, where Selim Pasha was thought to have been remiss in not attempting the relief of the besieged fortress.

Lord Stratford de Redcliffe to the Earl of Clarendon (received December 21)
Therapia, December 10, 1855

(Extract)
Enclosed in copy is a report of General Mansfield's conversation with the Seraskier Pasha, when he waited upon that Minister at my request after the arrival of the last despatches from Erzeroom.

Enclosure

Brigadier-General Mansfield to Lord Stratford de Redcliffe
Pera, December 8, 1855

(Extract)
Not having thought it advisable to defer making your Excellency's important communication to the Seraskier, in the absence of M. Pisani, I took the liberty of soliciting Mr Doria to accompany me to his Excellency, to which he willingly acceded.

I communicated the substance of the deplorable accounts from Erzeroom, and dwelt very urgently upon the reports of Mr Brant, on the conduct of Selim Pasha. His Excellency showed me the despatches of Selim Pasha, as well as the original ones of Vassif Pasha. The despatch of Selim Pasha, giving the account of the surrender, was not in the packet which had arrived from Erzeroom, although there was one from the Civil Governor alluding to it, and confirmatory of the account of the Consul.

In respect of the accusations preferred against Selim, it must be said that there has been no attempt at concealment on his part. The despatches of Vassif were laid before me, in which the former was strongly urged to come to the assistance of Kars, while attention was directed to the Russian moveable column on the side of Byazid.

Arrangements have been made by Selim for the collection of provisions at Olti and Penek, and the Kaimakam of Childir had, by his orders, collected 5,000 horses with arabas to convey them into Kars, if the vigilance of the enemy relaxed in any degree. I urged his Excellency to consider well the present position of Selim Pasha. Assuming that Vassif Pasha is in the hands of the enemy, on the Commander at Erzeroom now devolved the task of defending the country altogether. The relief of Kars was a single operation. The sphere of his duty would now be very largely extended.

He seemed to feel what I advanced, but said there must be inquiry to ascertain if he failed from want of forethought and energy, or whether he had been prudent in not risking incomplete action with imperfect means, which, while endangering his force, could produce no real result. He must have time to consider the question, prior to laying his views before the Council, which would assemble to consider the subject.

His Excellency was perfectly frank, and much time was spent in reading every despatch in the hopes of additional light being thrown on the matter. He repeated more than once that when they had sent Selim Pasha to Kars, their object was to send their best man.

When I expressed your Excellency's assurance that Her Majesty's Government would be much hurt if no effort had been made to save the fortress, his answer was: "And what must our Government feel?" The last advices from Omer Pasha himself are unimportant. But the messenger who brought the latest account said that the advanced guard of the army under his Highness was within four hours of Kutais, and the main body within six hours. According to him, Omer Pasha had signified to the Commanders that the advance was to be made immediately. Batoom had now become the base of operation. A large quantity of provisions had been thrown into Redoute-Kaleh. The road to that place was quite open from the camp of Omer Pasha. Mustafa Pasha was still near Ozurgheti, having been ordered by Omer Pasha not to advance till his Highness had crossed the Rhion.

Various advices go to show that the strength of the Russians before Kars is considerably under 20,000 men. Letters from one Arslan Bey in the fortress, which I saw, give details of a Russian division having left the army before Kars and gone to Ahkiska in consequence of the march of Omer Pasha. In like manner it is believed that the Cossacks who have been so long at Ardahan, blocking the road from Kars to Batoom, have gone to Akhalkhileh in two divisions. But this report having come from Kars, which is twelve hours' distance from Ardahan, perfect reliance cannot be placed on it.

When my very lengthened visit was brought to a close, the hour was too late for me to visit Fuad Pasha. But the Seraskier assured me that he would bring your Excellency's communication most seriously before the Council; and while I was with his Excellency, the despatches which had arrived from Erzeroom during my visit, were sent to the private residence of the Minister for Foreign Affairs.

Lord Stratford de Redcliffe to the Earl of Clarendon (received December 27)
Constantinople, December 14, 1855

My Lord,
We are still without intelligence of the actual surrender of Kars and its garrison into the hands of the enemy, but no doubt of the fact appears to have

been entertained at Erzeroom, when the last dispatches under date of the 29th ultimo, came away.

Though sealed reports, which may be presumed to contain the same statements as those addressed to me, are forwarded by the present occasion to your Lordship, yet, as I have no certain knowledge of their contents, I forward herewith copies of the despatches which I have myself received from Mr Brant and Major Stuart.

Your Lordship will observe that the number of men under arms in the fortress, which I fear is in Russian hands at this moment, is stated by the latter at 15,000 men, and the fall of the place from famine is the more to be deplored as the works appear to have been well provided with means of defence in other respects. Seventy pieces of field artillery, in addition to the guns in position, form a severe item of loss.

I have made a full communication of the painful correspondence to Fuad Pasha and his principal colleagues. M. Pisani informs me that they listened to it in silence. The conduct of Selim Pasha, as characterised by Mr Brant and Major Stuart, ought to produce his recall and consignment to a court-martial. I am not yet acquainted with the Porte's intentions.

STRATFORD DE REDCLIFFE

Enclosure 1

Consul Brant to Lord Stratford de Redcliffe

Erzeroom, November 28, 1855

(Extract)

I have the honour to inform your Excellency that the garrison of Kars contained, at the moment it was about to surrender, about 20,000 men receiving rations, out of which there was not above 10,000 combatants, 66 siege guns, with 70 beautiful pieces of field artillery, and 500 rounds per gun. There were about 2,000 good Minié rifles, and the muskets of the troops, with about 340,000 rounds of ball cartridge. Everything else had been used up.

This loss may be attributed to the dilatory proceedings of Omer Pasha, who about two months ago promised to relieve the Kars garrison, and to the cowardice of Selim Pasha, who, had he been courageous enough to have advanced, might have enabled the garrison to have made an effective sortie, or at least to have effected an honourable retreat.

There are now, and have been for months past, in this city, about 20 Pashas I believe, who literally may be said to do nothing but receive their extravagant appointments, and ruin the country by their exactions.

Enclosure 2

Major Stuart to Lord Stratford de Redcliffe

Erzeroom, November 28, 1855

My Lord,

I have the honour to inform you that yesterday afternoon General Kmety arrived here unexpectedly from Kars, with intelligence that leaves but little doubt that that place with its garrison, including General Williams and his immediate staff, and all the munitions of war it contained, are now in the hands of the Russians.

The circumstances communicated by General Kmety are as follows:

On the 23rd instant General Williams received a letter informing him that no succour would be sent to him by Selim Pasha, the Mushir in command here. On the morning of the 24th, he called together all the general officers holding commands in Kars, explained to them the position in which they stood, that there were but six days' provisions remaining in store, that matters were approaching to an extremity, and put it to them severally, if their troops were in a condition to attempt to cut their way through the Russian lines. The answer of all was to the effect that such an attempt would be utterly impossible, owing to the state of the men, debilitated as they were by long continued severe work and insufficient food. This being the case no alternative remained but capitulation, and accordingly at 2 or 3 p.m. of the 24th, Major Teesdale was sent to Mouravieff, to request he would appoint an hour for the settlement of terms. Major Teesdale had not returned at sunset, when General Kmety, in company with General Kolman, left Kars, with a few Koords as guides to make their escape; they succeeded with difficulty in getting through the lines, and riding day and night got in here, as I said, yesterday. I should observe that these officers being Hungarian refugees, were afraid of surrendering to the Russians, lest they should be handed over to the Austrian Government, and it was with General Williams' entire consent that they left Kars in the above manner.

The condition of Kars as described by General Kmety must have been deplorable. The hospitals were crowded; 70 or 80 men a day were dying of exhaustion, and all were reduced to an extreme degree of debility and emaciation: add to this that desertions in large numbers were of constant occurrence. With respect to the inhabitants of the place, their case was, if possible, worse; they had nothing but what was sparingly given them from the military stores, and General Williams had every day to endure the sight of women bringing their children to his door and leaving them there to die.

The garrison numbered, as nearly as I could learn, about 15,000; there were 70 field guns, 66 garrison guns, with 500 rounds of ammunition, and about 20,000 stand of small arms, including 2,000 excellent Miniés. I again affirm that this loss might have been averted had there been in command here a man of courage and ability. The number of troops at hand were sufficient for the purpose, but I greatly fear that Selim Pasha is altogether wanting in those military qualities which such an occasion called for.

Robert Stuart

Lord Stratford de Redcliffe to the Earl of Clarendon (received December 30)
Constantinople, December 14, 1855

My Lord,

I learn from M. de Thouvenel that permission has at length arrived from Paris for Marshal Pélissier to assent to the departure of the Egyptian Infantry at Eupatoria for Trebizond. I am informed, however, that the Turkish Commander had declared his determination to embark the troops without waiting for any further communication; and it is certain that English vessels, exposed by the delay to much tempestuous weather, were ready to receive them on board. If it be true, as stated on the alleged authority of the French Commander-in-chief, that out of the 10,000 Egyptians, 6,000 are affected by scurvy, I fear that little will be gained by the transfer of the healthy portion of them to Trebizond.

I avail myself of this opportunity to forward in copy for your Lordship's information the correspondence which has passed on this subject between Sir William Codrington and myself. I add the copy of a report from Her Majesty's Acting Vice-Consul at Trebizond, where a small reinforcement of about 800 Infantry had arrived.

Stratford de Redcliffe

Enclosure 1

General Sir W. Codrington to Lord Stratford de Redcliffe
Headquarters near Sebastopol, December 10, 1855

(Extract)

I wrote to Marshal Pélissier in the general tone of your letter, expressing to him the great object it seemed to be to get the Turkish troops to Trebizond, and that, if done at all, it should be done at once, and offering my assistance, if I could, by communications with our navy, further this object.

His answer was, that he could not consent to their leaving Eupatoria without the express sanction of the Emperor of the French.

Enclosure 2

Lord Stratford de Redcliffe to General Sir W. Codrington
Constantinople, December 12, 1855

The Turks are sadly mortified by the embargo which appears to have been laid on the Egyptian troops at Eupatoria.

Supposing the surrender of Kars to be confirmed, the Turks, I imagine, will still be anxious to send reinforcements to Erzeroom with all practicable speed, notwithstanding the lateness of the season.

Enclosure 3

Acting Consul Stevens to Lord Stratford de Redcliffe

Trebizond, December 3, 1855

My Lord,

I have the honour to inform your Lordship that 850 Turkish troops landed here yesterday from the steamer *Stella*, which vessel arrived the day before yesterday from Constantinople. I regret to state that the cholera manifested itself among these men; two fatal cases occurred on board, and two more since they landed, and there are 14 under treatment in Dr Farquhar's hospital.

G. A. STEVENS

General Williams to the Earl of Clarendon (received January, 1856)

Tiflis, December 14, 1855

(Extract)

I send these few lines, through General Mouravieff, to apprise your Lordship of the arrival of myself and Staff in this city. We were conveyed in carriages furnished by the Russian Government, and under the charge of Captain Baschmakoff, of the Imperial Guard, whose kind and friendly care of us demands our best thanks; indeed, nothing can exceed the warm and flattering reception which we have received from the authorities, military and civil.

We may, in ten days, hear the Emperor's decision as to the place of our abode during the time we shall remain prisoners of war; but, I believe, little doubt is felt by General Mouravieff that Moscow will be the point upon which we shall march.

The Earl of Clarendon to Lord Stratford de Redcliffe

Foreign Office, December 15, 1855

My Lord,

I have to state to your Excellency that Her Majesty's Government approve of the steps taken by you with reference to the precarious state of affairs at Kars, as reported in your despatch of the 3rd instant.

CLARENDON

Lord Stratford de Redcliffe to the Earl of Clarendon (received December 30)

Constantinople, December 17, 1855

My Lord,

Though I have nothing myself from Erzeroom of a later date than the end of November, I have seen a letter, copy enclosed, from Trebizond, which leaves no doubt that the fortress of Kars and its garrison had fallen into the hands of the Russians. It is a consolation to find that the conditions may fairly be termed honourable under such disastrous circumstances as we must conclude to have existed from the previous accounts.

The Porte has received intelligence similar in substance to what is stated in the letter from Trebizond.

STRATFORD DE REDCLIFFE

Enclosure

Extract from a letter from Trebizond, dated December 11, 1855

No authentic accounts had reached Erzeroom on the 4th of December, of the surrender of Kars, but it was known that the terms obtained by General Williams were most honourable. All the officers retained their swords in consequence of their heroic conduct on the 29th September. Redif and Bashi-Bozouks, all civil people and non-combatants, all Nogars, and 25 people to be named by General Williams, without any inquiry into reason, set at liberty. Dr Sandwith, Keane, and Rennisson, and Zohrab, the interpreter, were hourly expected at Erzeroom. Mr Churchill having fought in command of a battery on the 29th September, detained, and will be sent to Tiflis with General Williams. Some of the Nogars had reached Erzeroom; they left the evening before the Russians were to take possession. Omer Pasha is at a standstill in consequence of the heavy rains and swamps; he was on the Sieva, in tents, on the 30th of November.

Lord Stratford de Redcliffe to the Earl of Clarendon (received December 30)

Constantinople, December 18, 1855

My Lord,

I have the honour to transmit to your Lordship herewith, the copy of a despatch from Mr Consul Brant, dated the 3rd instant, stating the conditions of the capitulation of Kars as reported by some Hungarian officers recently arrived at Erzeroom.

STRATFORD DE REDCLIFFE

Enclosure

Consul Brant to Lord Stratford de Redcliffe

Erzeroom, December 3, 1855

My Lord,

I have the honour to inform your Excellency that yesterday some Hungarian officers arrived, and the conditions of the capitulation were learned from their report. They were sent off in haste to be out of the way before the Russian army entered the city, and Sir William Williams could not therefore write, but I am in momentary expectation of receiving a letter from him.

On the 24th at nightfall, Generals Kmety and Kolman left Kars. It was some time afterwards that Major Teesdale returned from the Russian camp; he was retained to dine, and was treated with most marked politeness. On the 25th

General Williams had his interview with General Mouravieff, which passed off satisfactorily. On the 26th Ekrem Effendi, first Secretary of the Mushir, Vassif Pasha, went to the Russian camp to make some arrangement, and on the 27th, Hafiz Pasha went. On that evening, the Hungarian officers left under a Russian guard, and they received everything necessary while thus escorted.

The conditions of the surrender are stated to be, that all non-combatants should be allowed to depart, as also all foreigners in the Turkish service whose countries are not at war with Russia. Also the Turkish Redif, with their officers, and the Bashi-Bozouks; private property is to be respected; all the British and Turkish officers, and regular troops are to remain prisoners of war; all the arms, guns, and ammunition to be surrendered, but the officers, in consequence of their heroic defence of the 29th of September, are allowed to retain their swords.

Thus far, if the report be true, the capitulation seems to be as favourable to the party surrendering as generous on the part of the victors, and I feel convinced these conditions are mainly attributable to the tact and noble bearing of General Williams. To the General and his Staff, General Mouravieff and his officers were most courteous, and it would appear that, for so heavy a calamity, everything was conducted in a manner creditable and satisfactory to both parties.

A Colonel, whose name I could not learn, was particularly attentive and communicative; he said it was a great fault for Omer Pasha to have invaded Georgia from the coast, and they had little apprehension of his successes on that side, and his army would probably be lost in the forests and marshes if it did not make a timely retreat, but if Omer Pasha had come by Erzeroom, things would have been changed.

Dr Sandwith will quit Kars when he has put in order and delivered over the hospitals.

Mr Zohrab was as yet too weak to be removed after his severe attack of typhus; Mr Rennisson will come with them. Mr Churchill, though free to retire, it is said will remain with General Williams. I will not attempt to give other details on mere hearsay, when, probably, everything will be soon reported in an authentic shape.

JAS. BRANT

The Earl of Clarendon to Lord Cowley
Foreign Office, December 19, 1855

(Extract)

I transmit to your Excellency herewith a copy of a despatch [dated November 19, 1855] from Lieutenant-Colonel Simmons.

Your Excellency will communicate this despatch to the French Government, and point out the danger to which the army of Omer Pasha is now exposed, and the urgent necessity for the formation of an army of reserve.

The Emperor and Marshal Vaillant have long been aware of the great importance attached by Her Majesty's Government to the relief of Kars, and the disastrous news which has recently arrived proves that their apprehensions as to its probable fate were but too well founded. But if prompt and decisive measures are not taken, the fall of Kars will be followed by the worst consequences. Masters of that strong fortress, threatening Erzeroom, and commanding all the mountain passes, the Russians may be able to force the whole of Koordistan and the Armenian population to assist them against the Sultan; and the allies may in a few months learn that far greater danger threatens the Ottoman Empire from the side of Asia than from Europe. In fact, the object of the war will be defeated if the integrity of that Empire is not secured from attack on every side, and at all events the military operations for next year must to a certain extent depend upon whether Asia Minor is placed in a position of adequate defence.

At the present moment and until the necessary measures are deliberated and determined upon, Her Majesty's Government have to suggest that the Turkish forces now at Eupatoria should, without delay, be conveyed to Trebizond, and placed under the command of Omer Pasha for the purpose of forming an army of reserve applicable either to the defence of Erzeroom or to serve as a reinforcement to the army now with Omer Pasha in Mingrelia.

The Earl of Clarendon to Major-General Williams
Foreign Office, December 22, 1855

Sir,

Her Majesty's Government have learned with the deepest regret that the garrison of Kars was reduced by famine to capitulate, and that in consequence yourself and the other British officers serving under you at that place have fallen as prisoners of war into the hands of the Russians.

Her Majesty's Government have observed with the utmost admiration the zealous and indefatigable exertions which you made for the defence of that important position under circumstances of no ordinary difficulty, as well as the judgment and energy which you displayed in overcoming the obstacles of every sort with which you had to contend, and in inspiring the Turkish soldiery with that confidence which enabled them, under your influence, signally to defeat on all occasions the attempts made by an enemy superior in numbers and military resources to make themselves masters by force of arms of the besieged town.

I trust that the applications which have been made to the Russian Government for your exchange may be successful, and that Her Majesty will soon again have at her disposal the services of an officer who has earned for himself so distinguished a reputation. Some time may elapse before you receive this despatch, but I think it right at once to place on record the sentiments of Her Majesty and of her Government in regard to your whole conduct during the time that you have been employed with the Turkish army in Asia; and, while sympathising with you in the unfortunate result of your honourable exertions, I have to express Her Majesty's entire approval of the manner in which you acquitted yourself throughout the whole period of your recent services.

I have at the same time to instruct you to signify to the officers and civilians serving under your orders at Kars, namely, to Colonel Lake, to Major Teesdale, to Captain Thompson, to Mr Churchill, and to Dr Sandwith, Her Majesty's entire approval of their conduct.

CLARENDON

Lord Cowley to the Earl of Clarendon (received December 24)
Paris, December 22, 1855

(Extract)

In compliance with the instructions contained in your Lordship's despatch of the 19th instant, which only reached me late at night on the 20th, I saw Marshal Vaillant this afternoon on the subject of permitting the Ottoman troops now at Eupatoria to proceed at once to Asia Minor.

The Marshal said that as far back as the 12th instant the French Government had consented to the departure of the Egyptian Division for Trebizond, and intelligence had been immediately sent by telegraph to Marshal Pélissier. On the other hand his Excellency had learnt by a telegraphic despatch of the 16th instant from the Crimea, which had crossed his of the 12th on the road, that the Egyptian Division must have left Eupatoria about that time.

To a further request made by me, in furtherance of your Lordship's instructions, to Marshal Vaillant, that the whole of the Turkish force now at Eupatoria should be set free and replaced by a part of the troops now before Sebastopol, his Excellency replied that he had no objection, if it were practicable.

The Earl of Clarendon to Lord Stratford de Redcliffe
Foreign Office, December 28, 1855

My Lord,

I need scarcely state to your Excellency that the news of the capitulation of Kars was received by Her Majesty's Government with the deepest pain and regret, and with a feeling of bitter disappointment that no attempt was made by Selim Pasha to save that place from the enemy.

It appears from the despatches of Her Majesty's Consul at Erzeroom, which have passed through your hands, that Selim Pasha was in command of a force which, under an active general officer, was capable of relieving Kars, but that he had shown no capacity or energy, and had evinced nothing but a steady repugnance to make any movements to rescue the brave garrison which was compelled at last to surrender to the Russian General, Mouravieff.

Mr Brant accuses Selim Pasha of incapacity, and even cowardice, and states, that although repeatedly urged in the strongest terms by Major Stuart, the senior British officer at Erzeroom, to advance and relieve Kars, he had returned a refusal to every entreaty addressed to him.

Her Majesty's Government, who are making such vast efforts and sacrifices to uphold the Ottoman Empire, are entitled to demand that a signal example should be made of an officer who has conducted himself as Selim Pasha is said to have done, and I have accordingly to instruct your Excellency to call upon the Porte to order an immediate and searching investigation into this case, and if the charges brought against Selim Pasha should prove to be well founded, to visit that officer with heavy punishment and disgrace.

CLARENDON

The Earl of Clarendon to Lord Stratford de Redcliffe
Foreign Office, December 31, 1855

My Lord,

I have to instruct your Excellency to make known to the Porte that, in the opinion of Her Majesty's Government, it is of urgent importance that reinforcements should be sent from Constantinople to Trebizond to go on to Erzeroom. Her Majesty's Government hope that the Turkish fleet, which has now nothing to do, may be employed on this service.

CLARENDON

Lord Stratford de Redcliffe to the Earl of Clarendon (received January 20, 1856)
Constantinople, December 31, 1855

My Lord,

With reference to my other despatch of this date, I have the honour to transmit herewith another despatch which I addressed to Her Majesty's Consul at Erzeroom, acquainting him with the Porte's intention to supersede the Mushir of Erzeroom by Vedgihi Pasha, formerly Governor of Saida.

STRATFORD DE REDCLIFFE

Enclosure

Lord Stratford de Redcliffe to Consul Brant
Constantinople, December 30, 1855

(Extract)

It will be agreeable to you to know that I have succeeded in obtaining from the Porte a promise that the two respective Mushirs of Erzeroom and of the army, Mehemet and Selim Pashas, shall be forthwith superseded.

The present intention, as announced to me from the Porte, is that Vedgihi Pasha, formerly at Saida, shall replace the former, and Ismail Pasha, who is now here from the Danube, the latter.

It is possible, however, that Omer Pasha, who has retired on Redoute-Kaleh, may take the command in person.

I have to request that you will consider this communication of the Porte's intentions as intended for the present for your own information alone.

P.S. The Porte has made me acquainted with its intention to send 10,000 men of Omer Pasha's army to Erzeroom.

I fear that the Egyptian troops landed from Eupatoria at Trebizond by means of transports furnished by Her Majesty's Naval Commanders, will suffer greatly from the fatigue of their march over such mountainous roads, and in an impaired state of health.

Lord Stratford de Redcliffe to the Earl of Clarendon (received January 20, 1856)

Constantinople, December 31, 1855

(Extract)

Selim Pasha, who has obtained so unhappy a distinction at Erzeroom, was recommended to his command there by Fethi Ahmed Pasha, the Master of the Ordnance. The Seraskier, who is now in office, made the official appointment under a persuasion, he declares, that he was qualified to render good service in the field. I understood when the appointment was communicated to me, that Selim Pasha was only invested with the command of the reinforcements destined for Erzeroom.

General Mansfield informs me that General Guyon, in speaking of Selim Pasha, described him as a man of undoubted courage; and I have heard the same character of him from another British officer. It appears that his intelligence is not rated so high as his bravery: and your Lordship is well aware how difficult it is to find among the candidates for high military employment in Turkey individuals distinguished for capacity and professional knowledge.

JANUARY 1856

Consul Brant to the Earl of Clarendon (received January, 1856)

Erzeroom, January 3, 1856

(Extract)

I have the honour to acknowledge your Lordship's despatch of the 10th of December, approving of the steps I took in endeavouring to persuade Selim Pasha to march to the relief of Kars. I only regret that all the endeavours of Major Stuart and myself failed; for, as your Lordship will have perceived by a subsequent despatch, had the Mushir advanced, General Mouravieff would probably have retreated, and Kars have been saved without even a battle.

The Earl of Clarendon to Lord Stratford de Redcliffe

Foreign Office, January 10, 1856

(Extract)

The Porte can neither hope for the success of the Sultan's arms, nor for the co-operation of his allies, if signal examples are not made of men like Selim and Tahir Pashas, of whose cowardice and treachery there now exist such overwhelming proofs.

Lord Stratford de Redcliffe to the Earl of Clarendon (received January 29)

Constantinople, January 14, 1856

My Lord,

I communicated to Fuad Pasha your Lordship's instruction requiring the trial and, eventually, the punishment of Selim Pasha. His Excellency's answer, after communicating with his colleagues, may be expressed in the following words: a searching inquiry into the conduct of Selim Pasha is already ordered by the

Porte, and should the charges brought against him prove to be well grounded, he will be punished accordingly.

STRATFORD DE REDCLIFFE

Lord Stratford de Redcliffe to the Earl of Clarendon (received January 29)
Constantinople, January 14, 1856

My Lord,

I have the honour to enclose herewith, for such use as your Lordship may please to make of them, a statement, drawn up by Brigadier-General Mansfield [Enclosure 2], and an abstract, compiled by Count Pisani, from my correspondence, exhibiting together the series of incidents which have taken place between the Turkish authorities, Her Majesty's Embassy, and the British Commissioner at Kars, from the autumn of 1854 [Enclosure 1].

These papers did not originate with me. I have not even looked through the abstract. General Mansfield and Count Pisani both felt of their own accord that public, and even parliamentary attention might be turned upon the matters in question; that erroneous or exaggerated impressions might possibly be entertained in England as well as elsewhere, and that by setting forth the facts in a clear and concise narrative, they might serve the cause of truth, and afford some eventual assistance to your Lordship's office.

So marked a testimony of good feeling and rightmindedness from persons who are intimately acquainted with all my proceedings on the subject referred to, is naturally gratifying to me, as chief of the Embassy, by Her Majesty's gracious indulgence. I cannot doubt that it will give them a fresh title to your Lordship's esteem.

It is unnecessary for me to fill up the only *lacuna* [missing part] which appears in either the statement or the abstract. I am content to leave the circumstances which are there passed over, to your Lordship's recollection and sense of justice.

STRATFORD DE REDCLIFFE

Enclosure 1

Abstract of correspondence [of Lord Stratford de Redcliffe] respecting the relief of Kars

FIRST EPOCH
From the arrival of General Williams to the departure of Vassif Pasha [August 1854 to January 1855]

August 15, 1854 Arrival of Colonel Williams. He is to go to the Crimea to communicate with Lord Raglan.

August 20, 1854   The town of Byazid is occupied by a Russian force. The Turkish troops in position there are stated to have fled on the approach of the enemy. The great commercial road between Turkey and Persia is thus placed at the mercy of the Russians. A battle has also taken place between the Turks and the Russians in that quarter: the loss very heavy and almost equal on both sides, but the Russians had remained in possession of the field of battle.

August 25, 1854 The more correct statements of the battle of Koorook-Dereh, which have recently arrived, represent the losses of the Turks as more considerable than they were at first believed to be.

I have had some conversation with Reshid Pasha and the Seraskier as to the means of repairing these losses, and I am assured that the Porte may be able to send a reinforcement of 15,000 men to Kars before the close of the season, and 10,000 more in the spring. It is the Porte's intention to place Ismail Pasha in command of the army at Kars, and Mustafa Pasha is preparing to take the command of the smaller army at Batoom, where disease is thinning its ranks to a frightful degree.

September 5, 1854 The most urgent want of the army at Kars at this moment is a Commander-in-chief. The Grand Vizier sent me word that Ismail Pasha was to take the command at Kars.

September 27, 1854 Ismail Pasha, who was lately appointed to the command of it, has been taken ill here. His complaint is an inflammation of the eyes, which may endanger his sight. A provisional Commander, by name Shukri Pasha, is appointed in consequence, with the rank of General of Division. To me the individual and his name are alike new. He is said to have been strongly recommended by Omer Pasha, and also by Ismail, to whom, when with the army, he is to act as Chef d'Etat-Major, superseding in that capacity General Guyon, and having as second in command a certain Hussein Pasha, who is stated to have been serving with Omer Pasha as General of Brigade. The arrival of those two officers at Kars will be followed by the departure of Mustafa Zarif Pasha, Kerim Pasha, and other superior officers, including General Guyon, for Constantinople, when they will be submitted to a Court of Inquiry.

It may be hoped that General Williams, who probably reached the army some days ago, will soon be able to throw a clearer light on its real state, its merits, its wants, and its prospects.

October 4, 1854 Immediately on the receipt of General Williams' despatches, I addressed an instruction to Mr Pisani for the purpose of bringing without delay the wants of the army at Kars to the knowledge of the Porte, and accelerating the transmission of the enumerated articles of supply, including specie, to the army at Kars.

Mr Pisani appears to have found no difficulty in obtaining the assent of the Turkish Ministers to my urgent recommendations, and I am led to hope that there will be no want of exertion on their part. He informs me on the part of the Grand Vizier and the Seraskier that orders for supplying the army with fuel and provisions had been transmitted to the Pasha of Erzeroom; that supplies of grain were to be furnished from Diarbekir, Sivas, Amasia, and the neighbourhood of Erzeroom; that 30,000 sets of winter clothing had been ordered, two-thirds of which had actually been forwarded, and that the rest would follow in a day or two; that 30,000 pairs of shoes and boots, and a similar number of worsted stockings, together with caps and linen, for the soldiers, were on their way to Trebizond; that a number of saddles, tents, and a certain quantity of ammunition had also been sent; that surgical instruments and medicines were ready for shipment; and finally, that 5,000 purses in specie were preparing for transmission to Erzeroom towards the pay of the soldiers.

October 14, 1854   I have much satisfaction in forwarding the clear and able reports of General Williams, who, on reaching the army of Kars, put himself at once into communication with the Commander-in-chief, and took his measures to obtain information calculated to afford a just presumption of the state of things in that neighbourhood.

In one respect I take upon myself to anticipate your instructions. I have already recommended strongly to the Seraskier's attention those improvements or objects of supply which were suggested by General Williams in his correspondence from Erzeroom, and I shall lose no time in pressing upon the Sultan's Government at large the urgent importance of giving immediate effect to those which figure in his subsequent despatch from Kars.

November 15, 1854   Feeling the importance of affording to General Williams all practicable support in the fulfilment of his arduous duties, I applied to Reshid Pasha that the military rank of Ferik, equivalent to General of Division, may be conferred upon that meritorious officer, and I am happy to say that I have His Majesty's authority, communicated to me through Mr Pisani, for informing your Lordship that my request will be complied with.

Agreeably, moreover, to your Lordship's suggestion, the new Commander-in-chief of the army of Kars will be directed to listen to such advice as General Williams may have occasion to offer.

Knowing the extreme importance which your Lordship attaches to the re-instatement of the Turkish army at Kars, I make no apology for transmitting the papers enclosed herewith, which I drew up myself from General Williams' voluminous despatches, and submitted to the Turkish Ministers with an instruction to Mr Pisani, recommending the whole of that officer's demands and suggestions to their most serious and immediate attention.

Later portions of the same correspondence have been conveyed in a similar form and with similar recommendations to the Seraskier Pasha and his colleagues.

I am assured that on the side of the Turkish Ministers there is every appearance of a sincere intention to comply with my demands; as soon as I am satisfied that the supplies are actually sent, and orders corresponding with General Williams' suggestions issued in strongest terms, I shall not fail to apprise your Lordship of so gratifying a result.

The subject being now relieved of much superfluous and exaggerated matter, the course is made clearer to Turkish apprehension, and I trust that the experience of last year, which certainly was painful enough in its most reduced proportions, will have the effect in contributing to the success of my endeavours, grounded on the strenuous exertions of General Williams, and aided by the pecuniary supplies derived from the Loan.

November 29, 1854   In obedience to your Lordship's instructions, I have demanded the trial and punishment of Mustafa Zarif Pasha, the late Commander-in-chief of the Turkish army at Kars. He arrived here a few days ago. I have suspended, meanwhile, a demand for the trials of the Generals of Division, Kerim and Veli Pashas, on account of the altered manner in which General Williams has spoken of the former in his latest despatches. It is desirable to know whether the appearance of amendment continues and extends. I have not, however, neglected the opportunity of remonstrating against the delays which have characterised the trial of Ahmed Pasha and Ali Ferik. I thought it necessary to give my complaint a formal character, by putting it into the shape of an official note. The Ottoman Secretary of State, after having perused it, said that the two last-mentioned criminals laboured under such manifest proofs of guilt that they could not possibly escape.

December 14, 1854   It will be satisfactory to know that some apparent progress is being made towards an improved state of things in what regards the Turkish army at Kars.

An intention has been entertained of sending Mustafa Pasha, Mushir commanding at Batoom, to take provisionally the chief command in place of Ismail Pasha, who is destined to command the army of the Danube during Omer Pasha's absence in the Crimea; but Vassif Pasha, late Commander-in-chief of the Arabian corps d'armée, being at liberty, it is intended to employ him for that purpose.

He will be instructed to attend to the advice offered to him by General Williams, and he will be also empowered to remove, if necessary, Shukri and Hussein Pashas, of whom General Williams has had occasion to complain. Letters of reprimand have been already addressed to those officers, at the same time that letters of approbation have been sent to Kerim and Hafiz Pashas, according to my application founded on the request of General Williams.

December 21, 1854   Among the despatches which I forward from General Williams by the present occasion is one which complains in no measured terms of my silence towards him, and supposed neglect of the interests committed to his care by Her Majesty's Government.

I have time at this moment only to remark that if the charge be correct, my reports to your Lordship must be a tissue of mis-statements. Silent, it is true, I have been, in so far as my correspondence with him is concerned, for the simple reason of my wishing to avoid any risk of disappointment arising out of the dilatory and sometimes illusive proceedings of this Government. But to what degree and with what success I have laboured for the accomplishment of those objects which General Williams has so properly pointed out and so strongly recommended, I hope to place in a clearer light on the departure of the next messenger.

The late Commander-in-chief of the Sultan's army of Kars, Mustafa Zarif Pasha, is placed under arrest, at my requisition, preparatory to an inquiry into his conduct.

His two predecessors are still awaiting their sentence in confinement. The illness of the President of the Council, who is not expected to live, has delayed the procedure.

I have not ceased to point out the necessity of following their conviction with example of condign punishment.

December 28, 1854 I think myself entitled to remark on the hasty manner in which General Williams has allowed himself to suppose that I have neglected the important interests committed to his charge. Because he did not hear from me as soon or as frequently as he expected, he rushed to the conclusion that I gave him no support, and under this inconsiderate impression he has made a deliberate appeal to your Lordship and Lord Raglan.

These circumstances do not in the least degree warp my judgment as to General Williams' excellent intentions and zealous exertions on behalf of the army at Kars, nor am I at all inclined to depreciate the somewhat voluminous correspondence which contains the result of his researches and remonstrances.

Your Lordship is already aware of the pains which I took on the receipt of his principal despatches to put their substance into a working shape, and to engage the Turkish Ministers to enter both promptly and fully on the correction of the abuses which he had denounced.

It is incumbent on me now to show that so far as official assurances go, I have succeeded in obtaining their assent to his leading suggestions, and in some instances a positive execution of the engagements thus contracted.

In order to place my conduct in a true light, independently of my own assertion, I have addressed a set of queries to Mr Pisani, by whose agency my representations, grounded on those of General Williams, have been urged on the Porte, requiring that he should give a distinct reply to each of them, according to the exact state of the case as known to him.

I have certainly to regret that the progress of the Turkish Ministers in acting on my suggestions has not kept pace with the desire of General

Williams, nor, indeed, I must say, with those requirements of the service which they concern. But winter, distance, roads scarcely passable, want of funds, the extent of evil to be cured, the scarcity of trustworthy officers, the greater interest of operations elsewhere, the illness of Ismail Pasha, all these causes of difficulty, and others which might be enumerated, have concurred to produce hesitation and delay. I regret the existence of such obstacles, and blame the Turkish Ministers for not surmounting them with more activity. But can I wonder? No; corruption, ignorance, prejudice, want of public spirit, and the instincts of selfishness, engender the same consequences wherever they prevail in long habitual exuberance. The real cause of the culpable inattention shown last year to the wants of the army in Asia is, I learn on authority on which I can rely, the jealousy entertained by the late Seraskier Mehmed Ali Pasha of Mehemed Rouchdi Pasha, at one time his colleague, and at another threatening to become his successor. Unhappily this is by no means a solitary instance. The present Seraskier and Omer Pasha have long been at variance with each other; mutual accusations take place; and while the Seraskier asserts that he has sent ample supplies to the army of Roumelia, the Generalissimo complains of being neglected, and all is contradiction and uncertainty, except one painful fact, the suffering of the soldiers.

If my silence towards General Williams continued longer than I intended, it originated in my anxiety not to occasion disappointment by announcing measures which might or might not be carried into effect. I knew that during the winter season little comparatively could be done, and I preferred, under the pressure of business flowing in abundantly from other sources, to give my correspondent an answer in full, rather than keep up a succession of partial communications.

December 31, 1854   Enclosed is copy of despatch to General Williams forwarding to him the Sultan's firman raising him to the rank of a General of Division in the Turkish service.

The list of articles of supply prepared for the army at Kars, or already transmitted thither, as I have received it from the Seraskier, is reserved for a future opportunity in consequence of the difficulty which has been experienced in translating some of the terms which are little known in ordinary composition.

January 11, 1855   I was visited the day before yesterday by Vassif Pasha, who has undertaken the charge of the army at Kars. I recommended General Williams to his confidence and attention in the most unreserved terms, and I endeavoured to impress upon his mind the importance of his acting in cordial concert with that officer, if he wished to render the army efficient, and to meet the views of Her Majesty's Government, identified as they were with those of the Sultan and the Porte. The assurances with which he replied to my injunctions were quite satisfactory, and I hope that his conduct will be such as to redeem the pledge which they conveyed. He spoke of the deficiencies existing in the War Department, and I am under an impression that further exertions will be necessary to have him properly instructed, and promptly sent forward to his destination. I have already expressed myself with earnestness to Reshid Pasha on this subject, and I hope that my words have not fallen on a barren soil. His Highness assured me that Shukri Pasha shall be recalled; that proper deference shall be paid to General Williams, as Her Majesty's Commissioner; and that a Council shall be formed at the War Department to assist the Seraskier, and to give a more steady and efficient direction to his operations.

SECOND EPOCH

From the departure of Vassif Pasha to the commencement of the siege [January to July 1855]

January 29, 1855   I forward herewith three documents calculated to throw light upon the conduct of the Ottoman War Department with respect to the army at Kars, and the points recommended by me for immediate adoption at the suggestion of General Williams. One of them is a report from the Council of the Seraskier's office to the head of that department. The second is an instruction addressed by the Seraskier, Riza Pasha, to the new Commander-in-chief *ad interim*, who embarked from Trebizond a few days ago. The third is an instruction addressed by the Grand Vizier to the same Commander, with the intention of supplying deficiencies in the former.

In pursuance of my instructions, Mr Pisani waited on Vassif Pasha on the 26th. His Excellency gave him positive assurances that he would attend to my recommendations to the best of his ability, and expressed a hope that General Williams would have reason to be satisfied with his exertions to put the army at Kars on an efficient and respectable footing.

Vassif Pasha embarked on the afternoon of the 26th on board the English steamer *London* for Trebizond.

January 31, 1855   The superintendence of the medical hospitals belonging to the Sultan's army at Kars has already been conferred, at my request, on Dr Sandwith, recommended by General Williams, whose requests with respect to Baron Schwartzenburg, alias Emin Bey, and Tashiar Bey, were also complied with some time ago.

February 5, 1855   I am informed by Her Majesty's Vice-Consul at Trebizond that Vassif Pasha, the new Commander-in-chief of the army at Kars, had arrived there on the 30th ultimo.

Mr Stevens states that the same vessel which conveyed Vassif Pasha to Trebizond had a large lot of military stores, chiefly for winter use, as also 220,000*l.* in specie and paper money for the use of the army.

March 21, 1855   Shukri Pasha, together with Hussein Pasha, has been arrested by order of Vassif Pasha; and the two accused Generals are now, it is to be presumed, on their way to Constantinople for trial.

Mr Pisani informs me that the Seraskier, on hearing of their arrest, declared his conviction that they had been arrested on insufficient grounds, and that he should think it his duty to send in a protest against the measure to the Porte.

Whatever may have been the demerits of the two accused Pashas since their arrival at Kars, they served with distinction under Omer Pasha; and in consequence of the latter's recommendation, had marks of approval and honour conferred on them.

April 16, 1855   Her Majesty's Commissioner to the army at Kars complains of the quarantine at Toprah-Kaleh being still maintained, in spite of my assurances to the contrary; I have also reason to complain of the delay. The explanation is contained in the accompanying report from Mr Pisani, who assures me that stringent orders have been issued again for its suppression.

The Porte has decided upon the removal of the veteran Mushir, Ismail Pasha, from Erzeroom. The Sultan's sanction remains to be obtained.

April 24, 1855   I have lost no time in acquainting the Porte with the desire entertained by Her Majesty's Government, that any reinforcements which can be spared from other more urgent services should be sent to the army of Kars. I shall take an early opportunity to inform your Lordship of the result of my application, which comes in support of my preceding instances with the weight derived from your Lordship's instructions in the name of Her Majesty's Government.

April 30, 1855   The enclosed report from Mr Pisani informs me that having communicated my instructions to the Turkish Ministers, he was told in reply that they are perfectly alive to the urgency of reinforcing the army of Kars, and that their Commanders repeatedly recommend that measure, but that it is utterly impossible, at least for the present, to spare any of the troops in actual service on the Danube, or in the Crimea.

May 17, 1855   It appears that neither of the two Pashas, Hussein and Shukri, sent down by Vassif Pasha from Erzeroom, on charges exhibited against them by General Williams, has yet been submitted to any legal sentence or judicial proceeding. The former has been applied for by Omer Pasha, as an officer distinguished heretofore by his good qualities, and thought to be capable of rendering good service under the orders of the Commander-in-chief.

On learning this intention, I sent a complaint to the Seraskier, and required that both the Pashas in question should be tried, or submitted to a legal inquiry, on the charges preferred against them. His answer having been less satisfactory than I thought myself entitled to expect, I renewed my application.

May 21, 1855   In reply to further representations in favour of General Williams' demands:

1. The Seraskier reminds me, through Mr Pisani, that the further supplies of the articles of provisions specified in the General's reports, have been forwarded to the army of Kars by the provinces.
2. That the old Ismail Pasha, Mushir of Erzeroom, has been removed.
3. That the Defterdar of that army has been superseded.
4. That orders to the Commander-in-chief to keep General Williams informed of the movements of the troops, and to take his advice, have been given to Vassif Pasha in writing and verbally.
5. That supplies of ammunition were forwarded in sailing vessels by the Ordnance Department more than two months ago.
6. That instructions were sent to Vassif Pasha for the removal and punishment of Injeh Arap and Hassan Yazidgi.
7. That further supplies of money (18,000 purses, or 9,000,000 piastres) have been sent for paying the arrears due to the army, and that more supplies of money are to be sent by the newly appointed Defterdar.
8. The Seraskier added, that he is aware of the necessity of taking into prompt consideration the requirements of the army, but that the state of the Porte's finances cannot allow her to act with the promptitude required.
9. That Salih Bey is not dismissed.
10. That camels are not to be got, but that the purchase of mules is in progress, and orders for the preparation of arabas have also been given.
11. That out of the 1,000 gunners required by General Williams, 400 have already reached Kars, and the remainder are to follow forthwith.
12. That the other matters recommended by General Williams in his report of February 18, to me, have been attended to, as proved by the Seraskier's report to Fuad Pasha, communicated to me by the latter.

June 14, 1855   I have again pressed the trial of Hussein and Shukri Pashas. The Seraskier contends that the charges brought against them have nothing to do with the service, and that they are purely personal quarrels. He also promises to answer me in writing, stating at the same time that Omer Pasha bitterly complains of the neglect shown by his predecessor in his omission to send Hussein Pasha to the Crimea, and insists upon having him there without loss of time; therefore that the Seraskier cannot refuse compliance with Omer Pasha's demand without incurring some responsibility.

The latest advices from General Williams intimate that the Russian movements at Gumri manifested an intention to attack the Turkish army at Kars. I had previously renewed my applications to the Porte, and urged the Turkish Ministers to send up further supplies and reinforcements if possible, even at this late hour. I most particularly urged the importance of forwarding a considerable sum of money without delay. The Seraskier asserted in answer, that some of the supplies forwarded by his predecessor had been acknowledged by the Acting Commander-in-chief. He added, that the larger portion of what had been required from his office had been transmitted, and that he was preparing to transmit the remainder by the earliest steamer. He admitted that according to the latest intelligence, the Russians appeared to be coming down in force.

June 15, 1855   On the receipt of a despatch from General Williams, informing me that appearances warranted an expectation that the Russian forces at Gumri were meditating an attack upon Kars, I lost no time in communicating with the Porte and the Seraskier, repeating my urgent remonstrances that reinforcements, with fresh supplies and money, should be sent out forthwith to Kars.

June 20, 1855   I went over to the Porte yesterday, and saw the Kaimakam, Fuad Pasha, and the Seraskier, who, with much civility, left the Council Chamber, where they were deliberating on the means of reinforcing the army at Kars, and afforded me an opportunity of again recommending to them in person, the urgent importance of making up for past delays by sending succour of every kind to that army with all practicable dispatch. These gentlemen had every appearance of entering fully into my views, and I trust that no time will be lost in carrying their intentions, late as they are, into effect. The Seraskier expressed a decided opinion that a body of 10,000 men might be detached from Batoom without danger to that establishment, which still has 4,000 or 5,000 for its protection. It was proposed, at the same time, that some vessels of war should be directed to cruise along the coast of Circassia; and I was requested to submit this plan to Rear-Admiral Sir E. Lyons, under an impression that a joint operation, in concert with the French, would be desirable.

The Turkish Ministers are under an impression that the position occupied by the Army at Kars would not enable it to withstand a vigorous attack on the part of the Russians, and that if the enemy appears in force Vassif Pasha will probably have to fall back on Erzeroom.

June 25, 1855   Enclosed herewith in translation, is an official memorandum addressed to me by the Porte, with reference to the charges brought against Shukri and Hussein Pashas by General Williams. After the representations which I had previously made to the Porte in support of General Williams' complaints, it would be useless for me to prolong the discussion without instructions from Her Majesty's Government. On the whole, I think it preferable to bring under your Lordship's unbiased judgment the excuses and arguments offered by the Porte. There is nothing in the meantime to prevent my informing Fuad Pasha that such is the course which I intend to pursue, and to submit to his cooler consideration the propriety of suspending any definite act of acquittal on behalf of the accused Pashas, until I can be put in possession of your Lordship's opinion.

June 28, 1855   Advices from Trebizond, which came round to me through Lord Raglan, describe the Russians from Gumri as being within a few days' march of Kars. Their force is stated at 36,000, a number which considerably exceeds the previous estimate. The Turkish forces, including all between Kars and Erzeroom, with the circumjacent stations, cannot safely be carried beyond an amount of 20,000, if so much, and the Seraskier has prepared me for a retrograde movement on their part, it being his declared opinion that the positions at Kars are not tenable against the enemy.

His Excellency and his colleagues are naturally desirous that no time should be lost in counteracting the Russian attack; and it is some consolation to me to find that even at this eleventh hour the necessity of listening to my advice and sending off reinforcements without further delay is recognised.

But where are reinforcements to be found in sufficient quantity? How are they to be provided with necessary supplies? What plan of operations offers the best chance of employing their service with efficiency?

Nothing can with prudence or consistency be detached from the army under Omer Pasha in the Crimea. At Batoom, Soukoum-Kaleh, and other neighbouring stations on the coast, it would be extremely difficult to muster more than 11,000 men, though a higher figure was quoted at first.

In Bulgaria I question the existence of more than 50,000 men, including garrisons. The other parts of the Empire afford no additional resources, with the exception of Bosnia, where it is still possible that a few thousand men might be detached. I speak of Regulars. Bashi-Bozouks may be procured; but your Lordship knows what little dependence is to be placed on such undisciplined hordes. There remains the half-formed corps of General Vivian, and the Irregular Cavalry of General Beatson, incompletely organised.

June 30, 1855   A meeting took place this morning at the Grand Vizier's house. In addition to his Highness, the Seraskier and Fuad Pasha were present. I was accompanied by Brigadier-General Mansfield.

We found that the Porte had received advices from Vassif Pasha, brought by an officer who had left Kars about eleven days before. Despatches from General Williams also came to hand at the moment we were entering into conference. Their latest date was the 19th instant.

It appears from both sources that the Russians advancing from Gumri with an amount of force varying from 20,000 to 30,000, had presented themselves before Kars; that a partial engagement of Cavalry had taken place, followed two days later by an attack, which had been repulsed, on the part of the enemy, and that the town was threatened with a siege.

I collected from the Turkish officer that when he left the scene of action rain was falling in torrents, the waters of the river were out, and the Russians had no choice but to encamp. It appears from the English statements that the defences of the fortress were deemed to be of considerable strength, that the place was provisioned for a month, and that the Turkish army may be calculated at 18,000 men.

It was clear to all present that, whether the Russians besieged or turned Kars, the Turkish army required the effort to be made for its relief with all practicable dispatch, and that of those possible modes of acting for that purpose, the only one likely to prove effective was an expedition by Kutais into Georgia. To send reinforcements by Trebizond would be, at best, a palliative. To establish an entrenched camp at Redoute-Kaleh, as formerly proposed by the Porte, would, at this unhealthy season, be equivalent to consigning the troops to destruction.

The real question was, whether a force numerically sufficient, and in all respects effective, could be collected in time at Kutais to make an incursion into Georgia and threaten the communications of the Russian army, placing it, indeed, between two hostile forces, should the Turkish army still be in a condition to take the field.

It was for the Turkish Ministers to solve this problem, and they proposed that the expeditionary force should be composed of 12,000 men from Batoom and the neighbouring stations, of the troops made over to General Vivian, and estimated at 10,000 of all arms, of General Beatson's Irregular Cavalry, of 10,000 men to be detached from the army in Bulgaria, as the complement of the Turkish Contingent, of 5,000 more derived from the same source, of an Egyptian Regiment of Horse, and of another regiment, expected from Tunis. To these the Seraskier proposed to add 2,000 Albanians by way of riflemen. These several forces, completed according to the figures, would furnish a total of 44,400 men, but perhaps to be reckoned with prudence, at not more than 36,000 effective.

Admitting the urgency of the case, and the consequent necessity of incurring a certain degree of hazard, I called attention to the importance of not exposing the Turkish Contingent or General Beatson's Horse prematurely to a trial beyond their strength. It was accordingly understood that, supposing the expedition to be resolved, neither of these corps would be required to embark for Redoute-Kaleh until the preparations were completed in other respects, and it is to be hoped that the interval thus gained for their benefit would suffice to secure their efficiency. I took, moreover, the liberty of remarking that the proposed expedition, besides being prepared with secrecy, and sanctioned by supreme authority, must finally depend for its adoption on our available means of providing it with all the requisite appliances. This indispensable field of inquiry might be investigated, with advantage, by General Vivian, the Seraskier Pasha, and General Mansfield, who, indeed, have undertaken to meet tomorrow for that purpose.

The Turkish Ministers having expressed their readiness to entrust the direction of the expedition, should it eventually take place, to a British Commander, and to accept General Vivian in that capacity, subject, of course, to the approval of Her Majesty's Government, I lost no time, after our separation, in communicating personally with that officer, and putting him in possession of all that had passed on the subject of our discussion.

July 6, 1855 The Seraskier informs me that most of the articles demanded for the army of Kars had been actually forwarded, and that more were preparing, and that 600 Artillerymen, besides those already sent, were preparing to embark with a large supply of ammunition.

July 12, 1855 The extreme importance of obtaining correct data before the expedition proposed for the relief of Kars be finally submitted to Her Majesty's Government, produces an unavoidable delay in the progress and preparation of the plan. The Porte has decided on sending confidential officers to examine the localities at Trebizond, Batoom, and Redoute-Kaleh, with a view of forming a more correct idea of their resources and difficulties. I hope that General Vivian and Sir E. Lyons will pursue the same course, and that an officer from each service will be sent in a suitable vessel to obtain the requisite information on the coast. I have already applied to General Vivian and Rear-Admiral Grey for that purpose, and I shall avail myself of the earliest opportunity to make a similar application to Admiral Sir E. Lyons.

On the same 12th July, the following telegraphic message was transmitted to the Earl of Clarendon:

> Preparations for an eventual expedition are in progress. It might save much valuable time if you would inform me at once by telegraph whether the Government is prepared to sanction a powerful diversion by Redoute-Kaleh and Kutais into Georgia, if local investigation and the engagement of Turkish and allied authorities as to the means of execution should warrant a calculation of success.

THIRD EPOCH
During the siege [July 1855]

July 16, 1855 On the night of the 14th instant I received despatches to the 2nd from Kars and Erzeroom. It results from their contents that Kars was surrounded by the Russians, who had established themselves on the high road leading to Erzeroom; that the garrison of the latter place was very weak, and that a portion of the provisions collected for the army was cut off; but that the troops and garrisons were in good heart, and to all appearance resolved on a foil performance of their duty.

With the view of ascertaining how far the advices received by the Seraskier from the same quarters corresponded with those addressed to me, and what real progress was being made in the preparation of measures calculated to operate in support of the beleaguered army, I requested General Mansfield to call upon that Minister. I am now informed, as the result of that interview, that the advices received by the Seraskier, though of the same date, and similar for the most part in substance to those received by me, are on the whole of a more encouraging character than the latter. They add to their confirmation of the resolute attitude assumed by the Ottoman troops at Kars, an assurance that the subsistence of the army was secured for three months; that 500 Irregulars had thrown themselves into Kars; that 300 artillerymen, with 20 guns, since followed by 500 from the Dardanelles and here, were on their way to the scene of action; that Hussein Pasha of Trebizond had taken the same direction, at the head of 10,000 Irregulars, and that plenty of ammunition was collected at Erzeroom.

It further appears from the Seraskier's statement to General Mansfield, that the inhabitants of Erzeroom had summoned the Pasha on his own responsibility to hasten to the assistance of Kars, and that he had in consequence assembled a body of Irregulars, and marched in that direction, without waiting for orders from Constantinople.

Another body of Irregulars, to the amount of 4,000, is to be raised by Toussoum Pasha, himself in former times a Bashi-Bozouk, and directed from Sivas into the country around Kars, with a view of controlling the operations of the Russian Cossacks in that quarter.

When General Mansfield expressed, in conversing with the Seraskier, his apprehensions as to the dangers of employing a numerous horde of Bashi-Bozouks, collected on the spur of the occasion, and probably ill-provided with everything, his Excellency replied that he had insisted on having the necessary funds wherewith to pay them, which was the main instrument of control, and that he had threatened to retire from office if his demand were not complied with.

With reference to the eventual diversion into Georgia, the Seraskier informed General Mansfield that the plan had been communicated to Omer Pasha, whose answer, however, had not yet reached his hands; that the 15,000 men in Bulgaria, destined to form part of the expedition, were in readiness to march to the coast with sufficient means of transport, and that, in general, his preparations were so far advanced as only to require the assent of Her Majesty's Government to be carried into practical effect.

July 19, 1855   Omer Pasha, apprised by the Seraskier of the danger to which Kars was exposed, and also of the plan for relieving it, which was under consideration here, had proposed to withdraw from the Crimea the 25,000 Turkish troops before Sebastopol, and to put himself at their head in order to operate a diversion from the coast in Circassia. Not finding among the English and French Commanders-in-chief any disposition to support him, he announced his intention of proceeding at once to Constantinople, with the view of submitting his opinions to his Government. He arrived here the night before last.

This impulsive resolution is by no means in keeping with the decided opposition offered by Omer Pasha to the late Seraskier's requisition for detaching 5,000 of his men for the Crimea. His Highness may account for the change of view by referring to the pressure at Kars, and to the suspension of active operations before Sebastopol. But the Generals, his colleagues, deprecate the latter ground of justification, and means might apparently be employed for the rescue of Kars without deranging the calculations of the allied armies in the Crimea.

Your Lordship is already acquainted with the plan which has been for some time under consideration here on the part of the Sultan's Government, in concert with Her Majesty's Embassy. An appeal has, moreover, been made by means of the electric telegraph to Her Majesty's Government, who were entreated to lose no time in making known its pleasure to the proposed diversion, supposing it to obtain the suffrages of the naval and military authorities in point of means for carrying it into effect. The answer may be expected from day to day, and a final decision may then be taken, with the advice and concurrence of the Commander-in-chief. It would have been idle to make any earlier communication to them of an official description: the state of the army at Kars was made known to the British Commander-in-chief by General Williams himself.

I have this day received the following telegraphic message from your Lordship:

> The plan of operations for reinforcing the army at Kars, contained in your Excellency's despatch of the 1st July, is disapproved. The reasons will be sent by the messenger today against employing the Turkish Contingent until it is fit for service.
>
> Trebizond ought to be the base of operations, and if the Turkish army of Kars and Erzeroom cannot hold out at the latter place against the Russians, it might be proper to fall back on Trebizond. It would easily be reinforced.

July 30, 1855 The unfavourable judgment passed by Her Majesty's Government on the plans which have been lately under discussion, with a view to the relief of Kars, has naturally increased the Porte's embarrassment. It was my duty to make it known to the Turkish Ministers, not only as an opinion, but, with respect to General Vivian's Contingent, as a veto. Her Majesty's Government not only withhold the Contingent, but express a decided preference for the alternative of sending reinforcements to Erzeroom by way of Trebizond. This opinion is not adopted by the Porte, or indeed by any official or personal authority here. The Seraskier, Omer Pasha, General Guyon, and our own officers, as far as I have means of knowing, agree with the Porte and the French Embassy in pressing a diversion on the side of Redoute-Kaleh, as offering the better chance of success, supposing, of course, that the necessary means of transport, supply, and other indispensable wants can be sufficiently provided. France is, at the same time, decidedly adverse to any diminution of force in the Crimea; and Omer Pasha, ready to place himself at the head of an Asiatic expedition, requires for that purpose a part of the troops now there.

Such being the present state of the case, I am precluded from contributing to the Porte's extrication from its difficulties, otherwise than by countenancing some new location of the Contingent, which without exposing the corps to a premature trial, might enable a force of the same amount to be detached for service elsewhere.

No final decision has yet been taken by the Porte. The French Ambassador has written for General Pélissier's opinion, and Omer Pasha is still in attendance on his Government.

Meanwhile the advices from Kars are not encouraging, and time, of precious value, is unavoidably wasted in doubt and uncertainty.

Enclosure 2

Memorandum by Brigadier-General Mansfield on the measures taken for the relief of Kars since his arrival at Constantinople

On the 26th of June, or about a week after my arrival at Constantinople, I visited the Seraskier Pasha by the desire of Her Majesty's Ambassador. The subject discussed was the relief of the army at Kars.

Two plans were talked over. The one being the march of a force from Trebizond, which would have been necessarily collected from various distant points. The second being the formation of a camp at Redoute-Kaleh, with the intention of making a strong diversion for the relief of Vassif Pasha by real menace of Georgia. A few days afterwards there was a meeting at the house of Aali Pasha, the Grand Vizier, at which were present his Excellency Lord Stratford, Fuad Pasha, the Seraskier Pasha, Mr Pisani (the head Dragoman), and myself.

The meeting was very secret. We sat for five hours in Council. The Redoute-Kaleh project was seriously discussed. It was proposed by the Turks to employ the Contingent, giving the chief command of the expedition to General Vivian.

The Turks were very confident of being able to find the necessary means, and there seemed to be general unanimity in the prudence of the Redoute-Kaleh project, if it were carried out at once. It was argued that the dispatch of slender reinforcements by way of Trebizond and Erzeroom would not only not effect the object, but would expose the people so employed to be cut off in detail.

That there was reason for this argument was shown by the after-movement of Mouravieff to Kupri-Keuy, the garrison of Kars being masked by 15 battalions left in position and a large body of Cavalry.

It was proposed, in consequence of the meagre Russian resources in Mingrelia, to land 20,000 men at Redoute-Kaleh, throw them boldly forward on Kutais, the remainder of the army to follow, as it could be gathered together from various quarters.

The strength of the entire force available for the campaign was estimated at about 44,000 men, with guns and horses in proportion. His Excellency having the greatest anxiety to relieve the besieged garrison, was in constant communication with the Porte. I was, on more than one occasion, dispatched to discuss the matter with the Seraskier Pasha. The project was formally communicated to General Vivian, who was requested to propose estimates of means required for the expedition.

That officer accompanied me to the Seraskierat early in July, and in my presence thanked the Seraskier Pasha for the honour conferred on him by the Government of the Sultan in the offer of the chief command. On the 9th of July I attended at a meeting of all the Ministers at the house of Fuad Pasha, when the details of the contemplated expedition were most carefully examined as regards men, material, provisions, land and sea transport.

By his Excellency's request, Major-General Smith was sent to reconnoitre Redoute-Kaleh and the neighbouring coast; and a report was also received from Captain the Honourable — Drummond, of Her Majesty's Ship *Tribune*, on the same subject. I have reason to believe that the movement of troops in Bulgaria towards Varna for shipment, was ordered at the same time by the Turkish Government, that is to say, that they were held in readiness, the whole scheme having been fully referred by the Ambassador to Her Majesty's Government for consideration. Various circumstances with which I have no concern, conspired to arrest the progress of the undertaking.

General Vivian did not consider his force ready for active service; Omer Pasha arrived suddenly from the Crimea; there was a disinclination to part with any troops from that quarter, and apparently an equal one to substitute for a portion of them the embodied regiments of the Turkish Contingent.

During this time urgent letters were constantly in course of arrival from General Williams and Vassif Pasha. It was alleged that the garrison could not hold out for more than two months. During the time lost its affairs were becoming more straightened, and we soon learnt that the daily ration was reduced. The well-appointed and numerous Russian Cavalry swept the whole country on a radius of twelve hours' march from Kars, and every magazine in the neighbourhood was cleared of its contents.

The Ambassador never ceased from making the most urgent representations to the Seraskier and the Porte. On the receipt of every fresh despatch from Kars and Erzeroom, either Mr Pisani or myself was sent to enforce the necessity of relief. My appearance at the Seraskierat might indeed have been considered an ill omen for the garrison of Kars, so frequently was I obliged to make the same representation. As may be seen from my numerous reports of the last four or five months, there was no want of alacrity on the part of the Turkish Government. There was a dilemma from which they sought to extricate themselves, but in vain. They could only accomplish reinforcements by driblets to the garrison of Erzeroom, and they were thwarted by the apathy of their own commanders.

If I may be allowed to offer an opinion on the real cause of the disastrous issue of the Turco–Asiatic campaign, I should say that it must be found in the nature of the alliance, which absorbed all the really available means of action, whether French, British, or Turkish, in the invasion of the Russian soil, to the exclusion of attention to the hostile operation on Turkish territory. The contest pursued in the former required every practicable means to ensure success, perhaps, may be said, even military safety.

The garrison of Kars performed a great duty in arresting the march of the Russian columns till the resources of the allies could be turned to Asia, either in consequence of a development they had not already reached, or of liberation from the Crimea.

Some months since I ventured to predict, in private conversation, that we should have to be satisfied with such an issue of the operations of the last year; and that, assuming the allies to be prepared to take advantage of what has been thus achieved by the devoted garrison, we should have no reason to be disappointed when viewing the two theatres of war as one comprehensive whole. I have no reason to depart from the opinion then expressed.

With regard to the proceedings of the Embassy, I may be permitted to add, that after a disposition was shown to enable Omer Pasha to go to Asia, no effort was spared to expedite his movements; and that if events had marched with the same rapidity as the wishes of his Excellency, we possibly might not now have to lament the surrender of Kars.

W. R. Mansfield,
Brigadier-General

Consul Brant to the Earl of Clarendon (received February 7)
Erzeroom, January 15, 1856

My Lord,

I have the honour to transmit to your Lordship, copy of a despatch which I have just addressed to Viscount Stratford de Redcliffe. I wrote it as an act of justice to Tahir Pasha, and to prevent his being made the scapegoat of Selim Pasha, who is infinitely more culpable. Tahir is, like all Turks, apathetic, but he is far superior to most in intelligence and honesty, and I hope he will not be allowed to be thus unworthily sacrificed.

Jas. Brant

Enclosure

Consul Brant to Lord Stratford de Redcliffe

Erzeroom, January 15, 1856

(Extract)

I have the honour to inform your Excellency that it is intended, at the Porte, to make Tahir Pasha the victim to cover the fault of those who, in reality, caused the fall of Kars, and I must, in justice, denounce this plot of the Seraskier Pasha's, as I believe it to be, to screen Selim Pasha from punishment.

It is pretended that, last winter, Tahir Pasha did not introduce stores into Kars, but I can state that the fault was not Tahir Pasha's, it was that of Shukri Pasha, the then President of the Medjlis, who lowered the carriage so much that no carrier would take grain to Kars at the rate offered. As soon as Shukri Pasha was removed, Tahir Pasha took his post, and immediately raised the carriage, and supplies were sent. That Tahir Pasha was energetic, and did all that might have been done, I will not pretend; but I assert that he did more than any other member of the Medjlis, and is certainly the least culpable of all the Pashas.

The Earl of Clarendon to Lord Stratford de Redcliffe

Foreign Office, January 21, 1856

My Lord,

In reply to your Excellency's despatch of the 31st of December, I have to acquaint you that Her Majesty's Government have learnt with satisfaction that you have obtained a promise from the Porte that Mehemet and Selim Pashas shall be forthwith removed from their respective commands at Erzeroom.

CLARENDON

Lord Stratford de Redcliffe to the Earl of Clarendon (received February 6)

Constantinople, January 24, 1856

My Lord,

I have sent Fuad Pasha an extract of your Lordship's instruction of the 10th instant, respecting the misconduct of Selim and Tahir Pashas.

The Seraskier told me yesterday that he believed the former of those two Pashas to be innocent, and he stated some particulars in support of his opinion. As the accused General is to come away from Erzeroom, and as an inquiry will be instituted into his proceedings, I thought it useless to repeat the charges which stand against him.

With respect to the deficiency of supplies, the blame is thrown upon a deceased Commissary, who had the position of Defterdar, and whose son has been thrown into confinement as an accomplice, to answer for the alleged malversation.

STRATFORD DE REDCLIFFE

At the close of these despatches, in January 1856, the main combatants of the Crimean War were poised to make peace. Final negotiations were agreed in March 1856 in Paris. The Treaty of Paris, however, which affirmed the integrity of the Turkish Empire, was to prove as futile as the war which had preceded it.

∘◦⬥❈⬥◦∘

THE BOER WAR:
LADYSMITH AND
MAFEKING, 1900

DESPATCHES FROM THE COMMANDERS
IN THE FIELD IN SOUTH AFRICA

∞⦿∞

CONTENTS

MAPS

GLOSSARY

abattis	defence formed by placing felled trees lengthwise with their branches towards enemy lines
biltong	sun-dried lean meat
Boer	European of Dutch descent, born in South Africa. Also known as "Dutch farmer"
breastwork	hastily constructed fieldwork
chess	parallel plank on a pontoon bridge
coolies	Indians
cossack post	small group of mounted troops on outpost duty
donga	gully
drift	a drove road
echelon	formation of troops, in parallel divisions
enteric fever	typhoid
epaulement	a cover raised to give protection from enemy fire
fagged	weary
feint	a mock assault
Field Cornet	regimental standard-bearer
get touch	reach
glacis	long gentle slope
heliographic, heliogram	signal using the sun's rays
hors de combat	disabled
impressed	put into service
invest	lay siege to
Kaffir	indigenous person
kopje	low hill
kraal	a hut or pen
laager	improvised fortification, e.g. made from ox-wagons
Lee-Metford (LM)	rifle
lodgment	position occupied by besieging army
Martini-Henry (MH)	rifle
Maxim-Nordenfelt	automatic machine gun
mealie, mealie meal	maize, finely ground maize
milch	milk-yielding
picquet	picket
raked	covered

redans	fieldworks forming an outward-pointing angle
retirement	retreat
salients	outward-pointing angles of a fortification or line of defence
sap	trench
scances, schanzes	backward-sloping trenches
shops	workshops
spruit	a watercourse, usually dry except after rains
stadt	a South African town or village
tell off	to detach on special duty
telling	effective
trunnions	gun supports

The Boer War of 1899–1902 was fought in South Africa between Great Britain and the two Boer republics, the South African Republic or Transvaal, and the Orange Free State. The conflict was sparked by the refusal of the South African Republic to grant voting rights to the "uitlanders" (the mainly English immigrant mineworkers). At the heart of the dispute, however, was the fact that the largest gold mines in the world were located in the Transvaal, beyond direct British control.

The war broke out on 11 October 1899, when the British attempted to reinforce their garrison in South Africa. Initially the British were weak, and the Boers took advantage of this, besieging Ladysmith, Mafeking and Kimberley within a few weeks of the outbreak of hostilities.

The following despatches describe the siege and relief of both Ladysmith and Mafeking, as reported by the commanders in the field. The reverses suffered at Spion Kop by the force sent to relieve Ladysmith are also included.

South Africa, 1899

PART I

∞∞∞∞∞

DESPATCHES RELATING TO THE SIEGE
AND RELIEF OF LADYSMITH

OPERATIONS AROUND LADYSMITH, NATAL, 24TH–30TH OCTOBER 1899

From Lieut.-General Sir George White, VC, GCB, GCSI, GCIE, Commanding the British Forces in Natal, to the Secretary of State for War

Ladysmith, Natal, 2nd December, 1899

Sir,

In continuation of my despatch of 2nd November, 1899, I have now the honour to report the occurrences of 24th October, referred to briefly in the last paragraph of my above-mentioned despatch. On that date I marched out of Ladysmith at dawn with the 5th Lancers, 19th Hussars, Imperial Light Horse, Natal Mounted Volunteers, 42nd and 53rd Batteries, Royal Field Artillery; No. 10 Mountain Battery, Royal Garrison Artillery; 1st Bn. Liverpool Regiment, 1st Bn. Devonshire Regiment, 1st Bn. Gloucestershire Regiment, and 2nd Bn. King's Royal Rifle Corps. The mounted troops were sent on in advance, and, after going about 6 miles along the Newcastle Road, came under rifle fire from the hills on their left on Rietfontein Farm. The 19th Hussars pushed on over the Modder Spruit and seized and held a ridge about 2 miles beyond that stream by dismounted fire, while watching the country to the front and flanks with patrols. The 5th Lancers similarly seized and held ridges south of the Modder Spruit, as also did the Imperial Light Horse. By this disposition of the mounted troops my right flank was entirely protected during the subsequent action.

At 8 am I arrived at Rietfontein at the head of the main body. At this moment the enemy opened artillery fire on my advanced Cavalry from a point high up on the Intintanyone Mountain, and about 5,000 yards to the west of the main road, at which he had apparently posted four guns. My Artillery was at once ordered to wheel off the road and come into action against these guns, which opened fire on them, but were quickly silenced. Leaving the 2nd Bn. King's Royal Rifle Corps with the baggage wagons, I moved the remainder of the Infantry under the shelter of a high ridge, parallel to the road, and facing the Intintanyone Mountain. The 1st Bn. Gloucestershire Regiment on the left, and the 1st Bn. Liverpool Regiment on the right were then advanced to the crest of this ridge, the Artillery also advancing and coming into action on the crest line between these two regiments. The position thus attained was one most suitable to my purpose, which was to prevent the enemy moving to the east, across the Newcastle Road, and attacking Brigadier-General Yule's force during its retirement from Dundee.

Our Artillery was entirely successful in preventing the enemy from making any further use of his guns, but a severe fire fight gradually developed between my troops and the enemy's infantry, and it became necessary to push the 1st Bn. Devonshire Regiment also to the crest of the ridge, half the 2nd Bn. King's Royal Rifle Corps being brought up from the wagons to take their place in reserve. In this Infantry fight our Artillery rendered great assistance, searching out the crest line and reverse slopes of the opposing ridges most effectively, and thus keeping down the enemy's rifle fire. Meanwhile the Natal Mounted Volunteers, who had been with the Cavalry, had been recalled, and, as the enemy showed some disposition to work round my left flank, as if to cut me from Ladysmith, I sent this force, under Colonel Royston, to work round the Boer right and cover my left flank, a movement which was most successfully performed. It was no part of my plan to deliver an attack on the enemy, posted as he was in ground exceptionally well suited to his tactics, and especially difficult for our troops; I contented myself, therefore, with maintaining the position I had gained. The Boers, on the other hand, were unwilling to attack us except by fire at long ranges, and as they could not approach Brigadier-General Yule's force without doing so, they gradually withdrew to the westward. By 2 pm firing had ceased, and as time had now been afforded for the Dundee column to pass the point of danger I returned with my troops to Ladysmith. Our casualties consisted of one officer and 11 non-commissioned officers and men killed, six officers and 97 non-commissioned officers and men wounded, and two non-commissioned officers and men missing. The enemy's loss was heavy, particularly from artillery fire.

On 25th October I sent out a force, under Lieut.-Colonel Coxhead, RA, to meet and, if necessary, to assist Brigadier-General Yule. This force got in touch with the Dundee column that afternoon, and, as already reported, both columns reached Ladysmith next morning (26th October) without any interference from the enemy.

On 27th, 28th and 29th October the enemy gradually approached Ladysmith from the west, north, and north-east. These days were spent by us in reconnaissances with a view to finding a favourable opportunity to strike a blow at him. On 29th October our Cavalry located a considerable Boer force with artillery on Long Hill, north-east of Ladysmith, and well within striking distance. I accordingly issued orders for an attack next day, which resulted in the action of Lombard's Kop.

My object was, in the first instance, to carry Long Hill, and, in the event of success, to similarly carry Pepworth's Hill, sending, at the same time, a considerable mounted force round over Nicholson's Nek to cut the enemy's line of retreat and endeavour to capture his laagers. To gain these objects I employed the entire force assembled at Ladysmith. 200 Natal Mounted Volunteers were sent out the evening before to hold Lombard's Kop and Bulwana Mountain. The 5th Lancers, 19th Hussars, and the remainder of the Natal Mounted Volunteers were ordered to move out, under Major-General French, at 3 am on 30th October, cross Lombard's Nek and the Modder Spruit and cover my right flank during the operations. A Brigade Division of Royal Field Artillery, the Natal Field Battery, 1st and 2nd Bns. King's Royal Rifle Corps, 1st Bn. Leicestershire Regiment, 1st Bn. Liverpool Regiment, and 2nd Bn. Royal Dublin Fusiliers, the whole under Colonel Grimwood, King's Royal Rifle Corps, were detailed for the attack on Long Hill, moving at night so as to be ready to commence the attack at dawn. An Infantry Brigade, under Colonel Ian Hamilton, CB, DSO, consisting of 2nd Bn. Gordon Highlanders, 1st Bn. Manchester Regiment, 1st Bn. Devonshire Regiment, and 2nd Bn. Rifle Brigade, together with the Divisional Troops, consisting of a Brigade Division, Royal Artillery 5th Dragoon Guards, 18th Hussars, Imperial Light Horse, and two companies, Mounted Infantry, were directed to rendezvous at the railway crossing on the Newcastle Road, and proceed to take up a position under cover of Limit Hill. This latter Brigade Division was directed, in the first instance, to assist in shelling Long Hill, the Infantry being intended for the attack on Pepworth's Hill. To cover my left flank and open a way for the action of the Cavalry after the position had been carried, No. 10 Mountain Battery, the 1st Bn. Royal Irish Fusiliers, and the 1st Bn. Gloucestershire Regiment, the whole under Lieut.-Colonel F. Carleton, Royal Irish Fusiliers, with Major W. Adye, DAAG, for Intelligence, as Staff Officer and Guide, were directed to fall in, at 11 pm on 29th October, and make a night march up Bell's Spruit to seize as strong a position as could be obtained towards Nicholson's Nek; if possible, the Nek itself.

The troops moved out in accordance with these instructions. The mounted troops, under General French, passed between Lombard's Kop and Bulwana Mountain, but failed to penetrate further than the line of kopjes north-east of the Nek, where at daybreak they came under the fire of the enemy's guns and rifles. They held the enemy in check here but could not advance further. The Infantry Brigade, under Colonel Grimwood, reached their appointed position, and the Artillery opened on Long Hill, which, however, was found to have been evacuated by the enemy during the night. At this moment Colonel Grimwood's force was attacked by guns and mounted infantry in large numbers from beyond the Modder Spruit, and had to change front to the right to meet this development, as the Cavalry, having been unable to get beyond the kopjes north-east of Lombard's Nek, were not in a position to cover that flank. Gradually the enemy's numbers increased, and made continual efforts to turn both flanks of the position occupied by Colonel Grimwood's force, necessitating a constant prolongation of his fighting line, and thus using up his supports and reserves, which, by 10 am, had all been absorbed in the firing line.

Meanwhile artillery fire had been opened by the enemy from Pepworth Hill, one of the guns employed being a 15-cm gun, throwing a shell of about 100 lbs weight, which commenced firing on the town of Ladysmith at a range of 8,000 yards. These guns were silenced by our Field Artillery, which also drove the enemy from the crest of Pepworth Hill. It was now about 8 am. At this period Major-General French reported that he was holding his position with difficulty against superior forces of the enemy, and I detached the 5th Dragoon Guards and 18th Hussars, under Brigadier-General Brocklehurst, to his assistance; the 69th and 21st Field Batteries being also moved to his support, and with this assistance he easily held his own till the end of the action. Of the remaining batteries, the 13th and 53rd were engaged in supporting Colonel Grimwood's force, while the 42nd and 67th were still firing on Pepworth Hill, from which the enemy had reopened fire, while he had also brought fresh guns on to Long Hill.

About 10 am I withdrew the Manchester Regiment from Colonel Hamilton's force and placed it in a position to support Colonel Grimwood. The fight now became stationary, our troops holding their positions without any great difficulty, but being unable to advance. The Boers, on the other hand, were unable to make any headway. This condition of affairs continued until 11.30 am, when, finding that there was little prospect of bringing the engagement to a decisive issue, I determined to withdraw my troops. I accordingly moved the 2nd Bn. Gordon Highlanders from my left to a strong position on Flag Hill, and sent Major-General Sir A. Hunter, KCB, my Chief of the Staff, to arrange a retirement in *echelon* from the left, covered by the fire of our Artillery. This was most successfully carried out, the Artillery advancing in the most gallant manner and covering the Infantry movement with the greatest skill and coolness.

Meanwhile the Naval Brigade landed from HMS *Powerful*, which had reached Ladysmith that morning, under Captain Hon. H. Lambton, RN, had moved out with their long 12-pr. guns on improvised field mountings, drawn by oxen, and had engaged the enemy's artillery on Pepworth Hill, directing their special attention to the heavy gun mounted there, which they temporarily silenced. The enemy did not follow up our retirement, and the whole force employed on this side returned to camp at 1.30 pm.

Turning now to this force, consisting of No. 10 Mountain Battery, Royal Irish Fusiliers, and the Gloucestershire Regiment, under Lieut.-Colonel F.

Carleton, Royal Irish Fusiliers, which proceeded by a night march up Bell's Spruit towards Nicholson's Nek to cover my left flank, I regret that, owing to the circumstances about to be related, I have no official report of their movements. My information has been obtained from subordinate officers, who, being severely wounded, were sent into my camp here by General Joubert. From this information it appears that the force moved off, as ordered, at 11 pm on 29th October, and proceeded for some distance without seeing signs of the enemy. When passing along the foot of a steep hill, known as Cainguba, stones were suddenly rolled down on them and some shots were fired. The Infantry at once fixed bayonets and carried the hill without difficulty, but unfortunately both the Mountain Battery mules and those carrying the Infantry ammunition took fright and stampeded. Mules carrying two guns eventually returned to camp, one was retained with the force, but no trace has been found of the other three, which presumably fell into the enemy's hands.

The force took up a position on Cainguba, which they strengthened with breastworks to some slight extent, and remained unmolested till daybreak. It was then found that the position was too large for them to adequately occupy, and that only the most pronounced salients could be held. The Boers appear to have gradually surrounded the hill, and after a fight extending over several hours, our men's ammunition began to fail owing to the ammunition mules having stampeded, as already described. The advanced parties holding the salients were driven back on the main body in the centre of the plateau, and the Boers gained the crest line of the hill, whence they brought a converging fire to bear from all sides on our men crowded together in the centre, causing much loss. Eventually it was seen that this position was hopelessly untenable, and our force hoisted a white flag and surrendered about 12.30 pm.

Including under the head of "missing" those thus taken prisoners, our losses this day amounted to six officers and 63 non-commissioned officers and men killed, 10 officers and 239 non-commissioned officers and men wounded, and 37 officers and 917 non-commissioned officers and men missing.

Next day, 31st October, General Sir Redvers Buller, VC, GCB, etc., arrived at Cape Town, and assumed the command in the whole of South Africa. My independent command in Natal consequently came to an end, and I therefore close this despatch with the events of 30th October. Subsequent events will be reported to the General Officer Commanding in South Africa in the ordinary course.

I desire to place on record my gratitude to the Government of Natal, and to all departments under the Government, for the most willing and hearty assistance which they have afforded me in every matter in which their co-operation was required.

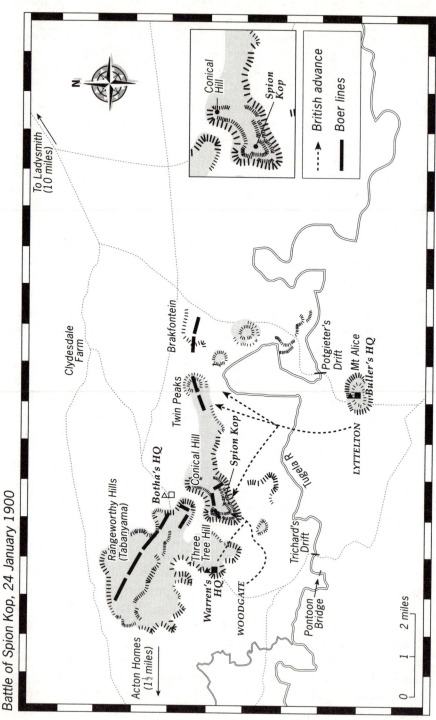

Battle of Spion Kop, 24 January 1900

Legend:
- ⇢ British advance
- ▬ Boer lines

Conical Hill

Spion Kop

To Ladysmith
(10 miles)

Clydesdale Farm

Brakfontein

Twin Peaks

Potgieter's Drift

Mt Alice
Buller's HQ

LYTTELTON

Tugela R

Conical Hill

Spion Kop

Rangeworthy Hills
(Tabanyama)

Botha's HQ

Three Tree Hill

Warren's HQ

WOODGATE

Trichard's Drift

Acton Homes
(1½ miles)

Pontoon Bridge

0   1   2 miles

ADVANCE ACROSS TUGELA RIVER
17TH–18TH JANUARY 1900
AND CAPTURE AND EVACUATION OF SPION KOP
23RD–24TH JANUARY 1900

From Field-Marshal Lord Roberts to the Secretary of State for War

Army Headquarters, South Africa, Camp, Dekiel Drift, Riet River
13th February, 1900

My Lord,

I have the honour to submit, for your Lordship's information, despatches from General Sir Redvers Buller, describing the advance across the Tugela River on the 17th and 18th January, 1900, and the capture and evacuation of the Spion Kop position on the 23rd and 24th January, as well as certain minor operations between the 19th and 24th January on the right or eastern line of advance.

The plan of operations is not very clearly described in the despatches themselves, but it may be gathered from them and the accompanying documents themselves that the original intention was to cross the Tugela at or near Trichard's Drift, and thence by following the road past Fair View and Acton Homes, to gain the open plain north of Spion Kop, the Boer position in front of Potgieter's Drift being too strong to be taken by direct attack. The whole force, less one brigade, was placed under the orders of Sir Charles Warren, who, the day after he had crossed the Tugela, seems to have consulted his General and principal Staff Officers, and to have come to the conclusion that the flanking movement which Sir Redvers Buller had mentioned in his secret instructions was impracticable on account of the insufficiency of supplies. He accordingly decided to advance by the more direct road leading north-east, and branching off from a point east of Three

Tree Hill. The selection of this road necessitated the capture and retention of Spion Kop, but whether it would have been equally necessary to occupy Spion Kop, had the line of advance indicated by Sir Redvers Buller been followed, is not stated in the correspondence.

As Sir Charles Warren considered it impossible to make the wide flanking movement which was recommended, if not actually prescribed, in his secret instructions, he should at once have acquainted Sir Redvers Buller with the course of action which he proposed to adopt. There is nothing to show whether he did so or not, but it seems only fair to Sir Charles Warren to point out that Sir Redvers Buller appears throughout to have been aware of what was happening. On several occasions he was present during the operations. He repeatedly gave advice to his subordinate Commander, and on the day after the withdrawal from Spion Kop he resumed the chief command.

In his note on Sir Charles Warren's report, accompanying despatch of 30th January, 1900 [see p. 165], Sir Redvers Buller expresses a very adverse opinion on the manner in which Sir Charles Warren carried out the instructions he had received. Without a knowledge of the country and circumstances it is difficult to say whether the delay, misdirection, and want of control, of which Sir Redvers Buller complains, were altogether avoidable; but, in any case, if he considered that his orders were not being properly given effect to, it appears to me that it was his duty to intervene as soon as he had reason to believe that the success of the operations was being endangered. This, indeed, is admitted by Sir Redvers Buller himself, whose explanation of his non-interference can hardly be accepted as adequate. A most important enterprise was being attempted, and no personal considerations should have deterred the officer in chief command from insisting on its being conducted in the manner to which, in his opinion, would lead to the attainment of the object in view, with the least possible loss on our side.

As regards the withdrawal of the troops from the Spion Kop position, which, though occupied almost without opposition in the early morning of the 24th January, had to be held throughout the day under an extremely heavy fire, and the retention of which had become essential to the relief of Ladysmith, I regret that I am unable to concur with Sir Redvers Buller in thinking that Lieut.-Colonel Thorneycroft exercised a wise discretion in ordering the troops to retire. Even admitting that due preparations may not have been made for strengthening the position during the night, reorganizing the defence, and bringing up artillery—in regard to which Sir Charles Warren's report does not altogether bear out Sir Redvers Buller's contention—admitting also that the senior officers on the summit of the hill might have been more promptly informed of the measures taken by Sir Charles Warren to support and reinforce them, I am of opinion that Lieut.-Colonel Thorneycroft's assumption of responsibility and authority was wholly inexcusable. During the night the enemy's fire, if it did not cease altogether, could not have been formidable, and, though lamp signalling was not possible at the time, owing to the supply of oil having failed, it would not have taken more than two or three hours at most for Lieut.-Colonel Thorneycroft to communicate by messenger with Major-General Coke or Sir Charles Warren, and to receive a reply. Major-General Coke appears to have left Spion Kop at 9.30 pm for the purpose of consulting with Sir Charles Warren, and up to that hour the idea of a withdrawal had not been entertained. Yet almost immediately after Major-General Coke's departure Lieut.-Colonel Thorneycroft issued an order, without reference to superior authority, which upset the whole plan of operations, and rendered unavailing the sacrifices which had already been made to carry it into effect.

On the other hand, it is only right to state that Lieut.-Colonel Thorneycroft appears to have behaved in a very gallant manner throughout the day, and it was doubtless due, in a great measure, to his exertions and example that the troops continued to hold the summit of the hill until directed to retire.

The conduct of Captain Phillips, Brigade-Major of the 10th Brigade, on the occasion in question, is deserving of high commendation. He did his best to rectify the mistake which was being made, but it was too late. Signalling communication was not re-established until 2.30 am on the 25th January, and by that time the naval guns could not have reached the summit of the hill before daybreak. Major-General Coke did not return, and Lieut.-Colonel Thorneycroft had gone away. Moreover, most of the troops had begun to leave the hill, and the working parties, with the half company of Royal Engineers, had also withdrawn.

It is to be regretted that Sir Charles Warren did not himself visit Spion Kop during the afternoon or evening, knowing as he did that the state of affairs there was very critical, and that the loss of the position would involve the failure of the operations. He was, consequently, obliged to summon Major-General Coke to his headquarters in the evening in order that he might ascertain how matters were going on, and the command on Spion Kop thus devolved on Lieut.-Colonel Thorneycroft; but Major-General Coke was not aware of this.

About midday, under instructions from Sir Redvers Buller, Sir Charles Warren had directed Lieut.-Colonel Thorneycroft to assume command on the summit of the hill, with the temporary rank of Brigadier-General, but this order was not communicated to Major-General Coke, who, until he left the position at 9.30 pm, was under the impression that the command had devolved on Colonel Hill, as senior officer, after Colonel Crofton had been wounded. Omissions or mistakes of this nature may be trivial in themselves, yet may exercise an important influence on the course of events; and I think that Sir Redvers Buller is justified in remarking that "there was a want of organization and system which acted most unfavourably on the defence."

The attempt to relieve Ladysmith, described in these despatches, was well devised, and I agree with Sir Redvers Buller in thinking that it ought to have succeeded. That it failed may, in some measure, be due to the difficulties of the ground and the commanding positions held by the enemy—probably also to errors of judgment and want of administrative capacity on the part of Sir Charles Warren. But whatever faults Sir Charles Warren may have committed, the failure must also be ascribed to the disinclination of the officer in supreme command to assert his authority and see that what he thought best was done, and also to the unwarrantable and needless assumption of responsibility by a subordinate officer.

The gratifying feature in these despatches is the admirable behaviour of the troops throughout the operations.

ROBERTS, *Field-Marshal,*
Commanding-in-Chief, South Africa

From General Sir Redvers Buller to the Secretary of State for War

Spearman's Hill, 30th January, 1900

Sir,

I have the honour to report that General Sir Charles Warren's Division having arrived at Estcourt, less two battalions, 10th Brigade, which were left at the Cape, by the 7th January, it moved to Frere on the 9th.

The column moved as ordered, but torrents of rain fell on the 9th, which filled all the spruits, and, indeed, rendered many of them impassable for many hours. To forward supply alone took 650 ox wagons, and as in the 16 miles from Frere to Springfield there were three places at which all the wagons had to be double spanned, and some required three spans, some idea may be formed of the difficulties, but these were all successfully overcome by the willing labours of the troops.

The 4th Brigade reached Springfield on the 12th, in support of the mounted troops who had surprised and seized the important position of Spearman's Hill, commanding Potgieter's Drift, on the 11th.

By the 13th all troops were at Springfield and Spearman's Hill, and supply was well forward.

On the 16th, a reserve of 17 days' supply having been collected, General Sir C. Warren, in command of the 2nd Division, the 11th Brigade of the 5th Division, the Brigade Division Royal Field Artillery, 5th Division, and certain corps troops, including the Mounted Brigade, moved from Springfield to Trichard's Drift, which is about six miles west of Potgieter's.

I attach a copy of the orders under which Sir C. Warren acted, and enclose his report of his operations.

On the night of the 23rd, General Warren attacked Spion Kop, which operation he has made the subject of a special report. On the morning of the 25th, finding that Spion Kop had been abandoned in the night, I decided to withdraw General Warren's force; the troops had been continuously engaged for a week, in circumstances entailing considerable hardships, there had been very heavy losses on Spion Kop. General Warren's dispositions had mixed up all the brigades, and the positions he held were dangerously insecure. I consequently assumed the command, commenced the withdrawal of the ox and heavy mule transport on the 25th; this was completed by midday the 26th; by double spanning the loaded ox wagons they got over the drift at the rate of about eight per hour. The mule wagons went over the pontoon bridge, but all the mules had to be taken out and the vehicles passed over by hand. For about 7 hours of the night the drift could not be used as it was dangerous in the dark, but the use of the pontoon went on day and night. In addition to machine guns, six batteries of Royal Field Artillery, and four howitzers, the following vehicles were passed: ox wagons, 232; 10-span mule wagons, 98; 6-span, 107; 4-span, 52; total, 489 vehicles. In addition to these, the ambulances were working backwards and forwards evacuating the sick and wounded.

By 2 pm, the 26th, all the ox wagons were over, and by 11.30 pm all the mule transports were across and the bridge clear for the troops. By 4 am, the 27th, all the troops were over, and by 8 am the pontoons were gone and all was clear. The troops had all reached their new camps by 10 am. The marches averaged for the mounted troops about 7 miles, and for the Infantry and Artillery an average of 5 miles.

Everything worked without a hitch, and the arrangements reflected great credit on the staff of all degrees; but I must especially mention Major Irwin, RE, and his men of the Pontoon Troop, who were untiring. When all men were over, the chesses of the pontoon bridge were so worn by the traffic, that I do not think they would have lasted another half hour.

Thus ended an expedition which I think ought to have succeeded. We have suffered heavily, very heavy losses, and lost many whom we can ill spare; but, on the other hand, we have inflicted as great or greater losses upon the enemy than they have upon us, and they are, by all accounts, thoroughly disheartened; while our troops are, I am glad and proud to say, in excellent fettle.

REDVERS BULLER
General Officer Commanding

From General Sir Redvers Buller to Lieut.-General Sir Charles Warren

Mount Alice, 15th January, 1900

The enemy's position in front of Potgieter's Drift seems to me to be too strong to be taken by direct attack.

I intend to try and turn it by sending a force across the Tugela from near Trichard's Drift and up to the west of Spion Kop.

You will have command of that force which will consist of the 11th Brigade of your Division, your Brigade Division, Royal Field Artillery, and General Clery's Division complete, and all the mounted troops, except 400.

You will of course act as circumstances require, but my idea is that you should continue throughout refusing your right and throwing your left forward till you gain the open plain north of Spion Kop. Once there you will command the rear of the position facing Potgieter's Drift, and I think render it untenable.

At Potgieter's there will be the 4th Brigade, part of the 10th Brigade, one battery Royal Field Artillery, one howitzer battery, two 4.7-inch Naval guns. With them I shall threaten both the positions in front of us, and also attempt a crossing at Skiet's Drift, so as to hold the enemy off you as much as possible.

It is very difficult to ascertain the numbers of the enemy with any sort of exactness. I do not think there can be more than 400 on your left, and I estimate the total force that will be opposed to us at about 7,000. I think they have only one or at most two big guns.

You will take 2½ days' supply in your regimental transport, and a supply column holding one day more. This will give you four days' supply, which should be enough. Every extra wagon is a great impediment.

I gathered that you did not want an ammunition column. I think myself that I should be inclined to take one column for the two Brigade Divisions. You may find a position on which it is expedient to expend a great deal of ammunition.

You will issue such orders to the Pontoon Troop as you think expedient. If possible, I should like it to come here after you have crossed. I do not think you will find it possible to let oxen draw the wagons over the pontoons. It will be better to draw them over by horses or mules, swimming the oxen; the risk of breaking the pontoons, if oxen cross them, is too great.

The man whom I am sending you as a guide is a Devonshire man; he was employed as a boy on one of my own farms; he is English to the back-bone, and can be thoroughly trusted. He thinks that if you cross Springfield flat at night he can take you the rest of the way to the Tugela by a road that cannot be overlooked by the enemy, but you will doubtless have the road reconnoitred.

I shall endeavour to keep up heliographic communication with you from a post on the hill directly in your rear.

I wish you to start as soon as you can. Supply is all in, and General Clery's Division will, I hope, concentrate at Springfield today. Directly you start I shall commence to cross the river.

Please send me the 10th Brigade, except that portion which you detail for the garrison at Springfield, as soon as possible; also the eight 12-pr. naval guns, and any details, such as ammunition column, etc., that you do not wish to take.

REDVERS BULLER, *General*

From Lieut.-General Sir Charles Warren to the Chief of the Staff
Hatting's Farm, 29th January, 1900

Sir,

I have the honour to make the following report on the operations on the north side of the Tugela, west of Spion Kop, from the 17th to the 27th of January, 1900.

On the 8th January field orders were published constituting the 10th Brigade of the 5th Division a Corps Brigade, and placing the 4th Brigade in the 5th Division. The 5th Division thus constituted marched from Frere on the 10th instant, arriving at Springfield on the 12th instant.

On the 15th January I received your secret instructions to command a force to proceed across the Tugela, near Trichard's Drift, to the west of Spion Kop, recommending me to proceed forward refusing my right (namely, Spion Kop), and bringing my left forward to gain the open plain north of Spion Kop. This move was to commence as soon as supplies were all in, and the 10th Brigade (except two companies) removed from Springfield Bridge to Spearman's Hill.

I was provided with 4 days' rations, with which I was to cross the Tugela, fight my way round to north of Spion Kop, and join your column opposite Potgieter's.

On the 15th January I made the arrangements for getting supplies, and moved the 10th Brigade on the following day; and on the evening of the 16th January I left Springfield with a force under my command, which amounted to an Army Corps (less one brigade), and by a night march arrived at Trichard's Drift, and took possession of the hills on the south side of the Tugela.

On the 17th January I threw pontoon bridges across the Tugela, passed the Infantry across by ponts, and captured the hills immediately commanding the drift on the north side with two brigades commanded by Generals Woodgate and Hart. The Commander-in-Chief was present during part of the day, and gave some verbal directions to General Woodgate.

The Mounted Brigade passed over principally by the drift, and went over the country as far as Acton Homes, and on the following day (18th) had a successful action with a small party of Boers, bringing in 31 prisoners.

During the night of the 17th, and day of the 18th, the whole of the wagons belonging to the force were brought across the Tugela, and the artillery were in position outside of Wright's Farm.

On the 19th two brigades advanced, occupying the slopes of the adjoining hills on the right, and the wagons were successfully brought to Venter's Spruit.

In the evening, after having examined the possible roads by which we could proceed, I assembled the General Officers and the Staff, and the Officer Commanding Royal Artillery, and Commanding Royal Engineer, and pointed out to them that of the two roads by which we could advance, the eastern one, by Acton Homes, must be rejected, because time would not allow of it, and with this all concurred. I then pointed out that the only possible way of all getting through by the road north of Fair View would be by taking 3 or 4 days' food in our haversacks, and sending all our wagons back across the Tugela; but before we could do this we must capture the position in front of us.

On the following day, 20th January, I placed two brigades and six batteries of Artillery at the disposal of General Sir C. F. Clery, with instructions to attack the Boer positions by a series of outflanking movements, and by the end of the day, after fighting for 12 hours, we were in possession of the whole part of the hills, but found a strongly entrenched line on the comparatively flat country beyond us.

On the 21st the Boers displayed considerable activity on our left, and the Commander-in-Chief desired me to move two batteries from right to left. At a subsequent date, during the day, I found it impossible to proceed without howitzers, and telegraphed for four from Potgieter's. These arrived early on the morning of the 22nd, and the Commander-in-Chief, arriving about the same time, directed me to place two of these howitzers on the left, two having already been placed on the right flank. I pointed out to the Commander-in-Chief that it would be impossible to get wagons through by the road leading past Fair View, unless we first took Spion Kop, which lies within about 2,000 yards of the road. The Commander-in-Chief agreed that Spion Kop would have to be taken. Accordingly orders were drawn up giving the necessary instructions to General Coke to take Spion Kop that night, but, owing to insufficient reconnaissance, he requested that the attack might be put off for a day.[*]

On the 23rd January the Commander-in-Chief came into camp, the attack on Spion Kop was decided upon, and Lieut.-Colonel àCourt, of the Headquarter Staff, was directed by the Commander-in-Chief to accompany General Woodgate, who was detailed to command the attacking column. The account of the capture of Spion Kop is given in another report.

On the morning of the 25th January the Commander-in-Chief arrived, decided to retire the force, and assumed direct command. The whole of the wagons of the 5th Division were got down to the drift during the day, and were crossed over before 2 pm on the 26th January.

The arrangements for the retirement of the 5th Division were exceedingly well got out, and the retirement was made in good order during the night of the 26th, the whole of the troops crossing to the south side of the Tugela before daylight, and the wagons were packed, and the troops bivouacked near the spruit about 2 miles to the east of the pontoon bridges. About 10 pm, previous to the retirement, heavy musketry was heard to the north of our position, which has been attributed to a Boer commando thinking we were going to make a night attack.

---

[*] I omitted to state that during the afternoon of the 22nd the Commander-in-Chief proposed an attack upon the enemy's position on our left flank that night. I summoned at once the General Officers available, namely, Generals Clery, Talbot, Coke, and Hildyard. General Clery, who was in command of the left attack, did not consider it advisable to make this attack, because, if successful, it would commit us to taking the whole line of the enemy's position, which he considered a hazardous proceeding, as we might not be able to hold it. In this I concurred, more particularly as it was evidently too late in the day to carry the operation out effectively. *CW*

I continually proposed to General Warren that he should attack the enemy's right, which was *en l'air* and not strong, and which it was part of the original programme to try and turn, but I never suggested doing this hurriedly or without adequate forethought and preparation. *RB*

I append reports from Lieut.-General Sir C. F. Clery, KCB, on the operations conducted by him on the 20th, 21st, and 22nd, also from Major-General Hildyard, CB, for his operations on those dates.

I propose to forward as soon as possible a more detailed report of the movements of brigades and units, and acts of individuals.

C. WARREN, *Lieut.-General,*
Commanding 5th Division

From General Sir Redvers Buller to the Secretary of State for War
Spearman's Camp, 30th January, 1900

In forwarding this report I am constrained to make the following remarks, not necessarily for publication.

I had fully discussed my orders with General Warren before he started, and he appeared entirely to agree that the policy indicated of refusing the right and advancing the left was the right one. He never though attempted to carry it out. From the first there could be no question but that the only practicable road for his column was the one by Fair View. The problem was to get rid of the enemy who were holding it.

The arrival of the force at Trichard's was a surprise to the enemy, who were not in strength. Sir C. Warren, instead of feeling for the enemy, elected to spend two whole days in passing his baggage. During this time, the enemy received reinforcements and strengthened his position. On the 19th he [Warren] attacked and gained a considerable advantage. On the 20th, instead of pursuing it, he divided his force, and gave General Clery a separate command.

On the 21st I find that his right was in advance of his left, and that the whole of his batteries, six, were crowded on one small position on his right, while his left was unprotected by Artillery, and I had come out to tell him that the enemy on that flank had received a reinforcement of at least 2,500. I suggested a better distribution of his batteries, which he agreed to, to some extent, but he would not advance his left, and I found that he had divided his fighting line into three commands, independent of each other, and apparently independent of him, as he told me he could not move any batteries without General Clery's consent.

The days went on. I saw no attempt on the part of General Warren either to grapple with the situation or to command his force himself. By the 23rd I calculated that the enemy, who were about 600 stong on the 16th, were not less than 15,000, and General White confirmed this estimate. We had really lost our chance by Sir C. Warren's slowness. He seems to me a man who can do well what he can do himself, but who cannot command, as he can use neither his staff nor subordinates. I can never employ him again on an independent command.

On the 19th I ought to have assumed command myself; I saw that things were not going well—indeed, everyone saw that. I blame myself now for not having done so. I did not, because I thought that if I did I should discredit

General Warren in the estimation of the troops; and that if I were shot, and he had to withdraw across the Tugela, and they had lost confidence in him, the consequences might be very serious.

I must leave it to higher authority whether this argument was a sound one. Anyhow, I feel convinced that we had a good chance on the 17th, and that we lost it.

REDVERS BULLER
General

From Lieut.-General Sir Francis Clery to the Assistant Adjutant-General, Sir Charles Warren's Force

Fair View Farm, 20th January, 1900

Sir,

I have the honour to forward the following report, called for this morning, on the operations conducted by me on the 20th, 21st, and 22nd instant.

In compliance with your instructions, I moved at 3 am, 20th January, with a force of four batteries Royal Field Artillery, 5th Brigade, and 11th Brigade, to occupy the heights to the west and north-west of Spion Kop. The eastern spur of those heights I occupied with two battalions of the 11th Brigade, and the spur immediately to the west of the latter I occupied with the two remaining battalions of the 11th Brigade. I explained in my report on the evening of the 20th that, on occupying these heights, I found myself in front of a semi-circular range of heights completely overlooking the heights I had arrived on. The left of this high ridge almost rested on the Spion, the right extended to the spur overlooking Fair View Farm. The road which we should have to use for wagons in our advance passes on the left end of this position, but the enemy's position here was very strong, with a glacis reaching down to the heights we were occupying. The ground on the other flank (left) seemed to afford a good deal more cover for advance, and I hoped if I succeeded in occupying that flank of the ridge, to swing round to the right, and take the remainder of the enemy's position in flank. I accordingly moved up the artillery to the eastern spur, and moved up the 5th Brigade to reinforce the two battalions of the 11th Brigade already on the western spur. I placed the whole of this latter force under Major-General Hart, and directed him to move forward against the left flank of the enemy's position. This was done, and a series of kopjes was occupied in succession, which brought the force that evening, within reach of storming the enemy's position.

The enemy evacuated the position that night, and it was occupied by General Hart's force the following morning. The previous evening two battalions had been detached from the 2nd Brigade to assist the troops on the heights, and I directed them to co-operate with General Hart by attacking the enemy's right flank.

When the enemy's position of the previous day had been occupied by our troops, I found that the enemy had fallen back to a second strong position in rear. The advance to this position was over open ground, and entailed a frontal attack. As this was a thing if possible to be avoided, I reported the situation to the General Officer Commanding, and suggested that some action should be taken against the enemy's right flank.

Two batteries were ordered by the General Officer Commanding to move from the hill on the right to ground on the left, where they came into action against the enemy's right flank. A fire was kept up with the enemy all day, but it was not considered advisable to make a frontal attack on his position.

On the morning of the 22nd, four howitzers arrived. Two were brought into action on the height close to the batteries already in action there; the remaining two came into action on the left. They both reached the enemy's position. Fire was kept up by both sides till about sundown. Both sides retained, generally, the same positions at the end of the day.

FRANCIS CLERY
Lieut.-General

Report from Major-General H. Hildyard on the 2nd Brigade operations on 20th, 21st, and 22nd January, 1900

Bivouac, Flat-topped Hill, near Fair View Farm
23rd January, 1900

20th January During the morning of the 20th, the 2nd Brigade remained in bivouac at Venter's Spruit Drift, no orders having been received for its movement. About 1 pm there was heavy musketry fire in north-westerly direction, where the mounted troops were engaged on the left of Sugar Loaf Hill at 4 pm. The 2nd Bn. Queen's was moved forward in that direction about 1½ miles, so as to be in a position to support the mounted troops and protect the left flank of the force.

At 2.50 pm some men of the mounted troops seized the top Conical Hill. This was reported to the Assistant Adjutant-General, 5th Division, and at 3.30 pm one company of the East Surrey was sent forward to support them.

At 4 pm three companies of the Queen's were also sent forward, and at 6 pm the remaining five companies of the Queen's. At 5.50 pm the 2nd Bn. West Yorkshire Regiment were sent up to the hill east of Conical Hill, in case General Hart, whose brigade was occupying the ground there, required support, with orders to report to him. Both the Queen's and 2nd Bn. West Yorkshire Regiments were in contact with the enemy during the night. The 2nd Bn. East Surrey Regiment protected the north-west of the camp with outposts day and night. The 2nd Bn. Devonshire Regiment placed outposts towards the east of Venter's Spruit Camp. There were no casualties.

21st January At 4.10 am the 2nd Bn. East Surrey Regiment were ordered to send up four companies to report to Colonel Kitchener in order to secure his left. Two companies of the 2nd Bn. Devonshire Regiment were sent at

2 am to Trichard's Drift on escort duty. By the personal order of the General Officer Commanding Field Force, General Hildyard was placed in command of the mounted troops, and was made responsible for the safety of the camp. In consequence of this the Officer Commanding Mounted Troops was directed to provide for the safety of the camp to the right bank of Venter's Spruit. The kopje on the left bank was held by the remaining three companies of the 2nd Bn. East Surrey Regiment. The 2nd Bn. Devonshire Regiment was ordered up to the Flat-topped Hill, about 1,000 yards southwest of Conical Hill.

At 8 am the remaining three companies of the East Surrey Regiment were ordered up to support the half battalion which was at this time on the western slope of Conical Hill.

At 7.50 am a report was sent to the Chief Staff Officer Field Force, on the dispositions of the 2nd Queen's on the night of the 20th, and the orders given to the Commanding Officer. It was at the same time suggested that some guns should be sent to the left flank of the general position. Between 11 am and noon, two batteries Royal Field Artillery, under Lieut.–Colonel Montgomery, arrived, and were placed under my orders. A position was selected for them with their left on Venter's Spruit, and they opened fire about 12.10 pm against the right of the enemy's position. Their fire had the effect of keeping down the enemy's long-range rifle fire on our left. At nightfall the 2nd Bn. Queen's and 2nd Bn. East Surrey Regiment were withdrawn from the firing line into camp and replaced by the 2nd Bn. Devonshire Regiment and the Lancashire Fusiliers, which had been ordered down to support the guns, and placed under my orders by the General Officer Commanding Field Force. About 7 pm the firing ceased all along the line.

In accordance with an order from the General Officer Commanding 2nd Division, communicated by Major-General Hart to him, Colonel Kitchener 2nd Bn. West Yorkshire Regiment took command of the force on Sugar Loaf Hill, and against the enemy's right flank. In this operation the 2nd Bn. Queens, 2nd Bn. West Yorkshire, and 2nd Bn. East Surrey Regiment were engaged. His plan was to work round the western slope of Sugar Loaf Hill with the four companies of the 2nd Bn. East Surrey Regiment, which had been sent up there at 4.30 am covering their advance by the fire of the 2nd Bn. Queen's from the neck east of the hill, and to attack the enemy's right. Simultaneously, two companies 2nd Bn. Queen's were to advance along the plateau, covered by the fire of the 2nd Bn. West Yorkshire Regiment were to push forward on the left of that portion of the enemy's position attacked by the 2nd Bn. Queen's.

The four companies 2nd Bn. East Surrey Regiment were unable to make headway in face of the fire brought against them for the enemy's position. They were, consequently, halted on the west face of the Sugar Loaf Hill in a fire position, where they remained. The two companies 2nd Bn. Queen's had, in the meantime, advanced, at 10.30 am, and immediately encountered a heavy fire. As soon as it was reported that the flank attack by the 2nd Bn. East Surrey Regiment had been stopped they were withdrawn. This advance and subsequent retirement occupied about half an hour. The two companies 2nd Bn. West Yorkshire Regiment had also advanced when the movement of the 2nd Bn. East Surrey Regiment was brought to a stand, and Colonel Kitchener then ordered the advance to be discontinued. One company 2nd Bn. West Yorkshire Regiment, which had reached the donga referred to above, remained there till the evening, so as to avoid loss in retiring.

22nd January The 2nd Bn. Devonshire Regiment and 2nd Bn. East Surrey Regiment held the positions occupied on the 21st. The two batteries occupied the same positions as they did on the 21st. At 10.30 am two howitzers arrived to reinforce the batteries, and were placed under my orders.

The batteries and howitzers kept up a steady fire all day, which was replied to by the Boer gun from the Acton Homes position. Towards evening the Boer guns opened a shrapnel fire on our Infantry line. About 8 pm all firing had ceased, and the batteries and howitzers were withdrawn to Venter's Spruit Camp.

The 2nd Bn. Lancashire Fusiliers were directed in Field Force Orders to rejoin the 11th Brigade. Three companies, which had acted during the day as escort to the guns, were relieved by the 2nd Bn. Queen's, and they bivouacked by Flat-topped Hill. It was too late for the Headquarters and five companies Lancashire Fusiliers to be called in from the front and rejoin.

H. HILDYARD, *Major-General,*
Commanding 2nd Brigade

Copy of instructions issued to Lieut.-General Sir C. F. Clery,
dated 19th January, 1900

General Officer Commanding 2nd Division,
I shall be glad if you will arrange to clear the Boers out of the ground above that at present occupied by the 11th Brigade, by a series of outflanking movements. In the early morning an advance should be made as far as the Hussars reconnoitred today, and a shelter-trench there made across the slope of the hill. A portion of the slopes of the adjoining hill to the west can then be occupied, the Artillery assisting, if necessary, in clearing the western side and upper slopes. When this is done I think that a battery can be placed on the slopes of the western hill in such a position that it could shell the scances of the Boers on Spion Kop and the upper portion of the eastern hill. When this is done a further advance can be made on the eastern hill, and artillery can be brought to bear upon the upper slopes of the western hill. It appears to me that this might be done with comparatively little loss of life, as the Boers can in each turn be outflanked. The following Cavalry are at your disposal: two squadrons Royal Dragoons and 5th Divisional Squadron.

C. WARREN
Lieut. General

Casualties during the operations around Spion Kop

Date		Officers			Men		
		Killed	Wounded	Missing	Killed	Wounded	Missing
January							
17th to 20th	5th Division	1	12	–	26	178	–
20th	2nd Division	–	8	–	4	102	2
21st	2nd Division	1	8	–	13	131	5
22nd	2nd Division	–	1	–	1	19	1
23rd	2nd Division	–	–	–	1	14	–
24th	2nd Division	1	1	–	4	12	–
24th	5th Division	21	22	–	139	388	279
24th	4th Brigade	6	11	6	32	120	2
25th	2nd Division	–	–	–	–	10	–
26th	2nd Division	–	–	–	–	3	–
21st, 22nd, 23rd, 25th 26th, 27th	5th Division	–	1	–	1	33	–
	Totals	30	64	6	221	1,010	289
			100			1,520	
23rd	General Barton's force is not included in above. He lost	1	1	–	4	5	11
20th	Lost by General Lyttelton, not shown above	–	1	–	2	13	1
		1	2	–	6	18	12
	Grand Totals		103			1,556	
Losses on 24th (included above)		28	34	6	175	520	281
	Totals		68			976	

There are said to have been 243 buried in Spion Kop, so no doubt many of those shown missing were killed.

Note appended by Sir Charles Warren to the instructions issued to Sir C. F. Clery on 19th January, 1900

20th January, 1900

After successfully carrying some of the hills, General Clery reported that he had now reached a point which it would be necessary to take by frontal attack, which he did not think would be desirable.

To this I replied:

I quite concur that a frontal attack is undesirable, and that a flank attack is more suitable. I intended to convey that we should hold what we get by means of entrenchments when necessary, and not retire, continuing the advance tomorrow if it cannot be done tonight; frontal attack, with heavy losses, is simply playing the Boer game.

C. WARREN

ACCOUNTS OF CAPTURE AND EVACUATION OF SPION KOP

From the General Officer Commanding, Natal, to the Secretary of State for War

Spearman's Hill, 30th January, 1900

Sir,

In forwarding Lieut.-General Sir C. Warren's report on the capture and evacuation of Spion Kop, I have the honour to offer the following observations.

Sir C. Warren is hardly correct in saying that he was only allowed 3½ days' provisions. I had told him that transport for 3½ days would be sufficient burden to him, but that I would keep him filled up as he wanted it. That he was aware of this is shown by the following telegram which he sent on the day in question. It is the only report I had from Sir C. Warren:

(Sent 7.54 pm. Received 8.15 pm.)

Left Flank, 19th January

To Chief of the Staff,

I find there are only two roads by which we could possibly get from Trichard's Drift to Potgieter's, on the north of the Tugela—one by Acton Homes, the other by Fair View and Rosalie; the first I reject as too long, the second is a very difficult road for a large number of wagons, unless the enemy is thoroughly cleared out. I am, therefore, going to adopt some special arrangements which will involve my stay at Venter's Laager for 2 or 3 days. I will send in for further supplies and report progress.

C. WARREN

The reply to this was that 3 days' supply was being sent.

I went over to Sir C. Warren on the 23rd. I pointed out to him that I had no further report and no intimation of the special arrangements foreshadowed by this telegram of the 19th; that for four days he had kept his men continuously exposed to shell and rifle fire, perched on the edge of an almost precipitous hill; that the position admitted of no second line, and the supports were massed close behind the firing line in indefensible formations, and that a panic or a sudden charge might send the whole lot in disorder down the hill at any moment. I said it was too dangerous a situation to be prolonged, and that he must either attack or I should withdraw his force. I advocated, as I had previously done, an advance from his left. He said that he had the night before ordered General Coke to assault Spion Kop, but the latter had objected to undertaking a night attack on a position, the road to which he had not reconnoitred, and added that he intended to assault Spion Kop that night.

I suggested that as General Coke was still lame from the effects of a lately broken leg, General Woodgate, who had two sound legs, was better adapted for mountain climbing.

As no heliograph could, on account of the fire, be kept on the east side of Spion Kop, messages for Sir C. Warren were received by our signallers at Spearman, and telegraphed to Sir C. Warren; thus I saw them before he did, as I was at the signal station. The telegrams Sir C. Warren quotes did not give me confidence in its sender, and, at the moment, I could see that our men on the top had given way, and that efforts were being made to rally them. I telegraphed to Sir C. Warren: "Unless you put some really good hard fighting man in command on the top you will lose the hill. I suggest Thorneycroft."

Colonel à Court was sent down by General Woodgate almost as soon as he gained the summit [therefore a Staff Officer was not present on the summit].

I have not thought it necessary to order any investigation. If at sundown the defence of the summit had been taken regularly in hand, entrenchments laid out, gun emplacements prepared, the dead removed, the wounded collected, and, in fact, the whole place brought under regular military command, and careful arrangements made for the supply of water and food to the scattered fighting line, the hills would have been held, I am sure.

But no arrangements were made. General Coke appears to have been ordered away just as he would have been useful, and no one succeeded him; those on the top were ignorant of the fact that guns were coming up, and generally there was a want of organization and system that acted most unfavourably on the defence.

It is admitted by all that Colonel Thorneycroft acted with the greatest gallantry throughout the day, and really saved the situation. Preparations for the second day's defence should have been organized during the day, and have been commenced at nightfall. As this was not done, I think Colonel Thorneycroft exercised a wise discretion.

Our losses, I regret to say, were very heavy, but the enemy admitted to our doctors that theirs were equally severe, and though we were not successful in retaining the position, the losses inflicted on the enemy and the attack generally have had a marked effect upon them.

I cannot close these remarks without bearing testimony to the gallant and admirable behaviour of the troops, the endurance shown by the Lancashire Fusiliers, the Middlesex Regiment, and Thorneycroft's Mounted Infantry was admirable, while the efforts of the 2nd Bn. Scottish Rifles and 3rd Bn. King's Royal Rifles were equally good, and the Royal Lancasters fought gallantly.

I am writing to catch the mail, and have not any particulars yet to enable me to report more fully on details.

REDVERS BULLER

Report by Lieut.-General Sir Charles Warren, KCB, upon the capture and subsequent evacuation of Spion Kop

Chief of the Staff,

I make the operations against Spion Kop in a separate report, because they did not enter into my original plans.

Under the original instructions of the General Officer Commanding-in-Chief, of 15th January, 1900, I was to act as circumstances required, but according to instructions, was generally to continue throughout refusing my right, and throwing my left forward until I gained the open plain north of Spion Kop.

Upon the 19th of January, on arrival at Venter's Laager, I assembled all the General Officers, Officers Commanding Royal Artillery and Royal Engineers of Divisions, and Staff Officers together. I pointed out to them that, with the 3½ days' provisions allowed, it was impossible to advance by the left road through Acton Homes. In this they unanimously concurred. I showed them that the only possible road was that going over Fair View through Rosalie, but I expressed my conviction that this could not be done unless we sent the whole of our transport back across the Tugela, and attempted to march through with our rations in our haversacks—without impedimenta.

The hills were cleared on the following day, and very strong entrenchments found behind them. The Commander-in-Chief was present on the 21st and 22nd January, and I pointed out the difficulties of marching along the road, accompanied by wagons, without first taking Spion Kop.

Accordingly, on the night of the 22nd, I ordered General Coke to occupy Spion Kop. He, however, desired that the occupation might be deferred for a day in order that he might make a reconnaissance with the Officers Commanding battalions to be sent there.

On 23rd January the Commander-in-Chief came into camp, and told me that there were two courses open: (1) to attack, or (2) to retire. I replied that I should prefer to attack Spion Kop to retiring, and showed the Commander-in-Chief my orders of the previous day.

The Commander-in-Chief then desired that I should put General Woodgate in command of the expedition, and detailed Lieut.-Colonel àCourt to accompany him as Staff Officer.

The same evening General Woodgate proceeded with the Lancashire Fusiliers, the Royal Lancaster Regiment, a portion of Thorneycroft's Horse, and half company Royal Engineers, supported by two companies of the Connaught Rangers and by the Imperial Light Infantry, the latter having just arrived by Trichard's Drift.

The attack and capture of Spion Kop was entirely successful. General Woodgate, having secured the summit on the 24th, reported that he had entrenched a position and hoped he was secure, but that the fog was too thick to permit him to see. The position was rushed without casualties, other than three men wounded.

Lieut.-Colonel àCourt came down in the morning and stated that everything was satisfactory and secure, and telegraphed to the Commander-in-Chief to that effect. Scarcely had he started on his return to headquarters when a heliogram arrived from Colonel Crofton (Royal Lancaster). The message was: "Reinforce at once, or all lost. General dead."

He also sent a similar message to headquarters. I immediately ordered General Coke to proceed to his assistance, and to take command of the troops. He started at once, and was accompanied by the Middlesex and Dorsetshire Regiments.

I replied to Colonel Crofton: "I am sending two battalions, and the Imperial Light Infantry are on their way up. You must hold on to the last. No surrender." This occurred about 10 am.

Shortly afterwards I received a telegram from the Commander-in-Chief, ordering me to appoint Lieut.-Colonel Thorneycroft to the command of the summit. I accordingly had heliographed: "With the approval of the Commander-in-Chief, I place Lieut.-Colonel Thorneycroft in command of the summit, with the local rank of Brigadier-General."

For some hours after this message I could get no information from the summit. It appears that the signallers and their apparatus were destroyed by the heavy fire.

I repeatedly asked for Colonel Thorneycroft to state his view of the situation. At 1.20 pm I heliographed to ascertain whether Colonel Thorneycroft had assumed command, and at the same time asked General Coke to give me his views on the situation on Spion Kop. Still getting no reply, I asked whether General Coke was there, and subsequently received his view of the situation. He stated that, unless the artillery could silence the enemy's guns, the men on the summit could not stand another complete day's shelling, and that the situation was extremely critical.

At 6.30 pm I asked if he could keep two battalions on the summit, removing the remainder out of reach of shells; also whether two battalions would suffice to hold the summit. This was in accordance with a telegram on the subject sent me by the Commander-in-Chief. Later in the evening I made arrangements to send two (Naval) 12-prs. and the Mountain Battery Royal Artillery to the summit, together with half company Royal Engineers (and working parties, two reliefs of 600 men each), to strengthen the entrenchments and provide shell covers for the men. I may here mention that the 17th Company Royal Engineers proceeded at the same time as General Woodgate's force, and were employed until daylight upon the entrenchments, then upon road making and water supply.

Sandbags were sent up early on the 24th instant.

While Colonel Sim was, with this party, ascending the hill, he met Colonel Thorneycroft descending, having evacuated the position. For the remainder of the account of the proceedings I attach the reports made to me by Colonel Thorneycroft and by General Coke, together with reports on the supply of food and water rendered by officers thus engaged. The supply of ammunition was ample.

I wish to bring to notice that I heard from all but one expression of the admirable conduct and bravery shown by officers and men suffering under a withering artillery fire on the summit of the slopes, and also of those who, with so much endurance, persisted in carrying up water and food and ammunition to the troops during this day.

During the day a Staff Officer of the Headquarter Staff was present on the summit, and reported direct to the Commander-in-Chief.

At sunset I considered that the position could be held next day, provided that guns could be mounted and effective shelter provided. Both of these conditions were about to be fulfilled, as already mentioned.

In the absence of General Coke, whom I ordered to come to report in person as to the situation, the evacuation took place under orders, given upon his own responsibility, by Lieut.-Colonel Thorneycroft. This occurred in the face of the vigorous protests of General Coke's Brigade-Major, the Officer Commanding the Middlesex Regiment, and others.

It is a matter for the Commander-in-Chief to decide whether there should be an investigation into the question of the unauthorized evacuation of Spion Kop.

CHARLES WARREN
Lieut.-General

Copy of a letter from General Woodgate to Sir C. Warren
Spion Kop, 24th January, 1900

Dear Sir Charles,

We got up about 4 o'clock, and rushed the position with three men wounded.

There were some few Boers, who seemed surprised, and bolted after firing a round or so, having one man killed. I believe there is another somewhere, but have not found him in the mist.

The latter did us well, and I pushed on a bit quicker than I perhaps should otherwise have done, lest it should lift before we get here. We have entrenched a position, and are, I hope, secure; but fog is too thick to see, so I retain Thorneycroft's men and Royal Engineers for a bit longer.

Thorneycroft's men attacked in fine style.

I had a noise made later to let you know that we had got in.

E. WOODGATE

Copy of letter from Lieut.-Colonel Thorneycroft to Sir C. Warren
Spion Kop, 24th January, 1900, 2.30 pm

To Sir C. Warren

Hung on till last extremity with old force. Some of Middlesex here now, and I hear Dorsets coming up, but force really inadequate to hold such a large perimeter. The enemy's guns are north-west, sweep the whole of the top of the hill. They also have guns east; cannot you bring artillery fire to bear on north-west guns? What reinforcements can you send to hold the hill tonight? We are badly in need of water. There are many killed and wounded.

ALEC THORNEYCROFT

If you wish to really make a certainty of hill for night, you must send more Infantry and attack enemy's guns.

Spion Kop, 24th January, 1900

3 pm: I have seen the above, and have ordered the Scottish Rifles and King's Royal Rifles to reinforce. The Middlesex Regiment, Dorsetshire Regiment, and Imperial Light Infantry have also gone up, Bethune's Mounted Infantry (120 strong) also reinforce. We appear to be holding our own at present.

J. TALBOT COKE, *Major-General*

From Colonel Thorneycroft to Chief Staff Officer to Sir Charles Warren
24th January, 1900

The troops which marched up here last night are quite done up—Lancashire Fusiliers, Royal Lancaster Regiment, and Thorneycroft's Mounted Infantry. They have had no water, and ammunition is running short. I consider that even with reinforcements which have arrived, that it is impossible to permanently hold this place so long as the enemy's guns can play on this hill. They have the long-range gun, three of shorter range, and one Maxim-Nordenfelt, which have swept the whole of the plateau since 8 am. I have not been able to ascertain the casualties, but they have been very heavy, especially in the regiments which came up last night. I request instructions as to what course I am to adopt. The enemy, at 6.30 pm, were firing heavily from both flanks with rifles, shell, and Nordenfelt, while a heavy rifle fire is kept up in front. It is all I can do to hold my own. If casualties go on occurring at present rate I shall barely hold out the night. A large number of stretcher bearers should be sent up, and also all water possible. The situation is critical.

ALEC THORNEYCROFT
Lieut.-Colonel

Note from Colonel Thorneycroft to Sir C. Warren

24th January, 1900

Regret to report that I have been obliged to abandon Spion Kop, as the position became untenable. I have withdrawn the troops in regular order, and will come to report as soon as possible.

ALEC THORNEYCROFT
Lieut.-Colonel

From Lieut.-Colonel A. W. Thorneycroft, Thorneycroft's Mounted Infantry, Commanding on Spion Kop, to the Chief Staff Officer to General Sir C. Warren

Camp, Trichard's Drift, 26th January, 1900

Sir,

On the night of the 23rd January, 1900, I rendezvoused with 18 officers and 180 men, Thorneycroft's Mounted Infantry, 2nd Bn. Lancashire Fusiliers, 2nd Bn. Royal Lancaster Regiment, and half company Royal Engineers, the whole under the command of General Woodgate. At 9 pm we started to march to the top of Spion Kop. I led the way with a small advanced party, crossed the dongas and advanced up the hill; on reaching the first plateau the force closed up in formation, and went on again. As the front broadened I got the Thorneycroft's Mounted Infantry into line, right across the hill, and the remainder followed in successive lines up the last slope, when we were suddenly challenged. I had ordered the men to lie down when challenged; they did so. The Boers opened fire from magazines, when I thought that they had emptied their magazines I gave the order to charge; an officer on my left gave the order to charge also, and the whole line advanced at the double and carried the crest line at 4 am, when I halted and re-formed the line. There were about 10 men wounded altogether.

Orders were immediately given by General Officer Commanding to form a trench and breastwork. There was a mist on the hill, and in the darkness and mist it was difficult to get the exact crest line for a good field of fire, and the boulders made it difficult to dig, but we made a rough trench and breastwork. At 4.30 a few Boers came up and began firing. The men lined the trench, but the picquets in front replied to the fire, and firing ceased for a time.

The Boers then returned with strong reinforcements from their camp, which lay concealed in a hollow on the side of the hill, and which was obscured in the mist; we sent out men in front to enable them to get a better field of fire; with two lulls in the firing, the mist rose about 8 am, when the rifle fire on both sides became heavy and the Boers opened fire from three guns and a Maxim-Nordenfelt.

The shrapnel fire was very accurate and burst well, sweeping the whole plateau. General Woodgate was wounded early in the action and Colonel Blomfield assumed command, but he, too, was wounded. At this time I was directing the movements of the Thorneycroft's Mounted Infantry, and sent out reinforcements to the firing line which was in advance of the trench; word was sent to me that General Sir C. Warren had heliographed that I was to assume command. I sent out more men to the flanks as the Boers were working round, and the replacing of casualties gradually absorbed all the men of the force. The firing became hotter on both sides, the Boers gradually advancing; twice the men charged out from the entrenchments in the centre and kept them back, but at length the entrenchment became the firing line in the centre (the left maintained their advanced position).

The Boers closed in on the right and centre. Some men of mixed regiments at right end of trench got up and put up their hands; three or four Boers came out and signalled their comrades to advance. I was the only officer in the trench on the left, and I got up and shouted to the leader of the Boers that I was the Commandant and that there was no surrender.

In order not to get mixed up in any discussion I called on all men to follow me, and retired to some rocks further back. The Boers opened a heavy fire on us. On reaching the rocks I saw a company of the Middlesex Regiment advancing, I collected them up to the rocks, and ordered all to advance again. This the men did, and we reoccupied the trench and crest line in front.

As the companies of the Middlesex arrived I pushed them on to reinforce, and was able to hold the whole line again. The men on the left of our defence, who were detached at some distance from the trench, had held their ground. The Imperial Light Infantry reinforced this part. The Boers then made a desperate endeavour to shell us out of the position, and the fire caused many casualties. The Scottish Rifles came up, and I pushed them up to the right and left flanks as they arrived. There was some discussion at this time as to who was in command, and the Officer Commanding Scottish Rifles said he would go and see General Talbot Coke, who was reported to be at the foot of the hill, to get orders. Up to this I had issued the orders, but as I only got a verbal message I did not understand that I had the temporary rank of Brigadier-General.

I continued to direct operations while the Officer Commanding Scottish Rifles went to see General Talbot Coke. General Coke said that Colonel Hill was in command, but I could not find him. The heavy fire continued, and the Boers brought a gun and Maxim-Nordenfelt to bear on us from the east, thus sweeping the plateau from the east, north, and northwest, and enfilading our trenches. The men held on all along the line, notwithstanding the terrific fire which was brought to bear on them, as the enemy's guns (which now numbered five and two Nordenfelts) were absolutely unmolested. When night began to close in I determined to take some steps, and a consultation was held. The Officer Commanding Scottish Rifles and Colonel Crofton were both of opinion that the hill was untenable. I entirely agreed with their view, and so I gave the order for the troops to withdraw on to the neck and ridge where the hospital was. It was now quite dark, and we went out to warn all to come in. The enemy still kept up a dropping fire. The regiments formed up near the neck, and marched off in formation, the Scottish Rifles forming the rear guard. I was obliged, owing to want of bearers, to leave a large number of wounded on the field.

In forming my decision as to retirement I was influenced by the following:

The superiority of the Boer artillery, inasmuch as their guns were placed in such positions as to prevent our artillery fire being brought to bear on them from the lower slopes near camp, or indeed from any other place.

By my not knowing what steps were being taken to supply me in the morning with guns, other than the mountain battery which, in my opinion, could not have lived under the long-range fire of the Boer artillery, and their close-range rifle fire.

By the total absence of water and provisions.

By the difficulty of entrenching on the top of hill, to make trench in any way cover from artillery fire with the few spades at my disposal, the ground being so full of rocks.

Finally, I did not see how the hill could be held unless the Boer artillery was silenced, and this was impossible.

Lieutenant Winston Churchill arrived when the troops had been marched off.

ALEC THORNEYCROFT
Lieut.-Colonel,
Commanding Thorneycroft's Mounted Infantry

Report of Major-General Talbot Coke, Officer Commanding 10th Brigade

Pontoon Bridge, 25th January, 1900

In accordance with your orders, General Woodgate assumed command of the column for the night attack, and settled his rendezvous near the Royal Engineer bivouac, for 7 pm, 23rd instant. I bivouacked on the hill upon which the Connaught Rangers' picquets are south of Three Tree Hill.

The first shots were fired at 3.40 am.

The valley between my position and Spion Kop, and also the top of that feature itself, was enveloped in mist until about 8 am, when it could be seen that our force held the schanzes on the summit. Shortly after it was seen to be exposed to a frontal fire from rifles, and to shell fire from its left front.

In accordance with orders communicated to me by you, to send a battalion to reinforce, a signal message was sent to the Imperial Light Infantry, which occupied a covering position towards Wright's Farm to proceed at once to support, moving by the right flank of the kop. The 2nd Bn. Dorsetshire Regiment was ordered to the place vacated by the Imperial Light Horse.

The position of Spion Kop was now seen to be exposed to a cross fire of artillery, and by your instructions I sent the Middlesex Regiment in support.

About 11.10 am, in consequence of the regrettable news about General Woodgate, at your order I proceeded to the kop myself. On arrival there, I found the track leading up very much congested, and, from information received, I formed the opinion that too many men were getting into the trenches and stone cover above, and becoming exposed to the artillery fire; I accordingly checked reinforcements. Soon after this, on my way up, an urgent message was received from Colonel Hill, who commanded at this time on the right, calling for reinforcements, as his line had actually fallen back before, and lost some prisoners to the Boers, who were pressing on in front. I accordingly sent up the rest of the Imperial Light Infantry available.

I now met Major Bayly, a Staff Officer, from the 4th Brigade, and he informed me that an urgent message for help had been received from Colonel Crofton, who commanded on Spion Kop, after General Woodgate was wounded. General Lyttelton had accordingly despatched the Scottish Rifles as an actual reinforcement, and a battalion of the King's Royal Rifles against the hill to the north-west of Spion Kop. It was on the further slope of this hill that one of the Vickers-Maxim guns was placed. (This battalion worked its way some distance up the hill, but its action did not materially affect the situation.)

I now again received an urgent appeal for support, this time for the centre and left. I sent the Scottish Rifles.

I now had only as a reserve Bethune's Mounted Infantry and the Dorsetshire Regiment. These I retained and they were not engaged at the actual front.

The shell fire was most galling, and was aimed not only at the summit, but at the crest of the spur leading up, along which reinforcements and parties bringing back wounded had to pass. The fire came:

1. From field guns firing shrapnel and common shell, situated, as I endeavoured to point out in a signal message to you, north–west of our position.
2. From a Vickers-Maxim, in about the same direction.
3. From a similar gun to the north-east.

All these were beyond the effective rifle fire, and our supporting Artillery on and about Three Tree Hill and on the Dragoon's Maxim position apparently could not see them, consequently they poured, unchecked, an uninterrupted cross fire on to our position from about 8 am till dark—10 hours.

Losses were very heavy, owing to the numbers necessarily assembled to hold back the Boer frontal attack, established under cover, and in which they showed gallantry in pushing forward to our lines. Colonel Crofton was now reported wounded, and the command of the troops in front devolved on Colonel Hill, Commanding 10th Brigade.

So the situation continued until 6 pm, when I wrote a report and despatched it to you by Colonel Morris, AAG [see p. 187]. I first showed this to Colonel Hill, and he concurred, even taking exception to my reference to a retirement. I had no doubt that the Infantry, which had so gallantly held its own all day, would be able to continue to do so when the shell fire abated at nightfall.

I accordingly went back to my reserves, having personally handed over command at the summit to Colonel Hill.

About 9.30 pm, in consequence of your orders, I left for your camp, leaving a Staff Officer (Captain Phillips) behind. The narrative must now be his.

About 11.30 pm this officer, who was sleeping, was awakened by the sound of men moving, and found a general retirement proceeding.

He allowed no one to pass after this, stopped the Scottish Rifles, and collected a large number of stragglers of the Dorset, Middlesex, and Imperial Light Infantry. Bethune's Mounted Infantry and the bulk of the Dorsets remained in position as posted in support to the front line. The other corps had gone down the hill.

He then published memorandum (*v*), attached, to all companies, except Lieut.-Colonel Thorneycroft, who had gone on; but they did not act upon it, urging that they had had distinct orders from Lieut.-Colonel Thorneycroft, who, as far as I knew, was only assisting Colonel Crofton in a portion of the front line, to retire.

We now held the spur to within about 300 yards of the summit, but the summit itself was evacuated. Signal communication could not be established at the moment, as the lamp which the signalling officer counted upon ran out of oil, and some time was lost in obtaining another.

About 1.30 am a person, not by his speech an Englishman, was brought in on suspicion by a picquet. He made a statement to the effect that a naval gun would shortly be brought up, and requested that it might not be fired on. This was the first intimation of any naval gun coming to Spion Kop.

About 2.20 am a naval officer reported that he had one 12-pr. gun below Spion Kop, near the donga on the west. He said he had orders to take this up to the summit. When asked whether he could do so before daylight, he said he could not. As it would be impossible to move the gun in any line after daybreak, on account of hostile fire, he was told to stand by in a place of safety. Signalling communication was now opened, and the attached message (*vi*) sent.

As Captain Phillips got no instructions, about 2.30 am he ordered vehicles back to a place of safety. All regimental wagons had been sent across by the Deputy-Assistant Adjutant-General (B), 5th Division.

Shortly after 4 am, there still being no orders, and a mass of transport, small-arm ammunition carts, etc., at the donga, steps were taken to cover this passage, and, with the concurrence of the Officer Commanding Dorsetshire Regiment, and Officer Commanding Scottish Rifles, certain dispositions were made with the latter battalion and about half the former. The other half of the Dorsetshire Regiment were employed in carrying away a large number of boxes (about 80) of small-arm ammunition, brought back from the front and elsewhere.

The Imperial Light Infantry, Middlesex, and Thorneycroft's had apparently gone home. Bethune's were dismissed.

It was now light, and Boer "sniping" commenced. Captain Phillips reported to me at the donga, about 4.45 am, when I was in possession of your order as to the pontoon crossing.

TALBOT COKE *Major-General,*
Commanding Right Attack

Attachments

(i)

Officer Commanding 10th Brigade, or any Officer:
Clear out left flank.

W. J. BONUS
Brigade-Major

(ii)

There are enough on the kopje, direct the others round the sides of the hill, 3.45 we hope to charge, at any rate at nightfall.

W. J. BONUS

(iii)

24th January, 1900, 5.05 pm

To General Talbot Coke,
We have now plenty of men for firing line, but the artillery fire from our left (west) is very harassing, I propose holding out till dark and then entrenching.

AUG. W. HILL
Lieut.-Colonel

(iv)

Officer Commanding Imperial Light Infantry:
Withdraw, and at once. 2 am.

W. J. BONUS
Brigade-Major

(v)

Officers Commanding Dorsetshire and Middlesex Regiments, Scottish Rifles, Imperial Light Horse:
This withdrawal is absolutely without the authority of either Major-General Coke or Sir Charles Warren.

The former was called away by the latter a little before 10 am.

When General Coke left the front about 6 pm our men were holding their own, and he left the situation as such, and reported that he could hold on.

Someone, without authority, has given orders to withdraw, and has incurred a grave responsibility. Were the General here, he would order an instant reoccupation of the heights.

H. E. PHILLIPS
Deputy-Assistant Adjutant-General

(*vi*)

Spion Kop, 25th January, 1900, 2.30 am
General Officer Commanding Three Tree Hill:
Summit of Spion Kop evacuated by our troops, which still hold lower slopes.
An unauthorized retirement took place.

Naval guns cannot reach summit before daylight; would be exposed to fire if attempted to do so by day.

PHILLIPS

(*vii*)

25th January, 1900, 2.30 am
Regimental Transport Officers:
All vehicles should be withdrawn to a place of safety, either towards Wright's Farm, or up the gully across the drift.

By order,

D. PHILLIPS

Extract from Commanding Royal Engineer's Diary, 5th Division, 24th January

Hatting's Spruit, 28th January, 1900
About 3 am (Commanding Royal Engineer, 5th Division) I was ordered by General Officer Commanding to take the second half company of the 17th Company Royal Engineers to Spion Kop, to make zigzag roads up the steepest parts for mules to take up water and the Mountain Battery.

The half company, under Captain Hedley, RE, and with Lieutenant Neill, RE, crossed the valley, and started work at dawn from the bottom of the slopes. I went to the top with Captain Hedley to choose out the best places, and on arrival we found the first half company, under Major Massey, RE, had almost completed their entrenching work, and he sent back all but a sub-section to assist in the road making. As the party was collecting tools and falling in, though the hilltop was in a thick cloud, the enemy opened musketry fire, and all troops took cover; the fire was not replied to and ceased after about 10 minutes. I then took the Royal Engineer party down. I also found water from small springs about halfway up the hill, and some men were set to collect it on the side of the hill that was not exposed to fire. Broad slides were also made down some of the boulder slopes up which guns might be dragged by hand. I returned to camp at 10.30 am.

At 10.30 Captain Buckland, RE, was sent to 17th Company to get sandbags taken to the hill. These (about 2,000) were taken by a small cart to the drift, and thence a rear company of a battalion going across (Dorsetshire Regiment), and the company native drivers of 17th Company Royal Engineers, carried about 1,000 up the hill. The remainder were left as a reserve at the drift to be taken up later. Captain Buckland returned to camp about 12.

At 12.30 Captain Buckland went to Venter's Spruit to procure three coils of 3-inch cable from 17th Company wagon, to enable the naval guns to be hauled up the hill at night. This was deposited at 17th Company camp about 2.30, to be ready for the guns when passing that way.

About 5 pm General Officer Commanding showed me a letter from Sir R. Buller, of which the following is an extract:

> If you send up either mountain guns or 12-pr. they should make some very strong epaulments, 8 feet thick, covering the gun from the line of its extreme fire. If this is done, any gun to attack it must come in front of it.

General Officer Commanding ordered me to be ready to do this, and also to take working parties at night to deepen the trenches on Spion Kop, so that they might screen the defenders from shell fire, being made 4 feet deep and sloping backwards inside, in the same form as the Boer "schanzes" are made.

I arranged with Officer Commanding 17th Company for the tools and for the half company that was now on Spion Kop to remain there, so that the officers and non-commissioned officers might superintend the working parties. At 9 pm General Officer Commanding ordered me to proceed and make epaulments for two naval guns (12-pr.), each to be 23 feet diameter, and to give 4 feet 3 inches cover; also epaulments as above for the Mountain Battery, and to improve the trenches. He gave me also a letter to Colonel Thorneycroft, urging him to hold the hill, and explaining the work I had been ordered to do. To carry the tools across, a party of 200 Somersetshire Light Infantry was detailed, and two reliefs, of 600 each, for the work were to be drawn from the reserve battalions on Spion Kop rear slopes.

About 12 pm [midnight], when I (with Captain Buckland, RE) had led the tool-carrying party about quarter the way up the slopes of Spion Kop, we met Colonel Thorneycroft coming down, having ordered a retirement. I gave him General Officer Commanding's letter, and he said it was too late, as the men, unsupported by guns, could not stay. He ordered me to take my party back. I sent them back with Captain Buckland, and then went forward to ascertain if the retirement was general. Finding it so, I walked up the valley to warn the officer in command of the naval gun of the altered situation, and prevent him risking his gun by moving it to the evacuated hill top.

The 37th Company Royal Engineers had been telegraphed for from Spearman's about 4 pm. It started at once, and arrived at the 17th Company camp about 1.30 am (25th). It then moved off with tools for Spion Kop, but was met by Captain Buckland, RE, who informed the Officer Commanding of the retirement. After proceeding a short distance, Major Cairnes, RE, Commanding, halted, and sent Captain Harper to the hill for information and orders. I found the company on my return about 2.30 am, and ordered it to bivouac where it was, and await further orders.

J. H. SIM, *Lieut.-Colonel, RE,*
Commanding Royal Engineer, 5th Division

From Major H. N. Sargent, DAAG (B), 5th Division, to General Officer Commanding, 5th Division
28th January, 1900

Sir,

With regard to the water supply on Spion Kop, I have the honour to report that the arrangements made were as follows:

All the available pack mules which could be procured—viz. 25—were utilized in carrying biscuit tins, filled with water, up the hill, the tins being refilled from water carts placed at the foot of Spion Kop. Each tin contained 8½ to 9 gallons of water. An officer was placed in charge of the water carts, and had a plentiful supply of spare tins, in addition to those carried by the mules. The mules were divided into two sections, each under an officer. These two sections of mules conveyed to the troops up the hill at each trip 425 gallons of water.

The water supply was kept going continuously during the day and late at night, with the exception of one break, caused by an order being given for one section of mules to bring up ammunition. In addition to the water conveyed on mules, there was a spring at the top of the hill, under Royal Engineer charge, which yielded a fair supply. I superintended generally the water supply myself, and made frequent enquiries as to whether the troops were getting sufficient quantity on top of the hill, and was told they were. A little delay was occasioned in the early part of the morning in looking for packalls, which I was told were in the camp, but which could not be obtained.

With regard to the food supplies, as soon as ever the drift near Spion Kop was made passable for our wagons, I collected the regimental wagons at the foot of the hill and instructed the regimental officers in charge to communicate with their units as to getting the supplies up the hill, which was done, and the boxes of biscuit and meat were taken up by hand.

H. N. SARGENT, *Major,*
DAAG (B)

From Major E. J. Williams, DAAG, to the General Officer Commanding, 5th Division
Springfield Camp, 28th January, 1900

Sir,

I have the honour to report for your information that, on the 24th January, I undertook to take water to the troops engaged at Spion Kop Hill. I guided 12 mules loaded with water to the trees near the top of the hill, arriving there about 12 noon. It was my intention to take the water to the field hospital on the top, but just as I arrived it was destroyed by shell fire, and the Medical Officer requested me to deposit the water where it was. The mules then made a second trip, and a water depot was established. After this all mules were seized to convey ammunition to the firing line. The Royal

Engineer company dug for water, which was found three-quarters of the way up the hill; it was thick, but fairly plentiful. At 3 pm I impressed some more mules, and from that time to 8 pm I continued to hurry up water to the water depot; also men were sent up with filled water bottles for distribution to the firing line. At 8 pm it was too dark for the mules to work, and although several fell over the cliff in getting up, there were at this hour several full boxes of water at different spots on the hill.

Supplies of all kinds were plentiful at the foot of the hill, and in conjunction with the water, I impressed all mules, horses, and straggling men to carry up rations before darkness came on, but it is impossible to say if these actually reached the front line, as it was impossible to see what was going on, owing to the troops going up and the stretcher bearers coming down.

E. J. WILLIAMS, *Major,*
DAAG

From Colonel A. W. Morris, AAG, 5th Division, to General Officer Commanding,
5th Division

28th January, 1900

Re the water supply on Spion Kop, I beg to report as follows:

I accompanied General Coke up Spion Kop, about 11 am, 24th instant. About half-way up the hill, just by the trees on the Kop, we came across a depot water supply, under a non-commissioned officer; I should say there were some 20 tins of water under this non-commissioned officer's charge. Numbers of men asked this non-commissioned officer for water, but he said it was reserved for the wounded. On this General Coke ordered a certain number of tins to be placed aside for the unwounded men, this the non-commissioned officer did at once; I think he set aside for the unwounded about five tins. No doubt many of the tins under his charge were empty, but I cannot say, as I was anxious to get further up the hill. However, when I got further up the hill, I saw several men bringing up by hand tins of water to the firing line. When I arrived at the firing line mules, loaded with ammunition, came up, and the General ordered the ammunition to be unloaded, and the mules sent back to the water supply depot to bring up more water tins. Whether these ever arrived I cannot say, as I shortly afterwards went down the hill to carry a letter to the General Officer Commanding, 5th Division.

Personally, I do not think the men were suffering very badly from want of water. I consider that, under the circumstances, nothing could have been better than the very difficult arrangements made for water supply; it was not plentiful, but sufficient for the purpose required.

A. W. MORRIS, *Colonel,*
AAG, 5th Division

From Field-Marshal Lord Roberts to the Secretary of State for War
Army Headquarters, South Africa, Camp Jacobsdal
17th February, 1900

My Lord,

In continuation of my letter, dated 13th February, 1900, I have the honour
to forward the enclosed telegram from General Sir Redvers Buller, requesting that certain words may be inserted in his despatch describing the
operations at Spion Kop.

ROBERTS, *Field-Marshal,*
Commander-in-Chief, South Africa

From the General Commanding-in-Chief, Natal, to the Military Secretary,
Cape Town

Spearman's Camp
31st January, 1900, 1.20 am

I posted my report on operations, 7th to 30th January, yesterday. When you
receive it, will you please insert after the words "enclose his report of his
operations", the following words:

As Sir Charles Warren does not allude to it, I may mention that on the 21st,
reinforced him by the 10th Brigade, made up to four complete battalions by
the addition to it of the 2nd Bn. Somersetshire Light Infantry and the
Imperial Light Infantry, a local corps 1,000 strong, for whose services he
particularly asked.—Buller

From General Sir Redvers Buller to the Secretary of State for War
2nd February, 1900

Secretary of State

I forward this. It is certain that General Warren did receive the message in
the terms he quoted, I saw it myself, and he also repeated it to General
Lyttelton, who has quoted it in his report. The signal station was not in or
very near the firing line.

I have an impression that the message referred to by Lieutenant Martin
was sent as well as that quoted by General Warren, but I have not been able
to verify this idea.

One thing is quite clear, about the time this message was sent, one portion of the front line did propose to surrender, and it was Colonel
Thorneycroft, and not Colonel Crofton, who refused the surrender and rallied the men.

REDVERS BULLER
General Officer Commanding

Hatting's Farm, 1st February, 1900

Chief of Staff,

With reference to my despatch on the "capture and evacuation of Spion Kop" already sent to you, I have now to forward a statement made by Colonel Crofton, Commanding 2nd Bn. Royal Lancaster Regiment, regarding the message which was signalled to me from the summit of Spion Kop, and which (as I have already reported) reached me in these words: "Reinforce at once, or all lost. General dead."

It seems certain that no message was written down at the transmitting station on Spion Kop, and the only written record is that of the message received at the receiving station with me.

C. WARREN, *Lieut.-General,*
Commanding 5th Division

From Colonel Crofton, Commanding 2nd Bn. Royal Lancaster Regiment, to the Brigade-Major, 11th Brigade

Hatting's Farm, 31st January, 1900

Sir,

I beg most strongly to protest against the message reputed to be sent by me from Spion Kop on the 24th, stating "All is lost." Such a message was never sent by me, nor did it ever enter my thoughts to send such a message, as the circumstances did not call for it. My message given to the Signalling Officer (Lieutenant Martin, Royal Lancaster Regiment) was: "General Woodgate dead; reinforcements urgently required." This I considered necessary, as the Boers were increasing in numbers every minute, and I had no means of ascertaining the numbers of the reserves that they had to draw upon.

I very much feared some error had occurred from the returned message, directing me under no circumstances to surrender, and I felt most deeply being superseded during the engagement by an officer so very much my junior.

MALBY CROFTON, *Colonel,*
Royal Lancaster Regiment

Hatting's Farm, 31st January, 1900

Officer Commanding Lancaster Regiment,

It would strengthen your case if you attached the message handed to Lieutenant Martin for despatch, and also call upon the signallers who signalled the message wrongly sent in your name to account for having despatched a message not properly authenticated by signature.

A. WYNNE, *AAG,*
Commanding 11th Brigade

31st January, 1900

Brigade-Major,
Lieutenant Martin's statement herewith.

MALBY CROFTON, *Colonel*

31st January, 1900

Lieutenant Martin, Signalling Officer,
Be good enough to let me have a full report hereon of the message I gave you to send from Spion Kop on the 24th, relative to General Woodgate's reported death, and asking for reinforcements.

MALBY CROFTON, *Colonel*

To Colonel Crofton, Commanding 2nd Bn. Royal Lancaster Regiment
Hatting's Farm, 31st January, 1900

Sir,
On 24th instant, soon after firing began, I was looking for some signallers, you met me, and said, "I must have a signaller;" I said, "I am looking for them."

You replied: "Get them at once, and send a message to Sir Charles Warren and say General Woodgate is dead, and ask for reinforcements at once."

I called for signallers, and two men of 2nd Bn. Lancashire Fusiliers ran up. We went to a spot that I selected, and found that there was already a signaller there, Private Goodyear, of the West Yorkshire Regiment (he was with Lieutenant Doomer, RA, observing the effect of artillery fire).

I said to Private Goodyear, "You might send a message for me whilst the helio is being put up."

I told him to call up "G.O.C." the station I wished to communicate with, and to say, "General Woodgate is killed; send reinforcements at once." I did not write the message down, as I had no paper.

A. R. MARTIN, *Lieutenant,*
2nd Bn. Royal Lancaster Regiment

Hatting's Farm, 31st January, 1900

AAG, 5th Division,
Forwarded. It is unfortunate that the message was not written. I believe the order is that signallers should not accept any message that is not written and signed.

A. WYNNE, *Major-General,*
Commanding 11th Brigade

FURTHER REPORTS ON TUGELA RIVER AND SPION KOP OPERATIONS

From the General Commanding-in-Chief, Natal, to the Secretary of State for War
Spearman's Hill Camp, 30th January, 1900

Sir,

I have the honour to forward to you the enclosed reports relative to recent operations in the vicinity of the River Tugela:

I ordered these operations to be undertaken on the eastern line, in order to free me as much as possible whilst operating on the western line.

I also forward a report from Major-General the Hon. N. G. Lyttelton, on the action taken by him during the operations of 24th January, but this should be read in connection with Sir C. Warren's of that day.

REDVERS BULLER, *General*

Chieveley Camp, 19th January, 1900

The Brigade Major,
Fusilier Brigade, Chieveley,

With reference to this day's operations towards Robinson's Drift, as the Mounted Infantry under my command got into difficulties down by the river, I beg to report, for the information of the General Officer Commanding, my orders to that unit.

Lieutenant Renton, two other officers, and 40 non-commissioned officers and men reported themselves to me at 5 am here. I told Lieutenant Renton, who had been out towards the drift with the General Officer Commanding and myself the previous evening, that I was going to move down with my Infantry and guns towards the drift, and that I wanted him to cover my advance and protect my flanks with his Mounted Infantry. I said, "Information is what I want, as I can tackle the enemy should they

191

come on." I told him I should like one officer and 15 men for each flank, and that 10 men would do very well for the front; on this he went away, and sent his men out. I told him my formation with Infantry and guns, and where I should be; I received no reports from him, but some two hours after, when I eventually arrived with my extended line on a ridge of hills overlooking the river and Robinson's Drift, some 3,200 yards from it, I met Lieutenant Renton, who reported to me that the enemy were not our side of the river, and that one or more of his men had been down to the drift and said it was unfordable. I then told him I much wanted to know for certain about the drift, and anything that could be seen of the enemy or their defences the other side, and suggested a place for a cossack post, where his men would be under cover and out of sight, and to try from there to get the information, but I repeated several times, "I do not want your men to get fired upon." Lieutenant Renton went down to this place, reported it suitable, and posted his men.

About that time I got the report of 1,000 of enemy on my left flank, which caused me to send Lieutenant Renton off to his men on that flank, and myself to watch it and give sundry orders; this report turned out to be false, and during this time we had seen the Boers moving down the hill the other side of the river and occupy different places. It was then that I found out that there were several Mounted Infantry scouts with their horses along the river in my front; they were, I believe, some of the 10 men who had covered my front in the morning, extended to some 200 yards, had gone down to the river and remained there; the Boers having come down towards the river they were in a very awkward position, as they could not withdraw without being under Boer fire. The difficulty was to extricate the men, I ordered up the two Mountain Battery guns and got them into action, and also requested the naval guns to shell a certain donga, which they did; further, my machine guns got into action, and tried some long-range volleys. The two latter methods were no good, but under cover of the guns several were got away; eventually, Lieutenant Renton reported to me that he had, as far as he could make out, four or five men away and three horses.

I left Lieutenant Renton and a sufficient force of Mounted Infantry to watch for his men, as I expected they would get away when the Boers retired back from the river or else under cover of darkness. I never gave Lieutenant Renton to understand he had to hold the river line or seize the drift; 10 men would not have been much good for such an undertaking. The cossack post from which I thought he could have reconnoitred the drift should, in my opinion, have been done by one or two men dismounted.

I commend the pluck of the men who came back from the river, two of them under a very hot fire. One man on foot made his way back across the open, and Lieutenant Jones, of the 8th Hussars, galloped down, picked him up, and brought him in on his horse, a plucky action, though, as it happened, he was not hotly fired on. Further, two men on the right, galloping on their horses, fell; one was left without a horse, and appeared to be wounded. Captain and Adjutant Braithwaite at once galloped out and picked the man up; he had damaged his foot, but had not been shot.

C. THOROLD, *Lieut.-Colonel,*
Commanding 1st Bn. Royal Welsh Fusiliers

Camp, Chieveley, 20th January, 1900

Chief of Staff,

Transmitted. I have communicated the same to General Officer Commanding Lines of Communication, Maritzburg.

I very much regret these most unnecessary casualties. It was distinctly explained to Captain Renton, and by him to his men, that they were going out to reconnoitre, not to fight.

It was not necessary for the scouts to go right down to the river bank, as a bare ridge overlooks the river at about 1,000 yards from the bank.

Having reached the river bank, however, the scouts should have withdrawn to high ground, as Colonel Thorold thought they had done. I have carefully questioned the sergeant who was in command of the scouts in front, and he says that five or six of his men dismounted on the bank and took good cover. He went along the river to examine the drift, and after a long time the Boers opened fire, and he shouted out to retire, and he and four of his men galloped back, being hotly fired upon. Two of the men led their horses wounded, and returning on foot, were helped back by two mounted officers. The remaining men apparently kept under cover, and lost their opportunity of retiring.

After the force had withdrawn, three Boers were seen to leave the trenches and go down to the bank, and the six men, South African Light Horse, were seen all together, and taking off their coats on the south bank. Shortly after, nine or ten men were seen on the north bank moving away from the river towards the hills. It is concluded our men waded across and surrendered, and they were not wounded.

G. BARTON, *Major-General,*
Commanding at Chieveley

Report of action near Potgieter's, 20th January, 1900

Camp over Potgieter's Drift

Sir,

Having received a telegram from Lieut.-General Sir C. Warren early in the morning of the 20th instant, that he was attacking the enemy north of Fair View, and that a demonstration by me against the Boer position opposite the drift might create a useful diversion, I ordered the 3rd Bn. King's Royal Rifles to advance and occupy some small kopjes on the left and a farmhouse on the right, about midway between my position and the Boers. This was accordingly done at about 10 am, and the balloon was also sent forward, in order to get a nearer and a better view. There was a donga to the right front of the farmhouse, about 300 yards in advance, which was occupied by one company, Captain Beaumont's. This company immediately came under a sharp fire at comparatively short range, and the party in the farmhouse were also fired on to a lesser degree. For some hours the damage done was quite trifling, one man only had been hit by 3 pm; but later on, one if not two machine guns were brought up, and casualties began to occur. It was very difficult to say from whence the fire came until the machine guns opened, probably from small parties concealed behind rocks and banks. To relieve the former, fire was opened by two naval 12-prs and two howitzers, assisted by the two 4.7-inch guns, and at about 5 pm the 64th Field Battery moved out and opened fire at about 2,400 yards from the Boers. The fire appeared singularly effective, searching the hillsides thoroughly, and the Boers were seen bolting in every direction from the shells. Their fire was promptly silenced, and there is good reason to believe that two machine guns were knocked out. As usual, it is impossible to say what loss the Boers suffered, but judging from their inability to face the shell fire and the accuracy of our fire, there must have been some; moreover, an ambulance was seen moving along the position.

At 5.30 pm the 2nd Bn. Scottish Rifles and the 1st Bn. Rifle Brigade moved out covered by artillery fire, and the whole force eventually withdrew under cover of night. I should add that the force on the left was also fired upon, but only one or two men were hit. It is hoped that the demonstration had some effect in forcing the enemy to their trenches, and preventing them from assisting the force fighting Sir C. Warren, which was the object aimed at. The King's Royal Rifles had a long and trying day, and I was quite satisfied with their behaviour.

The balloon was hit by a bullet, and Captain Phillips, RE, also had a narrow escape while in the air. Useful work in investigating the Boer position and in directing our fire was done by the balloon officers.

N. G. Lyttelton, *Major-General,*
Commanding 4th Infantry Brigade

From Officer Commanding Bethune's Mounted Infantry to Brigade-Major, 4th Brigade

Potgieter's Drift, 21st January, 1900

I moved out yesterday with two squadrons of my regiment in the direction of Swartz Kop, and skirmished towards the hills on the east of the enemy's position, opposite Swartz Kop. We drew the enemy's fire, and made them expose themselves. There were about 300 to 400 men on the hill. We killed one Boer and wounded one horse. Ammunition expended: 325 rounds. No casualties on our side. Returned to camp 7.15 pm.

The squadron that went over Wagon Drift reports that a heavy engagement was going on. A shell burst among them, killing one horse and wounding two others. Three rifles were lost by this squadron while crossing the river. I have ordered a Court of Enquiry to enquire into the matter.

E. BETHUNE, *Lieut.-Colonel,*
Commanding Bethune's Mounted Infantry

Chieveley, 23rd January, 1900

Chief of Staff,

Such persistent reports have reached the Intelligence Department at Headquarters, from various sources, regarding the Boers having left Cingol, Hlangwani, and even Colenso, that I determined to clear up the matter today by a reconnaissance in such force as I could muster. For this purpose (as I have only two battalions here) Colonel Blagrove brought from Frere 120 mounted men and two guns, and 400 men of the Rifle battalion, who were railed over.

I moved two guns (naval 12-prs) to the advanced gun position west of the railway, escorted by 300 Riflemen; left flank covered by 50 South African Light Horse. Colonel Blagrove, with 170 mounted men and two field guns, moved to Hussar Hill to reconnoitre. I supported him with 10 companies of Royal Fusiliers and Royal Welsh Fusiliers, and two naval 12-prs, which I moved forward far enough to the right front to shell Hlangwani and the Boer camp between Nât Hill and Bloy's Farm.

Work was continuing in the trenches about Colenso, and these were shelled. A pont and ferry boat were discovered above Colenso road bridge, and a landing stage; Boers were seen to cross to the south side, and they were shelled with effect.

Colonel Blagrove reconnoitred from the right in a masterly manner, and located a considerable number of Boers, who opposed him in trenches, which were peppered effectually by the field guns.

Unfortunately, a young officer of Bethune's Mounted Infantry, while reconnoitring, got 10 men into a stone kraal, and they were being surrounded when Colonel Blagrove succeeded in extricating the officer and seven men. Three appear to have been captured, as they are missing. The Boers showed considerable determination, and followed up the mounted men when withdrawing, but I was able to check their offensive movement by shell fire from the 12-prs, which were ably handled by Lieutenant Richards, RN. It is estimated that from 300 to 500 actually opposed Colonel Blagrove; his entire force was under a heavy fire, and there is no doubt the position is still strongly held by the Boers.

I saw numbers of Boers about the trenches at Fort Wylie and kopjes near there, but I did not take my Infantry within rifle range of the river.

My Cavalry scouts were fired at from Colenso, and from the river bank above Colenso.

The Boers' train steamed rapidly out of Colenso, and the 12-prs failed to hit it.

My casualties will be reported later. They are, I believe, four men missing, five wounded, including Captain de Rougemont, South African Light Horse, severely wounded, and not yet brought to camp, but an ambulance has gone to fetch him.

The Cingol camp is still occupied, and supplied today two Boer contingents to reinforce the Hlangwani force.

G. BARTON, *Major-General,*
Commanding at Chieveley

P.S. During the day the Boers did not reply with a gun, but, according to information of my scouts, there is still one on Hlangwani, and several at Colenso, the latter probably of no great value.

G.B.

From Officer Commanding Troops, Frere, to Chief of Staff
Frere, 24th January, 1900

Sir,

I have the honour to inform you that, on the 23rd instant, I co-operated with Major-General Barton in a demonstration in front of Colenso, with troops from Frere, as per margin.

Under instructions from General Barton, I reconnoitred with the mounted troops, via Hussar Hill, towards Hlangwani Mountain.

Having cleared the ridges in front by scouts of the South African Light Horse and Bethune's Mounted Infantry, the guns came into action on Hussar Ridge, and shelled the trenches on Hlangwani and slopes to the south-east, supported by a half squadron 14th Hussars. At the same time the South African Light Horse, Bethune's Mounted Infantry, and Mounted Infantry 4th and 5th Brigades, advanced and reconnoitred the enemy's position. The latter came on in considerable force, and after closely reconnoitring the enemy's position, the Colonial troops and Mounted Infantry were compelled to fall back, and I retired on Chieveley. The reconnaissance was completely successful in compelling the enemy to disclose their positions, and showed that Hlangwani Mountain is held in considerable strength. A small party of Bethune's Mounted Infantry was for a time isolated in a kraal somewhat far advanced, and in covering their retirement, casualties occurred.

I regret to say that Captain de Rougemont, of the South African Light Horse, from Chieveley, was dangerously wounded and is since dead. Captain Dalton, RAMC, proceeded, in the most gallant manner to his assistance, but was severely wounded whilst attending him.

H. BLAGROVE, *Lieut.-Colonel,*
Commanding Troops, Frere

Camp, Potgieter's, 25th January, 1900

Chief of Staff,

I have the honour to report as follows:

On my return from the kopjes at 10 am, I received a telegram from Sir C. Warren, marked A. This appeared to be so urgent that I ordered two squadrons of Bethune's Mounted Infantry, the Scottish Rifles, and the King's Royal Rifles, to cross at the Kaffir Drift, under Naval Gun Plateau, with these orders, the two first to join Sir C. Warren's extreme right and place themselves under the orders of the General Officer Commanding at that point.

Message B was received at 10.15 am. The first corps crossed—Bethune's at 11.45 am, Scottish Rifles, 12.30 pm, and King's Royal Rifles at 1 pm. As the first parties were crossing, I noticed that strong reinforcements were reaching Sir C. Warren's right, which was unduly crowded with troops. It seemed unnecessary to send more men then, and with a view of creating a diversion, I directed Colonel Riddell to move his battalion against Sugar Loaf Hill, and the hill between it and the right of the main position. I had misgivings that there was too wide an interval, and in instructing Colonel Riddell verbally, I told him to use extreme caution, sending out scouts and only extending two companies, and having a half battalion in reserve. I told him I could not give him definite instructions, and must leave a good deal to his discretion.

At about 2.30 pm I received message C from Major Bayly, and at once ordered, by signal, the Officer Commanding King's Royal Rifles to retire slowly until further orders. See message D. This order was again repeated by signal at 3.30 pm (message E), and by mounted orderly at 4.50 pm (message F). Considerable delay appears to have occurred before any of these were received, the hills being some distance in rear of the battalion, and it was not till 5 pm that I received helio message G.

At 5.15 pm I saw that a portion of the battalion had reached the top of the hill, and at 6 pm I received flag message H from Officer Commanding who was at top of Sugar Loaf. At 6 pm I sent message K by mounted orderly, ordering him to retire under cover of darkness, which was done without loss; I had no idea that the battalion was anywhere near the top of the hill. The advance was wonderfully well carried out, and the ascent of the precipitous hillside was a very fine feat, of which the battalion may be justly proud. I greatly regret the losses incurred, but I do not think they were fruitless. I have learnt that the men on Sir C. Warren's right say that without this diversion they could not have held their position, and I have heard from Sir C. Warren (message L) that my assistance had been most valuable.

N. G. LYTTELTON, Major-General,
Commanding 4th Infantry Brigade

Copies of telegrams, etc. of 24th January, 1900

(A)
From Sir Charles Warren to General Lyttelton (received 24th January, 1900, 10 am)

Give every assistance you can on your side. This side is clear, but the enemy are too strong on your side, and Crofton telegraphs that if assistance is not given at once all is lost. I am sending up two battalions, but they will take some time to get up.

(B)
From some person unknown to General Lyttelton (received 24th January, 1900, 10.15 am)

We occupy all the crest on top of hill, being heavily attacked from your side. Help us. Spion Kop.

(C)
From Major Bayly, Staff Officer to General Lyttelton (received 24th January, 1900, 2.30 pm)

Very hot fire here, near flag, which is our observing station; only just holding our own. Bethune's and Scottish Rifles are now coming up. Do not think that King's Royal Rifles can get up on right; it is held by Boers. We are only holding up to your left of saddle. A heavy fire from Boers on our north-west, where they have a gun, which is causing damage. Cannot see left of our line or the Boers. Water badly wanted.

(D)
From Brigade-Major, 4th Brigade, to Officer Commanding King's Royal Rifles (by heliograph) (sent 24th January, 1900, 3 pm)

Retire steadily until further orders.

(E)
From Brigade-Major, 4th Brigade, to Officer Commanding King's Royal Rifles (by heliograph) (sent 24th January, 1900, 3.30 pm)

Retire steadily till further orders. Please say how last message was transmitted.

(F)
From Brigade-Major, 4th Brigade, to Officer Commanding King's Royal Rifles (by mounted orderly) (sent 24th January, 1900, 4.50 pm)

No. 141. Unless the enemy has retired you will fall back, under cover of darkness, to the bridge just made, which is near the ford you crossed at, and where a fire will be lit, after dark, to guide you. Keep this orderly if of any use. Manners is at ford, with stretcher bearers, if you want any. Hope all is well.

(G)

From Officer Commanding King's Royal Rifles to Brigade-Major (by heliograph)
(received 24th January, 1900, 5 pm)

If I can recall the advanced sections I will do so, but it is difficult to communicate, and the hill is fearfully steep. I have two or three wounded to help down.

(H)

From Officer Commanding King's Royal Rifles to Brigade-Major (by flag)
(received 24th January, 1900, 6 pm)

We are on top of the hill. Unless I get orders to retire I shall stay here.

(J)

From Brigade-Major to Officer Commanding King's Royal Rifles (by flag) (received
24th January, 1900, 6 pm)

Retire when dark.

(K)

From Brigade-Major to Officer Commanding King's Royal Rifles (by mounted
orderly) (sent 24th January, 1900, 6 pm)

No. 144. I am sending you a signal lamp. The General Officer Commanding considers you could not hold the Sugar Loaf unsupported, and having no troops to support you with, he orders a retirement across the foot-bridge below ford, and bivouac on Naval Gun Plateau. Please report when you get in. I have rum, tea, and wood ready for you.

(L)

From General Warren to General Lyttelton (by wire) (received 24th January,
1900, 6.50 pm)

The assistance you are giving most valuable. We shall try to remain in status quo during tomorrow. Balloon would be of incalculable value.

From the General Officer Commanding, Natal, to the Secretary of State for War
Spearman's Hill Camp, 30th January, 1900

Sir,

In continuation of my letter of this date, I have the honour to enclose two additional reports from Major-General Barton, as under:

Report dated 24th January, relative to the action of a party of the enemy in firing upon and severely wounding Captain Dalton, RAMC, whilst attending to a wounded officer.

Report dated 25th January, relative to the same, and to the death of Captain de Rougemont, South African Light Horse.

This is a regrettable circumstance. As a rule the enemy treat our wounded with great kindness.

REDVERS BULLER, *General*

Camp, Chieveley, 24th January, 1900

The Chief of the Staff,
Headquarters,
I have the honour to make the following report for information of the General Commanding in Natal.

I have just seen Surgeon-Captain Dalton, RAMC, who was brought in wounded this morning, and he made the following statement to me, viz:

> I was out with a squadron of the 14th Hussars yesterday, and during the engagement near Hlangwani, Lieut.-Colonel Blagrove pointed to a man on the ground, and said, "There's a wounded man." I went across and found an officer of the South African Light Horse, and four men of the Mounted Infantry, who had carried the wounded officer to the spot for safety from fire. I dismounted, and was attending to the wounded officer, when some Boers rode up from the flank to within about 100 yards. I gave my white handkerchief to one of the men, and told him to wave it, which he did. I told another to take the Geneva Cross armlet off my arm and hold it up, which he did. In spite of this, they opened fire and shot two of us, myself and one of the men.

Apart from the signals made, there cannot possibly have been any shadow of doubt as to the meaning of the little group of men, kneeling and bending over the prostrate form of the dangerously wounded officer.

I fear that Captain Dalton's wound is very dangerous, as he was struck in the abdomen. He is a fine and gallant officer, wearing, besides war decorations, the medal of the Royal Humane Society.

I refrain from making any comment on the dastardly conduct of the Boers on this occasion.

G. BARTON, *Major-General,*
Commanding at Chieveley

Chieveley, 25th January, 1900

Chief of the Staff,
In continuation of my letter of the 23rd instant, I regret that my casualties on that date amounted to one officer and three men killed, one officer and five men wounded, and 12 men missing,.

It appears that as the officer of Bethune's Mounted Infantry (Lieutenant Coke) had returned from the kraal referred to in my letter, Colonel Blagrove had been informed that the officer and seven men had escaped. This, however, was not the case, as 11 of Bethune's Mounted Infantry are missing, and were no doubt taken prisoners.

As regards the other casualties, Captain Dalton's condition being more favourable, I again questioned him as to what occurred when he was wounded, and he has supplied the following further information:

> When the Boers fired upon the party attending to Captain de Rougemont, it appears that of the four men who had carried that officer away, one was killed, two were wounded, and one was taken prisoner. When the Boers came up to them, they took from the men's pockets all they required and went away. Of the two wounded men, one afterwards died.

Owing to the above circumstance, I deeply regret to say that Captain de Rougemont was not found until the following morning.

Captain Dalton, however, said that the wound was very dangerous, and the case hopeless from the first, and it appears that the deceased officer became delirious soon after he was wounded, and remained so until he died in the ambulance on his way to camp.

The Medical Officers with lanterns were searching the ground until a late hour on the 23rd to find Captain de Rougemont, not knowing that all his attendants were *hors de combat.*

G. BARTON, *Major-General,*
Commanding at Chieveley

OPERATIONS AFTER THE EVACUATION OF SPION KOP
25TH JANUARY–7TH FEBRUARY 1900

From General Sir Redvers Buller, Commanding in Natal, to the Secretary of State for War

Camp Springfield, 8th February, 1900

(Extract)

I have the honour to report that on the 25th January, as already reported, I decided it was desirable to withdraw my force from the west of Spion Kop. While they had been there, the enemy had very considerably strengthened his right, so that any attempt to advance our left would probably have been unsuccessful, while the failure to hold Spion Kop proved the strength of the enemy in front of our right.

I therefore withdrew the force and commenced preparations for a trial by another route. These preparations involved the formation of a road to the top of a very precipitous hill and the occupation of its summit by guns. Unfortunately the weather was very unpropitious and seriously retarded this work. Begun on the 27th, by the evening of the 3rd February it was completed—about 1½ miles of road through a very difficult country having been made up a steep hill-side, and six naval 12-pr, two 15-pr Royal Field Artillery, and six mountain battery Royal Artillery guns having been got to the top.

Unfortunately, the weather was too bad to admit of our getting up the two 5-inch guns which we had hoped to mount there. I must bear witness to the admirable way in which the Naval Brigade, the Royal Artillery, the Royal Engineers, and the Royal Scots Fusiliers worked at this arduous duty.

In the absence of any Officer Commanding Royal Artillery in Natal, I asked Majors Findlay and Apsley Smith, Royal Artillery, to advise me as to the best positions for the various guns at my disposal, and was much obliged by their advice.

The demonstration in front of Brakfontein was very well made by the 11th Brigade under General Wynne. The men in their extreme keenness got rather closer to the positions than I had wished, but though a very heavy fire both of shell and rifle was opened upon them, they retired when ordered in admirable order and with, I am thankful to say, but slight loss.

The batteries were also under heavy fire, the men fighting their guns as coolly as if on parade: their loss, fortunately, was small.

As soon as sufficient time had been given to get the Brakfontein trenches fully occupied, the batteries moved in succession from the left to the right over No. 2 Pontoon Bridge which had been constructed the night before, and the 4th Brigade under General Lyttelton supported by the 2nd Division advanced under cover of their fire to cover the construction of No. 3 Pontoon Bridge which was well and rapidly thrown under a well directed but long range fire.

As soon as it was completed the 2nd Durham Light Infantry supported by the 1st Rifle Brigade advanced on Vaal Krantz under a heavy fire from the hill and the dongas on the right, causing considerable loss, but the men would not be denied and the position was soon taken. It was later on occupied by the whole of the 4th Brigade, Mungers Farm being occupied by a battalion of the 2nd Brigade. The position thus gained was held till the following morning.

On the 6th, No. 2 Pontoon Bridge was taken up and reconstructed at the back of Vaal Krantz instead, to facilitate communication.

I should have mentioned that Vaal Krantz was occupied by a gun and some 120 of the enemy, of these the Field Cornet in charge went off with about half and the gun as we approached, most of the rest were killed by our shell and infantry fire, but we took six prisoners. I am sorry to have to report that among the men on the hill were several armed Kaffirs—Lieutenant Lambton of the Durham Light Infantry was wounded by one—and during the day we had ocular demonstration that the stories we had heard of the enemy arming natives to fight against us are not untrue.

We also all saw a gun detachment, and we thought the gun also, conveyed by the enemy to a gun position in an ambulance flying the Geneva flag.

On the evening of the 6th I relieved the 4th Brigade on Vaal Krantz by the 2nd Brigade, and all that and the following day I endeavoured to entrench a position on the hill but found the ground too rocky.

It was also raked by two guns which none of mine could silence, a 75 mm Creusot on Spion Kop, and a 15 cm Creusot on the top of the hill above Doorn Kloof. The first they could not see, the second was on a sort of truck mounting, its muzzle showed up when it fired and then it disappeared. Our

4.7, 12-pr naval, and 5-inch guns fired at it for the two days, they twice blew up its magazine or ammunition store, but failed to silence the gun.

As the safe tenure of Vaal Krantz was indispensable for further operations, and I could neither entrench there owing to the extremely rocky nature of the ground, nor protect it from Artillery fire, I concluded that an advance by that route would be impossible, and, recalling the 2nd Brigade at sunset, determined to try another passage.

As an illustration of the nature of the country I may mention that on the 5th the enemy were bringing what appeared to be a Maxim-Nordenfeldt gun drawn by eight horses on a galloping carriage across the back of the position from west to east—as they crossed the Mungers Farm–Klipport Road, they came under the fire of our guns on Swartz Kop. The first shell went very close, and the team turned sharp to the right and disappeared, they seemed to have fallen over into a donga, a shell followed them in, and we saw no more of them till they reappeared at least a mile off out of another donga, short of two horses and a man. The country was honeycombed with these dongas, all of which had been utilised for defence.

Of the prisoners we took, two, an Austrian and an Englishman, belonged to the Johannesburg Commando. They described their Commando as a mixture of all nationalities under the sun except Dutch, the common language being English. One of them said that in Johannesburg alone there were now over 2,000 widows who still believed their husbands to be alive.

EVENTS LEADING TO THE END OF THE SIEGE OF LADYSMITH

From Lieut.-General Sir George White VC, GCB, GCSI, GCIE, late Commanding the Ladysmith Garrison, to the Chief of the Staff to the Field-Marshal Commanding-in-Chief in South Africa

Cape Town, 23rd March, 1900

Sir,

In my despatch dated 2nd December, 1899, addressed to the Secretary of State for War, and forwarded through you, I brought down the history of events relating to the force under my command to the evening of 30th October, 1899. On the morning of the following day, General the Right Honourable Sir Redvers Buller, VC, GCB, KCMG, arrived at Cape Town and assumed command of the whole of the forces in South Africa. On the 10th January, 1900, Field-Marshal Lord Roberts took over the chief command. I have now the honour to report, for his Lordship's information, the events which have taken place from that date until the 1st March, 1900, on which day Sir Redvers Buller arrived in Ladysmith, having successfully carried out the relief of this long besieged town.

It will be remembered that during October, 1899, the forces of the Orange Free State and the South African Republic had been gradually converging on Ladysmith from west and north, and that, although my troops had successfully encountered portions of the enemy's armies at Talana, Elandslaagte, and Rietfontein, the battle of Lombard's Kop on 30th October had proved that the numbers and mobility of the Boer forces, when once concentrated, were too great to admit of any prospect of victory should I continue with inferior numbers to oppose them in the open field. The task before me was the protection from invasion by the Boers of

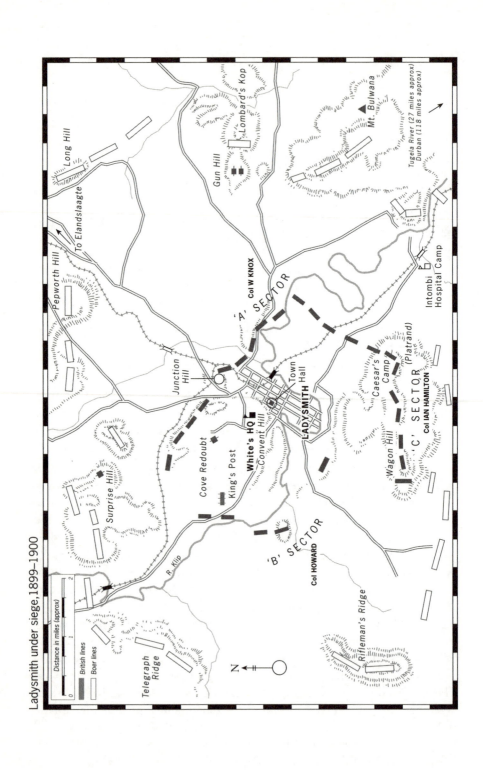

Ladysmith under siege, 1899–1900

Long Hill

To Elandslaagte

'Lombard's Kop

Gun Hill

Mt. Bulwana

Tugela River (27 miles approx)
Durban (118 miles approx)

Pepworth Hill

'A' SECTOR
Col W KNOX

Junction Hill

Intombi
Hospital Camp

Surprise Hill

Cove Redoubt

White's HQ
Convent Hill

King's Post

Caesar's
Camp

LADYSMITH
Town
Hall

Wagon Hill

'C' SECTOR (Platrand)
Col IAN HAMILTON

R. Klip

'B' SECTOR
Col HOWARD

Telegraph
Ridge

Rifleman's Ridge

N

Distance in miles (approx)

British lines

Boer lines

0   2

as large a portion as possible of the Colony of Natal, and especially of Pietermaritzburg, the capital of that Colony and the seat of its Government; and I had now to consider how this could be best ensured.

On 31st October General Sir Redvers Buller telegraphed to me as follows: "Can you not entrench and await events, if not at Ladysmith then behind the Tugela at Colenso?" On the same date I replied, stating my intention to hold on to Ladysmith, and on 1st November I received Sir Redvers Buller's approval of this course in a telegram which commenced as follows: "I agree that you do best to remain at Ladysmith, though Colenso and line of Tugela River look tempting."

It may be well to state here shortly the reasons which governed my choice of this position. Ladysmith is the most important town in northern Natal, and there was reason to believe that the enemy attached very great and perhaps even undue importance to obtaining possession of it. It was suspected then, and the suspicion has since been confirmed that the occupation of that town by the Boer forces had been decided on by the disloyal Dutch in both Colonies as the signal for a general rising; as, in fact, a material guarantee that the power of the combined Republics was really capable of dealing with any force the British Empire was able to place in the field against them. Our withdrawal would, therefore, have brought about an insurrection so widespread as to have very materially increased our difficulties. Strategically the town was important as being the junction of the railways which enter Natal from the Transvaal and the Orange Free State, and until the Republics could gain possession of that junction their necessarily divergent lines of supply and communication prevented their enjoying to the full the advantages of combined action. Tactically the place was already partially prepared for defence and offered a natural position of some strength; and although the perimeter which must be occupied was very great for the number of troops available, yet it afforded a possibility of maintaining a protracted defence against superior numbers. On the other hand, the mere fact of a retirement behind the Tugela would have had a moral effect at least equal to a serious defeat, and would have involved the abandonment to the enemy of a large town full of an English population, men, women, and children; and of a mass of stores and munitions of war which had been already collected there before my arrival in South Africa, and had since been increased.

The line of the Tugela from the Drakensberg to the Buffalo River is some 80 miles long, and in a dry season, such as last November, can be crossed on foot almost anywhere. Against an enemy with more than double my numbers, and three times my mobility, I could not hope to maintain such a line with my small force, and any attempt to prevent their turning my flanks could only have resulted in such a weakening of my centre as would have led to its being pierced. Once my flank was turned on the line of the river the enemy would have been nearer Pietermaritzburg than I should have been, and a rapid withdrawal by rail for the defence of the capital would have been inevitable. Even there it would have been impossible to make a prolonged defence without leaving it open to the enemy to occupy the important port of Durban, through which alone supplies and reinforcements could arrive, and for the defence of which another retreat would have become eventually essential; thus abandoning to the enemy the whole Colony of Natal from Lang's Nek to the sea. On the other hand, I was confident of holding out at Ladysmith as long as might be necessary, and I saw clearly that so long as I maintained myself there I could occupy the great mass of the Boer armies, and prevent them sending more than small flying columns south of the Tugela, which the British and Colonial forces in my rear, aided by such reinforcements as might be shortly expected, could deal with without much difficulty. Accordingly, I turned my whole attention to preparing Ladysmith to stand a prolonged siege.

With this object in view, I employed my troops during 31st October and 1st November in improving and strengthening the defences of the various positions surrounding Ladysmith, which together enclosed the area which I had determined to hold. During these days the Boers gradually pushed round from north and west to the south and east of the town, which underwent a slight bombardment on 1st November. On 31st October, General Koch, of the Army of the South African Republic, who had been wounded and taken prisoner at Elandslaagte, died, and his widow was permitted to remove his body for burial in the Transvaal. Before leaving she expressed her gratitude for the courtesy and kind treatment which both her late husband and herself had received at our hands. On the same date I despatched the 2nd Bn. Royal Dublin Fusiliers and Natal Field Battery by rail to Colenso to assist in the defence of the bridges over the Tugela. During the night of 1st–2nd November, the Boers brought several new guns into position, and although the Naval Brigade, under Captain the Hon. H. Lambton, RN, opened fire from one of the naval 4.7-inch guns on the morning of 2nd November, the bombardment of the town became much more severe than on the previous days. At about 4 am, the 5th Dragoon Guards, 5th Lancers, 18th Hussars, Natal Mounted Volunteers, and 69th Battery, Royal Field Artillery, moved out south into the Long Valley to reconnoitre the enemy and to endeavour to surprise one of his camps in the direction of Onderbook. Major-General French, who was in command, left Colonel Royston with the Natal Mounted Volunteers and two guns to hold the Nek between Wagon Hill and Middle Hill, and with the remainder of his force passed round the southern end of End Hill (where he left a squadron of the 5th Lancers to hold a ridge, dismounted), and gaining the plateau pushed on about 3,000 yards and opened an effective fire on the Boer camp. The enemy evacuated their camp and took up a position on a ridge to which they brought up field guns. Major-General French, having fulfilled his mission, withdrew his force, reaching camp by 10 am. Our casualties were one man wounded.

As he returned to Ladysmith a telegram was received from General Sir Redvers Buller, desiring that Major-General French and his staff might be sent to the Cape. Communications by wire and rail were still open, and although trains were constantly fired upon, advantage had been taken of the fact to send southward as many of the civil population of Ladysmith as were willing to depart. Major-General French and his staff left by train about noon on 2nd November, and a telegraphic report was received here that although the train had been heavily fired on near Pieter's Station, it had reached Colenso in safety. Immediately afterwards the wires were cut by the enemy, and railway communication was interrupted. Ladysmith was thus isolated from the world outside it, and from this date the siege may be held to have commenced.

On 3rd November, four squadrons, Imperial Light Horse, under Major Karri Davies, who were reconnoitring to the south, found a body of the enemy, with one gun, on Lancer's Hill, and asked for reinforcements to drive them off. The 5th Dragoon Guards, 18th Hussars, 19th Hussars, and 21st Battery, Royal Field Artillery (the whole under Brigadier-General J. F. Brocklehurst, MVO), were accordingly sent down the Long Valley to their assistance. The 19th Hussars seized Rifleman's Ridge and endeavoured to turn the enemy's left, while the 18th Hussars covered the right rear; two companies of Infantry, detached from Cæsar's Camp, occupied Wagon Hill, and a Mounted Infantry company seized Mounted Infantry Hill to protect the left rear; while the 5th Dragoon Guards and 21st Field Battery were moved straight down the Long Valley. Meantime two squadrons, Imperial Light Horse, were holding Middle Hill, while the remaining two squadrons were facing the enemy on Lancer's Hill. The squadrons on Middle Hill were opposed to a considerable body of the enemy, who were moving up from the east. The 21st Field Battery opened fire on Lancer's Hill and quickly silenced the enemy's gun. Believing that the enemy were evacuating the hill the two squadrons, Imperial Light Horse, made a gallant but somewhat ill-advised attempt to occupy it, but though they seized and held a portion of the hill the enemy was in too great strength for further progress. In the meanwhile I had sent out the Natal Mounted Volunteers and the 42nd and 53rd Field Batteries to join Brigadier-General Brocklehurst, and to cover his retirement, if necessary. General Brocklehurst sent the Natal Mounted Volunteers to reinforce the Imperial Light Horse squadrons on Middle Hill, and brought both batteries into action in the Long Valley. Finding, however, that the numbers of the enemy in his front and on both flanks were continually increasing, and that he could not hope to press his reconnaissance further without serious loss, he determined to withdraw. With the assistance of a dismounted squadron, 5th Dragoon Guards, under Major Gore, the squadrons, Imperial Light Horse, on Lancer's Hill were retired under cover of Artillery fire till they reached the main body, when the whole force engaged was gradually withdrawn to camp. Our loss was two officers and two non-commissioned officers and men killed, three officers and 23 non-commissioned officers and men wounded, and one man missing. The enemy's loss is reported to have been considerable, chiefly from our Artillery fire.

In the afternoon the enemy made demonstrations of an attack in force on Devonshire Post, which was reinforced as a measure of precaution, but the attack was not seriously pressed, and was repulsed with ease. The bombardment this day was very heavy, a large number of shells falling into the town, and especially in and around the hospitals, which were in various churches and public buildings near the centre of the town. In the evening a deputation of civilian residents of Ladysmith waited on me with the request that permission might be obtained for them to pass through the enemy's lines and proceed to the south. The Principal Medical Officer of the Force also represented that the effect of the bombardment on the large number of wounded in his hospitals was very bad, and asked that, if possible, an agreement might be arrived at for the hospitals to be placed outside the town.

Next morning I sent Major Bateson, RAMC, under flag of truce, with a letter to General Joubert, asking that these requests might be agreed to on grounds of humanity to sick, wounded, and non-combatants. In reply, General Joubert agreed to my hospitals being moved out of Ladysmith to a point on the flats, 4 miles down the railway and close to the Intombi Spruit. He refused to allow the civil inhabitants to go south, but permitted them to accompany the sick and wounded to the Intombi Camp. Food and all other requisites for this camp were to be supplied from Ladysmith, and, for this purpose, one train was to be allowed to run each way daily, and by daylight only, under flag of truce. On the same day General Joubert sent into Ladysmith six officers of the Royal Army Medical Corps, 10 Assistant Surgeons, and 98 of our wounded from Dundee; together with a number of Indian hospital attendants. There was a threatening of attack on Cæsar's Camp on this night, 4th November, but it was not pressed. Our first communications by pigeon post to Durban were sent off on this date.

5th November was Sunday. Throughout the siege Sundays have generally been observed by both sides, as far as possible, as days of rest from fighting. There has been no special arrangement on the subject, but a kind of tacit understanding came into existence that neither side would fire unless specially provoked to do so by the construction of fortifications or other signs of movement on the opposite side. 5th November was no exception to this rule, and advantage was taken of the day to send our sick and wounded and all such civilians, men, women, and children, as elected to go, to the Intombi Camp.

The defences of Ladysmith were, for the purposes of command, divided into four sections, A, B, C and D. "A" section, under Colonel W. G. Knox, CB, commenced at Devonshire Post and extended to the point where the Newcastle Road passes between Junction Hill and Gordon Hill. "B" section included all the defences from Gordon Hill round to Flagstone Spruit, and was commanded by Major-General F. Howard, CB, CMG, ADC. "C" section under Colonel Ian Hamilton, CB, DSO, comprised the ground from Flagstone Spruit to the eastern extremity of Cæsar's Camp. "D" section, under Colonel Royston, Commandant of the Natal Mounted Volunteers, included the thorn country north of Cæsar's camp and the Klip River Flats. The troops were allotted to these sections, and to the general reserve, and the variations in these arrangements which were, from time to time, found necessary.

On 6th November, 2nd Lieutenant R. G. Hooper, 5th Lancers, reached Ladysmith with despatches. Arriving in Natal too late to join his regiment before communication was cut off, he most gallantly made his way through the Boer lines at night, and on foot, accompanied only by a Kaffir guide.

All the provisions in the shops and stores in the town were taken over on this date and administered as part of the general stock, all civil residents being placed on rations which were issued free or on payment according to their means.

Next day, 7th November, Cæsar's Camp was subjected to a heavy fire of shells and long range musketry. Although no actual attack was made, it was found advisable to send the Imperial Light Horse to reinforce this point; while the 42nd Battery, Royal Field Artillery, under Major Goulburn, was placed in position on the plateau during the night, the horses returning to camp. A number of natives of India were sent into Ladysmith by the Boers.

On 8th November a 6-inch gun opened fire from the top of the Bulwana Mountain. Throughout the siege this gun has proved most troublesome to the defence. On the same day a number of refugees from Dundee, both English and Indian, were sent into Ladysmith by the Boers, and were located by us in the Intombi Camp.

9th November was ushered in by a very heavy fire at dawn on all sides of our defences from the enemy's artillery, which included several new guns, which now opened for the first time, and whose exact positions it was very hard to locate. This was followed by a general advance of their infantry and the development of a severe musketry action at Cæsar's Camp, in the thorn bush north of that ridge, at Devonshire Post and Observation Hill. The steady front shown by our troops prevented the enemy from trying to close, and although on Cæsar's Camp, where the 1st Bn. Manchester Regiment, under Lieut.-Colonel A. E. R. Curran, rendered very valuable service, the action lasted until darkness set in, yet elsewhere it had mostly died away at 12 noon. At that hour I proceeded, with my Staff, to the Naval Battery on Gordon Hill, whence a salute of 21 shotted guns, in honour of the birthday of the Prince of Wales, was fired at the enemy by Captain the Hon. H. Lambton, RN, and three cheers were given for His Royal Highness, which were taken up by the troops both in camp and on the defences. A message of congratulation, to be telegraphed to His Royal Highness, was despatched by pigeon post to Durban. Our casualties during the day amounted to 4 men killed, 4 officers and 23 men wounded. It is difficult to form any accurate estimate of the enemy's losses, but they certainly considerably exceeded our own.

From 10th to 13th November inclusive, very little of importance occurred, the fire both of guns and rifles being much less severe than usual.

An Irish deserter from the Boers gave himself up on the 12th November. From him we learnt that the total force then surrounding us here numbered about 25,000 men, that they were mounting more guns, and expected to be reinforced shortly.

On 14th November, I sent Brigadier-General J. F. Brocklehurst, MVO, with two regiments of Cavalry, two batteries of Artillery and detachments of the Imperial Light Horse and Natal Mounted Volunteers, across the Klip River, to try and work out on one or both sides of Rifleman's Ridge into the more open country beyond, to find out the enemy's strength in that direction, and, if possible, to capture one of their wagon convoys, of which several had recently been seen passing at a distance of some miles. The Natal Mounted Volunteers and Imperial Light Horse seized Star Hill, but after shelling Rifleman's Ridge for some time General Brocklehurst decided that it was too strongly held for him to leave it in his rear, while an attempt to storm it would have been more costly than the occasion would justify. He, therefore, returned to camp. On this night the Boers commenced for the first time to shell the town and camps at night, opening fire from their heavy guns about midnight for a few minutes, a practice which they maintained nightly for about a week, and then discontinued.

From this time nothing worth record took place until 19th November, when the Boers sent into Intombi Camp six privates of the 2nd Bn. Royal Dublin Fusiliers, who had been wounded in the attack on an armoured train near Colenso, on 15th November.

20th November was marked by an unusual number of casualties from shell fire, chiefly among the 18th Hussars and Gordon Highlanders.

Next day General S. Burger sent in a letter under a flag of truce, complaining that we had been running trains at night to the Intombi Camp, contrary to our agreement with General Joubert—a complaint for which there was no foundation whatever. He also enquired why a Red Cross flag was flying on the Town Hall although our hospital was at Intombi. I replied, on 22nd November, by giving my personal assurance that trains never had been and never would be, run to Intombi at night, and explaining that the Red Cross flag was hoisted on the Town Hall because that building was in use as a hospital for ordinary cases of sickness, and for slightly wounded men whom it was not worthwhile to send to Intombi. Before my answer could reach him the Boer guns were deliberately turned on the Town Hall, which was several times struck.

On 23rd November the enemy endeavoured, under flag of truce, to send into Ladysmith 230 Indian coolies. It became evident that the intention was to send in here as many non-combatants as could be collected who would be useless for defence, but would help to consume our supplies. For this reason I refused to receive them, and requested that they might be sent to the officer commanding our forces south of the Tugela. I understand that this course was eventually adopted. The same evening an attempt was made to wreck the only engine which the enemy possessed on the Harrismith line.

With this object an old locomotive was selected from those in the railway yard here and was sent off down the line, at night, with a full head of steam and with the safety valve screwed down. The Boers had, however, provided against such an attempt by destroying a culvert on our side of their temporary terminus, and here our engine was derailed and upset. The enemy evidently feared that it carried a cargo of explosives, as they did not approach it next morning until they had sent a number of shells into it from their artillery.

On the 24th November we had the misfortune to lose 228 oxen, which were captured by the enemy. Owing to lack of rain the grazing within our lines had become insufficient for all our animals, and a number of our cattle had to be grazed outside our defences, wherever a re-entrant gave them some protection from capture. Owing to the carelessness of certain civilian conductors, these oxen were allowed to stray too far out and seeing this the Boers commenced bursting shells on our side of the cattle in order to hasten their movements. In this they were successful, the Kaffirs in charge abandoning their animals in order to seek shelter. As soon as the occurrence was noticed, the Mounted Infantry Company of the 1st Bn. Leicestershire Regiment, under Captain C. Sherer, was sent out to try and head them back, but it was then too late, and though Captain Sherer did all that was possible and drove back a considerable number, under a heavy musketry fire from the enemy, yet, as already mentioned, the enemy obtained possession of 228 head.

Beyond the usual daily bombardment, nothing worth recording took place till 27th November, which was marked by the unmasking of a new 6-inch gun on Middle Hill, and a very evident increase in the number of Boers in our immediate vicinity. An attack on our positions seemed likely, and all precautions were taken accordingly, but next day news arrived of Major-General Hildyard's fight at Mooi River, and the consequent withdrawal of the Boers to the north of the Tugela, which fully explained the increased numbers visible from Ladysmith.

On the 28th November, two 6.3-inch howitzers were sent to occupy emplacements which had been prepared for them on the reverse slope of Wagon Hill; a naval 12-pr. was also placed on Cæsar's Camp. From this position they opened fire next day, and proved able to quite keep down the fire from the enemy's 6-inch gun on Middle Hill, which some days afterwards was withdrawn from that position. I arranged an attack on Rifleman's Ridge for the night of 29th November, but was compelled to abandon it, as just at sunset the enemy very strongly reinforced that portion of their line. There can, I think, be no doubt that my plan had been disclosed to them, and indeed throughout the siege I have been much handicapped by the fact that every movement, or preparation for movement which has taken place in Ladysmith, has been at once communicated to the Boers. The agents through whom news reached them, I have, unfortunately, failed to discover. I have sent away or locked up every person against whom reasonable grounds of suspicion could be alleged, but without the slightest effect.

Two civilians, who had volunteered to blow up the Sunday's River railway bridge, started on their perilous journey on 29th November, and returned here on 1st December. They reached the bridge without mishap, and duly placed the charges, but owing to not fully understanding the use of the fuse, only one out of four charges exploded.

On 29th November also we observed flashing signals on the clouds at night from Estcourt and were able to read a portion of a message. At a later period of the siege no difficulty was experienced in reading such messages, but we were without the means of replying in similar fashion.

30th November was a day of very heavy bombardment, a new 6-inch gun opening fire from Gun Hill and doing much damage. One shell in particular entered the Town Hall which we had hitherto used as a hospital, killing and wounding 10 persons. It was found necessary to evacuate the building and place the hospital under canvas in a gorge where the protection from shell fire was better. This severe bombardment continued throughout 1st and 2nd December, but fortunately proved comparatively harmless. On the latter date heliographic communication via Weenen was restored after having been interrupted for a long period.

On 3rd December General Joubert sent me a letter alleging that we had made unfair use of the Intombi Camp, and proposing that it should be broken up. In reply, I dealt in detail with the points raised, none of which had any foundation in fact, and as a result the breaking up of the camp was not pressed.

On 5th December, at 1.30 am, two companies of the 2nd Bn. Rifle Brigade moved out, under Captain J. E. Gough, to surprise Thornhill's Farm which the enemy were in the habit of occupying with a picket at night. The enterprise was very well conducted, but the farm was unfortunately found unoccupied.

On the night of 7th December, Major-General Sir A. Hunter, KCB, DSO, made a sortie for the purpose of destroying the Boer guns on Gun Hill, which had been giving us much annoyance. His force consisted of 500 Natal Volunteers, under Colonel Royston, and 100 men Imperial Light Horse, under Lieut.-Colonel A. H. M. Edwards, with 18 men of the Corps of Guides, under Major D. Henderson, DAAG for Intelligence, to direct the column, and four men Royal Engineers and 10 men No. 10 Mountain Battery, Royal Garrison Artillery, under Captain Fowke and Lieutenant Turner, Royal Engineers, with explosives and sledge hammers for the destruction of the guns when captured. Sir A. Hunter's arrangements were excellent throughout, and he was most gallantly supported by all his small force. Gun Hill was taken, a 6-inch Creusot and a 4.7-inch howitzer destroyed, and a Maxim captured and brought into camp. Our loss was only one officer and seven men wounded. I consider that Major-General Sir A. Hunter deserves the greatest credit for this very valuable service for which he volunteered. He brings to my notice specially the gallant behaviour of Colonel W. Royston, Commanding Volunteers, Natal, Lieut.-Colonel A. H.

M. Edwards (5th Dragoon Guards), Commanding Imperial Light Horse, Major D. Henderson, DAAG for Intelligence (wounded), Major A. J. King, Royal Lancaster Regiment, Major Karri Davies, Imperial Light Horse, Captain G. H. Fowke, RE, and Lieutenant E. V. Turner, RE, whose names I have much pleasure in bringing forward for favourable consideration.

The same night three companies of the 1st Bn. Liverpool Regiment, under Lieut.-Colonel L. S. Mellor, seized Limit Hill, and through the gap in the enemy's outpost line thus created, a squadron 19th Hussars penetrated some 4 miles towards the north, destroying the enemy's telegraph line and burning various kraals and shelters ordinarily occupied by them. No loss was incurred in this enterprise. At the same time five companies 1st Bn. Leicestershire Regiment, under Lieut.-Colonel G. D. Carleton, visited Hyde's and McPherson's farms, usually occupied by the enemy as night out-posts, but found them evacuated.

The slight opposition met with by these various operations of the night of 7th–8th December made it appear probable that the enemy had unduly weakened his force to the north of us in order to strengthen that opposing Sir Redvers Buller on the Tugela. Recognising that if this proved to be the case there might be an opportunity for my Cavalry to get far enough north to damage the enemy's railway, I ordered Brigadier-General J. F. Brocklehurst, MVO, to move out at dawn with 5th Lancers, 5th Dragoon Guards, and 18th Hussars and 53rd Battery, Royal Field Artillery, along the Newcastle Road, to feel for the enemy and discover his strength and dispo-sitions. The reconnaissance was carried out in a very bold and dashing manner by the 5th Lancers and 18th Hussars, the 5th Dragoon Guards being in reserve. The enemy, however, proved to be in considerable strength, and having obtained the information I required I directed Brigadier-General Brocklehurst to withdraw his brigade. The effect of these various enterprises was shortly evident in the return from the line of the Tugela next day of some 2,000 Boers.

On the 10th December, Lieut.-Colonel C. T. E. Metcalfe, Commanding 2nd Bn. Rifle Brigade, volunteered to carry out a night enterprise against a 4.7-inch howitzer on Surprise Hill. The undertaking was one of very con-siderable risk, as to reach that hill it was necessary to pass between Thornhill's and Bell's Kopjes, both of which were held by the enemy. Lieut.-Colonel Metcalfe moved off about 10 pm, with 12 officers and 488 men of his bat-talion, together with a destruction party under Lieutenant Digby Jones, RE, and succeeded in effecting a complete surprise, his advance not being dis-covered until he was within 4 or 5 yards of the crest line, which was at once carried, and the howitzer destroyed. The retirement, however, proved more difficult, since the enemy from Bell's and Thornhill's Kopjes, consisting apparently of men of various nationalities, closed in from both sides to bar the retreat. Lieut.-Colonel Metcalfe, however, fixed bayonets, and the com-panies, admirably handled by their captains, fought their way back to the railway line, where a portion of the force had been left in support, and from which point the retirement became easy. A number of the enemy were killed with the bayonet, and his total casualties must have been very considerable. Our own loss amounted to 1 officer and 16 men killed, 3 officers and 37 men wounded, and 6 men missing. The affair reflects great credit on Lieut.-Colonel C. T. E. Metcalfe and his battalion.

My attention was now chiefly directed to preparations for moving out a flying column to co-operate with General Sir Redvers Buller. All these preparations, including the movement of a 4.7-inch and a 12-pr. gun, both belonging to the Royal Navy, were completed by 15th December. Meanwhile the enemy had moved his 6-inch gun from Middle Hill to Telegraph Hill, and on 12th December I moved down the 6.3-inch howitzers to near Ration Post to oppose it.

The firing of Sir Redvers Buller's guns from the direction of Colenso had been audible for some days, and was especially heavy on 15th December. On 16th, Sir Redvers heliographed that he had attacked Colenso on the previous day, but without success. Although this news was naturally disappointing to the hopes of immediate relief which they had entertained, yet it was received by both soldiers and civilians without any discouragement, and with a cheerful readiness to wait until the necessary reinforcements should arrive. From this time up to the close of the year few other events of importance occurred, but on Christmas Day a telegram was received from Her Majesty and most gratefully appreciated by the garrison of Ladysmith. At this period a few of the many shells daily fired into our camps were especially destructive. One shell, on the 18th December, killed and wounded 10 men and 12 horses of the Natal Volunteers. Another, on 22nd December, killed 8 and wounded 9 of the Gloucestershire Regiment; and, on the same day a single shell wounded 5 officers and the sergeant-major of the 5th Lancers. On 27th December, again, one shell killed 1 officer of the Devonshire Regiment and wounded 8 officers and 1 private of that regiment. During this period, also, fresh complaints regarding the Intombi Camp were made by the enemy; and, by agreement with General S. Burger, Major-General Sir A. Hunter was sent to that camp to hold an inquiry. A few minor irregularities were discovered and corrected, and a copy of Sir A. Hunter's report was sent to General Burger, who was apparently satisfied that the complaints were without serious foundation.

At the close of the year my chief source of anxiety lay in the heavy and continuous increase in the number of the sick, which had risen from 475 on 30th November to 874 on 15th December, and to 1,558 on the last day of the year. Enteric fever and dysentery were chiefly responsible for this increase, there being 452 cases of the former, and 376 of the latter under treatment on 31st December.

The Boers opened the New Year by a fire of heavy guns at midnight, but beyond the daily long-range bombardment, nothing of importance occurred until 5th January, when we shelled, by indirect fire, two Boer camps, one behind Bell's Kopje, and one near Table Hill on the Colenso Plateau. In the latter case the fire probably had little effect, as the range was too great even for the naval gun employed, and the only possible observing station was very inconveniently placed. It was subsequently ascertained from the Boers themselves that the shells falling into the camp behind Bell's Kopje had been very effective, stampeding the horses and compelling the enemy temporarily to vacate the camp and seek shelter elsewhere.

On the 6th January the enemy made a most determined but fortunately unsuccessful attempt to carry Ladysmith by storm. Almost every part of my position was more or less heavily assailed, but the brunt of the attack fell upon Cæsar's Camp and Wagon Hill. On the night of the 5th–6th January, Cæsar's Camp was held by its usual garrison, consisting of the 1st Bn. Manchester Regiment; the 42nd Battery, Royal Field Artillery; a detachment of the Royal Navy; with a 12-pr gun; and a detachment, Natal Naval Volunteers. Wagon Hill was held as usual by three companies, 1st Bn. King's Royal Rifle Corps, and a squadron, Imperial Light Horse. A detachment, Natal Naval Volunteers, with a 3-pr Hotchkiss gun, had been sent there on the evening of the 5th January, and two naval guns, one a 4.7-inch and the other a 12-pr, were in process of transfer to the hill during the night. These guns were accompanied by naval detachments and a working party of Royal Engineers and Gordon Highlanders, who were consequently on Wagon Hill when the attack commenced at 2.30 am on the morning of 6th January.

This attack was first directed on the centre of the southern face of Wagon Hill, whence it spread east and west. It fell directly on the squadron of Imperial Light Horse, under Lieutenant G. M. Mathias, and the Volunteer Hotchkiss Detachment, under Lieutenant E. N. W. Walker, who clung most gallantly to their positions, and did invaluable service in holding in check till daylight the Boers who had gained a footing on the hill within a few yards of them. The extreme south-west point of the hill was similarly held by a small mixed party of Bluejackets, Royal Engineers, Gordon Highlanders, and Imperial Light Horse, under Lieutenant Digby Jones, RE. The remainder of the hill was defended by the companies of 1st Bn. King's Royal Rifle Corps.

Shortly after 3 am an attack was developed against the south-east end of Cæsar's Camp (which was garrisoned by the 1st Bn. Manchester Regiment), and on the thorn jungle between that Hill and the Klip River, which was held by the Natal Mounted Volunteers. As soon as the alarm reached me, I ordered the Imperial Light Horse, under Lieut.-Colonel A. H. M. Edwards, to proceed as rapidly as possible to Wagon Hill, and the Gordon Highlanders to Cæsar's Camp. Shortly afterwards, four companies, 1st Bn. King's Royal Rifle Corps, and four companies, 2nd Bn. King's Royal Rifle Corps, were ordered to march at once on Wagon Hill, and the 2nd Bn. Rifle Brigade on Cæsar's Camp. This section of my defences was under the command of Colonel Ian Hamilton, CB, DSO, who, judging that Wagon Hill was the point most seriously threatened, proceeded there himself, where he arrived about dawn, bringing with him a company of the 2nd Bn. Gordon Highlanders under Major Miller Wallnutt.

Perceiving that the close and deadly nature of the fighting made it impossible for one officer to adequately command on both hills, I directed Colonel Hamilton to devote his attention to Wagon Hill, while I entrusted the defence of Cæsar's Camp to Lieut.-Colonel A. E. R. Curran, 1st Bn. Manchester Regiment, who had been stationed there with his battalion ever since the commencement of the siege, and was specially acquainted with the locality. I ordered Major W. E. Blewitt's battery of Royal Field Artillery, escorted by the 5th Dragoon Guards, to move out by Range Post and endeavour to prevent reinforcements reaching the enemy from the west. Major A. J. Abdy's battery of Royal Field Artillery I sent to Colonel Royston, Commanding Natal Mounted Volunteers, to take up position on the Klip River flats and shell the south-eastern corner of Cæsar's Camp, where the enemy had effected a lodgment.

The Imperial Light Horse reached Wagon Hill at 5.10 am, and were at once pushed into action. They pressed forward up to and over the western edge of the flat crest of the hill to within a few yards of the enemy, who held the opposite edge of the crest. They thus afforded a most welcome relief to the small garrison of the hill, but they themselves suffered very severely in occupying and maintaining their position. The company of 2nd Bn. Gordon Highlanders, which arrived with Colonel Hamilton, was sent under cover of the western slopes to reinforce the extreme south-west point of the hill, and to endeavour to work round so as to outflank the enemy, but were unable to do so owing to the extreme severity of the fire kept up by the Boers from Mounted Infantry Hill and from every available scrap of cover in Bester's Valley, which they occupied in great numbers. At 7 am, four companies 1st Bn. King's Royal Rifle Corps and four companies 2nd Bn. King's Royal Rifle Corps arrived, and about 8 am, one of these companies, followed shortly afterwards by another, was sent to reinforce the extreme south-western point of the hill, but although gallantly holding their own under a rain of shells and bullets, no progress could be made either there or on the main ridge. Meanwhile the 21st and 42nd Batteries, Royal Field Artillery, and the naval 12-pr on Cæsar's Camp, were in action against Mounted Infantry Hill and the scrub on either side of it, and were of great assistance in keeping down the violence of the enemy's fire. Colonel Hamilton, seeing plainly that the only way of clearing out those of the enemy's marksmen who were established on the eastern crest of Wagon Hill, within a few yards of our men, was by a sudden rush across the open, directed Major Campbell to tell off a company of the 2nd Bn. King's Royal Rifle Corps to make the attempt, which however failed, Lieutenant N. M. Tod, who commanded, being killed, and the men falling back to the cover of the rocks from behind which they had started. The fighting continuing stationary and indecisive, at 10 am I sent the 5th Lancers to Cæsar's Camp and the 18th Hussars to Wagon Hill, two squadrons 19th Hussars having been previously posted on the ground near

Maiden Castle to guard against any attempt of the enemy to turn Wagon Hill from the west.

For some time the fighting slackened considerably, the Boers being gradually driven down below the crest line, except at a single point where they were favoured by excellent cover, with a flat open space in front of it. At 1 pm, however, a fresh assault was made with great suddenness on the extreme south-west point of the hill, our men giving way for a moment before the sudden outburst of fire and retiring down the opposite slope. Fortunately the Boers did not immediately occupy the crest, and this gave time for Major Miller Wallnutt, 2nd Bn. Gordon Highlanders, Lieutenant Digby Jones, RE, Lieutenant P. D. Fitzgerald (11th Hussars), Adjutant Imperial Light Horse, Gunner W. Sims, RN, and several non-commissioned officers, Imperial Light Horse, to rally the men; while Major E. C. Knox, Commanding 18th Hussars, brought up a portion of his regiment, which was in reserve at the foot of the hill, to act dismounted.

The top was reoccupied just as the three foremost Boers reached it, the leader being shot by Lieutenant Digby Jones, RE, and the two others by No. 459 Trooper H. Albrecht, Imperial Light Horse. Had they survived I should have had great pleasure in recommending both Lieutenant Jones and Trooper Albrecht for the distinction of the Victoria Cross. I regret to say that both were killed before the conclusion of the action.

At 3.30 pm, a storm of wind and rain of extraordinary severity set in and lasted for 3 hours. During its continuance the 5th Dragoon Guards, 5th Lancers, and 1½ squadrons 19th Hussars reinforced Wagon Hill, acting dismounted. About 4.45 pm, when the storm was at its worst, the portion of our troops holding the extreme south-west point of the hill were again driven from their position, but were rallied and reoccupied it; 2nd Lieutenant R. E. Reade, 1st Bn. King's Royal Rifle Corps, rendering himself conspicuous by his gallant service at this period.

At 5 pm, Lieut.-Colonel C. W. Park arrived at Wagon Hill with three companies 1st Bn. Devonshire Regiment, which I had ordered up as a reinforcement, and was at once directed by Colonel Hamilton to turn the enemy off the ridge with the bayonet. The Devons dashed forward and gained a position under cover within 50 yards of the enemy. Here a fire fight ensued, but the Devons were not to be denied, and, eventually, cheering as they pushed from point to point, they drove the enemy not only off the plateau but cleared every Boer out of the lower slopes and the dongas surrounding the position. Lieut.-Colonel Park went into action with four officers, but he alone remained untouched at the close. The total loss of the Devons was nearly 28 per cent of those engaged, and the men fired only 12 rounds per rifle. Captain A. Menzies, 1st Bn. Manchester Regiment, with a few of his men, accompanied the Devons throughout. He also was wounded.

I desire to draw special attention to the gallantry displayed by all ranks of the Imperial Light Horse, some of whom were within 100 yards of the enemy for 15 hours exposed to a deadly fire. Their losses were terribly heavy, but never for one moment did any of them waver or cease to show a fine example of courage and determination to all who came in contact with them.

I have already mentioned that at about 3 am, the south-east end of Cæsar's Camp was also attacked, as well as the pickets of the Natal Volunteers in the thorn scrub to the north of that hill. During the darkness the enemy succeeded in establishing themselves on part of that end of Cæsar's Camp, but the precise details of what occurred have not been made clear, as nearly all the defenders of this portion have been killed. It is believed, however, that taking advantage of a general similarity of dress to that of the Natal Volunteers and Police, and many of them having a perfect command of the English language, the Boers succeeded in deceiving the pickets as to their identity, and were thus able to effect a surprise.

As already stated, I sent the 53rd Battery, Royal Field Artillery, under Major A. J. Abdy, to Colonel Royston, Commanding Natal Volunteers; and these guns, most ably handled, came into action on the Klip River flats, and, though exposed to the fire of several Boer guns (including a 6-inch Creusot gun on Bulwana Mountain), to which they had no means of replying, shelled the south-east portion of Cæsar's Camp with great effect, and inflicted very heavy losses on the enemy. The 2nd Bn. Gordon Highlanders and 2nd Bn. Rifle Brigade were sent to Lieut.-Colonel A. E. R. Curran, who was in command here, and were gradually pushed into the fight, company by company wherever their services were most required. Gradually the Boers were pushed back over the crest line, but held on most stubbornly to the slopes, being continually reinforced or relieved from the dongas below and from the adjacent hills, whence a fire of very great intensity was kept up, while the whole of the plateau was swept by the Boer long-range guns from distant eminences. At last, after 15 hours of stubborn resistance by our men, and of continual effort on the part of the Boers, the enemy were driven off at all points during the same storm in which Wagon Hill was also cleared as already described, their retreat being hastened by the heavy fire poured on them as they retired.

Another attack was made before dawn on the 6th January on Observation Hill West, occupied by half battalion 1st Bn. Devonshire Regiment, under Major M. C. Curry. The enemy gained some dead ground near our works during the darkness, and at 9.30 am, and again at a later hour, they attempted to storm the works under cover of the fire of these men and of guns and rifles from all the surrounding kopjes. These, however, were repelled with no great difficulty by the wing 1st Bn. Devonshire Regiment, and the Artillery allotted to this portion of the defence, consisting of Royal Field Artillery and naval guns. The enemy, however, held on to the dead ground originally occupied all day, and only withdrew during the storm in the afternoon. The remainder of Section B and the whole of Section A of the defences were subjected to a heavy fire of guns and rifles all day, but no other attempt to press home an attack was made on these portions of our line.

Our losses, I regret to say, were very heavy, consisting of 14 officers and 135 non-commissioned officers and men killed, and 31 officers and 244 men wounded. I have not been able to ascertain the actual loss to the Boers, but 79 bodies found within our lines were returned to them next day for burial, and native spies report that their total casualties could not be less than 700.

On 8th January a thanksgiving service in commemoration of the repulse of the enemy on 6th idem was held by Archdeacon Barker, and very largely attended by such officers and men as could be spared from duty. From this time until the end of the siege, no further effort to carry Ladysmith by assault was made by the Boers, whose attention was fully occupied by the various attacks made by Sir Redvers Buller on the line of the Tugela, though the town and camps were exposed to a daily bombardment from the enemy's guns, and skirmishing between our outposts and those of the Boers went on all day and every day, and caused us small but continuous losses. During this period I shall only refer to a night enterprise undertaken by 2nd Lieutenant H. C. W. Theobald, and 15 non-commissioned officers and men, 1st Bn. Gloucestershire Regiment. The object was to set fire to the abbattis which the enemy had constructed at the foot of Gun Hill, and was carried out in a manner reflecting credit on the young officer in command, and without loss; while creating a considerable scare among the Boers who fired heavily in the darkness for a considerable time.

On 1st March I sent Colonel W. G. Knox, with the 1st Bn. Liverpool Regiment, 1st Bn. Devonshire Regiment, 2nd Bn. Gordon Highlanders, 5th Dragoon Guards, and the 53rd and 67th Batteries, Royal Field Artillery, to move out along the Newcastle Road to harass as much as possible the enemy whom we could see retiring before the successful advance of Sir Redvers Buller's force. Colonel Knox carried Long Hill and Pepworth Hill and opened fire with his guns on Modder Spruit Railway Station and the large Boer camp there, which the enemy at once evacuated. Both men and horses were too weak for rapid or prolonged operations, but several of the enemy's camps were captured, and the force returned after having very successfully carried out their object to as great a distance as their weakness permitted them to pursue. Our casualties were 2 officers and 6 non-commissioned officers and men wounded.

Colonel Lord Dundonald with a body of Colonial troops rode into Ladysmith on the evening of 28th February, and on 1st March General Sir Redvers Buller himself arrived, and the siege came to an end.

SIEGE CONDITIONS AT LADYSMITH

Sir George White's despatch of 23rd March 1900 continued

During the period from 6th January to 1st March, our struggle became one against disease and starvation even more than against the enemy. Our worst foes in this respect were enteric fever and dysentery, the former especially committing great ravages among the young soldiers of the garrison. Our deaths by disease from 2nd November, 1899, to 28th February, 1900, amounted to 12 officers and 529 non-commissioned officers and men. The officers of the Royal Army Medical Corps, the Army nursing sisters, the many ladies who voluntarily offered their services as nurses, and the hospital staffs of all ranks, maintained throughout the siege a brave and protracted struggle against sickness under almost every possible disadvantage, their numbers being most inadequate for the work to be done, and the supplies of drugs and of suitable food for invalids being entirely insufficient for so many patients for so long a period.

Even more important was the regulation and augmentation of the food supplies, as will be realised from the simple statement that 21,000 mouths had to be fed for 120 days; and the admirable manner in which all arrangements were made and carried out by the officers of the Army Service Corps and Indian Commissariat Department under the able and untiring superintendence of Colonel E. W. D. Ward, CB, my AAG (B), will be evident from the fact that at the date of the relief we still possessed resources capable of maintaining this great number on reduced rations for another 30 days.

At the commencement of the siege, it became necessary to augment as far as possible all food supplies, and, with this view, one mill and subsequently two, were taken over and worked under military supervision and with labour and mechanics obtained from the employees of the Natal Government Railway, who remained voluntarily with the garrison. From these mills we produced during the siege mealie flour, mealie bran and crushed mealies. The mills were worked under the personal supervision of Lieut.-Colonel Stoneman, ASC, DAAG, assisted by Major D. M. Thompson, Assistant Commissary-General, Indian Commissariat Transport Department.

When grazing and forage became scarce and the supply of cattle approached within a measurable distance of extinction, it was necessary to utilise for food the horses which would otherwise have died from exhaustion and weakness. From these slaughtered horses very considerable additions to the food supply were made, by the establishment of a factory from which were made: (i) "Chevril", a strong meat soup issued nightly to the troops; (ii) a condensed form of "Chevril" which took the place in the hospitals of various meat extracts which had been expended; (iii) a jelly similar to calf-foot jelly for the sick and wounded; (iv) "Chevril paste" made of boiled meat and jelly and issued as a ration to the men, and which being similar to the potted meats manufactured at home was much appreciated by the troops; and finally (v) "neats-foot oil", which was used for lubricating the heavy naval ordnance. The boiled meat was given to the soldiers at the rate of ½ lb per man.

The whole of this factory was under the management of Lieutenant C. E. J. MacNalty, ASC, whose untiring energy, ingenuity, and intelligence are deserving of high commendation. Captain J. R. Young, RE, RSO, converted a railway locomotive shed into a factory, and displayed very great skill in improvising the various appliances necessary for the manufacture of the different foods.

With the object of still further improving the rations a sausage factory was established which converted the horse-flesh into excellent sausages, issued to the men at the rate of ¼ lb per head. This factory was most efficiently worked under the supervision of Mr R. Beresford Turner.

As a safeguard against any serious loss of animals by disease or from other causes with a consequent reduction of our power of continuing the defence, a reserve of "biltong" was prepared, under the superintendence of Captain A. Long, ASC, who undertook it in addition to his onerous duties of Local Transport Officer.

The very large number of enteric and dysentery patients rendered it necessary to utilise all available sources of milk supply. All milch cows were requisitioned, and a dairy system established which provided milk, on medical certificate, for the sick, both military and civilian.

The feeding of the civil population was carried out by the Army Service Corps, a staff of civilian assistants being organised for distribution, and a large shed specially converted for the purpose. The two foregoing duties were carried out under the direction of Lieut.-Colonel Stoneman, DAAG, and Major Thompson, ACG.

On the investment of Ladysmith, the main was broken by the enemy, and the water supply for the camp and town became dependent upon the

Klip River. A system of filtration by Berkefeld filters was commenced, which answered well so long as the limited supply of alum lasted; as soon as it was expended the muddy condition of the water clogged the filters, and this method became unreliable. Three condensers were then constructed out of improvised materials by Mr Binnie, Maintenance Manager, Natal Government Railway, under the able direction of Engineer C. C. Sheen, RN, HMS *Powerful*. As a further means of obtaining pure water, apparatus for clearing water was constructed out of barrack sheeting placed on wooden stands, and having a deposit of wood ashes, through which the water was strained. It thus became possible to use the filters and also to provide all units with cleaning arrangements. It was possible, so long as the coal lasted, to supply at least 12,000 gallons of condensed or filtered water daily. The management of the water supply was carried out by Lieutenant H. B. Abadie, 11th Hussars, who performed the duties of Staff Officer for Water Supplies, and whose work is deserving of much praise.

Mr W. King, District Inspector, Public Works Department, Mr R. Brooke and the officials of that department, rendered most valuable assistance in every way possible.

With the object of reducing the number of orderlies employed in the conveyance of letters, a postal system, which included all the defences and the camp and town, was organised and most efficiently carried out by Captain P. C. J. Scott, ASC.

In order to supply the deficiency of hay, a corps of grass-cutters was formed and placed under the charge of Major W. J. R. Wickham, Assistant Commissary-General, Indian Commissariat Transport Department. This corps, which consisted of Indian refugees and Kaffirs, did excellent work, and collected grass under conditions of considerable difficulty.

I take this opportunity of publicly expressing my deep sense of the gallantry and patient endurance of hardships displayed by all ranks of all corps under my command.

The Naval Brigade of HMS *Powerful*, under Captain the Honourable Hedworth Lambton, RN, have rivalled the best of our troops in gallantry and endurance, and their long-range guns, though hampered by a most serious want of sufficient ammunition, have played a most prominent part in the defence, and have been most successful in keeping the enemy from bringing his guns to the ranges at which they would have been most efficient.

The Cavalry have not only performed their regular duties, but when their horses became non-effective have served as infantry, being re-armed with rifle and bayonet, and taking their regular share in holding the fortifications.

The Artillery have displayed their usual skill and gallantry, whether as mobile batteries or when used as guns of position in fixed emplacements as became increasingly necessary during the latter portion of the investment.

The Royal Engineers, both officers and men, have sustained the grand traditions of their corps, and whether engaged on the defences, in maintaining telegraphic and telephonic communication between all sections of the defences, in ballooning, or in any other work required of them, have done everything which they were called upon to perform in a manner which has afforded me the highest satisfaction.

The work of the Infantry especially, exposed day and night to all weathers on our lines of defence, almost continually under fire, and living latterly on a ration consisting of little more than a proportion of horse flesh with ½ lb per man of inferior and scarcely eatable mealie bread, has been of the most severe and trying nature, and has been carried out without a murmur and with the most cheerful steadfastness.

Of the Imperial Light Horse, specially raised in Natal at the commencement of the war, I have already expressed my opinion. No praise can be too great for the gallantry and determination which all ranks of this corps have invariably displayed in action.

The Natal Volunteers have performed invaluable service. Their knowledge of the country has been of the very greatest use to me, and in every action in which they have been engaged they have shown themselves most forward and daring. The Natal Naval Volunteers have proved themselves worthy comrades of the land forces of the Colony.

The civil inhabitants of Ladysmith, of all ages and both sexes, have uncomplainingly borne the privations inseparable from a siege, and have endured the long-continued bombardment to which they have been exposed with a fortitude which does them honour.

In conclusion, I trust I may be allowed to give expression to the deep sense of gratitude, felt not only by myself but by every soldier, sailor and civilian who has been through the siege, to General Sir Redvers Buller and his gallant force, who, after such severe fighting, so many hardships, and notwithstanding very severe losses, have triumphantly carried out the relief of my beleaguered garrison.

TELEGRAMS CONCERNING THE SIEGE OF LADYSMITH

From General Sir G. White to General Sir R. Buller (received at Estcourt and telegraphed to Pietermaritzburg, 4th December, 1899)

No. 20 P, 30th November. Flashing signals clouds seen last night for first time. Following portion only read: "I do not yet know which way I will come. How much longer could you hold out? From Maritzburg, from Buller." Commencement of message and date not read. Situation here unchanged; but enemy still mounting additional guns against some of our essential positions. I have provision for 70 days, and believe I can defend Ladysmith while they last. Hay or grazing is a difficulty; I have 35 days' supply of this at reduced ration. Small-arm ammunition, 5½ million; 15-pr guns, 250 rounds per gun; 4.7-inch naval guns, 170 rounds per gun; 12-pr naval guns, 270 rounds per gun; 6.3-inch howitzer, 430 rounds per gun.

Enemy learns every plan of operations I form, and I cannot discover source. I have locked up or banished every suspect, but still have undoubted evidence of betrayal. Native deserters from enemy and our native scouts report enemy much disheartened by news of advance on Free State, victory on Mooi River, and consequent retirement north of Tugela River. With regard to road of advance towards Ladysmith, I could give most help to a force coming via Onderbook Hotel or Springfield, but enemy is making his positions on that side stronger daily. If force south of Tugela can effect junction with me, I believe effect will be immediate and decisive. At present cannot go large as I am completely invested, and must reserve myself for one or two big efforts to co-oper-ate with relief force. It will be the greatest help to Ladysmith if relief force maintains closest possible touch with enemy. Hospital return: wounded, 225; dysentery, 71; enteric, 15; other fevers, 12; other diseases, 109. Additional portion of message deciphered "If you hear me attacking join in if you can." Please repeat entire message. I will keep a good look out and do all I can. Repeat General Clery.

From General Sir R. Buller to General Sir G. White (sent by messenger from Pietermaritzburg)

No. 58, 4th December. Your No. 20 P, 30th November, received. I shall have concentrated 4 brigades of Infantry, 5 batteries of Artillery, 1 regiment of Cavalry, 1,000 mounted Volunteers, by 6th December, and shall attack. I cannot yet say which route, but will (? communicate) with you in several cipher messages before I advance. I shall also send by searchlight messages in clear, but they will be false ones sent in order to deceive enemy.

From General Sir R. Buller, Natal, to Field-Marshal Lord Roberts, Cape Town (received 26th January, 1900, 12.03 am)

(Extract)

No. 169. Sorry to say I find this morning garrison had abandoned Spion Kop in the night. They lost up there yesterday, General Woodgate dangerously wounded, and 200 killed and about 300 wounded, mostly badly. I have gone over and assumed command, and am withdrawing the flank attack to Potgieter's Drift, which I shall reach morning 27th.

I mean to have one more try at Ladysmith, but fear that a great portion of the force is not in good spirits.

From Field-Marshal Lord Roberts, Cape Town, to General Sir R. Buller, Natal

Cape Town, 26th January, 1900

(Extract)

Your No. 169. I am much concerned to hear that the Spion Kop position has been abandoned. Unless you feel fairly confident of being able to relieve Ladysmith from Potgieter's Drift, would it not be better to postpone the attempt until I am in the Orange Free State? Strenuous efforts are being made to collect transport, and I am hopeful of having sufficient to enable me to move on or about 5th February. If White can hold out and your position is secure, the presence of my force on the north of the Orange River should cause the enemy to lessen their hold on Natal, and thus make your task easier. Reports from Boer camp point to their being fagged and unable to cope with our Artillery fire. It seems therefore most desirable to maintain as bold a front as possible for the next 10 days.

From Field-Marshal Lord Roberts, Cape Town, to General Sir R. Buller, Natal

Cape Town, 28th January, 1900

(Extract)

Please let me know exactly what your plan is for the next try to relieve Ladysmith, and about what date you think it would be possible to commence operations. I am deeply anxious that Ladysmith should be relieved, but unless you consider that you have a reasonable prospect of success, it would, I think, be infinitely better for many reasons for you to remain on the defensive behind the Tugela, until the operations I am about to undertake have produced the effect which I hope for. Early reply requested.

From General Sir R. Buller, Natal, to Field-Marshal Lord Roberts, Cape Town

Spearman's Camp, 29th January, 1900, 3.25 pm

(Extract)

My plan for next trial to relieve Ladysmith is to turn the Spion Kop position by the east, crossing the Tugela three times, and using a new drift just discovered, which makes all the difference by enabling me to reach a position I had hitherto considered inaccessible. I am only waiting for the Horse Artillery battery from India, and if it arrives I hope to attack Wednesday at 4 pm.

The death rate in Ladysmith is now 8 to 10 a day, and their hospital stores have run out, so delay is objectionable. I feel fairly confident of success this time, as I believe the enemy had a severe lesson last week, and are very disheartened, while we are all right.

One can never safely attempt to prophesy, but so far as my exertions can, humanly speaking, conduce to the desired end, I think I can promise you that I shall in no case compromise my force.

Please forward this to Secretary of State.

From Lord Roberts, by letter, Cape Town, to Sir R. Buller

26th January, 1900

(Extract)

I recognize what a very difficult operation you are now engaged in, and I should have been pleased beyond measure to hear that you had succeeded in relieving Ladysmith. You will now know from my telegram of today that, if you are not confident of forcing your way there, it would, in my opinion, be better that you should abandon the attempt, until I am in the Orange Free State, but I consider it is most desirable there should be no retirement from the line of the Tugela, for, as I mentioned in my telegram, reports from the Boer camp point to the enemy being harassed by the strain thrown on them, as they feel they are unable to cope with our artillery fire.

Letter from General Sir R. Buller, Natal, to Lord Roberts

Spearman's Hill, 4th February, 1900

... I have today received, per Captain Foot, your letter of the 26th January ... White keeps a stiff upper lip, but some of those under him are desponding. He calculates he has now 7,000 effectives. They are eating their horses, and have very little else. He expects to be attacked in force this week, and though he affects to be confident I doubt if he really is. He has begged me to keep the enemy off him as much as I can, and I can only do this by pegging away ... I do not think a move into the Free State will much affect our position here... If you would tell me how you propose to advance on Bloemfontein—from where that is—I should be better able to say what I could do.

The above extracts are published at the desire of Sir Redvers Buller, to explain the telegrams which follow:

From Field-Marshal Lord Roberts to the Secretary of State for War (received 6th February, 11.15 pm)

Cape Town, 6th February, 1900, 6.30 pm

(Telegram)

Following received from Buller:

> I have pierced the enemy's line after a fight lasting all of yesterday, without many casualties, and I now hold the hill which divides their position, and which will give me access to Ladysmith plain if I can advance. I shall then be 10 miles from White, with but one place for enemy to stand between us I must, however, drive back enemy either on my right or left to get my artillery and stores on to the plain. It is an operation which will cost from 2,000 to 3,000 men, and I am not confident though hopeful I can do it. The question is, how would such a loss affect your plans, and do you think the chance of the relief of Ladysmith worth the risk? It is the only possible way to relieve White, and if I give up this chance I know no other.

The following is my reply to Buller:

> Ladysmith must be relieved even at the loss you expect. I should certainly persevere, and my hope is that the enemy will be so severely punished as to enable you to withdraw White's garrison without great difficulty. Let troops know that in their hands is the honour of the Empire, and that of their success I have no possible doubt.

PART II

∞∞∞∞∞

DESPATCHES RELATING TO THE SIEGE OF MAFEKING

ENDORSEMENT OF MAJOR-GENERAL BADEN-POWELL'S COMMAND

From Field-Marshal Lord Roberts to the Secretary of State for War
Army Headquarters, South Africa, Pretoria
21st June, 1900

My Lord,

I have the honour to submit for your Lordship's consideration a despatch, dated 18th May 1900, with annexures and a letter dated 6th June 1900, from Major-General R. S. S. Baden-Powell, describing the siege of Mafeking which lasted from the 13th October 1899 to the 17th May 1900, and bringing to notice the officers and men, as well as the civilians and ladies, who rendered good service during the above period.

I feel assured that Her Majesty's Government will agree with me in thinking that the utmost credit is due to Major-General Baden-Powell for his promptness in raising two regiments of Mounted Infantry in Rhodesia, and for the resolution, judgment, and resource which he displayed throughout the long and trying investment of Mafeking by the Boer forces. The distinction which Major-General Baden-Powell has earned must be shared by his gallant soldiers. No episode in the present war seems more praiseworthy than the prolonged defence of this town by a British garrison, consisting almost entirely of Her Majesty's Colonial forces, inferior in numbers and greatly inferior in artillery to the enemy, cut off from communication with Cape Colony, and with the hope of relief repeatedly deferred until the supplies of food were nearly exhausted.

Inspired by their Commander's example, the defenders of Mafeking maintained a never failing confidence and cheerfulness, which conduced most materially to the successful issue; they made light of the hardships to which they were exposed, and they withstood the enemy's attacks with an audacity which so disheartened their opponents that, except on one occasion, namely, on 12th May, no serious attempt was made to capture the place by assault. This attempt was repulsed in a manner which showed that the determination and fighting qualities of the garrison remained unimpaired to the last.

In recording my high appreciation of the conduct of all ranks during this memorable siege, I desire cordially to support Major-General Baden-Powell's recommendations on behalf of those serving under his orders, and the civilians and others who co-operated with him in the maintenance of order, and in the care of the sick and wounded.

Roberts, *Field-Marshal,*
Commanding-in-Chief, South Africa

From Major-General Baden-Powell, Commanding at Mafeking, to the Chief Staff Officer to Lord Roberts

Mafeking, 18th May, 1900

My Lord,

I have the honour to forward herewith my report on the siege of Mafeking by the Boers, from 13th October 1899 till the 17th May 1900, for the information of his Excellency the Field-Marshal Commanding in South Africa.

R. S. S. Baden-Powell
Major-General

REPORT OF THE SIEGE OF MAFEKING, BY MAJOR-GENERAL BADEN-POWELL OCTOBER 1899–MAY 1900

RESUMÉ

I arrived in the beginning of August in Rhodesia, with orders:

1. To raise two regiments of Mounted Infantry.
2. In the event of war, to organize the defence of the Rhodesia and Bechuanaland frontiers.
3. As far as possible, to keep forces of the enemy occupied in this direction away from their own main forces.

I had the two regiments raised, equipped, supplied, and ready for service by the end of September.

As war became imminent, I saw that my force would be too weak to effect much if scattered along the whole border (500 miles), unless it were reinforced with some men and good guns. I reported this, but as none were available I decided to concentrate my two columns at Tuli and Mafeking, respectively, as being the desirable points to hold.

Of the two, Mafeking seemed the more important for many reasons, strategical and political:

1. Because it is the outpost for Kimberley and Cape Colony.
2. Also, equally, for the Protectorate and Rhodesia.
3. It threatens the weak flank of the Transvaal.
4. It is the head-centre of the large native districts of the north-west, with their 200,000 inhabitants.
5. It contains important railway stocks and shops.
6. Also large food and forage supplies.

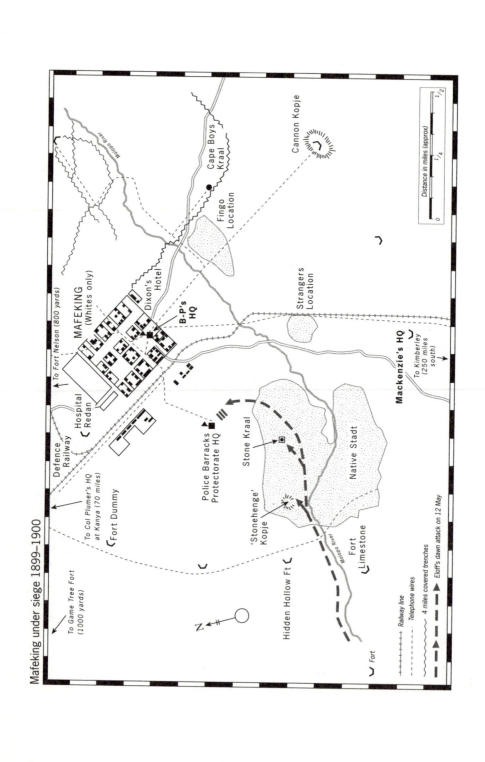

Mafeking under siege 1899–1900

To Game Tree Fort (1000 yards)

To Col Plumer's HQ at Kanya (70 miles)

Fort Dummy

Defence Railway

To Fort Nelson (800 yards)

Hospital Redan

MAFEKING (Whites only)

Dixon's Hotel

B-P's HQ

Molopo River

Cape Boys Kraal

Fingo Location

Cannon Kopje

Police Barracks Protectorate HQ

Stone Kraal

'Stonehenge' Kopje

Native Stadt

Strangers Location

Mackenzie's HQ

To Kimberley (250 miles south)

Fort Limestone

Molopo River

Hidden Hollow Ft

Fort

N

Railway line
Telephone wires
4 miles covered trenches
Eloff's dawn attack on 12 May

Distance in miles (approx)

0   1/4   1/2

Therefore, I left the northern column in charge of Colonel Plumer, and went myself to Mafeking, and organized its defence.

Mafeking

Mafeking is an open town, 1,000 yards square, in open undulating country, on the north bank of the Molopo stream. Eight miles from the Transvaal border. White population, about 1,000.

The native Stadt lies ½ mile south-west, and contains 6,000 inhabitants.

The defence force

700 whites, of whom 20 were Imperial Army, remainder Protectorate Regiment, British South Africa Police, Cape Police, and Bechuanaland Rifles (Volunteers). These were used to man the forts and outworks.

300 able-bodied townsmen enrolled as town guard. Employed to garrison the town itself.

300 natives enrolled as cattle guards, watchmen, police, etc.

Half the defenders were armed with L.M., half with M.H. rifles, with 600 rounds per rifle.

Total numbers:

White men	1,074
White women	229
White children	405
Natives	7,500

Our armament consisted of:

Four 7-pr M.L. guns
One 1-pr Hotchkiss
One 2-in Nordenfelt} (all old)
Seven 303 Maxims

To this armament we afterwards added:

One 6-pr M.L. old ship's gun
One 16-pr M.L. howitzer (made in our own shops)

I had two armoured engines promised from Kimberley. I had armoured trucks made at Bulawayo and Mafeking. One engine arrived, the other was cut off *en route* by the enemy and captured at Kraaipan.

The siege

On the 13th October the siege began. General Cronje with an army of 8,000 Boers and 10 guns, most of them of modern pattern and power, surrounded the place.

On the approach of the enemy we sallied out and, in a sharp little engagement dealt them a severe blow, by which they lost 53 killed and many more wounded, and which had a lasting morale effect.

During the first phase of the siege, October and November, General Cronje made various attempts to take the place. These attacks we beat off without difficulty in every case, and responded by sorties, varying their nature every time as far as possible, and making them so sudden and so quickly withdrawn as not to give the enemy's supports time to come up and overpower us. Of these "kicks" we delivered half-a-dozen, on 14th, 17th, 20th, 25th, 27th, 31st October, and 7th November (the Boers quote 14, but they include demonstrations and shelling of dummy forts, guns, and armoured trucks, etc., which we put up to draw their fire).

The enemy's losses in this period were very heavy as compared with ours:

Boers' losses: 287 killed, 800 wounded.[*]
Our losses: 35 killed, 101 wounded, 27 missing.

Cronje having lost a month of valuable time at Mafeking, now gave up the idea of taking the place by storm, and moved off south for Kimberley with 4,000 men and six guns (leaving General Snyman with the remainder, viz., 3,000 to 4,000 men and six guns including a 94-pr siege gun to invest us).

Seeing then that we could not be relieved for many weeks, if not months, I took over into our own management all details such as hospital, municipality, police, treasury, post and telegraph, railway, native affairs, water supply, ordnance shops, etc.

I also took over all food, forage, and liquor stores, and native supplies, etc., and put everybody on rations.

I had disposed my garrison over what some of my officers considered a rather extended perimeter (about 5 or 6 miles), but everything was arranged for drawing in our horns if necessary. However, in the event we were able to maintain our original position, and even further to extend it as became necessary.

The next phase lasted three months, November to January, during which Snyman pushed his works and trenches nearer to the place. He also drew a cordon of natives around the whole. His artillery kept up a continual bombardment on the town.

On our part, during January, February, and March, we pushed out counter-works and gradually gained point after point of ground till we obtained grazing for our livestock, and finally (after a hard tussle in the "Brickfields", in trenching and counter-trenching up to within 70 yards of enemy's works), we drove them back at all points out of range for rifle fire of the town.

During this period, owing to the careful and systematic sharp-shooting of our men the enemy's losses continued to be largely in excess of ours. 40 per month killed was admitted by the Boer medical officer.

In April the enemy withdrew the siege gun, and contented themselves with investing us at a distance, and shelling our cattle in the hope of starving us into submission.

[*] These numbers are quoted from Transvaal newspapers, but must, I think, be exaggerated. I think that about 600 killed and wounded would be nearer the mark.

On the 12th May the enemy made a bold night attack on the place, and succeeded in getting into the Stadt with their storming party, but we beat back their supports and surrounded the remainder, inflicting on them a loss of 70 killed and wounded, and 108 prisoners, including Eloff their commandant (grandson of President Kruger).

In the meantime, Colonel Plumer had near Tuli prevented a force of Boers from invading Matabeleland from the south. After their retreat the rising of the river made the border comparatively safe, and I called him down to defend the railway and the Protectorate border (which were already being held by a small force organized from Bulawayo by Colonel Nicholson).

Colonel Plumer accordingly pushed down the line, repairing it to within 40 miles of Mafeking, and pushing back the enemy who had been holding it. He then established himself in a good position 35 miles north-west of us, where he was in touch by means of runners and pigeons, was able to afford refuge to our natives escaping out, and he was also able to put a stop to enemy's depredations and to give security to the natives throughout the Protectorate, his force being too small to effect more till reinforced. His presence enabled us to get rid of nearly 2,000 native women and children, which materially relieved the strain on our food supply.

Early in May, he was reinforced by Canadian Artillery and Queensland Infantry, etc., and on 15th he joined hands with a relief column from the south under Colonel Mahon. And, on the 17th May, the relief of Mafeking was successfully effected by the combined columns, after a siege of 218 days.

One of the most noticeable features of the long and trying siege has been the loyalty, patience, and good feeling which have prevailed throughout the community, civil, military and native. The steadiness and gallantry of the troops in action, and their cheerful acceptance of hardships, are beyond praise.

The ladies, and especially those who acted as nurses in the hospitals, displayed the greatest patience and fortitude.

The significance of the siege

At Mafeking
1. A force of 8,000 Boers and 10 guns was contained at the first outbreak of war, and prevented from either combining with the Tuli column, and invading Rhodesia, or joining the forces against Kimberley. Cronje's commando was thus held here for a month.
2. From 2,000 to 3,000 Boers and eight guns (including a 94-pr) were kept employed here for over 6 months.
3. The enemy expended considerably over 100 tons of ammunition, and lost over 1,000 men killed and wounded, and had four guns disabled and one captured.
4. Large stores of food and forage, and general stocks, were prevented from falling into the enemy's hands.

5. Valuable railway plant, including 18 locomotives, rolling stock, shops, coal, etc., were saved.
6. Refuge was given to a large number of British from the Transvaal.
7. Most of the local neighbouring tribes, and all those of the Protectorate and South Matebeleland, remained loyal which they could not have continued to do had Mafeking fallen and they been at the mercy of the Boers.
8. Loss of prestige to Cronje's force, who had apparently expected to take possession at once on first arrival, and had had proclamation printed annexing the district to the South African Republic.
9. Eloff and 108 Boers and foreigners made prisoners of war.

The Rhodesian Column

During the same period the northern portion of my force under Colonel Plumer (in spite of its small numbers and the exceptionally difficult country and trying climate in which it was operating) succeeded:

1. In holding and sending back the enemy in their attempt to invade Rhodesia, via Tuli.
2. In holding the Bulawayo railway for some 200 miles south of the Rhodesian border.
3. In giving direct support and protection to the natives in Khama's and Linchwe's domains, and Bathoen's and the Protectorate generally when threatened by the enemy.
4. In pushing down and repairing the railway in the face of the enemy to within 40 miles of Mafeking, and there establishing a place of security for our natives escaping from Mafeking, and collecting supplies ready to effect our relief in Mafeking on arrival of reinforcements.

The Palapye Column

A small column organized by Colonel Nicholson, from Bulawayo, with armoured trains, etc., held Mangwe, Palapye, Mochudi, etc., on the railway until Plumer's column was available for the duty.

The whole of the frontier force, north and south columns combined, numbered under 1,700, while the Boers during the early part of the campaign had between 9,000 and 10,000 out on their northern and north-western border. Country operated over, between Mafeking and Tuli, 450 miles in length.

DETAILS OF THE SIEGE

Artillery

Our so-called artillery should of course have been entirely outclassed by the modern high-velocity guns of the enemy, but in practice they managed to hold their own in spite of their using powder, shells and fuzes all made in our own shops.

The artillery and also the ordnance shops were under Major Panzera, assisted by Lieutenant Daniell, British South Africa Police.

Communications

Local

Telephone All outlying forts and look-out posts were connected up with headquarters, under management of Mr Howat, postmaster, and his staff. I was thus able to receive reports and issue orders for all parts of the defence instantaneously.

Postal To cover the heavy expenses of runners, and for the convenience of the public, postage was established at: 1d for town, 3d for outlying forts, 1s for up country.

Signalling Heliograph, lamp and flag signalling was established for defence purposes by brigade signallers, under Major Panzera and Sergeant-Major Moffat.

Megaphones were also made and used in outlying trenches and posts.

Phonophores were also made and used on the armoured train, attached to ordinary telegraph lines.

Distant

Runners Native runners were employed twice weekly, or oftener when necessary, to take despatches, letters, etc., to our northern column. They had to be highly paid, as the risk of capture and death was very great. I was thus practically in touch with my force on the railway, and through them with Colonel Nicholson at the base, and Colonel Plumer's column at Tuli.

Civil administration

I established, for the trial of all cases not directly amenable to military law, a Court of Summary Jurisdiction:

Members
Resident Commissioner
Resident Magistrate
Town Commandant
Officer Commanding Protectorate Regiment
Chief Staff Officer

At first it was a little difficult to make the civilians appreciate the restrictions of martial law, and, as times grew more critical, there came a tendency to spread rumours and to grumble, this had to be stopped. I also published some explanatory remarks and advice on the working of martial law etc.,

Casualties in Mafeking

	Killed and died of wounds	Wounded	Missing	Died	Accident	Total
Combatants						
Whites						
Officers	6	15	1			22
NCOs and men	61	103	26	16	5	211
Total						
Whites	67	118	27	16	5	233
Coloured	25	68				83
				Total combatants		**316**
Non-combatants						
Whites	4	5				41
Natives	65	117		32		182
Baralongs	264					264
				Total non-combatants		**487**

Total all casualties during siege, 803.

Out of 44 officers, 21 were killed, wounded, or missing.
Out of 975 men, 190 were killed, wounded, or missing.

and these steps had a most marked effect, obedience to orders and a good spirit thenceforward prevailed.

Compensation

From the commencement of the siege careful record was kept of all shell fire damage to property, and claims of owners considered and assessed. Total assessed, £16,462 10s 2d. No promise was held out that Government would grant compensation, the proceedings were merely intended to assist the commission should one afterwards be assembled, and to protect Government against exorbitant claims.

A record was also made of losses suffered by refugees, in property, live-stock, etc. All livestock killed or wounded by shell fire was bought at a fair price and utilized for food, so that the owners have no claims on this head, at the same time the value of the animals is in many cases not represented by cash, and it would be far more satisfactory to the owners if they could be repaid in kind. This is a point which I venture to suggest be taken into consideration when dealing with the Boers after the war; a substantial fine in cattle would touch them heavily without leaving them destitute, and the bestowal of such cattle on deserving and looted loyalists would give great satisfaction and be far more acceptable to them, and less expensive to Government, than grants of money.

Correspondents

(Under Lieutenant the Hon. A. Hanbury-Tracy as Press Censor)
These gentlemen gave a certain amount of trouble at first, as for the most part they were more reporters than correspondents. Further reforms in the matter of correspondents in the field are very desirable. The enemy derived a great deal of information as to our circumstances from the newspapers, not only the local ones, but also from the Colonial and English papers, in spite of a strict censorship on our part.

Defence accounts

(Under Captain Greener, British South Africa Police)
These are detailed in the table 'Expenditure during the siege'.

Defence works

(Under direction of Major Vyvyan, for town and East Front; Major Godley, West Front)

Scheme General scheme at first was to secure the town and Stadt by clearing front, laying mines, fortifying outskirts, etc. Then to push out advanced trenches to drive back those of the enemy, and finally to establish a girdle of outlying forts. The scheme included the provision of bombproofs and

Expenditure during the siege

	£
To labour	13,024
To pay, local corps and trench allowance	20,777
To pay, clerical and civil staff	3,543
To foodstuffs, grain, rations, etc.	36,076
To material, clothing, equipment, etc.	10,801
To hospital staff, comforts, etc.	5,411
To local transport	890
Total	90,522
To payments other than defence, viz., frontier forces, special pay, etc.	32,729
Total	123,251

Receipts

	£
By foodstuffs, and grain sales	5,184
By soup kitchens	3,242
By sales of Government property	442
By local post office	238
By dog tax	67
By fines	127
Total	9,300
Weekly average expenditure in pay	1,550
Average receipts for rations	625
Soup	600
Total	1,225

extensive covered ways, gun emplacements, drainage, etc. In all some 60 works were made, and about 6½ miles of trenches. The perimeter of the works at first was approximately 7 miles, latterly it extended to a little over 10 miles.

Nature Generally semicircular redans, but no two works were similar in trace, they varied according to position, ground, etc. At first dug out and kept very low, latterly, owing to difficulties of drainage, long grass, inaccuracy of enemy's shell fire, etc., they were made more upstanding. Head cover was found to be essential. When trenches were near, steel loopholes had to be used, the ordinary sandbag and wooden ones being too good a target to the enemy.

Huts A good form of portable iron and wood hut was devised, and used for housing the fort garrisons.

Enemy's artillery, fighting, treachery, field works

Artillery   Guns employed:

> 1×94-pr Creusot, 15-cm, 20-lb charge
> 2×7-pr (Jameson's)
> 2×5-pr Armstrongs' B.L.
> 1×12-pr B.L.
> 1×9-pr Krupp, B.L.
> 2×Q.F. 14-prs, high velocity
> 2×1-pr Maxims
> Total 11 guns

The 94-pr fired 1,497 rounds, and the artillery altogether fired 2,000 rounds during the siege.

The damage done was very small, partly owing to the open nature of the town and lowness of our forts, but more especially on account of the want of intelligent directing of the fire.

Fighting The enemy's attacks invariably failed from want of discipline and pluck on the part of the men. In the attack on Cannon Kopje they got within 400 yards, and even started digging shelter trenches, but when the men began to fall the rest retreated promptly.

The night attack on the Stadt, on 12th May, was boldly led by Eloff and a number of foreigners, and had their supports come on with equal pluck we should have had a hard task to drive them out, but as it was the supports were easily beaten off and the storming party surrounded.

Treachery The enemy fired on numerous occasions on our hospital, convent, and women's laager, although these were conspicuously marked with Red Cross flags, stood in isolated positions, and had been fully pointed out by me to the Boer Generals.

The women's laager was deliberately shelled in particular on 24th and 30th October, 27th January and 11th April. The Red Cross flag was used to cover artillery taking up position on 24th, 30th, and 31st October. Convent deliberately shelled, 16th October, 3rd and 8th November. Our white flag, returning from a conference with the enemy, was deliberately volleyed, 17th January.

Field works The enemy's trenches were of a very good design, and made in well-selected positions. The typical trench or fort consisted of a chain of small chambers 10 feet square, partly excavated, partly built up with sandbags, having stout walls, loopholed to front and rear, the whole roofed in with corrugated iron and railway rails. Command, about 3 feet.

Finance

(Under Captain Greener, as Chief Paymaster)
I ordered all Government accounts to be kept settled up to date, so as to leave as little as possible for subsequent settlement; much work and confusion has thereby been saved.

The accounts were well kept by Captain Greener and his staff. An examiner of accounts was appointed to check accounts before payment, and also an auditor for the larger amounts.

Cash in bank amounted to £12,000, of which only £650 was in silver. Cash soon became scarce, because the public, especially the natives and Indian traders, concealed all the cash they could get, in anticipation of the place being taken by the enemy.

Paper money thus became necessary, and I issued coupons for 1s, 2s and 3s. Ultimately gold also became scarce, and £1 notes were printed in cyanotype and issued; but they never got into real circulation as people kept them as curios to the extent of £700. 10s coupons were issued with satisfactory result. For the convenience of the men, and to get cash from the public, a "Garrison Savings Bank" was opened. Deposits amounted to £8,800.

	£
Total Government expenditure to end of May	142,660
Total Government receipts to end of May	11,828

Food supply

(Under Captain Ryan)
Early in the siege, I took over all merchant stocks and put everybody on rations.

Beginning on the usual scale, I gradually reduced it to the lowest that would allow of the men being fit for duty. During the latter part of the siege no extras of any kind were obtainable. All lived strictly on the following scale:

	At first	Latterly
Meat	1 lb	¾ to 1 lb
Bread	1 lb	5 oz
Vegetables	1 lb	6 oz
Coffee	⅓ oz	⅓ oz
Salt	½ oz	½ oz
Sugar	2 oz	
Tea	½ oz	
Sowens		1 quart

We had a large stock of meat, both live and tinned. For livestock, we had to open up a wide extent of grazing ground. We ate the fresh meat first in order to avoid loss from enemy's fire, failure of grass and water, lung sickness, etc. The tinned meat we stored in bombproof chambers, and kept as reserve. During the last 2 months, we were on horseflesh three days a week.

Our stocks of meal were comparatively small, but we had a large supply of forage oats. These we ground into flour, and fermented the residue into sowens (a form of porridge) and the remaining husks went as forage to the horses. Fresh vegetables were largely grown within the defences, and for a greater part of the siege formed a regular portion of the ration.

The cost of feeding the troops was 1s 3d per ration, or, with fresh vegetables, 1s 6d; about 3d below the contract price in peace. Civilians paid 2s, and women in the laager 1s 2d.

All liquor was taken over and issued in "tots" to the troops on wet nights, and I think saved much sickness.

Natives For the natives, we established four soup kitchens at which horse stew was sold daily, and five sowen kitchens. Natives were all registered, to prevent fraud, and bought rations at 1 quart per adult, and 1 pint per child, at 3d per pint.

Defence watchmen, workmen, police, etc., and certified destitute persons were given free rations. The kitchens so managed paid their own expenses.

They were under Captain Wilson, ADC, with Mr Myers as cash taker and inspector.

Fuel

Coal 300 tons available at railway store, was used for armoured train, ordnance foundry, pumping station, flour mills, forage factory, forges, etc.

Wood 25,000 lb weekly for bakery, soup, and oat-sowen kitchens, cooking, etc. Procured from roofs of huts in the Stadt, old wagons, lopped trees, fencing, etc.

Petroleum Asbestos stove made, but was not a success.

Patent fuel Cow dung and coal dust, mixed in equal parts and baked, produced 20 tons good fuel.

Garrison

[Details of the garrison strength are given in the table on p. 248.]
Town Guard, 296 men (untrained)
Total garrison: 44 officers, 975 men

From the above Town Guard was formed the Railway Division, 2 officers, 20 men, under (local) Captain More.

Garrison strength

Force	Commander	Strength	
		Officers	Men
Protectorate Regiment	Lieut.-Colonel Hore	21	448
British South Africa Police	Lieut.-Colonel Walford	10	81
Cape Police, Division 1	Inspector Marsh	2	45
Cape Police, Division 2	Inspector Browne	2	54
Bechuanaland Rifles	Captain Cowan	4	77
Deduct missing at Lobatsi		1	26
Total drilled men		38	679

The following commanded sections of the defence:

Western defences, Major Godley
Stadt and south-western forts, Captain Marsh
Cannon Kopje and south front, Colonel Walford
South-eastern works (Brickfields), Inspector Marsh, at first, Inspector Browne, latterly
North-east works, Captain Cowan
Town, Colonel Vyvyan, at first, Major Goold-Adams, latterly

Hospital

(Under Major Anderson, Royal Army Medical Corps, as Principal Medical Officer)

Staff
Dr W. Hayes (acted as Principal Medical Officer during first part of siege)
Surgeon-Major Holmden, British South Africa Police
Dr T. Hayes, District Surgeon
Dr Elmes

Victoria Hospital (70 beds, base hospital)
Nursing staff: Miss Hill (Matron) and three nurses, assisted by four volunteer nurses; also by Mother Teresa and six sisters.
Convalescent hospital: At convent, Lady Sarah Wilson.
Women and children's hospital: Miss Craufurd.

On outbreak of war I took over the town hospital, but at first the administration was not satisfactory on account of want of supervision over expenses of stores, and sanitation. I therefore appointed an issuer and storekeeper, and a sanitary inspector. To existing accommodation I added a native ward, nurses' quarters, a ward for Colonial Contingent, and a boarded marquee for shell wounds, etc.

Both doctors and nurses did excellent work, always short-handed, and frequently under fire. (All the hospital buildings were struck by shells and bullets, and the first convalescent hospital was wrecked, and the second damaged by 94-pr shells.)

Natives

(Under Mr Bell, Resident Magistrate and Civil Commissioner)

Natives in Mafeking, during the siege, were:

Baralongs	5,000
Fingoes, Shangans, and district Baralongs	2,000
Total	between 7,000 and 8,000

The Shangans were refugees from the Johannesburg mines, and were sent into Mafeking by the Boers on the outbreak of war. Being accustomed to digging they proved useful for working gangs on the defences.

The district Baralongs, Fingoes, and Cape Boys, came into Mafeking when their villages were burnt and their cattle looted by the Boers. From among them we got about 300 men to act as armed cattle guards, watch-men, police, etc.

The local Baralongs living in the Stadt displayed their loyalty, and did some good service (especially after I had deposed their Chief Wessels for want of energy, and supplied good despatch runners, spies, cattle runners, etc.). Of the natives living in the district, Saani remained particularly loyal, and although a prisoner in the hands of the Boers he managed to send us information from time to time. Bathoen was loyal, but too timid to be of use. Copane, a subject of the Boers, although forced to supply them with men, offered us his allegiance. Hatsiokomo and Matuba (British subjects) joined the enemy, and the latter and his men fought with them.

Railway

(Under Captain More)
132 men, 46 women, 86 children.

Eighteen locomotives, only one of which was damaged by shell fire, as they were moved round to the "lee" side of the railway buildings with every move of the enemy's big gun. Also a large amount of rolling stock.

Value of railway plant, £120,000.

A defence railway 1½ miles long was laid round the north-east front. We made three armoured trucks, walls of steel rails, iron lookout tower, acetyline search light, speaking tubes, electric bells, water, medicine chests, stretchers, etc.

200 tons of rails were used in construction of bombproofs.

The armoured trains did much good service.

Specialities

Ammunition Mr Fodisch, our gunsmith, reloaded Martini-Henry cartridges, using ordinary gun caps fixed with plaster of Paris for detonators. Powder and bullets were home-made.

Armoured train We armoured ordinary long-bogey trucks with steel rails (iron ones not being bullet-proof) to a height of 5 feet, with loopholes and gun ports. I had three prepared at Mafeking under the able direction of Mr More, Resident Engineer Bechuanaland Railway, also three at Bulawayo by Mr Wallis, Resident Engineer.

Bombs Dynamite bombs were made up in small potted meat and milk tins for use as hand grenades, with slow match fuzes, with complete success by Lieutenant Feltham. Sergeant Page, champion bait thrower of Port Elizabeth, by using a whip stick and short line was able to throw these with accuracy over a distance of 100 yards.

Brawn was made from ox and horse hides and feet, and was much appreciated as meat.

Fuel When coal and wood began to run low a very satisfactory fuel was made up of coal dust and cow dung mixed.

Fuzes A simple and useful percussion fuze was invented by Lieutenant Daniell, British South Africa Police, in which the butt end of a Lee-Metford cartridge was used as detonator. This fuze was in regular use with our locally made shells.

Howitzer A 6-inch howitzer was made in our workshops, under the orders of Major Panzera, by Mr Conolly. The bore was a tube of steel, with iron rings shrunk on in two tiers. The breech was a block of cast bronze. The trunnions and ring were a similar solid casting. The gun threw a 18-lb ball (shell), and reached a distance of 4,000 yards.

Lookout poles Telescopic lookout poles were made of lengths of iron piping, and set up with steel wire stays, with a pulley and slung seat to hoist the man to the masthead. Height, about 18 feet.

Oat bread Mr Ellitson, our master baker, made up our forage oats into a good form of bread. The oats were winnowed, cleaned, kiln dried, ground, steam sieved (twice), and made into bread in the usual way, with a small admixture of Boer meal.

Search light Mr Walker, agent for the Acetyline Gas Company, under Captain More's direction, made a very effective and portable acetyline search light with an engine head-light and a theodolite stand. These we had stationed in the principal forts and on the armoured train.

Signalling lamp Sergeant-Major Moffat and Mr Walker devised a very effective and portable acetyline signalling lamp, which is reckoned to be readable at 15 miles. We had two in work.

Sowens This is a form of porridge, made from the fermented bran of oats after the flour had been extracted for making bread. 100 lb of bran in 37 gallons of water give 33 gallons of sowens. On this food we fed both natives and whites. We had five sowen kitchens, each capable of producing 800 gallons daily. It was sold at 6d per quart to those not entitled to it as a ration.

Sausages The horses which we used for meat were, as a rule, so poor in condition that we found it best to cut off the flesh from the bones and mince it for issue as ration. The remainder of the carcase then went to the soup kitchen. The mince was then mixed with spice and saltpetre, and made up into sausages, the intestines of the same animal being used for sausage skins. The meat thus treated lasted longer, and was more palatable.

Steel loopholes Finding that the enemy shot through ordinary loopholes at short distances, especially in trench work, I devised a form of steel loophole with two plates of ½-inch steel bolted together at an angle of 45 degrees, with a hole 2 inches square in the middle of the joint, the shield being 2 feet high and 2 feet wide.

Steel sap roller I also had a sapping shield made of two sheets of ⅜-inch steel, each 4 feet square, bolted together at an angle and mounted on wheels, to be pushed in front of a party pushing a sap under fire.

Relief committee

Numbers of the refugees and some of the townspeople, being without means during the siege, I formed a relief committee, consisting of the Mayor, the Base Commandant, the Chaplain, and other representative men, with myself as president, for disbursing funds for purchase of clothing and necessaries, etc., and for the issue of rations to deserving cases.

Sums received from England, from the various relief funds, were thus carefully and advantageously administered and accounted for, and there was no real suffering among the white population.

Staff

Headquarters
Colonel Commanding—Colonel Baden-Powell
Chief Staff Officer—Major Lord E. Cecil, DSO
Deputy-Assistant Adjutant-General (B)—Captain Ryan, Army Service Corps
Aide-de-Camp—Captain G. Wilson, Royal Horse Guards
Intelligence Officer—Lieutenant Hon. A. Hanbury-Tracy, Royal Horse Guards.

Local
Commanding Artillery and Deputy-Assistant Adjutant-General—Major Panzera, British South Africa Police
Base Commandant and Commanding Engineer—Major C. B. Vyvyan, "Buffs"
Principal Medical Officer—Dr W. Hayes (at first), Major Anderson, Royal Army Medical Corps
Chief Paymaster—Captain Greener, British South Africa Police
Town Commandant and Protectorate, Natives—Major Goold-Adams, CB, CMG
Local Natives—Mr C. G. H. Bell, Resident Magistrate and Civil Commissioner
Women and children—Mr F. Whiteley, Mayor
Transport—Lieutenant McKenzie

Post and telegraphs—Mr Howat, Postmaster

Chaplains—Rev W. H. Weekes (Church of England), Rev Father Ogle (Roman Catholic).

Spies

The enemy were well informed of all that went on in Mafeking during the siege. We had over 30 suspects in the gaol for the greater part of the time, but it was almost impossible to get proofs against them. The stationmaster had undoubtedly been in communication with an ex-fenian, Whelan, a prominent member of the Irish Land League. This man we arrested on the outbreak of war, and kept in gaol. He had among his papers a code for messages.

The natives acted as spies for the enemy; we caught two and tried them, and shot them. More than half the families in the women's laager were Dutch, and of pro-Boer sympathies. Four of our men deserted to the enemy at different times.

Transport

(Under Lieutenant McKenzie)

This department was very ably managed, and though at first much hired transport was employed, Lieutenant McKenzie gradually arranged so that the whole of the Army Service Corps, Royal Engineers, sanitary, etc., duties (as well as the regimental work) were carried out by the Government transport, available, viz.:

11 wagons
6 Scotch carts
2 trollies
3 ambulances
188 mules
12 oxen

The mules kept their condition wonderfully well, considering the absence of forage and the amount of work.

Water supply

(Under Major Vyvyan and Major Hepworth)

The enemy cut off our water supply from the waterworks during the first few days of the siege. Fortunately the season was unusually wet, and consequently the Molopo stream did not run dry, and house tanks kept fairly filled. But to make sure against contingencies, and to ensure a supply of wholesome water, we cleaned out various wells and dug a new one of great capacity. The water from these was issued to the town and garrison by tank wagons, filled nightly and posted at convenient points during the day.

Women's laager

(Under Mr F. Whiteley, the Mayor)

Formed at Mr Rowland's house, where everything was placed at the disposal of the refugees in a most kindly way by Mr Rowlands.

Number of whites: 10 men, 188 women, 315 children; also about 150 native servant girls.

Health fairly good considering the circumstances. Diphtheria made its appearance, but after four cases was stopped by isolation. Deaths, 24.

A large bombproof, 180 yards by 5 feet, was made for the accommodation of the whole of the inhabitants of the laager, with protected ways, latrines, etc.

The women and children were rationed, the supply and distribution being efficiently carried out by Mr Whiteley, without any kind of remuneration to himself. This gentleman carried out the entire management of the laager with conspicuous success, and was very ably assisted by Rev W. H. Weekes and Mr Rowlands.

The following were the cases dealt with by the Court of Summary Jurisdiction:

Charges	
House–breaking	14
Treason	35
Theft	197
Minor offences	184
Total	430
Punishments	
Death	5
Corporal punishment	115
Detention in gaol	23
Fines	57
Imprisonment with hard labour	91
Total	291

Total fines, £140 3s 6d.

ENGAGEMENTS DURING THE SIEGE

Action of 14th October

Six miles north of Mafeking on railway

Early in the morning of the 14th October our reconnoitring patrols exchanged shots with a strong party of the enemy, who were advancing along the railway 3 miles north of the town.

I ordered out the armoured train, under Captain Williams, British South Africa Police, to endeavour to rush the Boers and pour a heavy fire into them, as I wanted to make the first blow felt by them to be a really hard one. The train carried a 1-pr Hotchkiss and a .303-inch Maxim, and 15 men, British South Africa Police.

I sent out, in support of the train, a squadron of the Protectorate Regiment, under Captain FitzClarence.

On coming up with the train he found it heavily engaged with the Boers, who had been strongly reinforced from their laager, some 7 miles north; they had also brought up a 7-pr Krupp and a 1-pr Maxim.

Captain FitzClarence, dismounting his men, advanced to attack with his left protected by the train.

For a quarter of an hour he was held by the enemy under a very hot fire, and then, pressing forward, well backed up by the train, he drove the enemy back and successfully beat off their several attempts to encircle his flank. Meantime, I sent up an additional troop under Lord Charles Bentinck, and also a 7-pr. These also became hotly engaged and did good work. The fire from the armoured train put the enemy's gun out of action before it had fired a shot, and eventually also drove the 1-pr Maxim from the field.

The engagement lasted about 4 hours, and the enemy largely outnumbered our men, but Captain FitzClarence made up for this deficiency by the able handling of his men. Moreover, he kept his orders in mind, and when he saw the opportunity he got his wounded on to the train, and after driving the enemy back he withdrew his command quietly on Mafeking, covered by the train, without any attempt on the part of the enemy to follow him up.

In this their first engagement, the Protectorate Regiment showed a spirit and dash worthy of highly trained troops, and were most ably led by Captain FitzClarence and Lord C. Bentinck.

This smartly fought little engagement had a great and lasting morale effect on the enemy.

Their losses were afterwards found to amount to 53 killed (including four field cornets) and a large number wounded. They also lost a number of horses.

Our casualties were:

2 killed
16 wounded (including two officers)
1 missing (cyclist)
4 horses killed
12 wounded.

Enemy's attack on the Stadt

25th October, 1899

Enemy commenced shelling at 6.30 am till midday from the east and south with seven guns. At noon they commenced a general advance against the town from the south-west, east, and north-east; the south-west being the main attack directed against the Stadt. Their number about 3,000. The enemy commenced firing at extreme range, to which we made no reply, reserving our fire for close distances. So soon as our volleys and Maxims commenced the enemy stopped their advance, and soon began to withdraw at all points. Casualties on our side were one man wounded, and two horses and eight mules wounded. The Boers losses unknown, but probably considerable, as their ambulances were on the field picking up for over an hour.

It was afterwards (10th December) ascertained that the attack on the Stadt was intended as a feint while the main attack should come off to north-ward, on our western face. The Boers had expected the Baralongs not to fire on them, and so advanced more openly than they would otherwise have done; nor had they expected to find white men defending the Stadt. Their loss was, therefore, pretty heavy, and, surprised at their rebuff, they fell back altogether.

At one period of the action, a small mounted troop of Boers advanced at a gallop towards the western position, and came under fire of the Cape Police Maxim, which dropped five of them, the remainder rapidly dispersed.

During the afternoon some of our scouts near the Brickfields were moving, under fire, when one of them fell with his horse and lay stunned. Two Cape Police troopers in the works ran out and placed the injured man on his horse, and brought him in under heavy fire from the enemy: names, Troopers George Collins and W. F. Green.

Night attack on Boer trenches

27th October, 1899

During past two days enemy had moved their advanced trenches closer into the east face. I determined to make an attack on their main advanced trench with the bayonet, in order to discourage their advancing further.

A night attack was therefore organized with Captain FitzClarence's squadron, Protectorate Regiment, supported by a party of Cape Police. Guiding lights were hoisted, by which Captain FitzClarence was able to lead his party past the flank of the main trench.

The attacking force moved off at 9.30 pm in silence, with magazines charged, but no cartridges in the chamber, the order being to use the bayonet only. The men wore white armlets and used "FitzClarence" as their password. The night was dark, but still. The squadron attained its position on the left rear of enemy's trench without being challenged or fired at. Captain FitzClarence then wheeled up his men, and with a cheer charged into the main and a subsidiary trench, and cleared both with the bayonet.

The enemy's rearward trenches opened a heavy fire, to which the Cape Police replied from a flank, in order to draw the fire on to themselves, and so to allow Captain FitzClarence's squadron to return unmolested.

The whole operation was carried out exactly in accordance with instructions, and was a complete success. The more so as the enemy, being taken by surprise, were in much confusion, and, as we afterwards discovered, fired into each other. Their casualties, we heard on reliable authority, amounted to 40 killed and wounded with the bayonet, 60 killed and wounded by rifle fire. Our casualties were six killed, nine wounded, two missing.

Action at Cannon Kopje

31st October, 1899

The enemy opened a heavy concentrated shell fire from the south-eastern heights, from the racecourse (east), and from Jackal's Tree (south-west), directed against Cannon Kopje. The fire was well aimed, and the racecourse gun took the work in reverse. For a time little harm was done beyond knocking down parts of the parapet and smashing the iron supports of the lookout tower: most of the garrison were lying in the trenches some 80 yards in rear of the fort. The gun and two Maxims in the work had been previously dismounted and stowed away for safety during shell fire, to which, of course, they were powerless to reply. The telephone wire was cut away early in the proceedings. After half an hour's steady and accurate artillery fire, the enemy, who had been gradually massing on the high ground south and south-east of the fort, began to advance in line of skirmishers from three sides at once; they were backed up by other parties in support. A large force also collected in the Molopo Valley, south-east of the town, and were formed evidently with the idea of storming the town after Cannon Kopje had been captured.

As the enemy began to get within range of the fort, the garrison moved up from their trench and manned the parapets and Maxims. It was then that we suffered some casualties from shell fire. As the enemy continued their advance, I sent to Captain Goodyear's Colonial Contingent to advance a party on to a ridge above them, and so to take enemy's attacking line in flank, but they could not be got to move. One Maxim at Ellis's Corner now jammed, and I had to replace it by one from the reserve.

Meantime, I had a 7-pr run out under cover of houses near south corner of the town. This opened, under direction of Lieutenant Murchison, on the flank of the enemy's line as it began to get near the fort. The gun made excellent practice, every shell going in among them and effectually stopped the further advance of the Boers.

These now hesitated and began to draw off, and as they did so their guns reopened on Cannon Kopje to cover their retirement. The fire then died down, and enemy sent out ambulances under Red Cross flags to recover their dead and wounded. We lost six killed and five wounded.

During this fight, the Boers sent out a Red Cross flag on to a commanding point and then brought their guns up into position there. I visited Cannon Kopje after the fight and congratulated Colonel Walford and his men on the gallant and determined stand made by them in the face of a very hot shell fire. The intention of the enemy had been to storm Cannon Kopje, and thence to bombard the south-eastern portion of the town, and to carry it with the large forces they had collected in the Molopo Valley. Their whole scheme was defeated by the gallant resistance made by the garrison, and by the telling fire it brought to bear on them. We afterwards learnt that the attack was designed and directed by young Cronje. The enemy's loss was not known, but ambulances were seen about the field picking up for a considerable time, and native spies reported there was much mourning in the laagers, and that several cart loads of dead had been brought in and buried.

Surprise on enemy's western laager

7th November, 1899
At 2.30 am, Major Godley paraded his force, in accordance with a plan I had arranged, to attack the western camp of the enemy with a heavy fire at daylight, and then to retire again before enemy's guns and reinforcements arrived on the scene. The force in enemy's camp was reckoned at 200 to 250. Our force consisted of:

Two 7-prs
One 1-pr Hotchkiss, under Major Panzera
One squadron of 60 men, Protectorate Regiment, dismounted, under Captain Vernon
One troop of 30 men, Bechuanaland Rifles, mounted, under Captain Cowan.

The force moved out along the heights to about 1,500 yards in advance of Major Godley's position; Captain Vernon's squadron leading in attack order, with the guns on his left rear, and Bechuanaland Rifles covering his right rear.

At 4.15 am, our guns opened on enemy at 1,800 yards, and the squadron fired volleys by alternate troops into the enemy's camp, over which they had full command from the heights they were on. The surprise was complete, the enemy bolting in all directions to take cover. Their 1-pr Maxim and 7-pr Krupp in the Beacons Fort in a short time responded with a heavy and well-directed fire. Large bodies of reinforcements very soon began to come down from the main south-west laager. Major Godley thereupon commenced withdrawing his forces, artillery retiring first; the Bechuanaland Rifles occupying Fort Ayr to cover the retirement, which they did very effectively against a wing of mounted Boers, who had worked round to our right flank. The enemy brought a very heavy musketry fire to bear on our force, but the retirement was carried out with the greatest steadiness. Enemy's strength, about 800 or 1,000. Our retirement was further covered by 7-pr at the west end of the Stadt, and the Cape Police Maxim and escort. In the course of the retirement, our 1-pr Hotchkiss upset and broke the limber hook; her crew, Gunners R. Cowan and H. Godson, very pluckily stood up and repaired damage with rope, etc., and got the gun away safely under heavy fire from enemy's 1-pr Maxim and 7-pr Krupp and rifle fire.

Three of the enemy's ambulances were seen picking up their casualties after the action, and we afterwards learnt that they had lost a considerable number. On our side we had five men wounded, five horses killed, five wounded, and 36 cattle in the refugee laager killed and wounded by bullets.

On this day a commando of the Boers made a demonstration against Khama's men on the Limpopo, and opened fire upon them, but shortly after retired across the border.

Action at Game Tree

26th December, 1899

The Boers' work at Game Tree, 2,500 yards north of the town, had checked our grazing in that direction, and it commanded our line of communication northward. Some shells thrown into it a few days previously had caused enemy temporarily to vacate it, showing it to be a weak open work; this had been confirmed by reconnaissance by our scouts, but as the enemy had been seen strengthening it during the past few days, I determined to attack before they should make it impregnable. Accordingly, two squadrons Protectorate Regiment, supported by armoured train and Bechuanaland Rifles, were ordered to attack from the left flank of the work, under direction of Major Godley, while three guns and Maxim prepared the way from the right front of the work. This scheme was carried out at dawn on the 26th, the guns making good practice, and the two squadrons advancing in attack formation exactly as required. But on pressing home the attack a heavy fire killed or wounded most of the officers and the leading troops. These succeeded in gaining the parapet, but the work was found to have been strongly roofed in and so closed as to be impregnable.

The attack fell back upon the eastern face, and pushed forward again on the southern face, but eventually had to retire. If blame for this reverse falls on anyone it should fall on myself, as everybody concerned did their part of the work thoroughly well, and exactly in accordance with the orders I had issued. Both officers and men worked with splendid courage and spirit.

Boers' attack

12th May, 1900

At about 4 am on 12th May, a very heavy long-range musketry fire was opened on the town from east, north-east, and south-east. I sounded the alarm, and the garrison stood to arms. The fire continued for half-an-hour; I thereupon wired to the south-west outposts to be on the lookout.

At about 4.30, 300 Boers made a rush through the western outposts and got into the Stadt; this they then set fire to. I ordered the western defenders to close in so as to prevent any supports from coming in after the leading body, and sent the reserve squadron there to assist. They succeeded in driving off an attack of about 500 without difficulty, and returned to round up their station. In the meantime the Boers in the Stadt had rushed the British South African Police fort and made prisoners the men in it, viz. three officers and 15 men, staff of the Protectorate Regiment.

In the darkness the attackers had got divided up into three parties, and as it got light we were able to further separate these from each other, and to surround and attack them in detail. The first party surrendered, the second were driven out with loss by three squadrons, Protectorate Regiment, under Major Godfrey, and the third, in the British South African Police fort, after a vain attempt to break out in the evening, surrendered. During the whole of the day, while the struggle was going on in the Stadt, the enemy outside made demonstrations as if about to attack, and kept up a hot shell fire on the place, but without palpable effect.

We captured this day 108 prisoners, among whom was Commandant Eloff, Kruger's grandson. We also found 10 killed and 19 wounded Boers, and their ambulance picked up 30 more killed and wounded. Our losses were four killed, 10 wounded. Our men, although weak with want of food and exercise, worked with splendid pluck and energy for the 14 hours of fighting, and instances of gallantry in action were numerous.

Relief of Mafeking

16th–17th May, 1900

When relief became imminent, I formed a small force of 180 men and two guns, under Colonel Walford, capable of taking the field should it be desirable to make a diversion or counter attack during the probable encounter between the investing force and the relieving column.

On the evening of the 16th May, the enemy contested the advance of the relief column 6 miles west of the place. Colonel Walford's party moved out and demonstrated as if to attack the Boers in rear. This caused them to withdraw a 1-pr Maxim which had been posted on the probable line of advance of the column, and also a number of men with it. This move left the road open for Colonel Mahon's force to come into Mafeking, which it did during the night without the knowledge of the Boers.

Early next morning, seeing that the enemy were beginning to move wagons from the laager, I pushed forward Colonel Walford's force at once to attack, ordering the relief force to join in as soon as possible. This had a good effect, as our guns opened on their advanced trenches and prevented them from getting their 5-pr away, and our men from the Brickfields, moving up the river, took the trench in rear and cleared it, killing five Boers and taking their flag and gun. Meanwhile, Colonel Mahon and Colonel Plumer's guns came into action and shelled the enemy's laager with great effect, the Boers going off in full flight, abandoning several wagons, camp equipment, hospital, etc. Colonel Walford's men, who had been working up through the bush, quickly took possession and drove off the enemy's rear guard without difficulty.

The operations connected with the relief of the place have, I assume, been reported on by Colonel Mahon, but I would add that his clever move near Maritzani, when he shifted his line of advance suddenly from one road to another, quite unexpected by the Boers, entirely puzzled them, and discon-certed their plans. And again, after the fight outside Mafeking, when he bivouacked his column at nightfall, the Boers were prepared to renew the attack in the morning only to find that he had slipped into the place during the night, and was through the town and shelling their laager on the other side.

The whole operation of the two relief columns was exceedingly well conceived and carried out.

RECOMMENDATION OF STAFF AND OTHERS

Staff: Military

Major Lord Edward Cecil, DSO, as Chief Staff Officer, was of the greatest assistance to me. He stuck pluckily to his work, although much hampered by sickness during the first part of the siege. He did a great amount of hard work in the first organization of the frontier force, and at Mafeking, his tact and unruffled temperament enabled our staff dealings with the Colonial civilians to be carried on with the least possible friction.

Captain Ryan, Army Service Corps, as Deputy-Assistant Adjutant-General (B), proved an exceptionally capable and energetic Supply Officer. On his shoulders fell the whole work of feeding the entire community, gar-rison, non-combatants, and native, a duty which he carried out with conspicuous success (practically unassisted), as we took the food supply out of the hands of contractors and merchants; and he lost the services of his two chief assistants, Captain Girdwood, killed, and Sergeant-Major Loney, convicted of theft of Government stores. Captain Ryan's work has been invaluable, and has mainly contributed to the successful issue of the siege.

Lieutenant Hon. A. Hanbury-Tracy, Royal Horse Guards, as Intelligence Officer and Press Censor, has worked hard and successfully, and with tact and firmness in his dealings with the press correspondents. Captain G. Wilson, Royal Horse Guards, as my Aide-de-Camp, in addition to his other duties, had charge of the soup and sowens kitchens, and did most useful work. To both the above officers I am much indebted for their willing work and personal assistance to myself.

Honorary Lieutenant McKenzie as Transport Officer did excellent work in the organization of his departments, and in the purchase of mules and material, etc. In addition to his other duties he acted as extra Aide-de-Camp to me, and was an exceptionally energetic and useful Staff Officer.

Major Panzera, British South Africa Police, as Commanding Artillery, showed himself a smart and practical gunner, endowed with the greatest zeal, coupled with personal gallantry in action. The great success gained by our little guns, even when opposed to the modern armament of the enemy, was largely due to Panzera's organization and handling of them.

In addition to these duties he acted as my Brigade-Major, and proved himself a most reliable and useful Staff Officer.

Major (local Lieut.-Colonel) C. B. Vyvyan, "Buffs", was Base Commandant, Commanding Engineer, and (for 3 months) Town Commandant during the siege. As such, he organized the Town Guard and defences in the first instance. To his untiring zeal and ability the successful defence of the town is largely due. He carried out a very heavy amount of work, practically single-handed, and with conspicuous success.

Major Anderson, Royal Army Medical Corps, throughout the siege showed untiring zeal, coupled with coolness and gallantry, in attending the wounded under fire in action, in addition to his eminent professional ability. Latterly, as Principal Medical Officer, his unfailing tact and administrative capabilities rendered his services of greatest value. The strain of his devotion to his duty told heavily on his health.

Medical Staff Dr W. Hayes, Surgeon-Major Holmden, British South Africa Police, and Dr T. Hayes. All worked with conspicuous zeal and skill under a never-ending strain of work; all of them very frequently under fire in carrying out their duties, even in their own hospital.

Nursing Staff The work done by the lady nurses was beyond all praise. Miss Hill, the Matron of the Victoria Hospital, was assisted by a number of lady volunteers, in addition to her regular staff, consisting of Mrs Parmister and Miss Gamble.

Mother Superior Teresa and eight Sisters of Mercy also worked in the hospital.

Lady Sarah Wilson, assisted by other ladies, managed the Convalescent Hospital.

Miss Craufurd managed the Women and Children's Hospital.

The above ladies worked with the greatest zeal and self devotion throughout the siege. The protracted strain of heavy work, frequently carried out under fire (Lady Sarah Wilson was wounded), told on most of them, Miss Hill being at one time prostrated by overwork. It was largely due to their unremitting devotion and skill that the wounded, in so many cases, made marvellous recoveries, and the health of the garrison remained so good.

Captain Greener, Paymaster, British South Africa Police, as Chief Paymaster, rendered most efficient and valuable service throughout the siege. He kept account of all Government expenditures and receipts connected with defence, feeding population, etc., in addition to his ordinary police and administrative accounts. By his care and zeal I am convinced that the Government were saved much expense.

Regimental

Lieut.-Colonel Hore, Staffordshire Regiment, raised, organized, and commanded the Protectorate Regiment, which did invaluable service in the siege.

Major Godley, Royal Dublin Fusiliers, as Adjutant of the Protectorate Regiment, had much to do with the successful organization of the corps when it was first raised. As commander of the western defences of Mafeking throughout the siege, his services were of the highest value. His coolness, readiness of resource, and tactfulness in dealing with the Colonials, made him an ideal officer for such command in action. He was my right hand in the defence. I cannot speak too highly of his good work.

Colonel Walford, British South Africa Police, commanded the southern defences, with his detachment of British South Africa Police, throughout the siege with conspicuous success. Always cool and quick to see what was wanted, his services were most valuable.

Inspector Browne, Cape Police, commanded the detachment of Division 2, Cape Police. He and the splendid lot of men under his command did excellent work throughout the siege, especially in the occupation of the trenches in the Brickfields, where for over a month they were within close range of the enemy's works, and constantly on the alert and under fire.

Inspector Marsh, Cape Police, Division 1, commanded the detachment of Division 1 throughout the siege, and carried out his duties most efficiently and zealously.

Captain Cowan, commanding the Bechuanaland Rifles (Volunteers), had his corps in such a condition of efficiency as enabled me to employ them in all respects as regular troops. He was at all times ready and zealous in the performance of any duty assigned to him.

(Local) Captain More, Resident Railway Engineer, organized most effectively the railway employees into a paid division for the armoured train, and a division for the Town Guard. He managed their rationing, hospital, defence works, protection for their women and children, etc., in a most practical manner. His energy and resourcefulness were conspicuous throughout the siege. The armoured trains, defence railway, search light, etc., were made under his supervision.

Captain Marsh, Royal West Kent Regiment, commanded a squadron of the Protectorate Regiment, with very good results. He also had charge of the defence of the native Stadt, and displayed great tact and patience in his successful management of the natives.

Captain Vernon, King's Royal Rifle Corps, was a most successful officer in command of a squadron, and displayed the greatest gallantry in action. He was killed in action on 26th December.

Captain FitzClarence, Royal Fusiliers, commanded a squadron in the Protectorate Regiment. He distinguished himself on numerous occasions during the siege by his personal gallantry and exceptional soldierly qualities. He was twice wounded. I have reported more specially on his good work in a separate letter.

Lieutenant (local Captain) Lord C. Bentinck, 9th Lancers, commanded a squadron of the Protectorate Regiment, with very good results. He did good service by his zeal and readiness in action.

The following officers also did much good and useful work:

Captain A. Williams, British South Africa Police
Captain Scholfield, British South Africa Police
Lieutenant Daniells, British South Africa Police
Lieutenant Holden, Protectorate Regiment
Lieutenant Greenfield, Protectorate Regiment
Lieutenant Feltham, Protectorate Regiment.

Corporal (local Lieutenant) Currie, City Police, did exceptionally good service in command of the Colonial Contingent, to which he succeeded when Captain Goodyear (who originally raised the corps) was severely wounded while gallantly leading his men.

The following organized and commanded with most satisfactory results the native cattle guards, watchmen, etc.:

(Local) Captain McKenzie, Zulus, etc.
Mr D. Webster, Fingoes
Corporal (local Sergeant) Abrams, Cape Police, Baralongs.

These detachments all did most useful and loyal work at different times during the siege in spite of their privations.

Town Guard
Major Goold-Adams, CB, CMG, Resident Commissioner of the Protectorate, commanded the Town Guard during the last half of the siege. His extensive knowledge of the country and people (both native and white) was of the greatest value, and his advice was always most willingly at my disposal. I am greatly indebted for the great assistance he at all times afforded me. The fact that the natives of the Protectorate remained loyal to us at a very critical time is due in a great measure to his advice and great personal influence over them.

Civil

Mr C. G. H. Bell, Resident Magistrate and Civil Commissioner, had entire charge of native affairs, and he managed the chiefs with great tact, and very successfully, at a critical time when they were inclined to sit on the fence and see which side was going to win, and were being tempted with offers from the

Boers. As magistrate, he also rendered me great assistance during the siege.

Mr F. Whiteley, Mayor of Mafeking. This gentleman's services were invaluable during the siege. In a most public-spirited manner he took up at my request, the difficult task of arranging for the feeding and housing of all the women and children, and carried out their management with marked success throughout the siege, devoting himself to the task without any return whatever.

He was much assisted by Mr Rowlands, who gave up his house, garden, water supply, etc., to be used by the laager similarly without drawing any kind of compensation or return.

The Rev Mr W. H. Weekes also rendered valuable service in assisting in the management of the women's laager, etc.

Mr Howat, Post and Telegraph Master, with his staff, namely:

Messrs Campbell, Simpson, and McLeod did invaluable work in connecting up, and in keeping in communication with headquarters the whole of the defence works by telephone. Their duties were unceasing, by night as well as by day, and were frequently carried out under heavy fire and at great personal risk. The zeal, energy, and willingness displayed by these officers was most conspicuous throughout the siege, and their work had a large share in bringing about the successful issue of the siege.

Mr Heal, the gaoler, carried out most arduous and difficult duties most loyally and efficiently. In addition to ordinary prisoners, he had in his charge military offenders, and also a large number of Dutch suspects, spies, and Irish traitors.

He was unfortunately killed by a shell, 12th May, at his post in the gaol.

Sergeant Stewart, Cape Police, rendered valuable service as head of the civil police during the siege.

Mr Millar, head of the refugees' laager, displayed much zeal and did excellent work in the management of the refugees' laager and defences, etc.

Non-commissioned officers and men

Trooper (local Sergeant-Major) Hodgson, Cape Police, acted as Sergeant-Major to the Army Service Corps, and was of the greatest help to Captain Ryan. He proved himself to be a most thoroughly reliable, sober, and upright man, clever at his work, and particularly active and zealous in its performance.

Sergeant Cook, Bechuanaland Rifles, specially recommended for clever and plucky scouting, and for gallantry in action.

Sergeant-Major Moffat, Signalling Staff, for gallantry in action, in bringing a sergeant out of action under heavy fire. Also for good work as a signaller.

Sergeant-Major Taylor, Colonial Contingent, for gallantry and general good work in the Brickfields, scouting, blowing up a kiln occupied by the enemy, etc.

This non-commissioned officer was killed in action.

Conclusion

I should like to add that the conduct of the rank and file of the garrisons throughout the 31 weeks' siege, was beyond all praise. In all the long strain of privations, due to short rations and to the entire absence of all luxuries, as well as to living in the trenches month after month, there was no complaining, and the men took their hardships smiling. When there was fighting to be done they showed unexceptionable pluck and steadiness.

The Town Guard, formed of all the civilians capable of bearing arms, took to their duties as soldiers, and submitted themselves to military discipline with most praiseworthy readiness and success.

The self-devotion and good work of the ladies who acted as nurses in the hospitals, have already been alluded to, but the bravery and patience of all the women and elder children, under all the cruel dangers, anxieties, and privations to which they were exposed, were most exemplary.

The natives took their share in the defence of their Stadt, and showed great patience under their trials.

The notable feature of the siege was that the whole community was pervaded by a spirit of loyal endurance and cheery goodfeeling, under which all the usual local and private differences were sunk in the one great idea of maintaining Her Majesty's supremacy to the end. With such spirit to work on, the task of conducting the defence was an easy one.

R. S. S. BADEN-POWELL

THE SIEGE OF THE
PEKING EMBASSY, 1900

DESPATCHES RELATING TO THE BOXER REBELLION AND SIR CLAUDE MACDONALD'S REPORT

CONTENTS

BRITISH MINISTERS AND CONSULAR STAFF, 1900

Berlin, Germany	Viscount Gough
Chefoo, China	Consul Tratman
Hankow, China	Acting Consul-General Fraser
London, Great Britain	Lord Salisbury (Prime Minister)
Paris, France	Sir E. Monson, Mr Herbert
Peking, China	Sir Claude MacDonald
Rome, Italy	Lord Currie
Shanghae, China	Consul-General Pelham Warren
St Petersburgh, Russia	Sir C. Scott
Tien-tsin, China	Consul Carles
Tokio, Japan	Mr Whitehead
Washington DC, USA	Lord Pauncefote

At the Chinese Legation in London: Sir Chihchen Lofêngluh

The Boxer Rebellion of 1900 was the name given to a religious, fanatical uprising of Chinese people who believed that all western foreigners were bent on destroying their traditional Chinese culture. Chief among their targets were the Christian missionaries, many of whom were corrupt, who were particularly active in China at that time. By the spring of 1900 the Boxer movement was out of control, partly because the Dowager Empress (Tzu Hsi) herself didn't trust foreigners, and showed a certain amount of sympathy for Boxer ideals.

Events came to a head on 29 May, when the Boxers attacked two British missionaries, killing one of them. On 9 June they burnt down the racecourse, the first of many Boxer attacks against foreign property in Peking. Sir Claude MacDonald, the British ambassador in Peking, immediately lodged a protest with the Chinese government, and also wired for a relief force to be sent from the port of Taku.

By 10 June it was clear to the diplomats and their staff living in the Legation Quarter in Peking that they would be the next in line for attack. The Boxers cut the telegraph line to Tien-tsin, stopped the delivery of letters, and openly collaborated with the imperial troops guarding the city. On 19 June, all foreigners were ordered to evacuate Peking within 24 hours, as their safety could no longer be guaranteed. The order was not complied with.

The correspondence which follows is a unique collection of contemporary despatches and reports relating to the events of that turbulent period. They describe how the largest international force ever assembled in history fought its way from Taku to Peking in order to rescue the hundreds of diplomats and their families who were stranded inside the Legation buildings. The central part of the story, however, is the gripping diary kept by Sir Claude MacDonald, as he and the other diplomats bravely fought off the Boxers' daily attacks for two months.

It may help the reader to be aware of this incident in two contexts. At the turn of the century the British Army and the diplomatic service were engaged in several conflicts round the world. The use of the telegraph to maintain contact with the highest authorities in the government is evident throughout the siege, although the telegraph wires to the Legation Quarter were cut soon into the siege. The various consular staff in the region reported directly to the Prime Minister, Lord Salisbury, who was dealing with this matter personally, and effectively, as he was with several other major matters at the same time.

271

The other aspect of this conflict that may assist the reader is a wider understanding of the relationship between China and the western powers during the preceding century. The approach had been to lend money and missionaries in an attempt develop a European style of civilisation and a capitalist industrial society with its infrastructure, particularly in the form of railways. It was the same approach as had been used in Africa. Debts to foreign countries became impossible to pay, and effectively led to the forfeit of a number of coastal cities to various countries. Thus Britain acquired Hong Kong, Shanghae and Wei-hai Weh, and there were towns which were leased to or protected by the Germans, the Russians and the French.

It was against this loss of their own historic civilisation and the moral and financial domination that was such a powerful force in their country, that the Boxer movement rose with tremendous violence. In this light the behaviour of the Dowager Empress might indeed be seen as heroic.

PART I

CORRESPONDENCE CONCERNING THE BOXER REBELLION IN CHINA

1900

APRIL TO MAY 1900

Sir C. MacDonald to the Marquess of Salisbury (*received June* 11)

Peking, April 16, 1900

My Lord,

In my despatch of the 16th ultimo I enclosed a copy of the identical note addressed to the Yamên on the 10th March by myself and my colleagues of the United States, Germany, Italy, and France, reiterating our former demand for the publication in the *Official Gazette* of a Decree prohibiting certain anti-Christian Societies.

More than three weeks passed without a reply, and on the return of M. Pichon, the French Minister, from a visit to the south, a meeting of the five foreign Representatives was held on the 4th instant, at which it was decided that we should send the Chinese Secretaries of our respective Legations to the Tsung-li Yamên next day with a message to the effect that each of us expected to receive an answer within two days.

This was accordingly done, and on the 7th instant we received the note, of which I have the honour to enclose translation herewith. Although not entirely satisfactory in substance, this note contained an indication that the Chinese Government were prepared to meet our wishes as far as possible.

In acknowledging the receipt of the Yamên's note, which we did in similar terms on the 12th instant, we agreed not to press further for a special Decree in the *Gazette*, in view of the difficulties described by the Yamên; but at the same time we declared that we held the Chinese Government responsible for any further results which might follow their failure to comply with the measure we had recommended.

I had myself previously suggested informally to the Yamên that a way out of their difficulty might be found by the publication in the

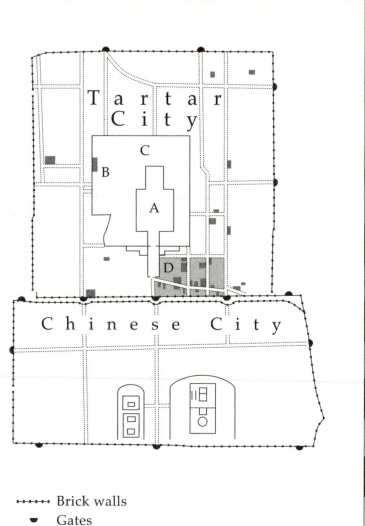

Brick walls
Gates
Streets

A. The Forbidden City
B. Pei T'ang Cathedral
C. The Imperial City
D. Legation Quarter in 1900

Gazette of Memorials from the Governor-General of Chihli and Governor of Shantung, respectively, embodying and reporting their action on the Imperial Decree denouncing the Societies which had already been issued at the instance of the Tsung-li Yamên.

For a translation of this satisfactory Decree, as embodied in a Proclamation of the Governor-General of Chihli, I have the honour to refer your Lordship to the Yamên's note of the 1st March enclosed in my despatch of the 5th March. The Governor of Shantung's Proclamation quoting the same Decree had also been sent to myself and my colleagues by the Yamên in a note of the 15th ultimo, of which I enclose translation herewith.

The Yamên have made no reference to my suggestion; but in the *Peking Gazette* of the 14th instant, there was published the Memorial from the Governor-General of Chihli, of which I have the honour to forward a translation to your Lordship. A similar Memorial from the Governor of Shantung may be expected to follow in due course.

In any case the fact that an Imperial Decree denouncing the "Boxers" or "Fist of Righteous Harmony" by name has appeared in the Gazette may be accepted as a practical concession of the demands made by my colleagues and myself, our only object all along having been to secure for such a Decree a publicity equal to that accorded to the disturbing and ambiguous Edict of the 11th January. It is true that the Ta Tao Hui ("Big Knife Society") is not mentioned by name, but all my recent information goes to show that I Ho Ch'üan ("Fist of Righteous Harmony") and Ta Tao Hui are but different titles of the same organization, and I therefore attach no significance to this omission.

I had the honour to report to your Lordship by telegraph today the publication of this Decree.

As an example of the constant reluctance of the Tsung-li Yamên to admit being influenced by the requests made by foreign Legations, I may instance a recent case in which representations made by me were apparently passed over in silence, although the result at which I aimed was in reality effected.

At the instance of Her Majesty's Consul at Tien-tsin I called the attention of the Yamên, on the 5th March, to the fact that the Magistrate of Tsao-ch'iang, whose dismissal from his post had been promised me by the Viceroy of Chihli as a punishment for his gross neglect of duty in connection with "Boxer" disturbances in his district, had been allowed by the Provincial Treasurer to take leave under plea of illness.

I pointed out that, in view of the expressed intention of the Throne of China to adopt effective measures for the complete suppression of the Societies in question, it amounted to an exhibition of extreme leniency to permit a Magistrate, guilty of allowing rebellious characters to escape and of neglecting to make arrests, simply to leave his post on the plea of sickness; and I requested that the Viceroy should be directed to carry out his original intention in dealing with this officer.

The Yamên made no reply to my communication; but a Memorial from the Viceroy of Chihli, published in one of the editions of the *Gazette* of the

2nd instant, has come to my notice, in which the Magistrate in question is severely denounced for conniving at the escape of the "Boxer" leader, whom he ought to have caught last January. The Imperial rescript to the Memorial orders him to be deprived of his rank.

I regret to have to conclude by stating that the continued activity of the "Boxer" Society in drilling and enlisting recruits in the neighbourhood of Peking and Tien-tsin indicates that the danger from this source is not yet passed; but, at the same time, I think I am justified in expressing the opinion that the Central Government is at last beginning to give evidence of a genuine desire to suppress this anti-Christian organization.

CLAUDE M. MACDONALD

Enclosure 1
The Tsung-li Yamên to Sir C. MacDonald

(Translation)

Peking, April 7, 1900

Sir,

The Yamên have the honour to acknowledge the receipt on the 10th of the moon (10th March) of your Excellency's despatch, requesting the insertion in the *Peking Gazette* of an Imperial Decree with regard to the "Fist of Righteous Harmony" and "Big Knife" Societies.

[Despatch summarized]

The Yamên have the honour to observe that, in the course of the first moon (February), they presented a Memorial to the Throne praying for the prohibition of the "Fist of Righteous Harmony" and the "Big Knife" Society, and had the honour to receive a Decree directing the Viceroy of Chihli and the Governor of Shantung to publish Proclamations. In these Proclamations, as stated by the Yamên in previous despatches, the Imperial Decree is quoted textually in full, while in that published by the Governor of Shantung the "Big Knife" Society is specified by name.

Thus it is evident that the important points covered by your Excellency's request have been already thoroughly dealt with by the Yamên as desired.

With regard to the Imperial Decree previously received, as it has already been directly transmitted to the provinces concerned as a message from the Throne ("t'ing chi": see Yamên's note of the 7th March), it is obviously out of the question that it should be again handed to the Grand Secretariat for publication in the *Peking Gazette*. [On this point] the Yamên have already stated the true facts in their previous despatch. The matter is one affected by Standing Regulations, and the Yamên believe that your Excellency will have appreciated their difficulties with regard to it. However, they will not fail, as soon as they have an opportunity, to take into further consideration what can be done to carry out the view expressed in your Excellency's despatch.

(Seal of Yamên)

Enclosure 2
The Tsung-li Yamên to Sir C. MacDonald

(Translation)

Peking, March 15, 1900

Sir,

On the 11th instant we received the following communication from the Acting Governor of Shantung:

> On the 22nd February I had the honour to receive the Imperial Edict severely denouncing the Society of the Fist of Righteous Harmony, etc. With reference to this, I have to report that in the month of January last, after my arrival at my post, I had already issued a Proclamation vigorously denouncing Boxer Societies, and published it throughout my jurisdiction. In obedience to the Imperial commands now received, I have, as in duty bound, again issued a trenchant Proclamation, and have expressly composed an ode in verses of five characters to be posted from village to village. I have also commanded the local authorities to lead the way in this matter with the gentry, Elders and Headmen of the towns and villages, and on all the market days to expound the ode carefully and truly.

With reference to the above communication, we beg to observe that in the ode composed by the Acting Governor the name of the "Big Knife" Society is definitely mentioned, and that the local authorities are to lead the gentry and Elders in expounding the ode on market days. This is a course of action indicating special zeal and sincerity.

We have the honour to forward herewith, for your Excellency's information, a copy of the draft of the Proclamation and of the ode referred to.

(Seal of Yamên)

Enclosure 3
Proclamation by Yüan, Acting Governor of Shantung

(Translation)

A stringent Proclamation and Admonition issued in obedience to Imperial commands.

On the 23rd February, 1900, a message was reverently received from the Grand Council transmitting the following Imperial Decree, received on the 20th February, 1900.

[Here follows Imperial Decree, as embodied in the Governor-General of Chihli's Proclamation.]

On receipt of the above message it was immediately, in obedience to Imperial commands, reverently written out and circulated. Again, on the 25th February, I had the honour to receive a communication from the Tsung-li Yamên forwarding a copy of their original Memorial and a copy of the Imperial Decree.

With reference to the above communications I have to observe that in the month of January last I printed a Proclamation strictly prohibiting the Society of the "Fist of Righteous Harmony", and issued it to be posted everywhere throughout my jurisdiction, that every household and every inhabitant might be made aware of its contents, and that evil practices might be eradicated.

Having now had the honour to receive the further commands above set forth, I have instructed all the officers under my jurisdiction to make continual and vigorous investigation and suppress this evil. To this end I have also expressly composed an ode in verses of five characters, and ordered it to be posted from village to village throughout my jurisdiction for the information of all. I have likewise commanded the local authorities, directing the gentry, Elders, and Headmen of the towns and villages on all occasions of public gatherings to engage the services of lecturers, and at the country and town markets and places frequented by traders and people to expound the contents of this ode carefully and accurately, and to exhort and admonish as required.

In addition to this a copy can be issued to every school and college, large or small, and the students directed to chant the ode from time to time. In this way the ode will be published throughout every village community, and even the women and children will know it. The natural disposition of men for good will thus assert itself and all will be clearly made to understand that they cannot believe in or follow after perverse Societies, and that the Imperial Decree cannot be disobeyed.

It is my most earnest hope that those who are already members of the Societies will tremble for the consequences, and those who are not members take warning from the fate of those in front of you; that both may strive to follow righteousness, and that joy and prosperity may be your reward.

Enclosure 4
Extract from the Peking Gazette *of April 14, 1900*
(Translation)

SUPPLEMENTARY MEMORIAL BY YÜ LU (GOVERNOR-GENERAL OF CHIHLI) On the 20th day of the first moon of the present year (19th February, 1900), Memorialist had the honour to receive the following Imperial Decree:

[Here follows Decree as embodied in Yü Lu's Proclamation enclosed in Yamên's note of the 1st March.]

Memorialist humbly submits that having learned some time ago that the Society of the "Fist of Righteous Harmony" (or "Boxers") had spread from Shantung into Chihli, in the neighbourhood of Ho-chien-fu, Shên-chou, and Chichou-Chihli districts bordering upon Shantung, that these centres had been established for the practice of boxing and that outrages were being committed on native converts, he immediately gave orders to Mei Tung-li, now Provincial Commander-in-chief of Kuei-chou, then commanding the right wing of the Huai army, and to Chang Lien Fên, expectant Taotai, to lead their forces to the scene, and in conjunction with the local officials act-ing under their directions, to suppress effectually and disperse (the rioters), and to station troops for the protection of places where there were Christian churches (or missionary establishments).

On repeated occasions the above-mentioned General and his colleague destroyed "Boxer" head-quarters by fire and arrested ringleaders of the dis-turbances, and handed them over to the local officials, by whom they were punished.

As for the ignorant folk, who had been enticed by evil-doers, to enter these societies and learn the "Boxers'" arts, they were ordered to find proper securities that they should in future refrain from such practices. Orders were also given to the local authorities that cases arising between converts and ordinary people should be promptly and impartially settled.

On receipt of the Decree above referred to, Memorialist has at once had the Imperial commands reverently transcribed, and has embodied them in a clearly worded prohibitory Proclamation, which has been issued to every Department and district and posted up everywhere. Orders have also been given to the bodies of troops stationed at various points throughout Memorialist's jurisdiction to act with energy in effecting arrests. If any secret Societies are organized or centres established for the practice of boxing, they are to be immediately and in every case suppressed, and not the slightest remiss-ness is to be exhibited.

The above supplementary Memorial reporting the action taken in obe-dience to the Imperial Decree, and the issue of a Proclamation strictly prohibiting the "Boxer" Societies is hereby humbly submitted for the inspec-tion of the Throne and the Imperial commands are solicited thereon.

Imperial Rescript

NOTED   It is hereby commanded that the utmost vigilance be shown in the work of suppression in every case, and that not the slightest remissness be permitted.

Sir C. MacDonald to the Marquess of Salisbury (received June 11)
Peking, April 18, 1900

My Lord,
In continuation of my despatch of the 16th instant, I have the honour to for-ward herewith to your Lordship a translation of an Imperial Decree which has since appeared in the *Peking Gazette* deprecating anti-Christian distur-bances.

No Societies are mentioned by name; but the reference to those village associations for self defence, which were spoken of with approval in the Decree of the 11th January, seems to indicate that this Decree is intended to correct the mischievous interpretation which had been put upon the former one.

CLAUDE M. MACDONALD

Enclosure

Extract from the Peking Gazette *of April* 17, 1900

(Translation)

IMPERIAL DECREE

The organization of trained bands in village communities throughout the provinces for self-preservation and protection of the inhabitants and their families has its foundation in the fitting principle enjoined by the ancients of "keeping mutual watch and giving mutual help", and, provided that the villagers are peaceful and abide by the law, there is no reason why they should not be allowed to act in this regard at their discretion.

But there is reason to fear that, the good and the evil being indiscriminately associated together in this way, there may be found some who make a pretext (of such organizations) to oppress converts, ignoring the fact that the Throne sets no bounds to its principle of regarding all men with equal benevolence. It is the duty of our subjects humbly to carry this principle into effect, and not to find vent for their private resentments, and so to create disturbances, and involve themselves in crime and punishment.

The High Provincial authorities are hereby commanded to give strict orders to the local officials under them to take every opportunity of making it clearly known to all that every man must attend to his own business, and live continually at peace with his fellow men, that so the reiterated and solemn injunction of the Throne may not be disregarded.

Sir C. MacDonald to the Marquess of Salisbury (received July 9)

Peking, May 21, 1900

In my despatch of the 16th April I had to report to your Lordship that in spite of the commencement of a firmer attitude on the part of the Chinese Government towards the anti-Christian movement in North China, there still existed indications of danger in this neighbourhood from the "Boxer" Society.

The activity of the "Boxers" has showed no signs of diminution; reports of depredations in country districts indicated that armed bands of them were approaching daily nearer to Peking; while in the city itself the frequent spectacle of numbers of young lads practising in a kind of hypnotic frenzy, the peculiar gymnastic evolutions inculcated by the craft, and the appearance of numerous virulent anti-foreign placards posted in conspicuous places, combined to create considerable alarm amongst the native Christians of all denominations, a feeling which they were not slow in trying to communicate to their foreign spiritual directors.

I take this opportunity of enclosing a translation of one of these placards as a specimen of the silly superstitions which the leaders of this movement work on to further their designs. Several similar documents have been forwarded to this Legation, most of them less literary in composition, and containing more scurrilous abuse of foreigners, but all having for their theme the necessity of putting all foreigners to death. I have called the attention of the Yamên more than once to the posting of such placards, and have been assured that steps were being taken to put a stop to this dangerous practice.

Your Lordship will observe that, in Mgr Favier's letter to M. Pichon [enclosed], the situation at Peking is painted in very dark colours. The Bishop declares that the conditions now are precisely similar to those preceding the Tien–tsin massacre of 1870, and asks that a guard of marines should be sent to protect the lives of French missionaries.

At the meeting of the Diplomatic Body which took place, accordingly, yesterday, the French Minister showed that he was profoundly impressed by the apprehensions of Mgr. Favier, and by reports which he had received from other sources. He expressed complete disbelief in the genuineness of the measures of which the Yamên had spoken to me, and declared that it was impossible to exaggerate the danger of the outlook.

Mgr. Favier has lived in Peking for over thirty years, and is in constant touch with Chinese of all classes, so that it was generally felt that, after making all due allowances for the colour which might have been lent to his words by the fears of his converts, his deliberately expressed opinion on the situation could not be treated with indifference. At the same time, we did not consider that the circumstances, so far as we were as yet in a position to judge, were such as to justify the bringing up of Legation Guards, and M. Pichon did not insist upon the immediate necessity for such a step. He produced the draft of a joint note which he proposed the doyen should be authorized to address to the Tsung-li Yamên, in which certain specific measures for the suppression of the "Boxers" were demanded, and, after some discussion, the terms of this note were accepted by the meeting.

As regards my own opinion as to the danger to which Europeans in Peking are exposed, I confess that little has come to my own knowledge to confirm the gloomy anticipations of the French Fathers. The demeanour of the inhabitants of the city continues to be quiet and civil towards foreigners, as far as my experience and that of my staff is concerned, although, from the undoubted panic which exists amongst the native Christians, it may be assumed that the latter are being subjected to threats of violence. I am convinced that a few days' heavy rainfall, to terminate the long-continued drought which has helped largely to excite unrest in the country districts, would do more to restore tranquillity than any measures which either the Chinese Government or foreign Governments could take. As this cannot be counted upon, my judgment as to the probability of continued security must be suspended until the Chinese Government shows by its action within the next few days, whether or not it has the will and the power to do its duty.

CLAUDE M. MACDONALD

Enclosure

<small>PLACARD POSTED IN WEST CITY, PEKING</small>

4th moon, 1st day (April 29, 1900)

(Translation)

In a certain street in Peking some worshippers of the I-ho Ch'üan ("Boxers") at midnight suddenly saw a spirit descend in their midst. The spirit was silent for a long time, and all the congregation fell upon their knees and prayed. Then a terrible voice was heard saying:

> I am none other than the Great Yü Ti (God of the unseen world) come down in person. Well knowing that ye are all of devout mind, I have just now descended to make known to you that these are times of trouble in the world, and that it is impossible to set aside the decrees of fate. Disturbances are to be dreaded from the foreign devils; everywhere they are starting Missions, erecting telegraphs, and building railways; they do not believe in the sacred doctrine, and they speak evil of the Gods. Their sins are numberless as the hairs of the head. Therefore am I wrath, and my thunders have pealed forth. By night and by day have I thought of these things. Should I command my Generals to come down to earth, even they would not have strength to change the course of fate. For this reason I have given forth my decree that I shall descend to earth at the head of all the saints and spirits, and that wherever the I-ho Ch'üan are gathered together, there shall the Gods be in the midst of them. I have also to made known to all the righteous in the three worlds that they must be of one mind, and all practise the cult of the I-ho Ch'üan, that so the wrath of heaven may be appeased.
>
> So soon as the practice of the I-ho Ch'üan has been brought to perfection—wait for three times three or nine times nine, nine times nine or three times three [meaning obscure]—then shall the devils meet their doom. The will of heaven is that the telegraph wires be first cut, then the railways torn up, and then shall the foreign devils be decapitated. In that day shall the hour of their calamities come. The time for rain to fall is yet afar off, and all on account of the devils.
>
> I hereby make known these commands to all you righteous folk, that ye may strive with one accord to exterminate all foreign devils, and so turn aside the wrath of heaven. This shall be accounted unto you for well doing; and on the day when it is done, the wind and rain shall be according to your desire.
>
> Therefore I expressly command you make this known in every place.

This I saw with my own eyes, and therefore I make bold to take my pen and write what happened. They who believe it shall have merit; they who do not believe it shall have guilt. The wrath of the spirit was because of the destruction of the Temple of Yü Ti. He sees that the men of the I-ho Ch'üan are devout worshippers and pray to him.

If my tidings are false, may I be destroyed by the five thunderbolts.

Enclosure

Père Favier to M. Pichon

Apostolic Mission of Peking and North Chih-li

Peking, May 19, 1900

(Translation)

The situation becomes daily more and more serious and threatening. In the Prefecture of Paoting-fu more than seventy Christians have been massacred; three other neophytes have been cut to pieces. Several villages have been looted and burnt, a great number of others have been completely deserted. Over 2,000 Christians are fugitives, being without food, clothes, or shelter; in Peking alone about 400 refugees—men, women, and children—have already been given shelter by us and the Sisters of Charity; in another week's time we shall probably have several thousands to look after; we shall be obliged to disband the schools, colleges, and all the hospitals, to make room for these unfortunate people. On the east pillage and incendiarism are imminent; we receive more and more alarming news every hour. Peking is surrounded on all sides; the Boxers are daily approaching the capital, being only delayed by their measures for exterminating all Christians.

I beg you will be assured, M. le Ministre, that I am well informed and am making no statements at random. The religious persecution is only a blind, the main object is to exterminate the Europeans, and this object is clearly indicated and written on the Boxers' standards.

Their accomplices in Peking are awaiting them; they are to begin by an attack on the churches, and are finally to assault the Legations. For us, indeed, here at Pei-t'ang, the day of attack has actually been fixed; the whole town knows it, everybody is talking about it, and the popular excitement is clearly manifest. Last night, again, forty-three poor women, with their children, flying from massacre, arrived at the Sisters' Home; over 500 people accompanied them, telling them that, although they had succeeded in escaping once, they would soon all perish here with the rest.

I will not speak of the numberless placards, M. le Ministre, which are posted in the town against Europeans in general; new notices appear daily, each more clearly expressed than the last.

People who were present at the massacres in Tien-tsin thirty years ago are struck by the similarity of the situation then with that of today; there are the same placards, the same threats, the same notices, and the same want of foresight. Then also, as today, the missionaries wrote and begged, foreseeing the horrible awakening.

In these circumstances, M. le Ministre, I think it is my duty to request you to send us, at least to Pei-t'ang, forty or fifty sailors, to protect us and our belongings. This has been done on much less critical occasions, and I trust you will favourably consider my humble supplication.

Alph. Favier

Seymour's Advance, 1900

Allied Operations against Peking, June to August 1900

Admiral Seymour's advance and retreat   10 June to 26 June

Final Allied Advance   4 August to 14 August

Railway lines

PEKING
Feng Tai
Tung Chou
Chang Chia Wan
Matou
Ho Si Wu
Tsai Tsung
An Ting
Langfang
Lofa
Yang-Tsun
Pei-Tsang
TIEN TSIN
Lutai Canal
Tangku
Lutai
Pei Tang
TAKU

RUSSIA

MONGOLIA

CHINA

Peking
Taku
Port Arthur
Chefoo
Wei-hai Wei
Shanghae
Hankow
Canton
Hong Kong

KOREA

JAPAN
Tokio

Bering Sea

Sea of Okhotsk

Sea of Japan

East China Sea

Pacific Ocean

JUNE 1900

Sir C. MacDonald to the Marquess of Salisbury
Peking, June 4, 1900

(Telegraphic)

I am informed by a Chinese courier who arrived today from Yung-Ching, 40 miles south of Peking, that on the 1st June the Church of England Mission at that place was attacked by the Boxers. He states that one missionary, Mr Robinson, was murdered, and that he saw his body, and that another, Mr Norman, was carried off by the Boxers. I am insisting on the Chinese authorities taking immediate measures to effect his rescue.

Sir E. Monson to the Marquess of Salisbury (received June 4)
Paris, June 4, 1900

(Telegraphic)

The French Minister at Peking has informed the Minister for Foreign Affairs that the situation has, in his opinion, improved.

Sir C. MacDonald to the Marquess of Salisbury (received June 5)
Peking, June 4, 1900

(Telegraphic)

Present situation at Peking is such that we may at any time be besieged here with the railway and telegraph lines cut. In the event of this occurring, I beg your Lordship will cause urgent instructions to be sent to Admiral Seymour to consult with the officers commanding the other foreign squadrons now at Taku to take concerted measures for our relief.

The above was agreed to at a meeting held today by the foreign Representatives, and a similar telegram was sent to their respective

Governments by the Ministers of Austria, Italy, Germany, France, Japan, Russia, and the United States, all of whom have ships at Taku and guards here.

The telegram was proposed by the French Minister and carried unanimously. It is difficult to say whether the situation is as grave as the latter supposes, but the apathy of the Chinese Government makes it very serious.

Vice-Admiral Sir E. Seymour to Admiralty

Tong-ku, June 4, 1900

(Telegraphic)

D'Entrecasteaux (French), *Kasagi* (Japanese), *Zenta* (Austrian), arrived. Twenty-four men-of-war here altogether.

A guard of 75 sent to Peking and 104 to Tien-tsin, matters being reported serious. I remain awaiting developments and further news from Minister.

Sir C. MacDonald to the Marquess of Salisbury (received June 5)

Peking, June 5, 1900

(Telegraphic)

My telegram of yesterday.

I went this afternoon to the Yamên★ to inquire of the Ministers personally what steps the Chinese Government proposed to take to effect the punishment of Mr Robinson's murderers and the release of Mr Norman.

I was informed by the Ministers that the Viceroy was the responsible person, that they had telegraphed to him to send troops to the spot, and that that was all they were able to do in the matter.

They did not express regret or show the least anxiety to effect the relief of the imprisoned man, and they displayed the greatest indifference during the interview. I informed them that the Chinese Government would be held responsible by Her Majesty's Government for the criminal apathy which had brought about this disgraceful state of affairs. I then demanded an interview with Prince Ching, which is fixed for to-morrow, as I found it useless to discuss the matter with the Yamên.

Sir C. MacDonald to the Marquess of Salisbury (received June 5)

Peking, June 5, 1900

(Telegraphic)

My preceding telegram.

I regret to say I have received confirmation of the reported murder of Mr Robinson. Her Majesty's Consul at Tien-tsin has been informed by the Viceroy of the murder on 2nd June of Mr Norman, who was supposed to be a prisoner.

★ Office or residence of a Chinese public official.

Consul Carles to the Marquess of Salisbury (received June 5)
Tien-tsin, June 5, 1900

(Telegraphic)
Urgent. I have today sent the following telegram to the Admiral:

> At a meeting of the Consuls held yesterday to form a home guard, a Resolution was passed asking for strong reinforcements. This step I consider to be absolutely necessary. Our passive position intensifies the danger of the situation hour by hour, and I strongly urge the advisability of the guard being permitted to take active measures of hostility.

> I am telegraphing to Her Majesty's Minister, but am doubtful how long communications may remain open with Peking.

Sir E. Monson to the Marquess of Salisbury (received June 6)
Paris, June 5, 1900

(Extract)
I asked M. Delcassé last evening what news he had from Peking, observing that the telegrams published in the French papers as to the dangerous situation in that capital were confirmed, as far as I knew, by the information sent to your Lordship by Her Majesty's Minister.

M. Delcassé replied that, on the contrary, his latest telegrams from M. Pichon represented that he considered that for the moment all imminent danger was over.

M. Delcassé could not tell me the date of M. Pichon's telegram, but his Excellency seemed to be convinced that it was subsequent to anything that had appeared in the newspapers, and to believe that all the Europeans at first reported missing had escaped.

Sir C. MacDonald to the Marquess of Salisbury (received June 6)
Peking, June 5, 1900

(Telegraphic)
As the wire to Tien-tsin may be cut at any moment, please send immediate instructions to the Admiral.

Sir C. MacDonald to the Marquess of Salisbury (received June 6)
Peking, June 5, 1900

(Telegraphic)
This afternoon I had an interview with the Prince and Ministers of the Yamên. They expressed much regret at the murder of Messrs Robinson and Norman, and their tone was fully satisfactory in this respect.

I pointed out that there was not the slightest indication that the Chinese Government intended to deal severely with the Boxer disturbances, and that insecurity of human life within a few miles of the capital and serious danger of an outbreak occurring within the city itself was the result of this attitude.

I said that this failure to suppress the Boxers was, as far as I could judge, leading straight to foreign intervention, however much friendly Powers might regret such a course.

No attempt was made by the Prince to defend the Chinese Government, nor to deny what I had said. He could say nothing to reassure me as to the safety of the city, and admitted that the Government was reluctant to deal harshly with the movement, which, owing to its anti-foreign character, was popular. He stated that they were bringing 6,000 soldiers from near Tien-tsin for the protection of the railway, but it was evident that he doubted whether they would be allowed to fire on the Boxers except in the defence of Government property, or if authorized whether they would obey.

He gave me to understand, without saying so directly, that he has entirely failed to induce the Court to accept his own views as to the danger of inaction. It was clear, in fact, that the Yamên wished me to understand that the situation was most serious, and that, owing to the influence of ignorant advisers with the Empress-Dowager, they were powerless to remedy it.

Sir C. MacDonald to the Marquess of Salisbury (received June 6)

Peking, June 6, 1900

(Telegraphic)

Since the interview with the Yamên reported in my preceding telegram I have seen several of my colleagues.

I find they all agree that, owing to the now evident sympathy of the Empress-Dowager and the more conservative of her advisers with the anti-foreign movement, the situation is rapidly growing more serious.

Should there be no change in the attitude of the Empress, a rising in the city, ending in anarchy, which may produce rebellion in the provinces, will be the result, "failing an armed occupation of Peking by one or more of the Powers."

Our ordinary means of pressure on the Chinese Government fail, as the Yamên is by general consent, and their own admission, powerless to persuade the Court to take serious measures of repression. Direct representations to the Emperor and Dowager-Empress from the Corps Diplomatique at a special audience seems to be the only remaining chance of impressing the Court.

At today's meeting of the foreign Representatives, it will probably be decided to ask the approval of their respective Governments for the demand for such an audience, unless it appears that the situation is so critical as to justify them in making it without waiting for instructions.

As no foreign Representative here has Ambassador's privileges it is probable that an audience will be refused, as against precedent, and it is certain to be delayed should the demand be refused, or unless there is an improvement in the situation (as there may be if the demand opens the Empress's eyes).

I am of opinion that strong measures should be taken to enforce compliance.

Sir C. MacDonald to the Marquess of Salisbury *(received June 6)*

Peking, June 6, 1900

(Telegraphic)

My preceding telegram.

A meeting of the foreign Representatives was held this afternoon, and it was decided to postpone till Saturday next the question of demanding an audience.

Vice-Admiral Sir E. Seymour to Admiralty

Tong-ku, June 6, 1900

(Telegraphic)

Situation having become more grave, I have ordered *Aurora* and *Phœnix* here from Wei-hai Wei; *Humber* to Shanhaikuan. Several Europeans in isolated positions have been murdered, and there is a strong feeling against all foreign elements. Chinese Government appear to be doing nothing to check outrages. Meeting of Senior Naval Officers of the French, German, Italian, Russian, Austrian, United States, and Japanese men-of-war held on board *Centurion* this afternoon to discuss situation and arrange concerted action if necessary.

Admiralty to Vice-Admiral Sir E. Seymour

June 6, 1900

(Telegraphic)

In case of danger to the foreign Legations at Peking, or to British subjects either there or at Tien-tsin and in the neighbourhood, take such steps, in concert with the Commanding Officers of the other squadrons, as you may consider advisable and practicable for their protection. Her Majesty's Government desire to leave you a wide discretion as to the measures to be adopted.

Foreign Office to Admiralty

June 6, 1900

Sir,

Her Majesty's Minister in China, in his telegram of the 4th instant, of which a copy was communicated to you yesterday, stated that the situation at Peking was such that Her Majesty's Legation might at any time be besieged, with the railway and telegraph lines cut. He requested that in the event of this happening, urgent instructions might be sent to the Commander-in-chief on the China station to consult with the officers in command of the squadrons of other Powers at Taku, with a view to concerted measures for the relief of the foreign Legations at Peking. Sir C. MacDonald added that his telegram was the result of a decision arrived at at a meeting of the foreign Representatives, and that similar telegrams had been sent by the Ministers of Austria–Hungary, Italy, Germany, France, Japan, Russia, and the United States to their respective Governments, all of whom have guards at Peking and ships at Taku.

In a further telegram received today, of which a copy has also been transmitted to you, Sir C. MacDonald states that the telegraph to Tien-tsin may be interrupted at any moment, and repeats his request that the instructions suggested in his first telegram may be sent to Admiral Seymour.

The Marquess of Salisbury would suggest that the Lords Commissioners of the Admiralty should telegraph to the Commander-in-chief in China, that, in case of danger to the foreign Legations at Peking or to British subjects either there or at Tien-tsin and in the neighbourhood, he should take such steps in concert with the Commanding Officers of the other squadrons as he may consider advisable and practicable for their protection; and that Her Majesty's Government desire to leave him a wide discretion as to the measures which, under the circumstances, it may appear to him expedient to adopt.

FRANCIS BERTIE

Vice-Admiral Sir E. Seymour to Admiralty

Tong-ku, June 7, 1900

(Telegraphic)

In view of the gravity of the situation, and it being unadvisable to distress ships for men, submit whether troops from Hong Kong may be sent for Tien-tsin and Peking. *Terrible* available for conveyance.

Admiralty to Vice-Admiral Sir E. Seymour

June 7, 1900

(Telegraphic)

Following telegram has been addressed by Secretary of State for Foreign Affairs to Her Majesty's Minister, Peking:

> The situation is difficult, and your discretion must be quite unfettered. You may take precisely what measures you think expedient.

Report any steps you may take in concert with Minister.

The Marquess of Salisbury to Sir C. MacDonald

Foreign Office, June 7, 1900

(Telegraphic)

With reference to your telegram of the 5th instant, I have to inform you that the following instructions were telegraphed yesterday to the Admiral:

[*See despatch from Admiralty to Vice-Admiral Sir E. Seymour, dated
June 6 1900*]

The Marquess of Salisbury to Sir C. MacDonald

Foreign Office, June 7, 1900

(Telegraphic)

Your telegram of the 6th June.

The situation is difficult, and your discretion must be quite unfettered. You may take precisely what measures you think expedient.

The Marquess of Salisbury to Sir C. MacDonald

Foreign Office, June 7, 1900

(Telegraphic)

With reference to your telegram of the 6th June on the subject of the crisis at Peking, I approve the proposal to demand an audience of the Emperor and Empress-Dowager.

Sir C. MacDonald to the Marquess of Salisbury

Peking, June 7, 1900

(Telegraphic)

There is a long Decree in the *Gazette* which ascribes the recent trouble to the favour shown to converts in law suits and the admission to their ranks of bad characters. It states that the Boxers, who are the objects of the Throne's sympathy equally with the converts, have made use of the anti-Christian feeling aroused by these causes, and that bad characters among them have destroyed chapels and railways which are the property of the State.

Unless the ringleaders among such bad characters are now surrendered by the Boxers they will be dealt with as disloyal subjects, and will be exterminated. Authorization will be given to the Generals to effect arrests, exercising discrimination between leaders and their followers.

It is probable that the above Decree represents a compromise between the conflicting opinions which exist at Court. The general tone is most unsatisfactory, though the effect may be good if severe measures are actually taken. The general lenient tone, the absence of reference to the murder of missionaries, and the justification of the proceedings of the Boxers by the misconduct of Christian converts are all dangerous factors in the case.

Vice-Admiral Sir E. Seymour to Admiralty

Tong-ku, June 8, 1900

(Telegraphic)

My telegram of 6th instant. In case of a sudden march on Peking as regards command, the best course might be for me to undertake it, with Russian Colonel as Chief of the Staff. I think all or most of the foreign officers here would agree to this. Request instructions.

Rear-Admiral would be left in the command of the squadron off Pei-ho.

Admiralty to Vice-Admiral Sir E. Seymour

June 8, 1900

(Telegraphic)

With reference to your telegram of the 7th instant, you are to place your-self in communication with the General Commanding at Hong Kong, and concert with him as to dispatch of any troops from there to the Pei-ho should it be considered desirable.

The Marquess of Salisbury to Sir C. MacDonald

Foreign Office, June 8, 1900

(Telegraphic)

I have been informed by the Spanish Government that, having no guard to send to protect their Legation at Peking, they would be glad if the British force could undertake that duty.

If the British force is sufficiently strong, you can comply with any application from your Spanish colleague to this effect.

Foreign Office to Admiralty

June 8, 1900

Sir,

With reference to the inquiry of the Commander-in-chief on the China station as to who should be in command of the force from the foreign ships of war in the event of a march on Peking becoming necessary, I am to state that, in Lord Salisbury's opinion, the Senior Officer should command the force, and Sir Edward Seymour should be so informed.

FRANCIS BERTIE

Foreign Office to Admiralty

June 8, 1900

Sir,

I have laid before the Marquess of Salisbury a copy of a telegram from the Commander-in-chief on the China station [Vice-Admiral E. Seymour to Admiralty, June 8, 1900] in which he proposes that, in the event of it being necessary for the forces from the foreign ships of war to march to Peking, he should take command of them, with the Russian Colonel as Chief of his Staff.

Lord Salisbury suggests that Admiral Seymour's proposal should be approved.

FRANCIS BERTIE

Foreign Office to War Office

June 8, 1900

Sir,

The Lords Commissioners of the Admiralty have communicated to the Marquess of Salisbury a copy of a telegram from the Commander-in-chief on the China station of yesterday, in which he suggests that, in view of the gravity of the situation in northern China, and the inadvisability of leaving Her Majesty's ships without sufficient crews, troops should be sent from Hong Kong for employment at Tien-tsin and Peking.

A copy of Admiral Seymour's telegram has been sent to Her Majesty's Secretary of State for War.

I am directed by Lord Salisbury to state that he considers it advisable that all the troops that can be spared, not only from Hong Kong, but also from Wei-hai Wei and Singapore, should be concentrated at Taku.

His Lordship would be glad to be informed what steps Lord Lansdowne proposes to take in the matter after communicating with the Lords Commissioners of the Admiralty.

FRANCIS BERTIE

Sir C. MacDonald to the Marquess of Salisbury
(*received June* 9)

Peking, June 8, 1900

(Telegraphic)

A very bad effect has been produced by the Decree reported in my immediately preceding telegram. There is no prohibition of the Boxers drilling, which they now openly do in the houses of the Manchu nobility and in the temples. This Legation is full of British refugees, mostly women and children, and the London and Church of England Missions have been abandoned.

I trust that the instructions requested in my telegrams of the 4th and 5th instant have been sent to the Admiral.

Sir C. MacDonald to the Marquess of Salisbury
(*received June* 9)

Peking, June 8, 1900

(Telegraphic)

I have received the following telegram, dated noon today, from Her Majesty's Consul at Tien-tsin:

> By now the Boxers must be near Yang-tsun. Last night the bridge, which is outside that station, was seen to be on fire. General Nieh's forces are being withdrawn to Lutai, and 1,500 of them have already passed through by railway. There are now at Yang-tsun an engine and trucks ready to take 2,000 more men.

295

Lutai lies on the other side of Tien-tsin, and at some distance. Should this information be correct, it means that an attempt to protect Peking has been abandoned by the only force on which the Yamên profess to place any reliance.

The 6,000 men mentioned in my telegram of the 5th instant were commanded by General Nieh.

Sir C. MacDonald to the Marquess of Salisbury (received June 9)

Peking, June 8, 1900

(Telegraphic)

I have sent the following telegram today to Tokio:

> I have been instructed by Lord Salisbury to inform you of the present position here by telegraph.
>
> The movement against foreigners—has been permitted to develop until it has resulted in the burning of railway stations, the interruption for the last five days of communication by rail, the murder in the country, near Peking, of two British missionaries and several foreigners, and in the surrounding districts the destruction of chapels and the pillage of numerous converts. In Peking itself British missionaries have been forced to quit their houses and come for refuge to the Legation, which has a guard of marines for its protection.
>
> The Chinese Government have been so far moved by these events as to depute high officials to hold parley with the 'Boxers,' but give no indication of any intention to suppress them summarily. Probably they still have the power to do so, but sympathy with the movement strongly influences the Throne, and the temper of the troops is uncertain.
>
> There is a disposition on the part of the Diplomatic Corps to request an audience, in order to represent the seriousness of the situation to the Throne, but as yet I am not aware whether this step will meet with the approval of Her Majesty's Government.

Sir C. MacDonald to the Marquess of Salisbury (received June 9)

Peking, June 8, 1900

(Telegraphic)

With reference to my telegrams of the 5th and 6th instant and my two immediately preceding telegrams, I have to report that the situation is now critical. To-morrow or next day we shall meet to decide the question of a personal audience with the Empress-Dowager and the Emperor. If the demand for an audience is made it is essential, first, that it should be insisted on, and that we should compel the Chinese Government to grant it; secondly, that a definite statement should be made to the Throne, when the audience takes place, putting in plain terms the existence of so deplorable a state of things in North China owing to the Boxers not being repressed, and concluding with a strong intimation that, unless the Chinese

Government immediately suppressed the Boxers and re-established law and order, the foreign Powers would be compelled themselves to take measures to that end, as the present state of things is fraught with so much danger to foreign interests.

Admiralty to Vice-Admiral Sir E. Seymour

June 8, 1900

(Telegraphic)
Yours of the 8th instant.
Your proposal is approved if agreement come to.

Admiralty to Vice-Admiral Sir E. Seymour

June 9, 1900

(Telegraphic)
With reference to Admiralty telegram of yesterday, War Office has authorized Hong Kong and Straits Settlements to give such military force as they can spare on your request, should they be required.

War Office to Foreign Office (received June 9)

Sir, June 9, 1900
I am directed by the Secretary of State for War to acknowledge the receipt of Foreign Office letter of 8th June relative to the situation in China.

In reply, I am to acquaint you, for the information of the Marquess of Salisbury, that the Admiralty has informed the Admiral on the station that the General Officers in command at Hong Kong and Singapore have been instructed to meet any demand for troops that he may make upon them to the extent that they can be spared.

The General Officers concerned have been instructed to comply as far as possible with the demands of the Admiral.

R. H. KNOX

The Marquess of Salisbury to Sir C. MacDonald

Foreign Office, June 9, 1900

(Telegraphic)
The Admiral has pointed out the inadvisability of unduly depleting the ships of war.

In consequence of his representation he has been informed that, in the event of his requiring them, troops from Hong Kong and Singapore will be placed at his disposal.

The Marquess of Salisbury to Sir C. MacDonald
Foreign Office, June 9, 1900

(Telegraphic)

I concur in the proposal contained in your telegram of yesterday with regard to the intimation to be made to the Emperor and Dowager-Empress at the audience it is proposed to demand.

Vice-Admiral Sir E. Seymour to Admiralty
Tong-ku, June 10, 1900

(Telegraphic)

Following telegram received from Minister at Peking:

> Situation extremely grave. Unless arrangements are made for immediate advance to Peking it will be too late.

In consequence of above, I am landing at once with all available men, and have asked foreign officers' co-operation.

Consul Carles to the Marquess of Salisbury (received June 10)
Tien-tsin, June 10, 1900

(Telegraphic)

At my request a meeting of Consuls and Naval Commandants was held last night to consider the urgent request of Her Majesty's Minister for the immediate arrangement for the dispatch to Peking of guards.

The Japanese, Italians, Austrians, and Americans agreed to join with us in dispatching all men available as guards for the protection of the working party which is restoring the railway and for the gradual advance for the relief of the Legations, which was to take place as the line was repaired.

The French and Russians refused to dispatch guards unless a force of at least 1,500 men was sent or the line was in working order. It was suggested that this or larger force could, if the situation was really as grave as was painted, be asked for from Port Arthur. It was agreed between us to ask the Viceroy to furnish a train, and the detachments will leave this morning, if possible, without awaiting the Russians and French.

Consul Carles to the Marquess of Salisbury (received June 10)
Tien-tsin, June 10, 1900

(Telegraphic)

The Commander-in-chief on the China station, with 300 British, 100 Americans, 60 Austrians, and 40 Italians left this morning by train.

Other detachments, including the Russian, French, and German, immediately follow.

Consul Carles to the Marquess of Salisbury (received June 11)

Tien-tsin, June 10, 1900

(Telegraphic)

This morning the second detachment, consisting of British, Germans, Japanese, French, and Russians, numbering about 600 in all, left for Peking. The total force sent was about 1,400 to 1,500 men. There is an interruption in the telegraphic communication with Peking.

Consul Carles to the Marquess of Salisbury (received June 11)

Tien-tsin, June 11, 1900

(Telegraphic)

Yesterday evening Admiral Seymour had advanced 30 miles with 1,078 men. He had met with no opposition, and he hopes, unless opposed, to reach Peking this evening. Probably total force is not less than 1,700 men. Last night the train reached Lofa Station.

Admiralty to Vice-Admiral Sir E. Seymour

June 11, 1900

(Telegraphic)

Afford protection to Spanish Legation at Peking on application from British Minister.

Consul Carles to Admiralty

Tien-tsin, June 11, 1900

(Telegraphic)

Following received from Admiral for transmission:

Force now increased by 450 Germans, 90 British.

Sir C. MacDonald to the Marquess of Salisbury (received June 12)

Peking, June 11, 1900

(Telegraphic)

It is reported that Admiral's party is at Langfang, half-way from Tien-tsin. All communication by telegraph with the latter place is interrupted.

On the 8th June the Boxers attacked student interpreters close to the city walls, who only escaped by using fire-arms.

Some soldiers yesterday assaulted the Secretary of the Belgian Legation at the end of Legation Street.

The summer Legation at the hills which I had officially handed over to the Chinese Government was last night totally destroyed by fire.

I am sending this telegram by the Kiachta route.

Vice-Admiral Sir E. Seymour to Admiralty

Tien-tsin, June 12, 1900

(Telegraphic)

Now nearly half-way to Peking; progress much delayed by damage still being done to railway as we advance.

Boxers found in considerable force yesterday afternoon near railway at Langfang, and were engaged. They fled, leaving about thirty-five killed.

No casualties on our side. Our force, increased by 200 Russians and fifty-eight French, who arrived yesterday, is now 2,000 strong.

Sir C. Scott to the Marquess of Salisbury (received June 12)

St Petersburgh, June 12, 1900

(Telegraphic)

The latest report received from the Russian Minister at Peking, dated the 10th June, confirms the alarming account of the situation there given in Sir C. MacDonald's telegrams of the 8th instant. An audience has not apparently been granted to the foreign Ministers, the Boxers have entered the capital, and the situation is one of danger for the Legations.

In Count Mouravieff's opinion, the real state of things has been concealed from the Empress-Dowager, and, since all the Chinese Councillors having any experience of Europe have been removed, there is none in authority on whose influence it is possible to place any reliance.

Authority has been given to M. de Giers to order up immediately any amount of military force he may consider necessary; but his Excellency understands that, while a very large additional force has been sent by us from Tien-tsin, Russia has only sent up thirty more men.

I replied that, according to the latest telegrams which I had seen from Tien-tsin, all the Commanders were dispatching sufficient forces to restore railway communication with the capital and keep it open, and to secure the safety of the foreign Legations, the primary importance of which his Excellency admitted.

Consul Carles to the Marquess of Salisbury (received June 12)

Tien-tsin, June 12, 1900

(Telegraphic)

Yesterday a further detachment of 300 men passed up. The total force which had left Tien-tsin up to last night is estimated to number 2,300.

Sir C. MacDonald to the Marquess of Salisbury (received June 13)

Peking, June 12, 1900

(Telegraphic)

Pressing. Inform relief party the mutinous Kansu soldiery, who are today in possession of the Peking terminus, may offer them some resistance there. The Government of China seems powerless. It is useless to wait till troops arrive from Singapore; if necessary, I hope Admirals will not have the least hesitation in depleting their ships.

Consul Carles to the Marquess of Salisbury (received June 13)
Tien-tsin, June 12, 1900

(Telegraphic)
The Admiral, who had been fighting with the Boxers yesterday, killing about fifty of them, was at Langfang this morning. Our side suffered no loss. The above-mentioned place is half-way on the road to Peking.

Vice-Admiral Sir E. Seymour to Admiralty
Tien-tsin, June 13, 1900

(Telegraphic)
Progress very slow; railway much broken up, only 3 miles during last twenty-four hours.

No further encounter with Boxers, who are said to be 2 miles in advance in force.

The Russians are landing an additional force of 1,700 troops, and I have requested General to send 650 troops now ready at Hong Kong to Taku in *Terrible*.

Trustworthy courier arrived from Peking reports great excitement there at our approach.

General Tung expected to oppose entry within city.

Mr Herbert to the Marquess of Salisbury (received June 13)
Paris, June 13, 1900

(Telegraphic)
Although last telegram received from French Minister at Peking was dated yesterday, M. Delcassé has received no news of presence of Boxers in the capital, reported in Sir C. Scott's telegram of 12th June.

Sir C. Scott to the Marquess of Salisbury (received June 13)
St Petersburgh, June 13, 1900

(Telegraphic)
Count Mouravieff, at his reception today, appeared to consider that, owing to the agitation of the Reform party, the situation was really more threatening in Southern and Central than in Northern China.

His Excellency counts on the large European force which is now forcing its way to Peking as sufficient to save the situation in the capital.

In his opinion, the Empress-Dowager is at the present moment powerless in the hands of fanatic and ignorant councillors, but she will be both willing to assist and amenable to sounder views when once she has been relieved from their control.

The foreign Representatives on the spot were possessed of the views of their respective Governments as to the necessity of not further endangering or complicating a position of affairs already very serious, and events were moving so rapidly that the only thing to be done was to trust to their judgment and prudence.

Mr Whitehead to the Marquess of Salisbury (received June 13)

Tokio, June 13, 1900

(Telegraphic)

Information has reached here that 1,700 Russian soldiers were landed yesterday at Taku, including 270 cavalry and 20 guns. Two more ships had arrived with a further contingent of 1,000 men.

The Minister for Foreign Affairs has inquired as to the intention of Her Majesty's Government, and wished to know whether British troops can be sent. He said that if foreign naval detachments which have been actually landed should be surrounded or otherwise in danger, the Japanese Government would be ready to send at once a considerable force to their relief, if Her Majesty's Government concurred in such a course, but that otherwise his Government do not intend to send soldiers.

Consul Carles to the Marquess of Salisbury (received June 13)

Tien-tsin, June 13, 1900

(Telegraphic)

A member of Japanese Legation at Peking, when on his way to station, was killed by General Tung's cavalry, and I believe that Her Majesty's summer Legation has been destroyed by fire. In private letters, dated Peking, the 11th instant, the situation is described as being extremely grave.

Prince Tuan and three other Manchu Ministers have been made members of the Tsung-li Yamên.

Lack of water, and continued injury to railway, delays to a great extent the advance of Naval Brigade, whose entry into Peking the Chinese expect will be resisted. I fear that the delay in their progress makes this more probable than before.

General Officer Commanding, Hong Kong, to the Secretary of State for War

Hong Kong, June 13, 1900

(Telegraphic)

I am sending 950 British and Indian troops, with Maxim and gun, to the Admiral, who has asked for every man available. Some will leave on the 14th instant, on a fast transport vessel; the rest on the 17th instant on Her Majesty's ship *Terrible*. The absence of these troops does not compel me to ask for reinforcements at once.

Admiralty to Foreign Office (received June 14)

June 13, 1900

Sir,

I am commanded by my Lords Commissioners of the Admiralty to request you will inform the Secretary of State that the following is a summary of the international forces now under the command of Vice-Admiral Sir Edward Seymour on their way to Peking, compiled from telegrams which have been received from him from time to time:

British	736
German	450
American	100
Russian	315
French	158
Austrian	25
Italian	40
Japanese	52
Total	1,876

It will, however, be observed that this does not agree with the total of 2,000 mentioned by the Vice-Admiral in his telegram of the 12th instant, copy of which has already been sent to you.

C. J. THOMAS
Pro Sec.

Sir C. MacDonald to the Marquess of Salisbury (received June 14)

Peking, June 14, 1900

(Telegraphic)

I am informed by Russian Minister that 2,000 men embarked at Port Arthur for Taku on 11th June. More probably the date should be 9th June.

The Japanese Secretary of Legation was killed yesterday by Tartar cavalry close to the city gate.

It may be assumed that the Japanese will also send troops to Taku.

Consul Carles to the Marquess of Salisbury (received June 14)

Tien-tsin, June 14, 1900

(Telegraphic)

I have received a letter from Sir C. MacDonald, written on the 12th instant in which he informs me that Ministers of Yamên had called to say that, if the force did not exceed 1,200 men, Chinese Government would not oppose their coming to Peking.

Consul Carles to the Marquess of Salisbury (received June 14)

Tien-tsin, June 14, 1900

(Telegraphic)

A report, which I do not think it right to disregard, has reached me from Chinese sources that on the 16th June the Empress-Dowager has resolved to destroy the Legations. Boxers here very menacing, and I understand that two bridges beyond Yang-tsun have been rendered impassable. Communications with Admiral are interrupted.

Acting Consul-General Warren to the Marquess of Salisbury (received June 14)

Shanghae, June 14, 1900

(Telegraphic)

I have received no exact information as to the situation in the north, but news seems to be worse.

I am convinced that, if there is any likelihood of it resulting in a breach with the Peking Government, we ought at once to come to an understanding with the Hankow and Nanking Viceroys. I have every confidence that they will do all they can to keep peace in their districts if they can rely on Her Majesty's Government for effective support.

There is no doubt that great loss would be caused and probably considerable loss of life would be entailed by any outbreak in the Yang-tsze Valley. It is necessary that prompt action should be taken; the situation is serious.

The Marquess of Salisbury to Mr Whitehead

Foreign Office, June 14, 1900

(Telegraphic)

China crisis: your telegram of the 13th June.

You should inform Japanese Minister for Foreign Affairs of the application for troops made by our Admiral, and of the numbers which are being sent from Hong Kong.

Admiralty to Rear-Admiral Bruce (communicated by Admiralty, June 15)

June 15, 1900

(Telegraphic)

Adequate means for protecting life and property on Yang-tsze should be provided, using ships from Philippines and Southern Division for this purpose.

Take action and inform Commander-in-chief when you can.

Consul Carles to the Marquess of Salisbury (received June 15)

Tien-tsin, June 15, 1900

(Telegraphic)

The native city is practically in the hands of the Boxers and the mob, who have burnt down the chapels and compelled Chinese officials to get out of their chairs in the streets.

The action of the Viceroy has been very correct.

Communication with the Admiral is cut off.

The situation here is more serious than he is aware of.

A portion of the Russian troops still remains in this place.

Consul Carles to the Marquess of Salisbury (received June 15)

Tien–tsin, June 15, 1900

(Telegraphic)

The Chinese Government are taking measures to concentrate troops along the approaches to Tien–tsin and on Taku.

I am informed that, in consequence of this, the Admirals may be compelled to seize the Taku forts without delay.

Consul Carles to the Marquess of Salisbury (received June 15)

Tien–tsin, June 15, 1900

(Telegraphic)

On the evening of 13th June the Boxers entered Peking and destroyed the old Custom-house quarters and the establishments of several Missions.

It appears that many Chinese were massacred, but that there were no casualties among the Europeans.

The Marquess of Salisbury to Mr Whitehead

Foreign Office, June 15, 1900

(Telegraphic)

Murder by Chinese troops of the Chancellor of the Japanese Legation at Peking.

Inquire what steps, if any, the Japanese Government contemplate taking.

The Marquess of Salisbury to Acting Consul-General Warren

Foreign Office, June 15, 1900

(Telegraphic)

Protection of British interests on the Yang-tsze.

Your telegram of the 14th June. We are in communication with the Admiralty as to the dispatch of a man-of-war to Nanking, and the message to the Viceroys there and at Hankow which you suggest, assuring them of British protection in maintaining order.

You are authorized, in the meantime, to inform the Viceroy at Nanking that he will be supported by Her Majesty's ships if measures are taken by him for the maintenance of order.

You should inform Her Majesty's Consul-General at Hankow that he may give to the Viceroy there a similar assurance.

Foreign Office to Admiralty

June 15, 1900

Sir,

I am directed by the Marquess of Salisbury to transmit to you, to be laid before the Lords Commissioners of the Admiralty, a copy of a telegram from Her Majesty's Consul at Tien-tsin [dated June 15, 1900] relative to the state of affairs at that place.

Mr Carles reports that the Viceroy has acted very correctly.

In these circumstances his Lordship proposes, should their Lordships see no objection, to instruct Mr Carles to inform the Viceroy that, in the event of his believing himself to be in personal danger, it will be open to him to take refuge on board one of Her Majesty's ships.

FRANCIS BERTIE

Foreign Office to Admiralty

June 15, 1900

Sir,

I am directed by the Marquess of Salisbury to transmit to you a copy of a telegram from Shanghae, which has been communicated by the China Association to this Department, relative to the importance of having a sufficient force on the Yang-tsze for the protection of the interests of this country during the present crisis.

Mr Pelham Warren, Acting Consul-General at Shanghae, in his telegram of the 14th instant, of which a copy has been sent to you, also urges the necessity of British interests on the Yang-tsze being efficiently protected, and states that it would, in his opinion, be advisable to send a large man-of-war to Nanking, and to assure the Viceroy that he will receive the support of Her Majesty's Government in maintaining order.

Lord Salisbury concurs in Mr Warren's view as to the desirability of arriving at some understanding on the subject with the Viceroys both at Nanking and Hankow, and he would be glad if arrangements could be made for the dispatch of one of Her Majesty's ships to Nanking with instructions to communicate with the Viceroy in the sense suggested, and for a similar intimation being conveyed to the Viceroy at Hankow.

FRANCIS BERTIE

Enclosure

Telegram from Shanghae Committee to General Committee

With a view to preventing possible disturbance Yang-tsze River, it is very important that there should be adequate force prepared to protect our interests. There are at present above Hankow the *Esk*, *Woodlark*, *Woodcock*, and *Snipe*. Nothing below.

Key to the situation—Kiang-yin.

Foreign Office to India Office

June 15, 1900

Sir,

In view of the considerable force of British and Indian troops which is being sent from Hong Kong to Taku on the requisition of the Naval Commander-in-chief on the China station, the Marquess of Salisbury desires to submit, for the consideration of the Secretary of State for India, the question of replacing them by the dispatch to Hong Kong of one or two battalions of native troops from India. It is possible that more may be required.

The men who have been landed from the British squadron at Taku cannot be spared for long from the ships; and having regard to the present state of affairs in China, and the impossibility of foreseeing the course which events in the Far East may take, it appears to his Lordship very desirable that the British garrisons should be maintained at their full strength.

A similar letter has been addressed to the War Office.

St John Brodrick

Admiralty to Foreign Office (received June 16)

June 16, 1900

Sir,

With reference to your letter of the 15th instant, I am commanded by my Lords Commissioners of the Admiralty to request you to state to the Marquess of Salisbury that they concur in his proposal that in the event of the Viceroy of Tien-tsin being in personal danger on account of his correct attitude, he should be allowed to take refuge on board one of Her Majesty's ships.

Copy of a telegram on the subject which has been this day sent to the Rear-Admiral at Taku is enclosed for information.

H. J. Van Sittart Neale

Enclosure

Admiralty to Rear-Admiral Bruce

June 16, 1900

(Telegraphic)

In event of Viceroy, Tien-tsin, being in personal danger owing to his loyalty to British, he is to be afforded an asylum on board one of Her Majesty's ships.

Foreign Office is informing Consul accordingly.

Admiralty to Senior Naval Officer, Shanghae

June 16, 1900

(Telegraphic)

Hermione proceed Nanking and communicate with Viceroy, assuring him of support of Her Majesty's Government in preserving order and protecting

British interests; in the event of disturbance, consult with Consul, Shanghae, before leaving.

Linnet to proceed to Hankow for similar purpose and to give similar assurance to Viceroy there, and to communicate with Consul there.

Undaunted leaves Hong Kong today for Woosung.

Mr Whitehead to the Marquess of Salisbury (received June 16)
Tokio, June 16, 1900

(Telegraphic)
Japanese troops are to leave Ujina on the 21st June, and should arrive about the 24th June at Taku. They will consist of one battalion with two or three guns, making about 1,200 men in all.

The cruiser *Yoshino* left for Taku this morning with Admiral Dewa.

Consul-General Warren to the Marquess of Salisbury (received June 16)
Shanghae, June 16, 1900

(Telegraphic)
The last intelligence we possess is that on the night of the 13th June there were serious disturbances in Peking, when hundreds of converts and servants of foreigners were murdered. It is stated that no Europeans were killed. Many buildings belonging to foreigners were destroyed.

It is not probable that communication with Tien-tsin, which is now interrupted, will be restored at any early date.

The Marquess of Salisbury to Consul Carles
Foreign Office, June 16, 1900

(Telegraphic)
If possible, communicate with Admiral by runner. You should inform him that 950 troops have been ordered to Taku from Hong Kong. You should also ascertain his position, whether he needs reinforcements or supplies, and what his prospects are.

The Marquess of Salisbury to Consul Carles
Foreign Office, June 16, 1900

(Telegraphic)
With reference to your telegram of the 15th June, you should inform Viceroy that it is open to him to take refuge on one of Her Majesty's ships in the event of his considering himself in personal danger.

The Marquess of Salisbury to Sir C. MacDonald
Foreign Office, June 16, 1900

Sir,
I have received your despatch of the 16th April, reporting further negotiations with the Chinese Government on the subject of anti-Christian

Societies in the Provinces of Shantung and Chihli.

I approve your proceedings in the matter. ,

SALISBURY

The Marquess of Salisbury to Mr Whitehead

Foreign Office, June 16, 1900

Sir,

The Japanese Chargé d'Affaires called at this Office on the 11th instant and communicated the substance of a telegram which he had received from Viscount Aoki, instructing him to ascertain the attitude of Her Majesty's Government in the present crisis in China, and to inquire confidentially what action Her Majesty's Government would take should the Chinese Government prove themselves incapable of restoring peace and order and of protecting foreigners in China.

By my direction, Mr Villiers informed Mr Matsui that a force from the various squadrons at Taku was advancing on Peking, and that it was impossible to predict what the position of affairs would be on its arrival; that Her Majesty's Minister and the British Admiral had been left a wide discretion as to the best course to pursue, and that it was the desire of Her Majesty's Government to act with Japan and the other Powers interested in the restoration of order.

SALISBURY

Sir C. Scott to the Marquess of Salisbury (*received June* 17)

St Petersburgh, June 17, 1900

(Telegraphic)

According to information I have received, either to-morrow or Tuesday the *Official Gazette* will announce the issue of orders for the immediate dispatch of a force from Port Arthur to relieve the situation in Peking; this force will vary from 2,000 to 5,000 strong, according to necessity. A statement of the exact number of troops to be sent will be made on receipt of a telegram which is expected.

An explanation will accompany the announcement to the effect that to co-operate in the general interest for the protection of European lives and property is the sole aim of this expedition, and that it in no way indicates any desire to depart from the Emperor's settled peaceful and unaggressive policy.

Commander Gaunt to Admiralty (*communicated by Admiralty, June* 17)

Luu-leun-tao, June 17, 1900

(Telegraphic)

Writing on the evening of the 15th instant, the Rear-Admiral tells me that the Commander-in-chief is cut off 40 miles from Peking by Chinese troops and Boxers. If 2,000 Chinese troops, which were stated to be trying to cut Tien-tsin off from Taku advanced, the Council of Admirals have decided to shell the Taku forts. Her Majesty's ship *Phœnix* is at Chifu, and Her Majesty's ship *Peacock* is here. The telegraphic communication with the north is interrupted.

I send the above because I am in doubt as to whether you have been informed of the present situation.

Count Mouravieff to M. de Staal (communicated by M. de Staal, June 18)

St Petersburgh, June 3 (16), 1900

(Translation)

From the moment of the occurrence of events of an alarming nature in China the Government has exerted every effort to draw the attention of the Chinese Ministers to the dangerous consequences which might result from the excessive national excitement, and to induce the Tsung-li Yamên to adopt more vigorous measures for the re-establishment of order and security in the country.

Unhappily, the friendly counsels of the Russian Representative, as well as those of the other Powers at Peking have failed. The revolt of the Boxers constantly assumes a more menacing aspect. The life and property of foreign subjects are in danger. Finally, the destruction of the railways and the cutting of the telegraph lines has rendered it impossible for the Governments to remain in direct communication with their Legations at Peking.

Consequently, it becomes imperative to take more effective measures to assure the safety of the Imperial Legation and of Russian subjects residing in the country. With this object, His Majesty the Emperor has deigned to order the dispatch of a contingent of 4,000 soldiers, to be placed at the disposal of the Russian Minister at Peking.

The danger of the existing situation is universally recognized.

The British Representative applied to our Legation to ascertain how far the Imperial Government was prepared to co-operate with the efforts now being made to put an end to the existing complications. Certain other colleagues of M. de Giers have on their part solicited the aid and protection of the Russian Legation for their countrymen.

It is agreed that the temporary dispatch of the detachment of Russian troops has for its primary object the security of the Imperial Legation and that of Russian subjects resident in the north of China, and is actuated by no hostile designs with regard to that country, with which we maintain friendly and neighbourly relations.

On the contrary, instructions have been given to the detachment to co-operate with the troops landed by the other Powers, and to assist the Chinese Government at the same time in the work of re-establishing order so necessary, in the primary interests of China herself.

Acting Consul-General Warren to the Marquess of Salisbury (received June 18)
Shanghae, June 18, 1900

(Telegraphic)
I have received the following from Her Majesty's Consul at Hankow:

> I have given Lord Salisbury's message verbally to the Viceroy. Should there be
> disturbances he will apply for assistance. He professed to be confident of the
> ability of the Nanking Viceroy, with whom he is in communication, and himself
> to preserve order and to be taking the necessary steps for that purpose.

Lord Pauncefote to the Marquess of Salisbury (received June 18)
Washington, June 18, 1900

(Telegraphic)
I learn from the United States' Secretary of State that orders have been sent
to an American Regular Regiment now at Manila to proceed to Tien-tsin,
and act in concert with the other Powers for the protection of foreign life
and property and the suppression of disorder.

They will be accompanied by suitable artillery.

India Office to Foreign Office (received June 19)
June 18, 1900

Sir,
I am directed to acknowledge the receipt of your letter of the 15th June, and
to state, for the information of the Marquess of Salisbury, that Lord George
Hamilton has on a requisition received from the War Office, requested the
Government of India to replace the regiments at Hong Kong and Singapore
by native regiments from India.

C. STEDMAN, *Major-General*
Military Secretary

Memorandum communicated by Chinese Minister, June 19, 1900
The Chinese Minister has been requested by the Viceroy of Huquang to
communicate to the Marquess of Salisbury the purport of a telegram which
he has just received from his Excellency with reference to a communication
which Her Majesty's Consul at Hankow had been instructed to make to the
Viceroy on the part of his Lordship.

The communication consisted of an offer of assistance which the Consul
said Her Majesty's Government would be prepared to give to the Viceroy in
preserving order and tranquillity in the provinces under his jurisdiction, in
the event of the "Boxer" movement now agitating the Provinces of Chihli
and Shantung extending to those on the Yang-tsze.

The Viceroy tenders his grateful acknowledgments to Lord Salisbury for
his friendly offer, and will gladly avail himself of it in case of need. He, however, is persuaded that he and his colleague, the Viceroy of Nanking, with

whom he has been in communication on the subject, will be more than able to cope with the "Boxers" or any other elements of disorder who, contrary to his expectations, may attempt to disturb the peace and tranquillity of the Yang-tsze provinces.

Both he and the Viceroy of Nanking have at their disposal very sufficient, well-equipped, and well-disciplined forces, on which they can implicitly depend; and these they will so dispose and employ as to give the fullest measure of protection to all residing within their respective jurisdictions, whether natives or foreigners, and of whatever religion.

Under these circumstances, the Viceroy would deprecate any obtrusive demonstration of British naval force on the Yang-tsze as being calculated rather to make difficulties for the Chinese authorities than to aid them in maintaining tranquillity and good order in the riverine provinces.

Commanding Officer of Endymion *to Admiralty*
Liu-kun-tau, June 18, 1900

(Telegraphic)

Taku forts opened fire at 1 o'clock in the morning of the 17th June on the ships of the allied squadron. After six hours' engagement forts were silenced and occupied by the allied forces. Additional men for storming forts were sent ashore from the ships previous afternoon. British ships up the river engaged were *Algerine*, *Fame*, and *Whiting*. Two latter captured four Chinese torpedo-boat destroyers. Casualties: *Algerine*, slight; storming party and others unknown. Chinese second-class cruiser flying Admiral's flag detained outside Taku by the allied Admirals. No information of Commander-in-chief. China's return to Tien-tsin Bay had been received by the Rear-Admiral by 2 p.m., 17th June. Rear-Admiral not desiring to detach Chinese regiment, *Peacock* remains Wei-hai Wei. All British ships at Taku much depleted by men landed. Am leaving at once for Taku.

Mr Whitehead to the Marquess of Salisbury (received June 19)
Tokio, June 19, 1900

(Telegraphic)

Besides the troops mentioned in my telegram of 16th June, it is stated by the Japanese Naval Department that, in four or five days, 1,300 additional troops will be sent to Taku.

Commanding Officer of Hermione *to Admiralty*
Shia-ku-an, June 19, 1900

(Telegraphic)

I have had interview with Viceroy, and saw telegram received from Viceroy, Hankow, in which latter suggested to him that it is undesirable for any ship to be in Yang-tsze Kiang at present time. Viceroy, Nanking, considered two ships should be sufficient. Viceroy claims they are quite able to preserve order should any disturbance take place, which, they assert, is extremely unlikely.

In my opinion, present strength in Yang-tsze Kiang should not be reduced, and I have made arrangements to send ships to each Treaty port. Purpose leaving 20th June for Wuhu to await arrival of *Snipe* there, then returning to Nanking.

Consul concurs.

Rear-Admiral Bruce to Admiralty

Taku (via Chefoo), June 20, 1900

(Telegraphic)

June 17. Taku fort captured by allied forces this morning. Bombardment commenced 12.50 a.m., ended about 6.30 a.m. Details later on. Chinese Admiral present with allied fleet; flag flying in cruiser. At Council meeting this morning he agreed to anchor with fleet, putting out fires.

June 18. Situation getting worse. All north China under arms. No news from Commander-in-chief and advanced guard. Tien-tsin now cut off. Heavy fire heard there last night.

My communications with allied authorities most harmonious.

Admiralty to Rear-Admiral Bruce (communicated by Admiralty, June 20)

June 20, 1900

(Telegraphic)

Eight hundred seamen and marines leave by freight as soon as possible for Hong Kong to wait orders, and ships on station will be reinforced.

Sir C. Scott to the Marquess of Salisbury (received June 20)

St Petersburgh, June 20, 1900

(Telegraphic)

Count Mouravieff explained to me today that the 4,000 troops mentioned in the telegram to the Russian Embassy consist of 2,000 who are understood to be already at Taku or the mouth of the river, and of the 2,000 at Tien-tsin who, last week, while the other foreign troops defended the foreign Settlements, attacked and dispersed with loss the Boxers threatening that town.

For the last four days no direct news from Taku or Tien-tsin, and for seven days no knowledge of the situation at Peking or confirmation of the reported return of Admiral Seymour's expedition, have been received by the Russian Foreign Office, but Count Mouravieff takes a sanguine view of the situation, and appears to expect that not only will communication for news from Tien-tsin and probably Peking be opened up at once by the capture of the Taku forts, but that it will also exercise a salutary impression on the

Empress-Dowager, who has been hesitating between her fear of the Boxers and her fear of the intervention of the foreign Powers.

His Excellency still regards the state of things in Central and Southern China as more threatening, and believes that in a fortnight the crisis will be over.

Consul Carles to the Marquess of Salisbury (received June 20)

Chefoo, June 20, 1900

(Telegraphic)

Much damage was done last night to the line north of Tien-tsin by Boxers, and a great number of Chinese houses, together with the Roman Catholic Cathedral and Mission chapel, were burnt. There was no visible effort made to restrain them by the Chinese troops. The Boxers attacked the Settlement, and about 100 were killed by the foreign guard.

Acting Consul-General Fraser to the Marquess of Salisbury (received June 20)

Hankow, June 20, 1900

(Telegraphic)

I am assured by the Viceroy that every possible measure to maintain order is being taken by him and the Viceroy of Nanking, and they have no doubt of their power. In view of the probability of popular alarm and suspicion being caused thereby he deprecates any naval demonstration, though, of course, understanding that this protest does not include the ordinary movements of Her Majesty's ships.

Foreign Office to Admiralty

June 20, 1900

Sir,

I am directed by the Marquess of Salisbury to transmit to you, to be laid before the Lords Commissioners of the Admiralty, a copy of a Memorandum [dated June 19, 1900] given to his Lordship by the Chinese Minister relative to the offer of assistance made by Her Majesty's Government to the Viceroys of Hankow and Nanking in preserving order.

Their Excellencies, while grateful for the offer, consider the forces at their disposal sufficient to cope with any disturbances which may arise, and deprecate any obtrusive demonstration on the part of the British naval force.

I am to suggest that instructions be issued to the Officer Commanding Her Majesty's ships on the Yang-tsze River to avoid any demonstrations, but to inform the Viceroys that Her Majesty's ships will be ready to co-operate with them whenever co-operation becomes necessary for the protection of the lives and property of Europeans, or to support the measures taken by the Viceroys for the maintenance of order.

FRANCIS BERTIE

Sir William Fenwick
Williams of Kars
(1800–83).

View of Kars in eastern Turkey, where the Turkish army, under the leadership of General Williams, was besieged by the Russians in 1855. Public Record Office.

Another view of Kars in eastern Turkey, this time clearly showing the fortress perched over a rocky ravine. Public Record Office.

An artist's impression of Kars. Hulton Archive.

COLONEL REDVERS BULLER, V.C., C.B.

*Sir Redvers Buller, c. 1879. An English
soldier, Sir Redvers Henry Buller (1839–1908)
was the commander-in-chief during the Boer War
and raiser of the siege of Ladysmith. From*
Illustrated London News, *11 October 1879.*
Hulton Archive.

*Lord Roberts, c. 1901. The English soldier
Frederick Sleigh Roberts (1832–1914) was
created Lord Roberts of Kandahar and
Waterford in 1892, and earl in 1901.
He became commander-in-chief of the
British Army in 1901.* Hulton Archive.

*Creuzot's field gun, known as "Long Tom", was used against the British at Mafeking during
the Boer War.* Archive: Corbis.

Major-General Robert Baden-Powell (1857–1941), founder of the Scout Association. He successfully defended Mafeking (1899–1900) during the Boer War.
Hulton Archive.

"Mournful Monday", 30 October 1899. On this day General White's troops were driven back by the Boers into Ladysmith. Horace Nicholls/RPS.

Boer soldiers relaxing outside their tent and displaying their firearms at Ladysmith, c. 1900.
Hulton Archive.

Armed Afrikaners on the veldt near Ladysmith, c. 1900. *Hulton Archive.*

A siege note, printed in March 1900. This ten-shilling Mafeking siege note shows Major-General Baden-Powell's drawing of a Briton and a Boer. Hulton Archive.

A Boer fortification at Mafeking, c. 1900. Hulton Archive.

The Boxer Rebellion, c. 1900. Cantonese men and boys crowd behind the gate of the English bridge, which barred the Cantonese from the English legation during the Boxer Rebellion in China.
Hulton Archive.

Lou Henry Hoover inspects the big guns that shelled the foreign community during the Boxer Rebellion in Tientsin. Archive: Corbis.

The Dowager-Empress of China, who did not trust the Europeans, Americans or the Japanese. Archive: Corbis.

British Legation building, c. 1900. This photograph shows a corner of the British Legation which was attacked during the Boxer Rebellion. Hulton Archive.

Rear-Admiral, Taku, to Admiralty

Chefoo, June 21, 1900

(Telegraphic)

Latest information from Tien-tsin by runner, 20th June.

Reinforcements most urgently required. Casualties have been heavy. Supplies of ammunition insufficient. Machine-guns or field-guns required. Beware ambuscades [ambush] near Tien-tsin. Russians at railway station hard pressed. Chinese maintain incessant fire with large guns on European Concession, nearly all of which burnt.

There are not reinforcements to send.

Rear-Admiral Bruce to Admiralty

Taku, via Chefoo, June 21, 1900

(Telegraphic)

No communication from Commander-in-chief for seven days or with Tien-tsin for five days. Allies hold Taku forts and Tongku securely, and they will advance for relief of Tien-tsin when in sufficient strength. Troops expected from Hong Kong tomorrow, and 300 from Wei-hai Wei day after to-morrow.

Believe that fighting is constantly going on around Tien-tsin. Our garrison there should be about 3,000.

Following Proclamation was agreed to this morning, to be at once [issued]:

> The Admirals and Senior Naval Officers of the allied Powers in China desire, to
> make known to all Viceroys and authorities of the coasts and rivers, cities, and
> provinces of China that they intend to use armed force only against Boxers and
> peoples who oppose them on their march to Peking for the rescue of their
> fellow-countrymen.

The Marquess of Salisbury to Sir Chihchen Lofêngluh

Foreign Office, June 21, 1900

Sir,

I have received a letter from the Upper Yang-tsze Syndicate (Limited), stating that they are anxious with regard to the safety of their staff now employed in the Province of Szechuen. Their staff consists of Mr Archibald Little, Mr Herbert Way, and Mr James W. Nicolson, and the last news received was a telegram from Mr Way, dated Chengtu, the 17th instant.

I have received a similar communication from Mr W. Pritchard-Morgan relative to Dr Jack and his assistants, Messrs Robert Jack, J. F. Morris, and T. H. Bush, who are employed by him in the same province. The latest news received from Dr Jack was dated Chengtu, the 16th instant.

I have the honour to request that, if you are able to communicate with the Viceroy at Hankow, you will be so good as to inform him by telegraph that the above-mentioned gentlemen are within the limits of his authority, and to request his Excellency to take measures for their protection.

SALISBURY

Foreign Office to Admiralty

June 21, 1900

Sir,

With reference to the telegram from the Officer Commanding, Her Majesty's ship *Hermione*, reporting the result of an interview with the Viceroy of Nanking relative to the preservation of order on the Yang-tsze, I am directed by the Marquess of Salisbury to request you to inform the Lords Commissioners of the Admiralty that his Lordship concurs in the opinion expressed by Captain Cumming, that the present strength of the British naval force on the Yang-tsze should not be reduced. Lord Salisbury would further suggest that the arrangements made by Captain Cumming for sending a ship to each Treaty port should be approved.

FRANCIS BERTIE

Consul Carles to the Marquess of Salisbury (received June 22)

Tien-tsin via Chefoo, June 21, 1900

(Telegraphic)

June 18.   No news yet received from the front. We have been attacked at various points, but have repelled the enemy.

The Chinese commenced shelling the Settlement yesterday afternoon at 3 o'clock, and a few buildings were slightly damaged. A force composed of Austrians, British, Germans, and Italians, and numbering 175, attacked the Military College, destroyed the guns, killed nearly all the occupants, and finally burnt the College, in which there was a considerable and valuable store of ammunition.

The behaviour of the Russians, who were throughout the day engaged in various quarters, was splendid, and their large force and heavy field-guns, of which they had four, saved the situation. During the day all were engaged on their respective sections. The following is list of casualties: Russians, 7 killed, 5 wounded; British, 1 killed, 5 wounded; Italians, 2 wounded; Germans, 1 killed.

Last night an attempt was made by the Chinese to seize a bridge of boats, but they were repulsed with loss, which included, it is said, one of their Generals.

Our communications have been cut.

Admiralty to Senior Naval Officer, Woosung

June 22, 1900

(Telegraphic)

With reference to Admiralty telegram of the 16th June to Senior Naval Officer, Shanghae, and with reference to telegram from *Hermione* of the 19th June to Admiralty, instruct Commanding Officers of Her Majesty's ships at Nanking and Hankow to avoid any obtrusive demonstration of naval force on the river, but to inform the Viceroys that Her Majesty's ships will be ready to co-operate with them whenever co-operation becomes necessary for the protection of European life and property, or in support of the measures taken by them for the maintenance of order.

Mr Whitehead to the Marquess of Salisbury (received June 22)

Tokio, June 22, 1900

(Telegraphic)

I learn that eleven large steamers averaging 3,000 tons gross, and four small steamers of 400 tons gross, have been chartered by the Japanese Government; of these, six of the large ones are to be used as colliers and store-ships for the navy, the remainder to serve as transports of the troops.

The *Akitsusima* has been dispatched to Chefoo to protect the telegraph.

According to the Foreign Minister, there is no present intention on the part of Japan of sending any more troops than the 3,000 now *en route* to Taku.

The Marquess of Salisbury to Mr Whitehead

Foreign Office, June 22, 1900

(Telegraphic)

You should inform Japanese Minister for Foreign Affairs of the critical condition of the foreign Legations at Peking, and also, I fear, of the international force sent to relieve them under Admiral Seymour. State that Her Majesty's Government have sent orders to the Government of India for the dispatch of a considerable number of troops to China, and ascertain whether it is not the intention of the Japanese Government to send a further force to their succour.

The urgency of immediate action and the favourable geographical situation of Japan makes her intentions a matter of very grave importance in this difficulty.

The Marquess of Salisbury to Lord Pauncefote

Foreign Office, June 22, 1900

(Telegraphic)

China. Strong appeals are being made to Her Majesty's Government for reinforcements, and the crisis at Tien-tsin and Peking appears to be urgent. Orders have been sent to India for the dispatch of a considerable body of troops, but some time must elapse before they can arrive.

You should suggest to Mr Hay that any troops which it would be possible to send from Manila would be of very great value, as it is probable that the United States' Legation is in great danger as well as those of other Powers.

The Marquess of Salisbury to Acting Consul-General Warren
Foreign Office, June 22, 1900

(Telegraphic)
You should inform Viceroy, with reference to your telegram of today's date, that he may count on the fullest support of Her Majesty's ships in any efforts he may make to restore order.

The Marquess of Salisbury to Consul Scott
Foreign Office, June 22, 1900

(Telegraphic)
Li Hung-chang's departure from Canton.
The Chinese Minister, at an interview today, communicated to me a message which he had received from Li Hung-chang to the effect that he had received a summons to proceed to Peking in order to bring about a solution of the crisis in North China. He wished to know whether, notwithstanding the fact that the Taku forts had fired on the international forces without orders from the Government at Peking, the Powers consider themselves at war with the Chinese Government. His visit to Peking would be without utility if it were considered that a state of war existed. In the contrary event, he felt sure of being able to restore order and to suppress the Boxers.

In reply, I informed the Chinese Minister that there is no reason that it should be considered that a state of war exists if the Taku forts had fired without orders from the Government at Peking, and if the attacks on the international troops are without authority; and I strongly advised that if he could be of use in suppressing disorder, and if he could do so with safety to himself, Li Hung-chang should go to Peking, but that he must be judge as to the risk to be run in doing so.

The Marquess of Salisbury to Sir C. MacDonald
Foreign Office, June 22, 1900

The Chinese Minister called on me this morning, and stated that the Viceroy of Nanking entirely adopted the Memorandum which he handed to me on the 19th instant. He was greatly obliged for our offer of assistance which he would make use of if required, but he was anxious on account of his people to avoid anything like a demonstration.

The Minister went on to say that Li Hung-chang had been ordered to go to Peking, and rather wanted our advice. I strongly advised that he should go there if he could be of any use in suppressing disorder so long as he could do so with safety, but that we should be sorry if his life should be in danger.

I said that he must be the best judge of the risk, as he knew his own countrymen better than I did.

Sir Chihchen replied that Li knew his own countrymen, and was quite convinced of his power of repressing disorder amongst them, and had not the least fear that the Boxers would not submit to him. But before he acted in that sense, he wanted to know, and the Empress also wanted to know, what were the intentions of the Powers and especially of Her Majesty's Government who could influence the Powers with reference to the political conditions after the suppression of the outbreak. What were the changes or revolutions, if any, which the Powers intended to introduce?

I replied by disclaiming energetically any responsibility for the acts of other Powers, but said that Her Majesty's Government had no intention whatever at present of taking any steps to affect the existing political position at Peking. Their one object was to restore order and secure life and property. I was obliged to say that their action could not but be affected by the action of the Chinese Government and in some degree of the other Powers, so that he must take my assurances as not necessarily applying beyond the present time. The sooner the Empress had quelled the disorder which had broken out at Peking, the safer she would be from any such changes as those she apprehended.

The Minister told me that the attack by the Taku forts had been made without any order from above.

I replied that if that were so, and that the attacks on the international troops were without authority, there was no reason for considering that a state of war existed, but I warned him that the destruction of property which had taken place would have to be met by an indemnity on the part of the Chinese Government.

SALISBURY

The Marquess of Salisbury to Mr Herbert
Foreign Office, June 22, 1900

Sir,

The French Ambassador came to this Department in the forenoon today to inform me of a message received by M. Delcassé from the Viceroy Li, and to inquire what my opinion on it might be.

M. Cambon stated to Mr Bertie that M. Delcassé had spoken to the Chinese Minister at Paris on the grave state of affairs in Yünan, and the perilous position of French officials and private individuals in that province. This had probably caused the Chinese Minister to communicate by telegraph with Li Hung-chang, the result being that the Viceroy had sent a message to M. Delcassé to the following effect:

The Government at Peking had summoned the Viceroy to Peking with the view of bringing about a solution of the crisis in the north of China. He would be ready to go to Peking and take measures for the suppression of the Boxers, and felt confident of his ability to do so, provided that the Powers would not consider themselves in a state of war with the Chinese Government. Li Hung-chang stated that the Taku forts had fired on the international forces without orders from the Government at Peking, but that if notwithstanding this act having been unauthorized the Powers considered themselves at war with China his mission to Peking would be without utility, and he should not go.

Soon after M. Cambon had left the Foreign Office, and just before the meeting of the Cabinet, the Chinese Minister brought to me a message from Li Hung-chang, generally to the same effect as the one sent by his Excellency to M. Delcassé, and I have informed the French Ambassador that the answer which I made was that if the forts at Taku fired without orders from the Government at Peking, and the attacks on the international troops are without authority, there is no reason that it should be considered that a state of war exists; and that if Li Hung-chang thinks that his life will be safe at Peking, and that he can suppress the Boxers and restore order, his mission will be viewed favourably by Her Majesty's Government.

The details of my conversation with Lofêngluh are given in my despatch of today to Sir C. MacDonald, of which I have sent to you a copy.

SALISBURY

Foreign Office to M. Cambon

June 22, 1900

Since I saw your Excellency this morning Lord Salisbury has received from Li Hung-chang a message generally to the same effect as the one sent to M. Delcassé.

Lord Salisbury has replied that if the forts at Taku fired without orders from the Government at Peking, and the attacks on the international troops are without authority, there is no reason that it should be considered that a state of war exists, and that if Li Hung-chang thinks that his life is safe at Peking and that he can suppress the Boxers and restore order his mission will be viewed favourably by Her Majesty's Government.

FRANCIS BERTIE

Sir Chihchen Lofêngluh to the Marquess of Salisbury (received June 23)

Chinese Legation, June 22, 1900

I have the honour to acknowledge the receipt of your Lordship's letter of yesterday's date, expressing the anxiety felt by the Upper Yang-tsze Syndicate (Limited) and Mr Pritchard-Morgan with regard to the safety of their employees in the Province of Szechuen, and, in reply, I beg leave to inform you that, conformably to your Lordship's request, I have telegraphed to the Viceroy of that province requesting that proper measures may be taken for their protection.

LOFÊNGLUH

Lord Pauncefote to the Marquess of Salisbury (received June 23)
Washington, June 23, 1900

(Telegraphic)
The Secretary of State, to whom I communicated the substance of your telegram of the 22nd instant, informs me that in addition to a full regiment, 300 marines have been ordered from Manila to Tien-tsin, and that telegraphic inquiries are being made as to what further force can be spared. His Excellency states that the Chinese Minister here reports assurances from the Viceroys of their ability to maintain order in their provinces.

The Circular of the French Government to the Powers respecting Li Hung-chang's message has been delivered by the French Ambassador to Mr Hay, who has replied that the United States' Government are favourable to the offer being accepted, and that, all the facts not being known, they do not think that a state of war necessarily exists.

Lord Pauncefote to the Marquess of Salisbury (received June 23)
Washington, June 23, 1900

(Telegraphic)
I am informed by the Chinese Minister that, in reply to his inquiry as to the safety of the United States' Minister, he has received a telegram from the Viceroy of Nanking, dated 22nd June, in the following words:

"All the Ministers are well," but how the news reached the Viceroy he could not say.

Mr Whitehead to the Marquess of Salisbury (received June 23)
Tokio, June 23, 1900

(Telegraphic)
At 9 this morning I attended a meeting, convened by the Japanese Minister for Foreign Affairs, of the Representatives of Powers who have naval forces at Taku.

Two telegrams from the Japanese Admiral at Taku describing the extreme gravity of the situation, and urgently demanding the immediate dispatch of troops, were read to us by his Excellency.

The Minister, while refusing to make any suggestion himself, said that in view of the imminent danger of the situation and the critical position of international forces, his Government, desirous of conforming their resolves to those of the Powers interested, were anxious to know what measures our Government proposed to take immediately to meet the actual necessities of the case.

Mr Whitehead to the Marquess of Salisbury (received June 23)
Tokio, June 23, 1900

(Telegraphic)
I at once personally communicated to the Minister for Foreign Affairs the substance of your telegram of the 22nd instant, which I received after the

meeting reported in my immediately preceding telegram. Though doubtful as to what decision would be taken, his Excellency promised to submit it to the Cabinet without delay.

The second time I visited the Foreign Office the Minister said that, of course, Japan has troops at her disposal, but that it was impossible to foresee the consequences of sending them.

Rear-Admiral Bruce to Admiralty

Chefoo, June 23, 1900

(Telegraphic)

Received your telegrams. The allied Admirals are working in perfect accord with Russian Vice-Admiral as Senior Officer, and as the Council of Admirals has supreme control over all the operations, in order to avoid opportunities of friction, the Officer Commanding land forces should belong to same nation, as Senior Admiral, President of Council, as is case now.

A Russian Major-General, with the Russians, and German second in command, and Captain Warrender, are in charge of the operations from Taku forts for relief of Tien-tsin under general control of Russian Major-General. All Admirals in command are together off Taku bar.

Have just received news that Americans and Russians attempted yesterday to relieve Tien-tsin, and were repulsed by Chinese with some loss. Expect Hong Kong regiments to-morrow, and know of no more reinforcements coming.

Russians have landed altogether about 4,000. Russian Admiral told me yesterday he expected no more troops, Germany has landed about 1,300, and expects no more. Other forces landed besides ours small numerically.

Consul Scott to the Marquess of Salisbury (received June 24)

Canton, June 24, 1900

(Telegraphic)

With reference to your telegram of the 22nd instant:

I had yesterday an interview with Li Hung-chang. That morning he had sent a message to Peking asking for definite instructions as to going or remaining, and saying that, unless the Central Government were prepared beforehand to follow his advice, his Mission to the north would be absolutely futile. According to what his Excellency told me he will remain if the matter is left to his own decision; but that, if he is unconditionally ordered to go, he must do so at any risk.

His Excellency does not expect a reply within a week, as telegraphic communication with Peking and Tien-tsin is closed. I was requested by him to convey to your Lordship his thanks for your thoughtful consideration of his position and for your advice.

Consul Scott to the Marquess of Salisbury (received June 24)
Canton, June 24, 1900

(Telegraphic)

On being informed by the French Consul that he had received official intelligence of the bombardment of the Concessions at Tien-tsin by Government troops, I considered it advisable, in view of the probable effect of the news here, to apply for a gun-boat as a precautionary measure, and to allay excitement and anxiety among the foreign community.

Otherwise the state of things here is fairly quiet.

Sir C. Scott to the Marquess of Salisbury (received June 24)
St Petersburgh, June 24, 1900

(Telegraphic)

Under instructions from his Government yesterday, the French Minister was to inform the Russian Government that his Government had learnt from Canton that Li Hung-chang had been summoned to Peking by the Dowager-Empress, but before proceeding there, he had desired to be informed whether the action at Taku was regarded by the foreign Powers as constituting a state of war with the Chinese Government. The French Government desired to ascertain the view of the Russian Government on the subject.

The opinion of Count Lamsdorff was that, as it was not to be assumed that the Chinese troops were acting on instructions from the Chinese Government, but by compulsion of the Boxers, the Powers were not in a state of war with China.

I met M. de Witte yesterday, and he took the same view as that expressed on Wednesday by Count Mouravieff with regard to the situation in the north of China. The summons to Li Hung-chang he regarded as a favourable sign of the Empress's desire to arrange matters with the Powers.

He said that he expected that before any reinforcements from Europe could arrive the whole trouble would be over.

Rear-Admiral Bruce, at Taku, to Admiralty (communicated by Admiralty, June 25)
Port Arthur, June 17, 1900
(Delayed on Chinese lines)

(Telegraphic)

Council of Admirals this morning decided to attack Taku forts 2 o'clock in the morning 17th June, if not previously surrendered, for purpose of trying to relieve Commander-in-chief and allied forces marching on Peking, and situation of affairs at Tien-tsin.

Presented ultimatum to Chinese Governor at Tien-tsin and Commandant of forts this afternoon.

Chinese telegraph lines interrupted. Situation of affairs over all China very critical. Towns on the Yang-tsze-Kiang anxious for protection. Commander-in-chief is still cut off from all communication.

Report arrived today that the Legations at Peking have been attacked. Tuan, new Head of Foreign Affairs in China, in my belief is head of the Boxers. [Am] saving such missionaries as I hear reach coast.

Rear-Admiral Bruce to Admiralty (communicated by Admiralty, June 25)
Chefoo, June 24, 1900
(Telegraphic)

Total force which left Tien-tsin with Commander-in-chief for Peking about 2,000, composed of detachments of the allied ships.

German and American Flag Captains were with Commander-in-chief.

Captain Bayly, *Aurora*, has been the commander, heart and soul, of the defence of Tien-tsin, assisted by Captain Burke, *Orlando*.

No action could be possibly taken to relieve the Commander-in-chief, because it was only known he was cut off by Tien-tsin being invested. Tien-tsin has been fighting for its life ever since. It was on receipt of information that Chinese army had ordered trains for attacking Tien-tsin, ravaged Tongku, and were reinforcing Taku, as well as mining the mouth of the Peiho, that it was promptly determined to seize Taku just in time, since when every effort has been made to relieve Tien-tsin.

Have commandeered small coasting steamer for taking troops sick and wounded across the bar and to Wei-hai Wei, where I intend making temporary base hospital and asylum for refuge until South China has settled down.

The Marquess of Salisbury to Sir C. Scott
Foreign Office, June 25, 1900
(Telegraphic)

I request that you will inquire of the Russian Minister for Foreign Affairs whether his Government will give their approval to dispatch of a Japanese force of from 20,000 to 30,000 men, if Japanese Government are willing to undertake it, for the restoration of order at Tien-tsin and Peking.

The Marquess of Salisbury to Sir C. Scott
Foreign Office, June 25, 1900
(Telegraphic)

In your conversation with the Minister for Foreign Affairs on the subject mentioned in my telegram of today, you may draw his Excellency's attention to the following considerations: Her Majesty's Government assume that the Russian Government will further reinforce their troops speedily, and are themselves sending some 10,000 troops from India; but it is clear that these reinforcements will not arrive in time to rescue the two forces at present surrounded or the Legations at Peking.

The Marquess of Salisbury to Mr Whitehead
Foreign Office, June 25, 1900

Sir,

The Japanese Chargé d'Affaires requested to see me today. He asked me what arrangements the Powers were making with respect to the China crisis. I informed him of the troops that were being sent by the various Powers, and that the officers on the spot were left to arrange with each other the measures that were most suitable for relieving the nationals of the various Powers who were in danger. I pointed out to him that considerable time must elapse before the relief from India or Europe could arrive, and that Japan was situated in a manner more favourable for immediate action. I asked him how long it would take to send a considerable force from Japan. He said that would depend upon the locality in Japan from which the force was sent, but he thought that if all preparations were complete, four days would be required for the passage. He did not, however, intimate that there was any chance of an immediate completion of the preparations. He said that he had received no instructions from his Government, but that, in his own opinion, it was not likely they would send a very large force.

He thought some assurance would be required that there was no objection on the part of other Governments which have interests in the East.

I have telegraphed to St Petersburgh to ascertain whether the Russians would approve of an expedition of 25,000 or 30,000 troops, and have urged upon the German Government that they should support us in this appeal.

SALISBURY

The Marquess of Salisbury to Viscount Gough
Foreign Office, June 26, 1900

(Telegraphic)

The crisis in China. Please inform Minister for Foreign Affairs that I have telegraphed to Her Majesty's Ambassador at St Petersburgh to inquire whether the Russian Government would approve of a force of from 20,000 to 30,000 men being sent by Japan to Taku.

I gather from the Japanese Chargé d'Affaires, with whom I had an interview late last night, that his Government, unless they receive some assurance that it will not lead to complications with other Powers interested, will not give effective assistance.

I hope the German Emperor will concur in our wish to procure such an assurance from Russia, and that His Majesty will be willing to lend us his assistance in obtaining it.

Acting Consul-General Warren to the Marquess of Salisbury (received June 26)

Shanghae, June 26, 1900

(Telegraphic)

A telegram has been received from the Governor of Shantung, Yuan-shih-Kai, to the effect that he has frequently sent out scouts to get news, but that, as a rule, the Boxers have killed them all. According to his latest information the foreign Ministers in Peking were unharmed up to the 20th instant.

Mr Whitehead to the Marquess of Salisbury (received June 26)

Tokio, June 26, 1900

(Telegraphic)

Japanese reinforcements.

Your telegram of the 22nd instant. I received official information this morning from the Minister for Foreign Affairs that it has been decided by the Japanese Government to mobilize and hold ready one division, which, including the force already sent, will make a total of about 13,000 men. If emergency arises, he states that transports will be available at any moment.

Sir Chihchen Lofêngluh to the Marquess of Salisbury (received June 26)

Chinese Legation, June 26, 1900

Referring to my letter of the 22nd instant, I have the honour to inform your Lordship that, in reply to the telegram I sent requesting that special precautions should be taken in the Province of Szechuen for the protection of the foreigners there employed by Mr Pritchard-Morgan and the Upper Yang-tsze Syndicate, I have received the following telegram from his Excellency the Viceroy of Huquang:

> Your telegram has been received, and the Viceroy of Szechuen has been requested to give the desired protection.
>
> In the Upper and Lower Yang-tsze, the Viceroy of Nanking and myself will, under any circumstances, afford adequate protection to foreign merchants, missionaries, and native Christians residing in our respective Governments. Please assure Lord Salisbury that no apprehension need be entertained as to this.
>
> LOFÊNGLUH

Sir Chihchen Lofêngluh to the Marquess of Salisbury (received June 26)

Chinese Legation, June 26, 1900

The Chinese Minister presents his compliments to the Marquess of Salisbury, and, at the request of the Viceroy of Huquang, has the honour to communicate to his Lordship the following translation of a telegram he has received from his Excellency, dated 6 a.m., the 23rd June:

> The rebels in the northern provinces, called by the name of "Boxers", have, in defiance of the Imperial Decree, overrun and devastated a large tract of country

in the vicinity of Peking, taking the lives of many persons, natives as well as foreigners of various nationalities, including a member of the Japanese Legation at Peking.

The present lamentable state of affairs, which the Imperial Government deplore as a national calamity, is doubtless attributable to the culpable negligence of the provincial authorities, who surely could never have foreseen the large proportions which the Boxer movement was fated to take; otherwise they would have suppressed it in the commencement.

I am very apprehensive lest the continued occupation of the Taku forts should lead to a breach of harmonious relations between China and the Treaty Powers. The Empress-Dowager and the Emperor have summoned Li Hung-chang to Peking by telegraph, in order to concert measures with the Government to the end that an understanding may be come to with the Treaty Powers; but a fortnight must necessarily elapse before he can arrive, and meanwhile the Treaty Powers are dispatching additional troops to China, which may have the effect of aggravating the gravity of the situation, and of, perhaps, precipitating matters beyond recall; thus creating new opportunities for other disaffected factions to join the Boxers, or even to act independently of them in their fell work of murder, rapine, and plunder.

The intentions of the Imperial Government are entirely pacific and in favour of friendly relations with the Treaty Powers. This is shown by the absence of any instructions to the provincial authorities to take measures with a view to defence.

You should endeavour to induce the Governments to whom you are accredited to instruct their respective naval Commanders in the neighbourhood of Tien-tsin to remain on the defensive until such time as Li Hung-chang shall have arrived in Peking and memorialized the Throne, with respect to the satisfaction to be given to the Powers. In this way, freed from the dread of drifting into war with them, we shall be at liberty to devote all our energies to the suppression of the rebellion.

The Viceroys of the provinces bordering on the Yang-tsze having taken precautions against the possibility of any troubles occurring within their respective jurisdictions, no apprehension need be entertained as to their ability and readiness to afford the fullest measure of protection to foreigners residing at the riverine ports. It might, however, be otherwise, should hostilities be continued at Tien-tsin.

The situation, then, being so critical, I would impress on you the necessity of your exerting yourself to the utmost in order to induce Great Britain to be forbearing, and not to press matters unduly in the north. The provincial authorities of the central provinces all agree with me as to the extreme desirability of these recommendations being attended to, and join me in requesting you to bring to the notice of the Foreign Secretary all the considerations I have given expression to in this telegram.

Sir Chihchen Lofêngluh to the Marquess of Salisbury (received June 26)

Chinese Legation, June 26, 1900

With reference to the telegram from the Viceroy of Huquang, dated Woochang, the 23rd June, which I have had the honour of communicating to your Lordship, I beg leave to state that I have received another telegram from his Excellency, instructing me to inform you that the under-mentioned Viceroys and Governors of provinces, being in complete accord with him as to the views expressed by him in the said telegram, have expressed a desire to be considered as co-Signatories with him of that communication:

Li Hung-chang, Viceroy of the Two Kwangs
Lieu Kwun Yih, Viceroy of the Two Kiangs
Wang Chi Chün, Governor of Anhwei
Yüen Shi Kai, Governor of Shantung
Yü Lin San, Governor of Hunan

In requesting your Lordship to take note of this, I venture to express the hope that the adherence of these important functionaries to the telegram of the Viceroy of Huquang may be viewed by your Lordship as lending additional weight to the considerations advanced by him in favour of a policy of abstention, on the part of the Treaty Powers, from extreme measures in the present unhappy condition of a part of Northern China.

LOFÊNGLUH

Rear-Admiral Bruce to Admiralty (communicated by Admiralty, June 26)

Chefoo, June 26, 1900

(Telegraphic)

Commander Cradock, commanding British contingent, Tien-tsin relief, reports Tien-tsin communicated with and reinforced 23rd June. Commander-in-chief reported 10 miles from Tien-tsin, hampered by sick and wounded, and engaged with enemy.

Force landed: German 1,340; American 335; Russian Naval Brigade 235, troops 3,500; Japanese Naval Brigade 602, troops 1,050, expected 26th June 2,100; Austrians 26; Italian 138; French 421, 3 p.m. 25th June French expect one battery artillery, one battalion infantry.

Acting Consul-General Warren to the Marquess of Salisbury (received June 27)

Shanghae, June 27, 1900

(Telegraphic)

Acting under instructions from the Viceroy, the Taotai of Shanghae asked the foreign Consuls to meet him yesterday in order to discuss the situation. He asked the Consuls at the meeting to telegraph to their respective Governments, suggesting that they should declare neutral all the districts other than those north of where fighting is actually in progress, and that if that were done they would then be able to guarantee the maintenance of order.

The allied Admirals' Proclamation, dated the 20th June, was the Consuls' reply. They declared that the foreign Powers were only fighting against the Boxers and those persons who opposed the forces sent to Peking to rescue their countrymen there. That the duty of keeping the peace rested with the Chinese officials, and that they need have no apprehension of any attack on our part if no breach of peace or act of war was committed by China.

Consul Carles to the Marquess of Salisbury (received June 27)
Tien-tsin, via Chefoo, June 27, 1900

(Telegraphic)
British column, under Major F. Morris, R.W.F., and Naval Brigade, under Commander Cradock, arrived at noon, 550 men strong; 1,500 Russians are reported to be at Tien-tsin Railway Station; 150 Americans and 50 Italians have also arrived 23rd June.

Consul Carles to the Marquess of Salisbury (received June 27)
Tien-tsin, June 27, 1900

(Telegraphic)
Heavy firing has been heard for thirty-six hours north of Tien-tsin, where the Commander-in-chief is believed to be at a place named Pei-tsang, about 9 miles from here.

A note was received yesterday morning by the Commissioner of Imperial Customs from the Inspector-General, dated 19th June, 4 p.m., stating that the Legations had been ordered to leave Peking within twenty-four hours.

Sir C. Scott to the Marquess of Salisbury (received June 27)
St Peterburgh, June 27, 1900

(Telegraphic)
Count Lamsdorff has been at Peterhof with the Emperor all day, and early to-morrow morning he has to return there, but I have been able to communicate in writing to him the sense of your Lordship's telegrams of 25th June, and he promises that as soon as he is enabled to do so he will give me an immediate reply.

There is an utter absence of news at the Russian Foreign Office with regard to the present situation in and near Tien-tsin.

Sir E. Monson to the Marquess of Salisbury (received June 27)
Paris, June 27, 1900

(Telegraphic)
M. Delcassé informs me that, beyond the two declarations he has already made in the Chamber, he has no statement to offer for the information of the Government of Japan in connection with the meeting of the foreign Representatives which the Japanese Minister for Foreign Affairs convoked at Tokio.

On the question of the co-operation of Japan on a large scale, his Excellency did not give me any intimation of his opinion.

On the whole, M. Delcassé's language was less optimistic than that which seems to have been held at St Petersburgh to Her Majesty's Ambassador.

The Marquess of Salisbury to Acting Consul-General Warren
Foreign Office, June 27, 1900

(Telegraphic)

Your telegram of today. Your answer to the Taotai is approved.

The Marquess of Salisbury to Sir Chihchen Lofêngluh
Foreign Office, June 27, 1900

Sir,

I have the honour to acknowledge the receipt of your note of yesterday's date, containing a telegram received by you from his Excellency the Viceroy of Huquang relative to the protection of foreigners and native Christians residing in the Yang-tsze provinces.

I have to thank you for your action in the matter.

SALISBURY

Consul Carles to the Marquess of Salisbury (received June 28)
Tien-tsin, via Chefoo, June 24, 1900

(Telegraphic)

News was brought yesterday by Bigham's servant, who is quite trustworthy, of the Commander-in-chief. He was being bombarded by a large number of guns in a small arsenal called Wuku, north of Tien-tsin, which he had seized. His losses were about 40 killed and 70 wounded, and relief was urgently needed. Force to succour him leaves tonight.

Comparatively slight damage was done to the foreign Settlements, which were shelled from the 18th to the 23rd June, except in the French Concession, which suffered severely; the British Consulate was also a good deal knocked about. The British casualties up to date of relief are 4 killed and 50 wounded, among the latter being 6 officers.

Admiralty to Rear-Admiral Bruce (communicated by Admiralty, June 28)
June 28, 1900

(Telegraphic)

It is proposed to make Wei-hai Wei the base for troops in the north of China, and all ships containing stores will be directed to call at Hong Kong for orders.

Sir C. Scott to the Marquess of Salisbury (received June 28)
St Petersburgh, June 28, 1900

(Telegraphic)

Following official telegram from Admiral Alexieff, dated Port Arthur, the 26th June, published by Russian War Office this evening:

On 24th June, General Stessel forced his entrance into Tien-tsin and effected junction with Anisimoff. Losses not great; details later.

Sir C. Scott to the Marquess of Salisbury (received June 28)
St Petersburgh, June 28, 1900

(Telegraphic)
Further official telegram from Admiral Alexieff, Port Arthur, 27th June. During night of 26th, detachment from Tien-tsin, commanded by Lieutenant-Colonel Shirinsky, and consisting of four Russian companies and similar number of foreigners, liberated Seymour detachment, escorting it to Tien-tsin; 200 of Seymour detachment wounded.

Sir C. Scott to the Marquess of Salisbury (received June 28)
St Petersburgh, June 28, 1900

(Telegraphic)
I communicated your Lordship's telegram of the 25th June to Lamsdorff, and have just received his Excellency's reply. The Russian Minister at Tokio has been instructed by telegraph to make the following reply to the Government of Japan:

> We can only highly appreciate the sentiments expressed by Japan in present circumstances, as also her view of Chinese affairs. We have no desire to hinder her liberty of action, particularly after her expression of a firm intention to conform her action to that of the other Powers.
>
> As regards Russia, her intentions have been clearly defined by the official communiqué published on the 24th instant.
>
> Admiral Alexieff has further received orders to regulate the measures which he might find necessary eventually to take in accordance with the developments in North China.

Acting Consul-General Warren to the Marquess of Salisbury (received June 28)
Shanghae, June 28, 1900

(Telegraphic)
I have received the following telegram from Her Majesty's Consul at Chungking for transmission to your Lordship:

> In order to have a possible means of escape for the women and children, I have taken it upon myself to detain the British merchant-steamer Pioneer at Chungking. A state of great anxiety prevails here owing to there being no gun-boat. I communicated with the Admiral by telegraph on the 19th June through the Consulate General at Shanghae, but I have not as yet received any reply. There are no means of communicating with Sir C. MacDonald. I am sending by mail a full report of what has been done.

Acting Consul-General Warren to the Marquess of Salisbury (received June 28)
Shanghae, June 28, 1900

(Telegraphic)

I have received the following message from the Nanking Viceroy:

I received the following Imperial Rescript on 25th June by telegraph:

'The Imperial Government continues as usual to accord every protection to the foreign Legations at Peking.'

Mr Whitehead to the Marquess of Salisbury (received June 28)
Tokio, June 28, 1900

(Telegraphic)

I have today been informed by Viscount Aoki that the division now mobilized would probably be very shortly embarked.

Viscount Aoki further stated that the communication, which in accordance with the instructions contained in your Lordship's telegram of the 22nd instant I made to the Japanese Government, was considered by them to be not so much a mere inquiry as a suggestion. It was possible for them to reply directly or indirectly, and they have chosen what seemed the preferable course by mobilizing their troops.

Consul Scott to the Marquess of Salisbury (received June 28)
Canton, June 28, 1900

(Telegraphic)

I am informed by Li Hung-chang that he has received an Imperial Edict, by which he is commanded to remain in residence for the present, so as to ensure the preservation of order in the district.

The Marquess of Salisbury to Sir C. MacDonald
Foreign Office, June 28, 1900

Sir,

The Chinese Minister called on me today, and said that the Viceroy Li Hung-chang had requested him to inform me that the foreign Representatives at Peking were safe at Pei-tsang, a station on the Tien-tsin–Peking Railway, some 16 miles to the north of Tien-tsin.

SALISBURY

Count Lamsdorff to M. de Staal (communicated by M. de Staal, June 29)
St Petersburgh, June 15 (28), 1900

(Translation)

We have been informed of the intention of Japan to take part in the re-establishment of order in China by Sir C. Scott and M. Isvolsky. The latter has been furnished with the following instructions in regard to the matter:

While appreciating the friendly sentiments which animate Japan, and which have suggested to Mr Aoki the overtures made by him to you, as well as the perfectly correct attitude adopted by that Power in view of the events which have occurred in China, we do not wish to hinder the liberty of action of the Tokio Cabinet, especially as the latter is quite disposed to act in harmony with the other Powers. As to the intentions of Russia, the Imperial Government has stated them in the recently published official communiqué.

Lord Currie to the Marquess of Salisbury (received July 2)

Rome, June 28, 1900

I asked M. Visconti-Venosta today what steps the Italian Government intended to take with regard to events in China.

He said that they wished to take part in any concerted action that may be taken by the Powers for the protection of Europeans, and for the re-establishment of order. They could not contribute as largely to these ends as most of the other Powers interested in the Far East, but small contingents had already been landed from the Italian ships, and had acted with the international forces. There were at present only two Italian men-of-war in Chinese waters, but another was on its way, and two more would start in a few days, and would be provided with extra crews, so as to strengthen the ships already on the station and provide men for landing parties. Another vessel would be got ready with all dispatch. So that in a short time the Italian Squadron in Chinese waters would be composed of six vessels.

It was not decided to send any soldiers at present, as it was uncertain whether they would be required, but, in the event of circumstances making it desirable that Peking or any other point should be occupied by an international force, Italy would be ready to send a contingent to take part in such occupation, and would reserve her decision as to any larger force that might be eventually required.

It was impossible at present to judge how far the movement in China was likely to spread, and what efforts might be required to cope with it.

It was the wish of the Italian Government, M. Visconti-Venosta said, to co-operate with Great Britain and the other Powers, and he would be very glad to learn whether the course which they proposed to follow met with the concurrence and sympathy of Her Majesty's Government.

CURRIE

Viscount Gough to the Marquess of Salisbury (received June 29)

Berlin, June 29, 1900

(Telegraphic)

Dispatch of Japanese expedition to China.

Your telegram of 26th June. The Minister for Foreign Affairs is absent with the Emperor, and the German Government has not yet given any answer.

Consul Carles to the Marquess of Salisbury
Tien-tsin, via Chefoo, June 29, 1900

(Telegraphic)

A message to the effect that the Legations are still in Peking has been received by a foreign Resident through the Customs Taotai.

Admiral Seymour's force, together with the relief force, arrived on the 26th instant. The casualty returns of the foreign detachments are incomplete; the British casualties are: killed, Captain Beyts and twenty-four men; wounded, seven officers and ninety-one men.

Vice-Admiral Sir E. Seymour to Admiralty (communicated by Admiralty, June 29)
Chefoo, June 29, 1900

(Telegraphic)

Have returned Tien-tsin with force, unable to reach Peking by rail. On the 13th June two attacks on advanced guard made by Boxers, repulsed with considerable loss to Boxers, none our side. 14th June Boxers attacked train at Langfang in large numbers with great determination, but were repelled with loss of about 100 killed. Our loss, five Italians.

Same afternoon Boxers attacked British guard left to protect Lofa Station. Reinforcements were sent back and enemy driven off, 100 being killed—two of our seamen wounded. Guards pushed forward to Anting, engaged enemy 13th and 14th June, inflicting loss of 175—no casualties our side.

Extensive destruction of railway in our front having made further advance by rail impossible, it was decided, 16th June, to return to Yangtsun, where proposed to organize advance by river to Peking.

After my departure from Langfang two trains left to follow on were attacked 18th June by Boxers and Imperial troops from Peking, who lost 400 to 500 killed. Our casualties: six killed, 48 wounded. These trains joined me at Yangtsun same evening. Railway at Yangtsun found entirely demolished, and train immovable, forces short of provisions, and hampered with wounded, forcing us to withdraw on Tien-tsin, with which there had been no communication for six days, and supplies cut off 19th June, wounded and necessaries started by boats, forces marching alongside river.

Opposition experienced during whole course of river from nearly every village, rebels when defeated in one village retiring on next, and skilfully retarding advance by occupying well-selected positions, from which they had to be forced, often at point of bayonet, in face of galling fire difficult to locate.

23rd June made night march, arriving at daylight opposite Imperial Armoury, above Tien-tsin, where, after friendly advances, treacherous heavy fire was opened while men were exposed on opposite bank.

Enemy kept in check by rifle fire in front, while position was turned by party of marines and seamen under Major Johnstone, who rushed and occupied one of sallied points, seizing a gun.

Germans lower down silenced two guns, then crossed river, capturing them. Armoury then occupied by combined forces. Determined attempt to retake it made same and following days, unsuccessful. Found immense stores of guns, arms, ammunition, latest pattern.

Several guns mounted for our defence and shelled Chinese forts lower down—having found ammunition and rice could have held out some days, but being hampered by large number of wounded, sent to Tien-tsin to ask for relieving force, which arrived morning of 25th June. Armoury evacuated, and forces arrived Tien-tsin, 26th June. On leaving armoury destroyed it by fire.

Casualties to date:

	Killed	Wounded
British	27	97
American	4	25
French	1	10
German	12	62
Italian	5	3
Japanese	2	3
Austrian	1	1
Russian	10	27

Consul Carles to the Marquess of Salisbury

Tien-tsin, via Chefoo, June 29, 1900

(Telegraphic)

At a Consular meeting held today it was unanimously agreed to make the following suggestion to our respective Governments, viz., that the Chinese Government should be informed that in case the persons of the foreign Ministers are touched, the Mausolea of the dynasty will be destroyed by the European troops.

The Commander-in-chief gave his support to this decision on the 26th instant, and it is to be communicated to all the Admirals.

Consul Tratman to the Marquess of Salisbury (received June 29)

Chefoo, June 29, 1900

(Telegraphic)

Nothing definite is known of Ministers, but they are supposed to be still in Peking. The damage done to Tien-tsin has been exaggerated; English ladies are still there and likely to remain. Admiral Seymour has been relieved, and has returned to Tien-tsin with a loss of 62 killed and 212 wounded.

Acting Consul-General Warren to the Marquess of Salisbury (received June 30)

Shanghae, June 29, 1900

(Telegraphic)

The following has been received from a reliable source, and the language of the Viceroy Liu and the Shanghae Taotai confirms its general terms:

> The Viceroy has received through the Governor of Shantung a Secret Decree dated the 20th June. This Decree, which is very curiously worded, is considered by the Chinese as the testamentary command of a dying Government. The Governors and Viceroys are ordered to protect the provinces under their administration, and to render assistance at the same time in the critical situation of affairs at Peking. The Chinese are of opinion that its language practically gives absolute authority to the Viceroys.
>
> A message has been received by Li Hung-chang from Jung-lu dated the 21st June, telling him to pay no further attention to Decrees from the capital. In combination with the Yang-tsze Viceroys, Li-Hung-chang has agreed no longer to recognize the Peking Government.
>
> A copy of the Secret Decree is in my possession. The language employed is non-committal, but I consider that Prince Tuan probably usurped the Imperial power about the 21st June. It is reported that Jung-lu is attempting to co-operate with the Chinese Viceroys and is opposed to him.

Viscount Gough to the Marquess of Salisbury (received July 2)

Berlin, June 29, 1900

I have the honour to inform your Lordship that the Emperor has appointed Major-General von Hoepfner, Inspector of the Marine Infantry, to the command of the reinforcements which have been ordered to China. In the Imperial Order notifying this appointment it is directed that when the General arrives on the East Asiatic Station he is to place himself under the orders of the Commander of the Cruiser Squadron. In any land operations, however, General von Hoepfner is to assume the command of the forces employed.

I have the honour to transmit to your Lordship a translation of an Imperial Order, published in yesterday's papers, directing the formation of the expeditionary corps for China, and specifying the number of officers and men, etc., of which it is to consist.

GOUGH

Enclosure

Imperial Cabinet Order respecting the Formation of an Expeditionary Corps for China

June 25, 1900

(Translation)

I command:

1. An expeditionary corps to be dispatched to China, is to be formed from my navy, consisting of the 1st and 2nd Marine Battalion, of a horsed field battery, and of a detachment of Pioneers.
2. To the Commander of the expeditionary corps I grant the jurisdictional and disciplinary authority of a Commander of a division.
3. His Staff consists of—one Staff Officer as Chief of the Staff, one Captain, one Lieutenant, one Staff Surgeon, one Paymaster, one Evangelical and one Catholic Naval Chaplain, and the necessary subordinates.
4. A reserve battalion is to be formed as soon as possible in Kiel and in Wilhelmshaven for the 1st and 2nd Marine Battalion. Executory orders are issued by the Secretary of State for the Imperial Department of Marine.
5. The dispatch of and arrangements for transport devolve upon the North Sea Naval Station.

Kiel, on board my yacht *Hohenzollern.*

WILLIAM

Rear-Admiral Bruce to Admiralty

Via Chefoo, June 30, 1900

(Telegraphic)

The conduct of Commander Stewart, *Algerine,* and Commander Lanz, *Iltis* (German), at bombardment Taku forts was magnificent, and elicited admiration of allied ships.

River route to Tien-tsin, 51 miles from Taku, now open. Railhead now 9 miles from Tien-tsin, and road inwards not [now?] quite safe. Communication with Commander-in-chief, Tien-tsin, difficult. Force with Cradock had to fight way into Tien-tsin. Cradock also Commander storming party previously forts at Taku. Fort which commanded river 13 miles above Taku was found deserted by Lieutenant and Commander Keyes, and blown up by him, leaving passage up the river free. Keyes reports today arsenal Tien-tsin captured 27th June.

Naval brigade losses: five men killed. Lieutenant Colomb, *Endymion,* slightly wounded; Gunner May and twenty-one men wounded. No further details. Warrender quite well, doing very good work, taking charge of all our forces on river and along lines of communication.

Vice-Admiral Alexieff, Governor-General of Port Arthur and Liaotung Province, Commander-in-chief of all Russian forces in the East, has just arrived on his way to Tien-tsin, taking supreme command of Russian forces. Captain Jellicoe shot through lung, doing very well.

Forces landed to date:

	Officers	Men
Germany	44	1,300
British	184	1,700
Austria	12	127
America	20	329
France	17	387
Italy	7	131
Japan	119	3,709
Russia	117	5,817
Total	520	13,500

With 53 field guns, 36 machine guns.

No details yet of killed and wounded with Commander-in-chief.

JULY 1900

Viscount Gough to the Marquess of Salisbury (received July 1)

Berlin, July 1, 1900

(Telegraphic)

With reference to your Lordship's telegram of the 26th June respecting the Japanese expedition, I have the honour to state that the German Government have sent me the following reply:

> No particulars (*modalitäten*) of the proposed Japanese intervention are in their possession; they are unable to judge whether the interests of third Powers would be affected by it, or whether the responsibility of supporting it could be undertaken by Germany.
>
> Order can be restored in China, and the Empire's existence and the peace of the world be continued only by the maintenance of the accord which has hitherto existed among the Powers.
>
> Germany would therefore only take part in the steps which Her Majesty's Government have proposed, if, from the outset, she felt certain that the above-mentioned indispensable accord would not be thereby endangered.

I am sending by post tonight copy and translation of the reply of the German Government.

Acting Consul-General Warren to the Marquess of Salisbury (received July 1)

Shanghae, July 1, 1900

(Telegraphic)

This morning news has been received here from Peking up to the 26th ultimo; all the power is in the usurper Tuan's hands and the situation is very grave. The Empress-Dowager and the Emperor are both in Peking but powerless. Tung-fu-hsiang, the Mahommedan General with 15,000 well-drilled Kansu men and Tuan with Manchu troops, are determined to resist foreign troops. Jung-lu beseeches foreign Powers to rescue their subjects while there is time. Viceroys and Governors of all the southern and central provinces have united to resist the usurper and ask for assurance from Powers that the war shall not spread south however bad the situation at Peking may become. I have again given them assurances that Her Majesty's Government will not land troops except in the north while the Chinese authorities continue to maintain order. News has reached Shêng from Paoting-fu that German Minister has been murdered. I consider the position of foreigners in Peking extremely critical. They are said to have taken refuge at the British Legation.

Acting Consul-General Warren to the Marquess of Salisbury (received July 1)
Shanghae, July 1, 1900
(Telegraphic)
I telegraphed today to Yuan-shih-Kai, Governor of Shantung, for the purpose of urging him to follow the example of the three great Viceroys in standing firm in the cause of order.

His reply is as follows:

> With regard to your telegram of today: My views are the same as those of the Viceroys. The rebels have reached Peking, have for a long time interrupted communication and have overrun the country. A messenger reached me on the 26th June with information that the foreign Representatives were still in the capital.

Vice-Admiral Sir E. Seymour to Admiralty (communicated by Admiralty, July 1)
Chefoo, July 1, 1900
(Telegraphic)
Arsenal north-east of Tien-tsin Settlement captured the 27th June by combined forces. British engaged were Naval Brigade and 1st Chinese Regiment.

Consul Tratman to the Marquess of Salisbury (received July 1)
Chefoo, July 1, 1900
(Telegraphic)
On the 13th June the German Minister at Peking was murdered by native troops. On the 23rd June there were only three Legations remaining. It is not stated which they were.

Rear-Admiral Bruce to Admiralty
Chefoo, July 1, 1900
(Telegraphic)
German Admiral reports Chinese runner, three days from Peking, arrived Tien-tsin yesterday; brought despatches to say all Europeans in great distress;

situation desperate; hoping for relief every hour. German Minister has been murdered by Chinese regular troops, and large Chinese army advancing on Tien-tsin. Have had long conversation with Russian Governor-General. He agrees with me that, with all reinforcements expected, Russian and Japanese, it will only bring total to about 20,000 men, which would enable us to hold the base from Taku, Tien-tsin, and probably Pei-ta-ho, but impossible to advance beyond Tien-tsin.   4 p.m., 30th June.

Viscount Gough to the Marquess of Salisbury (received July 2)

Berlin, July 2, 1900

(Telegraphic)

Count von Bülow left here for Wilhelmshafen in order to consult with the Emperor, upon receiving the official confirmation of the murder of the German Minister at Peking.

I was sent for this morning by Baron von Richthofen, who informed me as follows:

The German Consul at Tien-tsin has sent a telegram, dated the 29th June, in which it is stated that a Chinese messenger had arrived from Peking that day, bringing the following message, addressed to the Commander of the international forces, which had been dispatched by the Second Secretary in the German Legation, Herr von Bergen:

> Foreign community besieged in the Legations. Situation desperate. Hasten your coming.   Sunday, 4 p.m.
>
> ROBERT HART

The 24th June is assumed to be the date of the above message.

A further telegram has been received from the German Consul at Tien-tsin, stating that a second messenger, sent by a missionary, arrived on the 29th ultimo, having left Peking on the 25th. He reported that the military escorts of the Legations are suffering from want of ammunition, and he confirmed the murder of the German Minister and the burning of the majority of the Legations.

In view of the above information, and of that contained in Reuter's telegrams, the situation of all foreigners in Peking would appear to be most critical, if, indeed, they are still living. It is believed in the German Foreign Office that the foreign women and children, among them being the wife of the late German Minister, still remain in Peking.

Taking these facts into consideration, Baron von Richthofen then asked me, though he had not received any positive instructions from his Government to do so, whether Her Majesty's Government were prepared to propose any better measure, the effect of which would be immediate, than the one which the Consuls at Tien-tsin had proposed, namely, that a threat to destroy the Imperial tombs should be made, and whether to refuse a proposal which the best-informed persons on the spot had unanimously made, would not be to assume a great responsibility.

The Marquess of Salisbury to Viscount Gough

Foreign Office, July 2, 1900

(Telegraphic)

With reference to your telegram of the 2nd July respecting proposal of Consuls at Tien-tsin to threaten destruction of the Imperial Mausolea, you should inform Baron Richthofen that the proposal reaches us without any information as to the manner in which it is viewed by the Naval or Military Commanders on the spot.

We believe the Mausolea to be situated near Moukden and Hingking, in Manchuria, and it is probable that their destruction could only be effected by the dispatch of an expedition of considerable strength from Talienwan or Newchwang. The distance which would have to be covered would vary, according to the route and place of departure, from 100 to 200 miles.

We therefore feel unable to sanction a measure which would be so offensive to European opinion.

The threat appears, at first sight, very unlikely to have any effect upon mutinous soldiery or a riotous mob, and these are the factors which place the Legations in so perilous a situation.

Vice-Admiral Sir E. Seymour to Admiralty (communicated by Admiralty, July 4)

Tien-tsin, June 30

via Chefoo, July 3, 1900

(Telegraphic)

Chinese couriers arrived from Peking with short message dated 24th June, stating that condition there desperate, and asking for help at once. Couriers interrogated state all Legations except British, French, German, and part of Russian destroyed. Europeans gathered in British Legation, have provisions, but ammunition scarce. One gate of city near Legation held by Europeans with guns captured from Chinese. Five of Marine Guard killed and one officer wounded; not much sickness at present. I propose to remain at Tien-tsin at present unless naval operations in Yang-tsze or elsewhere. Vice-Admiral Alexieff is expected. Chinese inundated country near here yesterday from Grand Canal; object probably for defence of city to the south. No injury to us. General health good. All agreed that no advance on Peking possible for many days at least, owing to want of force and transport.

The Marquess of Salisbury to Mr Whitehead
Foreign Office, July 4, 1900

(Telegraphic)

Following just received from Admiral Seymour:

[*Repeats Admiral Seymour, 30th June, communicated by Admiralty 4th July.*]

This indicates a position of extreme gravity. You should communicate telegram at once to Japanese Ministers. Japan is the only Power which can send rapid reinforcements to Tien-tsin. No objection has been raised by any European Power to this course.

The Marquess of Salisbury to Mr Whitehead
Foreign Office, July 6, 1900

(Telegraphic)

Japan is the only Power which can act with any hope of success for the urgent purpose of saving the Legations, and, if they delay, heavy responsibility must rest with them. We are prepared to furnish any financial assistance which is necessary in addition to our forces already on the spot.

Her Majesty's Government wish to draw a sharp distinction between immediate operations which may be still in time to save the Legations and any ulterior operations which may be undertaken. We may leave to future consideration all questions as to the latter.

The Marquess of Salisbury to Mr Whitehead
Foreign Office, July 6, 1900

(Telegraphic)

Japanese troops for China: my telegram of today. In the circumstances we are prepared to undertake this financial responsibility, since a fatal expenditure of time would result from international negotiations on the point.

Mr Whitehead to the Marquess of Salisbury (received July 6)
Tokio, July 6, 1900

(Telegraphic)

I have just received a visit from the Japanese Minister for Foreign Affairs, who informs me that reinforcements to make up the Japanese force to 20,000 men will be sent as rapidly as possible.

The Marquess of Salisbury to Sir E. Monson
Foreign Office, July 6, 1900

(Telegraphic)

We have suggested to Japanese Government that they should dispatch reinforcements to China as soon as possible.

Inform French Government.

The Marquess of Salisbury to Sir C. Scott
Foreign Office, July 6, 1900

(Telegraphic)

The crisis in China. You should inform Russian Government that Her Majesty's Government have suggested to the Japanese Government that they should, with as little delay as possible, dispatch reinforcements to China.

Admiralty to Senior Naval Officer, Woosung (communicated by Admiralty, July 6)
July 6, 1900

(Telegraphic)

Austro-Hungarian Government ask that Her Majesty's ships may afford protection to Consulate Shanghae, and, if necessary, receive staff on board. You are to afford such protection as may be possible.

Sir Chihchen Lofêngluh to the Marquess of Salisbury (received July 12)
Chinese Legation, London, July 11, 1900

I have the honour to forward your Lordship the enclosed translation and Chinese text of a telegram from the Emperor of China to Her Majesty the Queen-Empress, and to request that you will have the goodness to have them presented at their high destination as soon as possible.

LOFÊNGLUH

Enclosure
The Emperor of China to Her Majesty the Queen
Peking, July 3, 1900

(Translation)

The Emperor of China to Her Majesty the Queen of England, Empress of India, sendeth Greetings:

Since the opening of commercial intercourse between foreign nations and China, the aspirations of Great Britain have always been after commercial extension, and not territorial aggrandizement.

Recently, dissensions having arisen between the Christians and the people of Chihli and Shantung, certain evilly disposed persons availed themselves of the occasion to make disturbances, and these having extended so rapidly, the Treaty Powers, suspecting that the rioters might have been encouraged by the Imperial Government, attacked and captured the Taku forts. The sufferings arising from this act of hostility have been great, and the situation has been much involved.

In consideration of the facts that of the foreign commerce of China more than 70 per cent belongs to England, that the Chinese Tariff is lower than that of any other country, and that the restrictions on it are fewer. British merchants have during the last few decades maintained relations with Chinese merchants at the ports as harmonious as if they had both been members of the same family. But now complications have arisen, mutual distrust has been engendered, and the situation having thus changed for the worse, it is felt that, if China cannot be supported in maintaining her position, foreign nations, looking on so large and populous a country, so rich in natural resources, might be tempted to exploit or despoil it; and, perhaps, differ amongst themselves with respect to their conflicting interests.

It is evident that this would create a state of matters which would not be advantageous to Great Britain, a country which views commerce as her greatest interest.

China is now engaged in raising men and means to cope with these eventualities, but she feels that if left to herself she might be unequal to the occasion should it ever arrive, and therefore turns to England in the hope of procuring her good offices in bringing about a settlement of the difficulties which have arisen with the other Treaty Powers.

The Emperor makes this frank exposure of what is nearest to his heart, and hopes that this appeal to Her Majesty the Queen-Empress may be graciously taken into her consideration, and an answer vouchsafed to it at the earliest possible moment.

Mr Whitehead to the Marquess of Salisbury (received July 12)
Tokio, July 12, 1900

(Telegraphic)

I have informed Admiral Seymour by telegraph that Lieutenant-General Teranchi, second in the General Staff, is being sent by Japanese Government to discuss with him and Admiral Alexieff a scheme of combined operations.

Chinese Imperial Edict (communicated by Sir Chihchen Lofêngluh, July 13)

Translation of an Imperial Edict dated Peking the 29th June, received by the Privy Council, and by the Board of War forwarded to the Provincial Treasurer of Chihli for transmission to the Chinese Ministers residing at the various Courts in Europe, America, and Japan, through the Taotai of Shanghae.

In view of the circumstance that the Treaty Powers have unexpectedly assembled considerable forces in China, it is expedient that the Chinese Ministers accredited to foreign countries should be made acquainted with the situation of affairs at present, and the causes that have led to it.

We therefore command that the following account of what has recently taken place in Peking be communicated to them, in order that they may the better be the interpreters of our intentions with respect to the Treaty Powers.

The present unsatisfactory state of affairs originated in the formation of a Society consisting of disorderly persons in the provinces of Chihli and Shantung. The ostensible object of the Society was the practice of athletics, attended by strange rites founded on the pretended possession by its members of supernatural powers.

At first the authorities, viewing it as harmless, took no notice of the Society or sect with any measures for its suppression, but soon, spreading like wild-fire, branches of it were found everywhere, and in the matter of a month great numbers of its adherents were found even in Peking, where they were considered as a mystical sect to which crafty and designing persons introduced anti-Christian proclivities.

About the 10th June its enmity towards Christianity was no longer a matter of doubt. In spite of every effort to control them, they then set fire to some of the missionary buildings in Peking, and at the same time killed some of the native Christians.

When things began to assume a serious aspect, the foreign Representatives in Peking requested permission to bring up some soldiers for the protection of the Legations, and, the situation appearing critical, this was agreed to, and the Legation guards were accordingly increased by the number of about 500 men of the different nationalities. This is an evidence of the desire of the Chinese Government to maintain friendly relations with foreign Powers.

On other occasions, when foreign soldiers had been called up to Peking for the protection of the Legations, the men were confined to the premises of the several diplomatic establishments, so no collision ever occurred between them and the populace, but on this occasion, no sooner had they arrived than they were sent with their arms to patrol the streets, and sometimes they used their arms to fire on the people. Nor did they seem to be kept under proper control, but were allowed to roam, apparently at their own will, wherever they liked; some of them having been stopped in an attempt to enter the Tung Hwa mên, a gate leading to the Imperial Palace, by which entrance is strictly forbidden. These acts on the part of the foreign soldiers so incensed the people that, lending ear to the false rumours that were being industriously disseminated amongst them by members of the Society, many of the people joined the latter, and, setting the law at defiance, proceeded to assist them in murdering the Christians and committing other outrages.

At this point the foreign Representatives called for more troops, but the advance of the reinforcements that were sent having been opposed by the combined forces of the Shantung and Chihli rebels, they have not, as yet, succeeded in reaching Peking.

It was not from any reluctance on the part of the Imperial Government that they did not adopt stronger measures for the suppression of the Boxer movement as soon as its real object became evident, but because of the danger to which, in the meantime, the Legations and Europeans in the disturbed districts would have been exposed. It was necessary to temporize, in order that the Society should not be provoked into attacking the Legations and committing further acts of hostility towards the Christians whilst the Imperial Government were preparing to deal an effectual blow. Any failure to do this at the first blow, might have led to the perpetration by the Boxers of acts which the Imperial Government would have viewed as a national calamity.

It was in view of these considerations that the Imperial Government thought of the expedient of requesting the Diplomatic Body to temporarily absent themselves from Peking, and it was whilst this project was being debated by the Tsung-li Yumên that Baron von Ketteler, the German Minister, was killed whilst on his way to the Yamên. On the previous day he had written to the Yamên asking for an appointment, but in consequence of the menacing attitude of the populace who then thronged the streets, it was not considered safe for him to be seen outside of the Legation. The Yamên, therefore, declined his request for an interview. The wisdom of this course was seen in the lamentable result of his attempting to come to the Yamên the next day. The increasing audacity of the crowd now then knew no bounds. It was now too late to send the foreign Ministers to Tien-tsin under the protection of a sufficient well-armed escort as the Yamên had intended doing; so, the only other course open to the Yamên was to continue the Ministers in Peking under the protection of an adequate guard of Chinese troops. And this was done, the officer in command of the guard having stringent orders to protect the Legations effectively in every possible emergency.

On the 16th June the officer in command of the allied fleets at Taku, much to our surprise, demanded of General Lo Yung Kwang the surrender of the forts under his command, at the same time informing him that, in case of non-compliance, they would be attacked and taken at 2 o'clock next day. It was the duty of Lo Yung Kwang to hold the forts, so he had no alternative but to refuse the demand.

At the appointed time the allied Commander opened fire on the forts and eventually captured them.

These hostilities were not of China's seeking. No false estimate of her power led her to measure her forces with those of the combined fleets. She fought because she could not do otherwise than resist.

This point the Ministers must make unmistakably clear to the respective Governments to whom they are severally accredited. They will also take occasion to explain to the different foreign Secretaries the action of the Chinese Government and the motives by which it was actuated under the ever-changing circumstances which have led to the present complicated state of our foreign relations.

Orders of a very imperative character have been given to the officer charged with the protection of the foreign Legations to exert himself to the utmost in order that nothing untoward may happen to them.

Our Ministers are to remain at their respective posts in foreign countries, and to continue to discharge their official duties with unremitting care and assiduity.

Let this be transmitted to them.

Respect this.

PART II

SIR CLAUDE MACDONALD'S DIARY
OF THE SIEGE, 20TH JUNE TO
14TH AUGUST, 1900

WEEK ONE (20TH–26TH JUNE)

EVENTS UP TO AND INCLUDING 20TH JUNE

Before the 20th June, barricades, but not of a very substantial nature, had been erected across the road which runs between the Imperial Maritime Customs compound and the Austrian Legation, in front of the Italian Legation in Legation Street, facing east. This was composed mainly of upturned Peking carts, and was to meet any attack from the east, whilst against an enemy advancing along the street from the west, one had been put up between the Russian and American entrance gates.

The British marines held the North Bridge over the canal with a picket; the other detachments also patrolled the roads in the vicinity of their Legations and pickets were stationed at various points.

The German detachment had made a barricade in the street between their Legation and the Tartar city wall facing east, and the Americans one at the back of their Legation facing west.

Immediately the death of the German Minister became known, it was clear that we had a different foe to deal with, and preparations were made to defend the Legations in grave earnest.

A plan which had been sketched out previously by the commandants of the Legation guards was immediately put into execution; all barricades were hastily strengthened and outlying pickets withdrawn. All women and children were ordered into the British Legation. This order was pretty generally carried out, only a very few remaining at the Peking Hôtel, situated in Legation Street. More than 100 women and children came in during the afternoon, for all of whom accommodation had to be found. This does not

Legation Quarter, Peking, in 1900

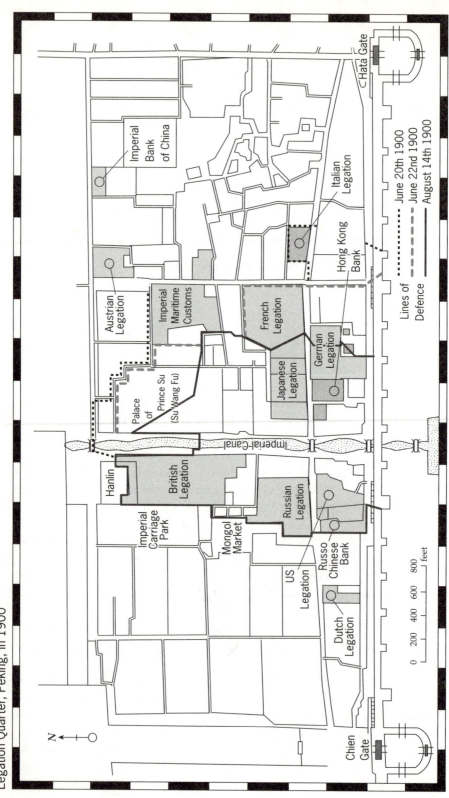

Imperial Bank of China

Italian Legation

Hong Kong Bank

Austrian Legation

Imperial Maritime Customs

French Legation

German Legation

Japanese Legation

Palace of Prince Su (Su Wang Fu)

Hanlin

British Legation

Imperial Canal

Imperial Carriage Park

Mongol Market

Russian Legation

US Legation

Russo Chinese Bank

Dutch Legation

Hata Gate

Chien Gate

N

Lines of Defence

June 20th 1900
June 22nd 1900
August 14th 1900

0   200   400   600   800   feet

include some 600 to 700 Chinese Christians, servants, converts, etc., of whom more than half were women and children.

The student interpreters gave up their quarters and slept in the "tingerhs", or open reception halls; most of the staff also gave up their houses. The Second Secretary's (Mr Dering's) was handed over to the Russian Legation and bank. The Accountant's was handed over to the members of the French Legation and their wives and families. The ladies of the American Legation occupied the doctor's quarters, and one block of the students' rooms was given over to the Imperial Maritime Customs. Fifteen ladies were accommodated in the ball-room of the Minister's house, twelve others lived in the smoking-room, two families occupied the billiard-room, whilst many missionaries slept in the corridors. The Belgian, Japanese, and Italian Ministers and their families, together with the widowed Baroness Ketteler, were also accommodated in the Minister's house. In all, 78 Europeans slept in this building, which usually accommodated a dozen; whilst nearly 900 lived within the four walls of the Legation during the eight weeks' siege, the normal number being about sixty.

The whole day [June 20] was occupied in bringing in and storing provisions and making further arrangements for the defence. Punctually at 4 p.m. the Imperial troops opened fire from the north and east, mostly on the Austrian and Italian barricades, and then commenced the organized attack on the Peking Legations by the forces of the Chinese Government.

So far as the Boxers were concerned, the garrisons of the various Legations could have routed their entire force in Peking, for the *bona fide* Boxer believed implicitly in his supernatural powers, and disdained to use a fire-arm; but, with Mauser and Mannlicher bullets humming through the air, we knew that a different order of things had begun. Captain Strouts withdrew the picket from the North, or Yu Ho Bridge, to a barricade which we had erected at the main gate of the Legation; the enemy, from the roofs of houses, opened fire on this barricade, and the fire was at once returned. The removal of this picket was in accordance with the plan decided upon by the military authorities; it was in a very exposed position, useful against Boxers, but untenable against rifle fire.

Across the canal, which runs from the Imperial city past the main gate of the Legation, is situated the Su Wang Fu, or Palace of Prince Su, a direct descendant of one of the Ironcapped Princes. This Prince had been friendly and helpful, allowing part of his Fu enclosure to be used as a shelter for the Christian refugees. I had, on this account, had some communication with him through a Mr Hubert James, a professor at the Peking University, one of the refugees in the Legation. When the firing commenced, Mr James informed me that Prince Su seemed very much distressed at hostilities having broken out, and asked him to convey a message to me, stating that he was convinced that if he could carry the Court an assurance that the foreign Powers had no intention of partitioning the Empire, orders would be given for a cessation of the attack. I authorized Mr James to say that the mission of all the foreign

Representatives in Peking was to maintain friendly relations with the Chinese Government and that Great Britain, and so far as I knew, none of the other Powers had any designs whatsoever on the integrity of the Chinese Empire.

Mr James departed with my message and returned shortly afterwards saying that he had delivered it to the Prince, who had immediately mounted his horse and galloped off in the direction of the Palace. Mr James returned to the Fu; suddenly, to the consternation of the small detachment holding our barricade at the main gate, he was seen to run out on the North Bridge, which at that time was swept by the enemy's fire and our own; instantly three Chinese cavalry soldiers charged the unfortunate man and with blows of their sabres drove him before them off the bridge; he was not actually seen to fall, but there is no doubt that he was then and there cut down. A hurried volley was fired at the cavalry, but owing to the failing light it was impossible to see with what result. Mr James, who spoke Chinese well, had without doubt left the north gate of the Fu and proceeded on to the bridge to expostulate with the soldiery, but orders had evidently now been given to kill all foreigners at sight, orders which Tung fu Hsiang's men were only too ready to obey.

The attack now became fairly general and if pressed home must have been attended with disastrous results for, as I have stated, none of the Legations had at that time been put into a thorough state of defence. Desultory attacks took place during the night, all of which were repulsed. On the following day work was continued on the barricades and the provisioning of the British Legation was proceeded with.

21ST JUNE

The Austrian Legation was vigorously attacked; a French marine was killed and an Austrian wounded behind the Austrian barricade; this led to the Austrians falling back on the French Legation, thereby exposing the entire east side of the large block of Customs buildings, which up to this had been held by volunteers belonging to the Maritime Customs. Before long, immense volumes of smoke arose, and the roar of flames and crash of falling timbers were heard, denoting that the Chinese had not been slow in taking advantage of this retirement. The incendiarism continued, and during the day the Austrian and Dutch Legations were burnt, as well as the greater part of the Customs quarter and the Chinese Bank. The enemy were particularly bold in their attacks, exposing themselves freely, and suffering in proportion; it was noticed that nothing fanned their failing courage so much as a conflagration. From the French and German Legations it was reported that some troops, presumably Prince Ching's, were seen to open a heavy fire on the Boxers in the neighbourhood of the Hata Gate. Meanwhile, Tung-fu Hsiang's troops, noticeable by their uniforms—red, with black velvet facings, the cavalry having on their breast three characters denoting "the cavalry of Kansu"—were very busy in their attacks on us from the north and west.

At 9 a.m. a determined onslaught was made on the Students' Mess, a two-storeyed building overlooking the Imperial Carriage Park; the upper storey of this building, which formed the library, had been barricaded, and was held by a garrison of marines and volunteers. The enemy were driven off, leaving six of their number, making picturesque dots of colour in the long grass. German marines reported that Prince Ching's troops had entered into conversation with them on the wall; these troops said that they had orders to prevent any Boxers coming on the wall of the city, and Prince Ching had issued the strictest injunctions to shoot any Boxers doing so; they added that foreign soldiers could come up there as much as they pleased.

All day the garrison not actually engaged in repelling the attacks of the enemy were busy in assisting the organization of the defence within the British Legation; a Committee of Public Comfort was appointed, the members consisting of representatives of the various Legations, the Maritime Customs, and the various missionary bodies. Various Sub-Committees were also appointed, one of the most important being the Fortification Committee, under the Rev. F. D. Gamewell, of the American Methodist Mission; this Committee, under its intelligent and energetic Head, subsequently rendered the most invaluable services; the Food Supply Committee, to look after and regulate the stores and supply of food; the Water Committee, in charge of the five wells in the Legation, to measure each day the depth of water and regulate its consumption; the Committee on Native Labour, a most important one, very ably presided over by the Rev. W. Hobart, an American missionary; by the proper management and organization of native refugees splendid results were obtained. There was, of course, some little confusion at first, but before many days everything worked smoothly, and by applying to the proper Committee even watches could be mended and boots repaired free of charge.

22ND JUNE

In the forenoon it was reported to me that, owing to a mistaken order, the garrisons of the various Legations were all falling back on the British Legation, and on going to the main gate I found this to be the case.

Fortunately, the Chinese were not aware of the critical state of affairs, or, at any rate, did not take advantage of it. Before it was too late the matter was rectified, and the various marine detachments marched back to their respective Legations, the Germans, however, losing two men in so doing.

While this was going on, a certain amount of confusion naturally prevailed, as a result of which the Russian, French, and Italian Ministers begged me, as having some previous military experience, to take general command of the defence of all the Legations, and I accepted the task. I subsequently saw the American and Japanese Ministers, who confirmed the above request. I would take this opportunity of stating that during the remainder of the siege I was throughout supported with the greatest loyalty and willingness by my colleagues, and also by the Commanders of the various detachments. I would also beg to acknowledge the splendid assistance given to the defence in general, and myself in particular, by the missionaries, especially the Americans, to whose powers of organization the comfort and comparative safety of the British Legation were mainly due.

The Italians, who, previous to their enforced retirement, had gallantly, by a bayonet charge, repulsed an attack of the enemy, found, on returning, that their Legation was in flames. Their Commander immediately reinforced the nearest post, which was the German, and together with their detachment held a barricade on the city wall above the German Legation, and also one in the street below. By my direction the Italians subsequently occupied, together with the Japanese, the Su Wang Fu. This Palace or Fu subsequently formed one of the principal parts of the defence; it consisted of an enclosure of some 12 to 14 acres, surrounded by walls 20 feet high. Inside were some thirty buildings of various sizes, beautiful gardens, houses, pavilions, rockeries, summer-houses, etc.

The garrison of the Fu now consisted of the Japanese detachment of one officer and twenty-three men, besides nineteen volunteers, most of whom had served in the army; the Italian detachment of one officer and twenty-eight men, the whole under the command of Lieutenant-Colonel Shiba, Japanese Military Attaché; also twelve British marines and the same number of volunteers, mostly from the Maritime Customs, a small garrison to hold so extensive a post. This was the weak point of the entire defence, the garrison being altogether too few in numbers for the area defended; it was, however, under the circumstances, unavoidable, as it would have been impossible to have surrendered any single point of the defence without seriously endangering the rest.

A general glance at the position held may here be useful.

The garrison were fighting practically with their "backs against a wall", in this instance the wall being that of the Tartar city, 50 or 60 feet high, and 30 feet wide at the top.

The German and American Legations were the two which abutted on to this wall, a narrow street only dividing them from it. The line of defence on the 21st June commenced on the east at the German Legation, and, crossing Legation Street, took in the French Legation, a compound of 5 or 6 acres, containing the Minister's residence and those of his staff.

The line then followed the wall of, and included, the Su Wang Fu; from there it crossed the canal, and took in the British Legation going south. It included the Russian and American Legations, finishing again at a point on the wall some 500 yards from where it commenced.

In the defence the French Legation formed a sort of salient, open to close attack from the north and east, and also from the city wall and houses to the south-east. By the burning of the Customs quarter the Su Wang Fu, generally called the "Fu", became open to attack from the east; its north wall faced the enemy, its west side was covered by the British Legation.

On the south of the Fu were situated the Spanish and Japanese Legations, which were included inside the lines of defence and never suffered from a direct attack. The British Legation was completely open to attack from the north and west; abutting the north face were the buildings, temples, examination halls, and library, of the world-renowned Hanlin Yuan or Hanlin College, commonly called "The Hanlin". On the west was the Imperial Carriage Park, consisting of an enclosure 12 acres in extent, with handsome trees and capacious storehouses tiled with Imperial yellow, in which were stored the Imperial chairs and carriages.

This Carriage Park was held throughout the siege by the enemy; it was noticeable that the yellow-tiled roofs of the store-houses, though they commanded the British Legation at close range, were never utilized by the enemy; to the south of the Carriage Park, and abutting the west wall of the Legation, in some places actually built against this wall, were the houses which surrounded an open space some 2 acres in extent, which went by the name of the Mongol Market; as its name implied, this enclosure was used by the Mongols, who visit Peking in the winter, as a market-place for their wares.

The south of the Legation was defended from direct attack by the Russian Legation, but between these two, which are some 50 yards apart, was a large collection of Chinese and Mongol houses. These houses were a source of grave danger to both Legations, on account of the ease with which they could be set on fire. South of the British Legation was situated the Russian, the north-east half of which was protected from direct attack by the British, but the north-west formed part of the Mongol Market, and was under fire from the north and west; abutting the west of this Legation were Chinese houses, the whole of the south wall faced Legation Street, on the opposite side of which was the American Legation, which was separated from the Tartar city wall by a narrow street. It was commanded at close range from the wall.

At the commencement of the siege the west of the American Legation was protected by the Russian Bank, which for some few days was held by Russian and American marines and volunteers. It was evident from the commencement that to the general defence the most important points were the Tartar city wall and the Fu, the former because an enemy holding it commanded easily the entire circle of defence, and the Fu, because its loss would render the British Legation almost untenable, and here were assembled, by the decision of the Military Commandants, the women and children, spare ammunition and provisions, also; an enemy holding the Fu would menace the retreat of the German and French Legations. The wisdom of the above-mentioned decision on the part of the Commandants was amply borne out by subsequent events.

Late in the afternoon the enemy developed their attack from the west, opening fire from the Mongol Market, the houses surrounding which had been loopholed. A private of the marines was shot dead on the west wall of the Legation whilst returning the enemy's fire. Two 9-pr. Krupps also opened fire from the Chien Gate of the city, doing damage to the Russian Bank and American Legation.

The buildings in the Hanlin College were, from a military point of view, a source of great danger to the British Legation, owing to the possibility of their being set on fire, and it was proposed to destroy them. As the buildings were, however, of a very substantial nature, it would have been difficult to do this without explosives, of which we had none; to set them on fire would have been the best course, but one attended with very great danger to ourselves. One could only hope, therefore, that the Chinese, a nation of *literati*, would hesitate to commit this act of vandalism and destroy their national library. By way of precaution, however, a hole was made through the wall which separated us from the Hanlin enclosure, and a search party sent out under Captain Poole; the various buildings were found unoccupied by the enemy, neither were any signs of preparation for setting them on fire visible.

23RD JUNE

Communication with the Russian Legation was established through a hole in the South Wall, and the work of destroying the shops and small buildings situated between the two Legations was commenced; this was a most important necessity in order to establish safe communication between the two Legations, and to ward off all danger from incendiarism; the enemy kept up a heavy rifle fire on the working party, some of whom were wounded, including Mr Peachy, a student interpreter, but considerable progress was made.

A brisk fire was now commenced and kept up by the enemy from some high roofs belonging to the recently established Electric Light Company, as also from the adjoining premises of the Chinese Colonial Office; these buildings lie some 300 yards to the north-east of the British Legation; the Italian quick-firing 1-inch gun was brought up and together with our sharpshooters from the north stable picket returned the fire with telling effect. This Italian quickfirer was by far the most useful of the machine-guns brought by the various detachments. The others were an Austrian Maxim, a British five-barrelled Nordenfelt, very old pattern; and an American Colt automatic. Unfortunately, there were only 150 rounds brought up with the Italian gun. In the course of the siege the entire gun detachment of this quickfirer, consisting of five men, were either killed or wounded.

At 11.15 a.m. a determined attack was made on the Hanlin enclosure. It was preceded by a sharp infantry fire from the Imperial Carriage Park; the greater part of the Hanlin was then set on fire by the enemy; the fire bell rang and all hands were soon at work endeavouring to extinguish the flames; the Chinese had carefully selected their day and had evidently no qualms whatever as to the vandalism they were committing; a fresh north wind was blowing and the flames were carried nearer and nearer to the Legation buildings; a stubborn fight was maintained until late in the afternoon when the flames were got under, but not before more than three-quarters of the temples, examination halls, and libraries, forming the Hanlin College, had been destroyed. There remained only one building entirely intact, the heavy wooden eaves of which overshadowed and almost touched the students' quarters in the Legation; had these caught fire, the Legation would most probably have been doomed, but owing to the splendid efforts of the garrison, men, women, and even children, joining in the work of passing water to the engines, as well as to a providential change of the wind to another quarter, the danger was averted. Orders were given to save as many of the valuable books in the Hanlin as possible; the greater part had, however, been destroyed either by fire or water; a good many were taken away as mementoes by members of the garrison.

The enemy pursued these incendiary tactics at other parts of the defence, and at 3 p.m. a fire was reported from the Russian Legation, but M. de Giers reported that he thought he could cope with it with the resources at his command. Late in the afternoon the American detachment reported a determined attempt to set fire to their Legation buildings. I sent over immediately a reinforcement of twenty-five men and some members of the fire brigade. The Russo-Chinese Bank next to the American Legation was on fire, and partially burnt down, but the Legation escaped. For the next five days the enemy endeavoured to burn out the garrison, and a daily and hourly fight took place, resulting in a complete victory for the defenders.

The practice from the enemy's Krupp 9-pr. battery on the Chien Gate now became very accurate, and for a time they paid particular attention to the national standards flying over the entrance gates of the Russian and American Legations. The American flag-staff was shot away,★ and a considerable hole made in the gate-way. The Russian flag had also some narrow escapes, and they were both eventually removed to places where they could not be seen from the wall. This battery also shelled the barricade on the wall at the back of the American Legation, bursting two shells in the barricade itself, the range being about 800 yards. Unfortunately we had no artillery heavy enough to silence these guns, and our riflemen were so scattered it was all we could do to keep in check those of the enemy. The 9-pr. which was to have accompanied the Russian detachment had most unfortunately been left behind on the platform of the railway station at Tien-tsin, though the ammunition had been brought.

24TH JUNE

Early on this morning an attack was made on the American and Russian Legations, resulting in some casualties on our side. A determined attack was

★N.B. Sir C. MacDonald telegraphed on the 29th January, 1901, to the effect that this incident took place not on the 23rd June, but later, on the 6th July.

also made on the Fu, the Chinese trying to breach the high wall on the north-east corner, but were driven off with loss. They also effected a lodgment on the Tartar city wall immediately behind the American Legation, where they displayed their banners, and seemed to be waiting for orders to fire. A brilliant charge along the top of the wall by a small force of Germans and Americans, led by the intrepid Lieutenant von Soden, put the enemy to flight, and the pursuit was kept up almost to the Chien Gate. Here the pursuing party had to retire, finding themselves face to face with a Chinese barricade. In this gallant affair the enemy lost from eight to ten killed and three banners.

While this was going on the British Legation was attacked in a determined manner from the Mongol Market, the attack being directed against the south stable quarters, the enemy working their way through the Chinese houses up to the wall of the Legation. They then set fire to part of the stables, and threw stones and other missiles into the stable-yard. A sortie was instantly decided upon, a hole was made in the wall, and a party of marines headed by Captain Halliday dashed into the burning buildings, and cleared them at the point of the bayonet. Unfortunately Captain Halliday was almost immediately wounded very severely by a rifle-shot through the shoulder and lung, and had to give up the command. Notwithstanding the severe nature of his wound, Captain Halliday shot three of his assailants, and, refusing all aid, walked to the hospital, a distance of some 200 yards. I regret to say, owing to the severity of the wound, the services of this excellent officer were lost to the defence for the rest of the siege.

Captain Strouts now took command of the sortie, and inflicted considerable loss on the enemy, killing thirty-four in one house. One marine was mortally wounded, and others slightly in this affair, which had a most excellent effect, as it destroyed some 200 yards of cover which the enemy possessed, and drove them back to their barricades situated at the same distance from the Legation wall.

During the morning an equally brilliant sortie was made by Colonel Shiba from the north-east corner of the Fu at the head of ten French, ten Italians, and ten Japanese marines, and some British and Japanese volunteers, driving the enemy out of and past the Customs buildings. In the meanwhile the American detachment under Captain Myers had effected a lodgment on the Tartar wall, and a barricade had been commenced, a special gang of coolies to work on it being told off under an American missionary. By the following morning this barricade was completed. Unfortunately it was constructed at the head of the east ramp leading up to a bastion, thus leaving the bastion and the west ramp to be taken possession of by the enemy should they be so minded. The ramp leading up to the barricade was under fire from the Hata Gate, and many casualties occurred in going up to it. I myself saw three "converts" shot on the ramp in the space of five minutes. The enemy maintained a smart fire on this position, as also on the barricades across the street below. The fire on the wall was so severe that any casualties which occurred could not be attended to until nightfall, and the dead had to remain where they fell.

The French and German Legations had meanwhile been keeping up a stubborn defence. The Germans held a barricade facing the Hata Gate, on the wall, and also on the road between the Legation and the foot of the ramp, and the French a barricade across Legation Street looking east. As evening closed in a British marine was dangerously wounded whilst walking inside our Legation compound. At the time he was shot down several ladies and children were within a few yards. It is a noticeable fact that during the entire siege only three casualties took place in the actual grounds as distinguished from the defences of the Legation. A marine was shot dead coming out of the guard-room by a bullet which skimmed the roof of the constables' quarters; the third casualty was a lady seriously wounded on the tennis lawn.

25TH JUNE

During the night and early morning the barricades on the wall and in the street at the back of the American Legation were badly damaged by shell fire from the Chien Gate; ten Germans and ten British marines were sent to reinforce, two British marines were almost immediately wounded by shell fire, one of whom subsequently died.

French reinforcements, together with Customs and Legation volunteers, under Captain Poole, were sent to the Fu, which was hard pressed; in this attack one French marine and two Japanese were killed and two Italians wounded.

Shortly after 4 p.m. great excitement was caused in the British Legation by the appearance of a small group of men carrying a board on the North Bridge, and word was passed to the northern defences and to the Fu to cease fire. By means of glasses from the north stable the board was made out to be an Imperial Decree stating that the Chinese troops were sent to protect the Legations and stop the firing, and adding that a despatch would be handed to the Legations on the North Bridge. One of the garrison, a Chinaman, volunteered to go out and receive the despatch; he was furnished with a notice board with black characters painted thereon, to the effect that the Imperial Decree had been understood, and that the despatch would be received; wearing an official hat the messenger sallied out watched by an expectant garrison; on arrival at the bridge he was received with cries of "Lai, la" ("He has come"), whereupon his courage seemed to fail him, and dropping the board he retreated hurriedly back to the Legation, arriving unhurt.

Two Mandarins accompanied by soldiers appeared round the corner of the bridge and everybody hoped that communications with the enemy were about to be opened, but some dropping shots were heard and the Mandarins and soldiers quickly disappeared. It was thought at the time that some too zealous sentries in the Fu had been unable to resist the temptation of shooting a Mandarin, and had disobeyed orders; but I have subsequently ascertained that the shots were fired by Tung fu Hsiang's soldiers at the party bearing the Imperial Decree, and that one of the bearers was actually shot dead, the rest taking to flight. The board with the Imperial Decree inscribed thereon remained for many days on the bridge, a curious commentary on the thousands of bullets which swept over it and pattered on the roofs and defences of the Legations.

The immediate effect, however, of this notice was a sounding of horns in the Imperial city, which was taken up all round the defences and the firing immediately ceased, thus showing very clearly the complete command the *de facto* Government, whether Dowager-Empress, Prince Tuan, or both had over the troops. The lull in the firing was the signal for increased activity in the British Legation on the part of Mr Gamewell and his Fortification Committee, and soon some hundred of converts were busily at work strengthening weak places and adding to the defences. Our advanced posts in the Hanlin entered into conversation with the Chinese soldiers; from the latter it was gathered that Yung Lu had ordered the "cease fire", and that a communication was coming from him to us, but it never came.

Previous to the appearance of the board, the Germans and Americans had been hotly engaged, and the Italian gun had been sent to the wall barricade to endeavour to keep down the shell fire from the Chien Gate, but had itself been put out of action, both gunners having been seriously wounded and carried to the International Hospital. By 8 p.m. the firing had altogether ceased; shortly after a few shots were exchanged between the French in their Legation and the opposing barricades; a few desultory shots were also fired on the wall. On this day the Chinese took to building barricades of a more substantial nature and scientific design; up till now they had fired from barricades hastily constructed, from roofs of houses, and from behind ruined walls, and must have suffered severely.

About midnight, Prince Tuan and the war party having presumably again got the upper hand a tremendous fusilade was opened from all sides, but principally from north and north-west. This was the heaviest fire to which we had yet been subjected, and the bullets struck and ricochetted off the roofs of the various buildings like hailstones; this fire was kept up all through the night, and very few of the garrison obtained any sleep. The Americans were badly pressed in the barricade below the wall and reinforcements were called for from the French Legation, but Captain D'Arcy was unable to send them, his own post being hotly attacked; ten British marines were accordingly sent as soon as they could be spared.

26TH JUNE

In the morning the enemy, exhausted evidently by their efforts of the previous night, kept fairly quiet, allowing the worn-out garrison to snatch a few hours sleep. At 9.30 desultory sniping took place all round the defences.

Mr Cockburn, Chinese Secretary, and Mr Ker, Assistant Chinese Secretary, remained with the picket in the north stables the whole day, in case any message should come from the Imperial city, but in vain, and it was now evident that the war party was in the ascendant, and that a policy of extermination of the Legations had been decided on. The enforced retreat of Admiral Seymour and the successful blockade and bombardment of Tien-tsin, of which we were, of course, unaware, would be sufficient to account for this decision.

Today was organized the last reserve, and the following order was posted on the Bell Tower:

> In case of heavy firing, all men with guns of any description who are not on special duty at the time are to assemble at once at the Bell Tower and there await the orders of Captain Strouts.

Subsequent instructions were given that the assembly should only take place at the ringing of the "general attack bell".

The French Legation was severely attacked towards evening, and heavy volleys were fired into it from the enemy's barricades.

WEEK TWO (27TH JUNE–3RD JULY)

27TH JUNE

This promised to be a lively day. The firing became very heavy all round as early as 2 a.m. At 8 a.m. the firing slackened somewhat; but a smart attack was made on the Fu, and Colonel Shiba sent for the Italian gun. Fresh gunners having been procured, the gun was sent to him.

At 2.30 the American Legation called for reinforcements, and a reserve of five British marines, which were now always kept ready at the main gate, were immediately dispatched with a promise of ten more, if necessary. Ten British marines were already in the American barricade; this made twenty-one British marines, rather more than one-third of the available force, on duty outside the British Legation.

At 4 p.m. a heavy fusilade commenced on all sides, and the bugle sounded to general quarters. There was also heavy firing from the north-east corner of the Fu, and a Japanese orderly came hurriedly over with a note for me from Colonel Shiba. It ran thus:

> Dear Sir, They are nearing to break down the Fu's wall. I want to crush them when they come in. Will you please send some more reinforcements to me with the bearer.

Five marines and five volunteers were immediately sent. Shortly afterwards Colonel Shiba came over and reported that the enemy, having breached a hole in the north-east corner of the wall, had poured through into the Fu. He was, however, prepared for this incursion, and opened a murderous fire on them from surrounding loop-holes. The enemy fled in panic, trampling each other down in their efforts to escape through the hole by which they had entered, and leaving over twenty of their dead in the enclosure.

To cover their retreat they set fire to a temple at the corner of the Fu, and for the rest of the afternoon occupied themselves in dragging their dead through the hole in the wall by means of long poles with hooks attached to the ends.

At 8 p.m. the American detachment reported that 200 Boxers, compelled by Chinese soldiers to advance, had attacked the street barricade, but had been forced to retire with a loss of fifty killed. This number is, I think, somewhat excessive.

At 10.30 the "general attack" bell was sounded. The reserves turned out smartly and in very creditable numbers. The firing ceased shortly after 11, and a fairly quiet night ensued.

28TH JUNE

The enemy had evidently constructed gun platforms during the night for their two Krupp guns in the Fu, and with these they devoted themselves to bombarding the north wall at close range (about 10 yards) in order to breach the wall further. They also turned their attention to the "Hôtel de Pékin". The upper storey of this building was struck twenty-six times by shell, without, however, doing any harm to the occupants, who were in the lower storey. The ruins of the Russo-Chinese Bank were occupied this day by the enemy.

At 6.30 p.m. the "general attack" bell was again sounded. The enemy had manned their loophole in the Mongol Market; and opened a heavy musketry fire against the stable quarters. Suddenly a gate at the north-west corner of the market flew open, and two Krupp guns opened fire at the top story of the stable quarters at a range of about 200 yards. Shell after shell crashed into the building, completely wrecking one window, shattering the barricades of the next, and driving the defenders out of the two upper rooms down below into the stable yard. Our men were not slow to return the fire, but having been driven out of the top storey of the building we could only bring a few rifles to bear. These, however, delivered an effective fire into the gateway, where, through the smoke, we could see the gunners at work. These, however, stuck to their guns, and it was only when it seemed as if the upper storey of the house must come down, that the fire suddenly ceased.

Experts say that two or three more rounds and the supporting walls would have given way, sending the heavy Chinese roof crashing into the storey below. The Chinese gunners must have suffered severely, for they were considerably exposed, and they never again attempted an artillery attack upon the Mongol Market.

The food supply suffered considerably during this bombardment, two mules and a pony having been killed by exploding shells. Several of the men had narrow escapes, but only two were wounded.

The wall behind the American Legation and the Legation itself were hotly attacked during the day. Mr Conger, writing from his Legation, says:

> Besides the attack of last evening our people on the wall and in the street below had two heavy attacks during the night. This morning they can be seen in largely increased numbers; they have occupied the inclined ramp opposite ours, and have planted a banner near the top, within 100 yards of our position, but we cannot touch them. If they attack, Captain Myers can repulse them, if not in great numbers. I have instructed him to hold on to the last minute, and am sure he will.

The enemy did not leave their barricade, but contented themselves with a continuous fusillade from their loopholes.

29TH JUNE

Two sorties had been arranged for this morning: one under Captain Wray and one under Captain Poole. The former consisted of 26 British, 10 Russians, 5 French, and 5 Italians, and the latter, of 5 marines and 10 volunteers. Captain Wray's party attacked the Mongol Market with a view, if possible, of capturing the two Krupp guns which had done such damage the day before; the guns had, however, been removed, and the sortie retired, setting fire to some houses; there were no casualties.

This sortie would have effected more, but so many nationalities were represented on one spot that orders given were not understood and some confusion resulted. Captain Poole's party penetrated into the Carriage Park, but were brought up by a high barricade; when near the same they came under a heavy cross-fire at close range, and had to retreat, fortunately without any casualties, though the fire was very hot, the bullets pattering like hail all round the hole in the wall through which the retreat had to be effected.

During the forenoon the enemy's artillery at the north-east corner of the Fu was particularly energetic; the gunnery, however, was erratic, several of the shells coming over the Legation, and finding a home in the Chinese city south of the Tartar wall. Reinforcements were sent into the Fu, 5 marines and 5 volunteers. Shortly after 10 the Chinese set fire to a large pavilion at the north-east corner of the Fu, and effected a lodgment in the grounds. They crept up under cover of ruins, etc., with long poles, at the end of which tow dipped in kerosene was tied. With these they set fire to the heavy overhanging wooden eaves of the Chinese buildings, which were very old, and burnt like tinder. It was only by being burnt out that the plucky defenders were forced to fall back.

Dr Lippett, surgeon of the American detachment, was dangerously wounded whilst talking to his Minister.

Captain D'Arcy, the gallant defender of the French Legation, was severely attacked and sent for reinforcements: 5 British marines, 5 volunteers, and 10 Japanese were immediately sent and assisted in repelling this attack. The British detachment was cheered by their French comrades when leaving the Legation.

Lieutenant Herbert, second in command of the French detachment, was killed whilst directing the defence, and two French marines were brought in wounded to the International Hospital, which had been established in this Legation under Drs Poole and Velde, surgeons of the British and German Legations respectively.

This had been a bad day for the defence: every single nationality had to deplore the loss of some of its members, and the French and Japanese, after hard fighting, had lost ground.

It had always been supposed that heavy rain would have the effect of driving the Chinese under shelter, and that a rainstorm while it lasted would result in quiet times for us. At 10 p.m. heavy rain commenced, and was the immediate signal for a most tremendous fusillade that quite surpassed anything that had ever taken place before. There was little or no artillery fire, but the roar, for it can be called by no other name, of musketry continued without intermission until daylight. There was no necessity to ring the alarm bell, for the entire garrison stood to arms during the whole night, thinking that this waste of ammunition must be the precursor of something more serious. Nothing, however, happened, and the damage done, except to trees and roofs, which were badly cut about, was practically nil. To maintain so continuous a fire I am of opinion that the Imperial regiments must have relieved each other in the firing line. The vast majority of the hail of bullets were going very high, and again the Chinese city must have suffered seriously. At a low computation 200,000 rounds must have been fired by the Chinese during the night.

30TH JUNE

Up till 9 a.m. the enemy remained quiet, having without doubt passed a sleepless night, but shortly after 9 they showed in large numbers opposite the German posts and, in reply to a communication from the German Chargé d'Affaires, a reinforcement of ten British marines was sent to assist in repelling the attack; two of this reinforcement were soon carried back severely wounded by splinters from shells; one has since died. Fighting had now become severe, and three German marines were killed and two wounded, but the enemy were repulsed having suffered heavily; the French, also, though attacked and hard pressed, drove off their assailants with loss.

At 11 p.m. the picket in the south stable reported what looked like a search-light far away on the southern horizon. I watched the light in question for some time; it certainly had the appearance of a search-light, or rather lighthouse, low down on the horizon; its resemblance to a search-light, however, was not sufficiently pronounced to warrant a notice being put up on the Bell Tower, where all events of interest were posted.

1st JULY

This morning began quietly, but at 9 a.m. the enemy, notwithstanding their lessons of the previous day, showed in force towards the Hata Gate, and creeping up in the ramps surprised the German guard of ten men, under a non-commissioned officer, who retired down the reverse ramp, thereby exposing the rear of the American barricade some 450 yards distant; the latter coming under a reverse fire also left the wall, and the situation for a time was very critical; the Chinese, however, did not realize or at any rate did not avail themselves of the advantage they had gained: Russian reinforcements were at once sent to the Americans, and shortly afterwards they reoccupied their barricades, but the German barricades on the wall remained in the hands of the enemy until the end of the siege.

At 10.30 a further reinforcement consisting of ten marines, under Captain Wray, was sent to relieve Captain Myers on the wall; seven marines also went to the German Legation; whilst this was going on a fierce attack was made on the French Legation; Mr Wagner, one of the Customs volunteers, was shot dead and the garrison momentarily fell back to their last line of defence, leaving the German Legation in a somewhat exposed and critical position. M. von Below, German Chargé d'Affaires, sent word to me informing me of the state of affairs and asking for reinforcements; though the Kansu troops were busy attacking our north and north-west defences, Captain Strouts was able to detach six men and a corporal to the relief; the French had in the meanwhile advanced and reoccupied their Legation.

The enemy had during the night built formidable barricades in the north of the Carriage Park; to cope with this the Italian quickfirer was with some difficulty hauled up into the Students' Library, a large upper storey room, and opened with deadly effect on the said barricade, completely silencing its fire.

At 2 p.m. Captain Wray who, it will be remembered, had been sent to Captain Myers' assistance on the wall, was brought in with a Mauser bullet through the shoulder. I had given this officer orders whilst on the wall to commence a barricade some 200 yards east of the American one in order to hold the enemy in check from the Hata Gate side and to cover the rear of the Russo-American position. On advancing towards the spot indicated he and his party were met by a severe cross-fire from both the Hata Gate and Chien Gate, the Mauser bullets from the latter just clearing the top of the American barricade in rear of the little party, and ricochetting along the wall, they nevertheless continued to construct the work. Captain Wray, whilst directing his men, was wounded soon after; one of his party was also shot down. The fire now became so hot that it was quite impossible to continue the work; Captain Wray, therefore, ordered a retreat, which was carried cut with most exemplary coolness under a severe fire.

At 3.15, Lieutenant Paolini, the officer commanding the Italian detachment in the Fu, reported that the Krupp gun, which had been firing all day, had been moved nearer, and he thought, by making a sortie, he might be able to take it; he asked for assistance, and also for permission to make the attempt. Thinking the proposition rather risky, I consulted Colonel Shiba, in whose judgment of affairs in the Fu I had the fullest confidence.

Colonel Shiba replied that he thought the capture of the gun practicable, and that the sortie should be made. I accordingly gave orders that the desired reinforcements should be sent to Lieutenant Paolini, and that he might proceed. There was no time to discuss the details of the sortie, as the position taken up by this gun was evidently only temporary, but the general idea was for Lieutenant Paolini's party to attack from the west, while Colonel Shiba attacked from the east. The reinforcements detached by Captain Strouts consisted of seven British marines and five volunteers, the latter all student interpreters in the Consular service. I ordered all firing to cease from the north stable picket and main gate, and waited results.

The attacking party sallied out of the gate of the Fu, and going along the wall, disappeared round the corner, up a lane which forms the north boundary of the Fu. A heavy fusillade was heard, and a marine was seen staggering back, waving his hand as if to attract attention; he had not gone very far when he fell. Three of the garrison instantly dashed out and brought him in. No man of the attacking party returned, and it was hoped that the attack had proved successful; this, however, proved subsequently not to be the case. Lieutenant Paolini was severely wounded, two Italian marines killed, and seven marines wounded, two of the latter being British. Mr Townsend, one of the student interpreters, was also severely wounded. It appeared that when the party turned into the lane they were met by a severe fire from a barricade some forty yards in front, as well as from the left wall of the lane, which was only some 18 to 20 feet broad. Lieutenant Paolini was shot almost immediately, whilst gallantly leading the party; two Italian marines also fell, one shot dead, the other mortally wounded (he died almost at once). The barricade in front, some 8 feet high, was a blaze of fire, as well as the side wall.

The little party, finding themselves in a death trap, sought to escape through a hole or breach in the wall of the Fu, which was, however, only large enough to allow of two passing through at a time; it was whilst getting through this breach that two other men were wounded. Mr Russell, a young student interpreter, with great presence of mind, ordered his party of four volunteers to take cover behind a small heap of earth and bricks, and wait till the regulars had got through the hole. As soon as all had passed through, the students dashed across the lane one at a time; it was in doing this that Mr Townsend was shot in the shoulder and thigh, and fell. He was, however, pulled through the hole, still retaining possession of his rifle. Mr Bristow, another of the party, with great coolness and presence of mind, picked up and brought in the rifle belonging to the Italian marine, whose dead body was lying in the lane. But for Mr Russell's cool action, the confusion and consequent loss amongst the attacking party would most certainly have been greater.

A fight now took place over the dead body of the marine, but the fire was so deadly in the lane it was found impossible to recover it; three of the enemy, tempted, doubtless, by the reward offered by the Chinese Government for the head of a foreigner, came out from behind their defences, but were instantly shot down by the north stable picket from an advanced post on the other side of the canal.

Lieutenant-Colonel Shiba came over to me at once and reported the ill-success of the sortie, for which he very generously took the entire blame.

It was impossible to reconnoitre the ground outside our defences, so that sorties were at all times very risky, and, with so small a garrison, only to be undertaken under very special circumstances. Colonel Shiba's party had also encountered an unexpected barricade, and been forced to retire. Had we been able to capture the enemy's gun and its ammunition, the loss we suffered would have been small in comparison to the addition to our strength in the shape of even one piece of artillery. Lieutenant Paolini's wound was found to be severe, and he was detained in hospital; his place was immediately taken by Mr Caetani, Secretary of the Italian Legation, an ex-officer of Italian cavalry.

The evening passed fairly quietly. At 10.30 the light I have alluded to was again reported. I went, together with the signalman of Her Majesty's ship *Orlando*, to the upper storey of the First Secretary's house, and the light was plainly visible; the signalman said it was evidently a flash-light. As it might possibly belong to the force which was on its way (we hoped) to relieve us, and by way of cheering up the spirits of the garrison, the following Notice was posted up the next day on the Bell Tower:

> Last night, between 10 p.m. and 2 a.m., an electric flash-light was seen on the south-eastern horizon; its approximate distance from Peking, 25 miles. The flashes were regular, and occurred at intervals of almost a second, with a pause of between five to ten seconds between forty or fifty flashes.

2ND JULY

Gangs of coolies were at work all night on the American barricades on the Tartar city wall, and some excellent work was put in, the barricades being very considerably strengthened. Spies coming in to Colonel Shiba stated that troops were being withdrawn from Peking towards the south. These statements were received with caution.

Up till 10 o'clock, however, very little firing took place, and it seemed as if the enemy were either withdrawing part of their force or engaged in making fresh plans for attack. At 10.30 the Krupp guns opened fire on the Fu, and an occasional shot took effect on the defences; the majority, however, were going high. During the forenoon the enemy commenced to construct a large barricade in front of the main gate of the Hanlin, about 60 yards from our northern barricades. A few well-placed shells from the invaluable Italian quickfirer, which had again been hauled up to the Students' Library, demoralized their working party, and they did not continue.

Various important defences were commenced today in the British Legation. It was evident that the enemy were concentrating their attack on the Fu, either because they knew how important a point it was in the defence, or because they were aware from their spies that the buildings immediately to the south of it had been allocated to the converts, and it was against these latter that the Chinese seemed especially incensed. Should the Fu fall into the hands of the enemy, the British Legation would be completely commanded by its west wall, and the enemy would be able to bring up their Krupp guns to within 40 yards of the east wall of the British Legation and batter it down, in the same way as they had done to the north wall of the Fu. By my orders the Fortification Committee, under Mr Gamewell, commenced to strengthen the east defences; the wall itself was furnished with a doubled row of loopholes and thickened to a breadth of 10 ft, so as to render it proof against artillery, and traverses were erected to protect the western defences from reverse fire.

At 9 p.m. the American Minister and Mr Squiers, his Secretary of Legation, both of whom had seen military service, and whose experience was invaluable to the defence, came over to report that the Chinese had advanced across the bastion in front of the Russo-American barricade on the wall under cover of a species of sap or stone wall, and had erected a tower at the end of the sap, from which they could actually throw stones at the defenders of our barricade, from which the tower was only distant some 25 feet. They pointed out that it was absolutely necessary to take this tower and the Chinese barricade by assault, to prevent the enemy rushing our position on the wall, which was in imminent danger.

I immediately fell in with their views, and promised a reinforcement of fifteen men, which, with the ten marines already on duty, made up a total of twenty-five; with them went Mr Nigel Oliphant, who volunteered for the sortie. The attacking party, under Captain Myers, United States' Army, collected behind the wall barricade at 1.30 a.m. on the 3rd July; the party consisted of Captain Myers and fourteen American marines, a Russian officer, Captain Vroubleffsky, and fifteen Russian marines, Mr Nigel Oliphant and twenty-five British marines. No marine officer was available, two, Captains Halliday and Wray, being in hospital wounded, and Captain Strouts could not be spared from the British defences.

Captain Myers addressed the men in a short speech, pointing out clearly the plan of attack: the Anglo-American detachment, under his immediate command, was to attack the tower, follow along the sap, and then assault the barricade on its left or southern side; the Russian detachment was to attack the Chinese barricade on the right or northern end, where it abutted on to the top of the ramp.

At a given signal the whole party swarmed over the American barricade; the night was very dark and threatening rain. The English and Americans, with Captain Myers at their head, entered the tower, which they found unoccupied. They followed along the sap. Here Captain Myers received a severe spear wound in the knee and was disabled. At the south end of their barricade the Chinese had left a small lane or opening to connect with the sap. Through this the Anglo-American party streamed and engaged the enemy, hand to hand, Mr Oliphant shooting two with his revolver. A small encampment of tents was found behind their barricade. The enemy was cleared out of these, and driven down the ramp, leaving twenty-five of their dead on the wall.

The Russians, gallantly led by Captain Vroubleffsky, had in the meanwhile climbed over the right of the barricade and joined in the combat.

The enemy's position, including the whole bastion, was now in our hands, and work was commenced to strengthen what we had taken. A tremendous musketry fire was opened on the working party from a second barricade some 60 yards further along the wall, severely wounding a non-commissioned officer of marines. Just before dawn heavy rain came on which lasted several hours and caused great discomfort to the men. Our losses were two American marines killed and Captain Myers wounded; one Russian killed and two wounded; and three British marines wounded, all severely.

The above was one of the most successful operations of the siege, as it rendered our position on the wall, which had been precarious, comparatively strong. Work was continued day and night, and every opportunity taken to improve the advantage gained. At dawn the Krupp guns again began pounding away at the Fu defences, which were severely knocked about, and several casualties took place. The rain which had set in at dawn continued until sunset; the canal which separated the British, American, and Russian Legations from the remainder of the defence came down in flood, and threatened to carry away the covered way and barricade which had been constructed across it; as soon as the water subsided, which it fortunately did next morning, work was started, and a culvert to carry off the water was constructed.

The heavy rain had an excellent effect from a sanitary point of view, as it helped to clear out the canal, which from the number of decaying bodies of horses, mules, and dogs, which had been killed in or near the same by the wild fire of the enemy, had become very offensive and insanitary; but it played havoc with the earthworks and defences generally, and the fortification gangs were hard at work repairing damages. The enemy's works were also much impaired, and they lost heavily when repairing them.

During the afternoon the halyard of the Union Jack flying over the British Legation gatehouse was cut by a bullet and the flag came down with a run. Attempts were made to rehoist it by the signalman and armourer of Her Majesty's ship *Orlando*, but the fire on the top of the gate-house was too hot; the flagstaff was let down to the ground through the tower, the flag nailed to the staff and then rehoisted into its old place. Amongst the small crowd of bystanders who helped with a will to hoist the heavy staff were the Representatives of three of the Great Powers.

At 9 p.m. heavy firing began against the Russian Legation and our new position on the wall, resulting in a few casualties. One of the enemy crept up in the dark to the Russian barricade and thrust a spear through one of the loopholes, narrowly missing a Russian sailor. The owner of the spear was instantly fired at from the neighbouring loopholes, but owing to the darkness it was impossible to see with what result. The flash-light was again seen, but clearer and with more movement. It was particularly bright at 2 a.m.

At my request a Return was furnished to me this day by the various officers commanding the detachments of the number of casualties which had taken place since the 20th June. They were as follows:

British marines: 2 killed, 15 wounded, including 2 officers.
Bluejackets, Italian: 5 killed, 7 wounded,
1 officer.
Bluejackets, Russian: 3 killed, 11 wounded.
Bluejackets, Japanese: 5 killed, 11 wounded.
German marines: 8 killed, 7 wounded.
Bluejackets, French: 6 killed, including 1 officer, 5 wounded.
Bluejackets, Austrian: 3 killed, 3 wounded.
American marines: 6 killed, 6 wounded, 1 officer.

All the wounds were severe and necessitated removal to hospital. Total, thirty-eight killed and fifty-five wounded.

WEEK THREE (4TH–10TH JULY)

4TH JULY

This being the anniversary of American Independence, the Anglo-Saxon community amongst the besieged had decided that the relieving force would appear today; knowing the difficulties of transport I did not share in their anticipations, though when appealed to, I did my best to encourage their hopes. Several attempts had been made through the converts to communicate with the outside world, from whom we had received no news whatever since the commencement of the siege. Our messengers were at first let down over the Tartar city wall or went through the canal sluice gate under the same. None had succeeded, so far as we knew, in piercing the strict cordon, drawn round us; some had returned baffled in their efforts; and some we feared had been killed.

To-day a Shantung lad of about 14, well known to the American missionaries, volunteered to go; he took a letter from me to the British Consul sewed up in a piece of oil-cloth; the package was flat, just an inch long and half-an-inch broad; instead of concealing it in the thick sole of his shoe or sewing it into his clothes, hiding places with which the enemy had become well acquainted, he concealed it in a bowl of rice which he carried with him, after the fashion of some Chinese mendicants. As this was the first of our messengers who got through, his adventures are worth recounting.

He left the water gate at night, and after having narrowly escaped capture, reached the south gate of the Chinese city; watching his opportunity he slipped through with some mendicants and gained the open country, working his way with great caution from village to village. As he was not certain of the road to Tien-tsin, and fearing to excite suspicion by making inquiries, he used, on arrival at a village, to join the children at play and from them ascertain by degrees the general lie of the country, the names of adjoining villages, and the direction of Tien-tsin. The country was overrun with Boxers, and the villages were full of wounded, the result of the fighting with Admiral Seymour. When within sight of Tien-tsin he was commandeered by the enemy and made to work for them for over a week; at last he managed to escape and slipping through the allied sentries, which was undoubtedly the most risky part of the journey, he arrived at Tien-tsin on the 19th, five days after the taking of the Chinese city by the allies. He wandered about for a couple of days before he met any European who could talk Chinese, but at last he was fortunate enough to do so and was at once taken to the British Consul, where he delivered his letter on the 21st instant, which, though dated the 4th, was the latest news received from Peking. He started back on the 22nd and made the return journey in six days.

The lad stated that when he arrived in the vicinity of Tien-tsin the enemy were in the greatest state of demoralization, flying in every direction and leaving their artillery in ditches and hidden in the millet fields. On the return journey he noticed that, finding they were not pursued, they had recovered most of their guns and were entrenching themselves at Pei-tsang and other places. All the above we ascertained on the 28th instant, when the lad returned.

The letter which was received on the 21st by the British Consul was the *facsimile* of several others I had sent on previous occasions, the number of casualties only being altered from day to day. On this day, the 4th July, we had forty-six killed, including civilians, and about double that number severely wounded; of these, eight civilians had been killed and eleven wounded. The slightly wounded were not entered in the Returns and only went to hospital to have their wounds dressed and then returned to duty. The letter gave the relieving force, for of course we always counted on a relieving force, all needful information with regard to the position we held, and also pointed out that the water or sluice gate through the Tartar city wall afforded the easiest means of entering the Legation quarter.

5TH JULY

At a European shop within our lines were found some Japanese fireworks. The light-hearted Japanese garrison amused themselves at night by a pyrotechnic display, but one of their number discovered that a very effective missile might be constructed by opening these fireworks and filling them with nails, scrap iron, etc.; this was accordingly done and used against the Chinese with considerable effect.

The upper storey of the "Hôtel de Pékin" was again severely knocked about by the enemy's shells from the Chien Gate; the Secretary's quarters in the German Legation were rendered untenable from the same cause. The enemy were during the morning very active in the Hanlin. A party under Captain Poole were out clearing the ruins, when the fire became very severe and a retreat was ordered. Mr David Oliphant, of my Consular staff, was busy cutting down a tree in company with the signalman of the *Orlando*, and before he had time to obey the order, was shot through the body and fell; the signalman stayed behind him under a shower of bullets until a stretcher was brought. The wound was mortal and the poor young fellow died and was buried the same afternoon; his loss was deeply felt by the whole British community, with whom he was an immense favourite; owing to his coolness under fire, and his knack of commanding men, I had appointed him in charge of the eastern defences of the Legation and I felt his loss very keenly.

At midday the sentries in the upper storey of the Students' Library and quarters reported the enemy at work amongst the yellow tiles on the top of the Imperial city wall, which is distant some 200 yards from the north wall of the Legation. At first it seemed as if they were loopholing it for musketry, but by means of field-glasses through the foliage of the trees two guns could plainly be made out. How the enemy had succeeded in getting them up to their position it was difficult to ascertain, for the wall was over 20 feet high and only some 3 feet thick. Fire was instantly opened upon the battery by our riflemen. The position, owing to the foliage and the very small part of the wall disturbed, was not easy to locate with the naked eye, but with glasses the gunners could clearly be seen getting their guns into position.

We were not long left in doubt as to the enemy's intentions, for the first missile, a 7-lb round shot, came crashing into the students' quarter, where a group of riflemen were endeavouring to pick off the gunners. The bricks were sent flying in every direction but no harm was done. This was the introduction to several more, all of which took effect on the buildings in the Legation, the Minister's house and upper students' quarters being particularly favoured.

The round shot were of two sizes, one weighing 7 lbs and the other 14 lbs. The bombardment continued with intervals day and night for the next ten days, and over 150 rounds of shot were fired into the Legation and the Hanlin buildings alone. Curiously enough, the only casualty resulting from this fire was an old Chinese woman, whose leg was broken by a round shot, from the effects of which she died. Some people were hurt by falling bricks, displaced by the shot, but no one seriously.

There were, of course, some narrow escapes. The British Nordenfelt, which was temporarily in action on the balcony of the nursery in the Minister's house, was struck by a round shot, which came through the wall and broke the wheel; the seaman who was working the gun escaped uninjured. Another struck a chimney high up, fell down the same and rolled out of the grate on to the floor occupied by three young ladies of the garrison. One crashed through the smoking-room of the Minister's house and fell amongst the occupants, all ladies, but without touching any of them. Another, after carrying away part of the coping of one of the bed-rooms in the Minister's house, smashed its way through a thick wall in the escort quarters occupied by the Maritime Customs and fell between two ladies without touching either. And lastly, one entered the big dining-room through the north wall, and passing behind a large picture of the Queen without in any way injuring it, pierced the south wall of the dining-room and fell into the little central garden, where the children were playing at Boxers, barricades, and mimic warfare generally.

Though the enemy's fire from these two batteries—for very shortly a second appeared some 30 yards to the right of the first, also furnished with two smooth bores—was ineffective, the same cannot be said of our return fire, which seemed to annoy the enemy considerably. The invaluable Italian gun was got into position and the second shell exploded in the westernmost battery, completely silencing one gun for the rest of the siege; the others continued to fire at intervals. Our rifle fire was so searching, however, that the gunners were unable to take aim; on the other hand, at that short range they could not help hitting some part of the Legation. The rifle practice, nevertheless, prevented the enemy from concentrating their fire on any one part of our defences and thus making a breach. Very shortly, owing doubtless to their losses at the guns, each embrasure was provided with an iron door, which opened at intervals; the muzzle of the gun was hastily protruded and the gun fired. The opening of these doors was a signal for a volley from our people, who had the range to a nicety. These volleys must have rendered the firing of the gun a somewhat unhealthy occupation.

After the siege was over these batteries were found to consist of very elaborate gun platforms, 20 feet by 16 feet, made of scaffolding strong enough to hold guns of a much heavier calibre than those actually used. They could accommodate from thirty to forty men, and were made of timbers 9 inches in diameter, some 700 to 800 being employed to make each battery. The constructing of the platforms must have taken from a week to ten days, and occupied from thirty to forty workmen a-piece. Ramps 12 feet broad led up to the platforms. A small gallery supported by scaffolding ran along to right and left of the batteries just below the yellow-tiled coping on top of the wall. This gallery was loopholed for musketry. The place where the guns stood was roofed over as a protection from sun and rain. The iron doors mentioned consisted of folding doors on hinges of wrought iron half-an-inch thick, but had been pierced over and over again by our rifle fire, and the left battery had a hole through its door as if made with a punch. This was the work of the Italian gun.

Towards evening the sound of big guns was heard to the west of the city. This was not the bombardment of the Roman Catholic missionary establishment known as the Peitang. The sound came from further off, and was almost due west of the Legation.

6TH JULY

The morning commenced by a severe shell fire against the Fu. The Chinese, emboldened by the failure of our last sortie in this direction, moved one of their Krupp guns up to within a few yards of the wall of the Fu, through which they had made a breach. Colonel Shiba seized the opportunity to make a sortie to capture the gun. Previous to so doing he came to me for orders, and to explain the situation. The gun was located some 10 yards in a lane to the right of the breach above mentioned, and the idea was to dash through the breach and seize the gun and limber. Several Chinese converts provided with ropes for dragging the gun away were to follow the attacking party, which was composed entirely of Japanese marines and volunteers, headed by an ex-officer of the Japanese army serving as a volunteer. A feint attack was to be made from the west by the Italian detachment, reinforced by a corporal and ten British marines.

The Japanese detachment charged through the breach. Unfortunately their leader was almost immediately shot through the throat and fell, but the men pressed on, and actually seized the gun, the Chinese gunners taking to flight. The converts were, however, panic-stricken and refused to advance. The enemy, taking more advantage of their hesitation, rushed back to their loopholes, and a terrific fire was opened upon the attacking party, causing them to retire through the breach with three more of their number *hors de combat*.

The gun and limber were now standing disconsolately in the lane, which formed a *cul de sac*. To venture into the lane was certain death, as every wall and building which commanded it was loopholed, and at every loophole stood one of Tung-fu Hsiang's men with a magazine rifle. On the other hand, any of the enemy who attempted to pass the breach in the wall to get at the gun was shot down by the Japanese. This state of affairs lasted till dark, when the Chinese from their side of the wall threw bricks and stones in front of the breach, gradually filling it up, and during the night they withdrew the gun.

The Russian and French Legations were severely shelled from the Chien Gate, the fire being mainly directed against the American flag, which could be seen from the enemy's battery. At the fourth or fifth shot the flagstaff was struck at the base by a shell, which exploded and shot away a large portion of the roof of the gate-house, bringing down the staff, flag and all. It was rehoisted in a neighbouring tree, the roof of the gate-house being too damaged to allow of it being rehoisted there. The Russian flag was also attracting the fire of this battery, the shooting from which was very true. The flag was therefore removed to another building. It is to be noted that the flags of such Legations as remained unburnt were kept displayed throughout the siege. These were the flags of America, Russia, Great Britain, France, Germany, Japan, and Spain, the Chinese gunners distributing their favours amongst them with absolute impartiality.

A Russian Consular student, whose mind, it appeared, had been somewhat affected by the strain of the siege, suddenly left the French barricade in Legation Street, and, before he could be stopped, advanced alone and unarmed towards the Chinese barricade some 60 yards distant. The enemy allowed him to approach to within 10 yards, and then shot him down. Instantly several Chinese soldiers rushed forward to seize the dead body, but the French sharpshooters were on the alert, and man after man of the enemy dropped, until eleven had paid the penalty of their temerity with their lives. During the night his body was removed by the Chinese. Since the commencement of the siege this was the third and last European whose dead body fell into Chinese hands. The gallant garrison of the Fu were this day burnt out of some more of the buildings held by them. Since the fighting began they had lost by this means about one quarter of the Fu.

7TH JULY

A quiet morning, but matters became lively as the day advanced. At 9.15 a sharp attack was made against the Fu defences, but repulsed. At 9.30 the French Legation was bombarded by the guns north of the Fu, and also from the Hata Gate. Firing of heavy ordnance was heard to the south and south-west of the city in the direction of the railway terminus. This firing had been distinctly heard throughout the night, and had been reported to me by the officers commanding the French, Austrian, and German detachments, and a notice to this effect was posted on the Bell Tower, and greatly cheered the garrison. The enemy started a fresh barricade near the North Bridge at the end of the road known as "Dusty Lane", but one or two well-placed shells from the Italian gun, which had been brought to the main gate of the Legation, made them desist. The ammunition for this gun was unfortunately getting very low. The cannonading from the Imperial city wall became very brisk; a round shot came through the north corridor of the Minister's house, and fell on the roof of the cellar, which had been converted into a magazine; as this contained some 20,000 rounds of Lee-Metford and Mannlicher ammunition, as well as ninety rounds of shell, common and shrapnel, for the Russian field gun, it was considered advisable to have the cellar further protected by a roofing of sandbags.

There were now only fourteen shells remaining for the Italian quick-firer, so this gun was only used when the case was urgent. The armourer of Her Majesty's ship *Orlando*, with considerable ingenuity, devised a new cartridge for the same; taking one of the empty copper cases, most of which had been converted into playthings by the children, but which were now collected, he cast some conical solid shot made from pewter vessels, tea-pots, candlesticks, etc., which had been found in the neighbouring houses; the charge consisted of pebble powder taken from the Russian shells. The difficulty was the percussion cap; this was surmounted by removing the cap of a 45-inch revolver cartridge, which exactly fitted the hole made in the copper case by the removal of the original percussion cap. One of these projectiles was used experimentally in the Italian gun, and answered admirably; the shot being solid pewter, and weighing more than the old shell, the shooting was not so accurate, neither was the effect of the solid shot so good as the explosive shell, but as a makeshift it was excellent. As soon as the shells were finished, these projectiles were taken into use, and continued until the end of the siege; so far as I know, though upwards of seventy were utilized, not one missed fire.

Towards evening much shouting and firing could be heard in the Chinese city; it seemed as if the Boxers and Chinese troops, or different factions of the latter, had fallen out and were settling their differences. Our guards on the wall reported skirmishing between what seemed to be Boxers and Imperial troops, and several of the former were seen to fall.

8TH JULY

At 2 a.m. a very heavy fusillade took place, but lasted only fifteen minutes; it was so severe that the "general attack" bell was rung, and the garrison stood to their arms; the smooth bores on the Imperial city wall joined in the chorus, and the din was deafening.

The morning passed quietly until shortly after 10, when the rattle of musketry burst out all round the north and east of the Fu, accompanied by the fire of the two Krupp guns, which were so close that they made the windows of the British Legation rattle again. At 10.15 the following note was brought to me by a Japanese volunteer:

Pressed hard; please send a strong reinforcement—SHIBA.

Warned by the musketry fire, a reinforcement was in readiness; a non-commissioned officer and six marines, also six volunteers, were at once hurried over. I also wrote to the Russian Legation, and they sent ten sailors; the attack had, however, in the meanwhile, been repulsed, and their services were not required. The French Legation, to whom Colonel Shiba had also applied, had not been able to help, as they were themselves hard pressed, being subjected to a severe shell and rifle fire from the Hata Gate. Captain Thoman, of the Austrian frigate *Zenta*, who had come up to Peking as a visitor, and had been unable to return to his ship, was killed on this occasion in the French Legation by a fragment of shell; he was a courteous and gallant officer, and his loss was much felt by those who knew him.

On the previous day one of the gangs of Chinese converts at work under the supervision of Dr Dudgeon discovered at an old foundry within our lines what appeared to be an old piece of iron but proved on closer examination to be a small cannon. The trunnions had been knocked off, and it was one mass of rust and dirt; it was handed over to Mr Mitchell, the master gunner of the American detachment, and after much hard work, scraping and cleaning, it presented quite a creditable appearance. It was at first lashed to a heavy spar; when this was found unsatisfactory, it was mounted on a spare set of wheels belonging to the Italian gun; the shell of the Russian gun, when removed from its projectile, fitted, with some coaxing, the bore of this new gun, which was found on closer examination to be rifled and apparently either made of steel or fitted with a steel lining, and probably dated back to 1860, when the Anglo-French forces were in Peking.

As the gun was found by Chinese converts in charge of a British subject, and was probably of either British or French manufacture; as it fired Russian ammunition, was mounted on an Italian carriage and further was put together and fired by an American, it was with much truth christened the "International" gun, though our marines more often called it the "Dowager-Empress" or "Betsy". The performances of this piece of ordnance were erratic, but owing to the close quarters at which the fighting was carried on, eminently satisfactory.

The first shot was aimed at the corner battery on the Imperial city wall, about 240 yards distant (as there were no sights, the aiming consisted of pointing the gun generally in the direction of the object aimed at). The projectile went screaming over the battery into the Imperial city; the result was received with great cheering by the onlookers in the Legation, who, truth to say, had not much confidence in their new acquisition, and by an astonished silence on the part of the enemy, who were apparently startled to find that after so many days we had at length opened fire with comparatively heavy ordnance. The second shot went woefully short, but the third landed in the battery. This woke the enemy up from their astonishment, and the Mauser bullets began to whistle all round in uncomfortably close proximity; the "International" was therefore temporarily withdrawn, and transported, not without considerable difficulty, over to the Fu, where it was twice fired under Colonel Shiba's orders with telling effect at a barricade some thirty yards distant. The first shot carried away one of the enemy's standards, and the second discharge, which consisted of old nails and bits of scrap iron, was fired into the barricade, and judging from the yells which followed did considerable damage. One drawback to this gun was that immediately the enemy located its whereabouts (which was not at all difficult to do, as the noise and smoke created by it were out of all proportion to its size), they opened a heavy rifle fire on the spot and the gun could not be used for more than three or four shots in succession from the same place. From this evening on, a corporal and five British marines and five volunteers were permanently stationed in the Fu, as affairs were very critical there; the Japanese detachment having been reduced by casualties from one officer and twenty-five men to one officer and seven men, and the Italian detachment had suffered in like manner.

The British marines also supplied a permanent guard of ten men to the American and Russian barricades on the Tartar city wall; this had been the case since the 1st July and lasted till the 17th July; this guard was changed every twenty-four hours. During the afternoon the enemy had been very persistent in their attacks from the Mongol Market and Carriage Park side, they brought up a 1-inch quickfirer and shelled the British Legation; in the space of fifteen minutes three shells exploded inside the roof of the Chinese Secretary's house, the fragments coming through the ceiling in a very unpleasant manner; several of these shells exploded in the trees round the tennis ground, some struck the hospital, which fortunately was well barricaded, and one exploded in front of the Second Secretary's house, then occupied by the Russian Minister's family; the fragments entered a room full of children and buried themselves in the wall and furniture, but happily touched no one. It was impossible to locate this gun as it was skilfully concealed amongst the ruins of the Mongol Market houses and was using smokeless powder; fortunately it never returned to this particular position.

9TH JULY

The "International" gun again changed position. This time it was unlashed from its carriage and hauled up into the Students' Library and fired at a barricade which the enemy had erected in the Carriage Park. Considerable damage was done to the enemy, but nearly every pane of glass was smashed in the library, although the windows were open, and the wall of the mess-room below was cracked. The whole of this day the firing all round was incessant, but nothing of particular interest in the fighting-line occurred. All our positions were maintained; constant work was kept up on the fortifications, repairing the old and making new.

A Christian convert volunteered to go into the city and, if possible, obtain news of what was going on. The American missionaries stated that the man in question was reliable. Towards the evening he returned, having had many narrow escapes. He said that the soldiers that surrounded us were Yung-lu's and Tung-fu Hsiang's men. In the north of the city business was proceeding as usual, the hucksters crying their goods in the streets. He had himself bought some small articles, which he brought back with him. The Emperor and Empress were both at the Palace, only a few hundred yards from us. The *Peking Gazette* was published as usual. The Chinese troops had lost heavily, and were afraid of the foreigners in the Legations. He could hear nothing of any foreign troops coming to our rescue.

10TH JULY

The forenoon was quiet after a night of incessant fusillade. It was evident that the Chinese troops indulged in a siesta between the hours of 11 and 1. During the night they never seemed to sleep; the above hours were, therefore, in future, reserved for demonstrations on our part.

Shortly after 2 a fierce fusillade commenced against the Fu, and the enemy seemed to be concentrating all their efforts on this part of the defence. Twenty marines under Captain Poole were sent over; also ten Russian marines. One of the Krupp guns suddenly turned its attention from the Fu to the Union Jack over the Legation gateway. Three shells in quick succession struck the gateway, and several exploded on the tennis lawn, just missing the staff.

As the latter was apparently drawing the enemy's fire and thereby endangering the women and children's lives, the question of hauling the flag down, or at any rate, moving it to another position, was mooted to me by the missionaries. Captain Strouts, whom I consulted, was of the opinion that this would only encourage the enemy to further efforts, and would lead to great discontent on the part of the British marine guard. Fortunately the enemy settled the difficulty by turning their attention to other parts of the defence, and never again made a deliberate target of the flag.

WEEK FOUR (11TH–17TH JULY)

11TH JULY

A message carried by one of the Christian refugees was sent out through the water gate. He was received with a volley from a loopholed house opposite, and beat a hasty retreat. The enemy had evidently discovered this means of exit from our lines and were prepared.

During this afternoon Baron von Rahden reported to me that Chinese soldiers had been seen leaving their defences carrying away their bedding, and that heavy firing had been heard south of the Chinese city.

No satisfactory reason for this heavy cannonading to the south and west of the city has ever been given. Rumour said that Prince Ching's troops had fought with Tung-fu Hsiang's and been defeated, but no corroboration of this came to hand.

Mr Nigel Oliphant, who, as already mentioned, had been with the sortie on the Tartar city wall, was brought in from the Fu this afternoon shot through the leg. The day's casualties in the Fu alone amounted to 1 Japanese marine killed and 2 wounded, 2 British marines and 2 volunteers wounded.

The temperature today registered 102° in the shade; it had not fallen below 90° for some days. The heat and a perfect plague of flies, together with the stench from dead bodies of men and animals, was very trying, especially for the wounded. The poor living—pony and mule broth—was beginning to tell on the children.

12TH JULY

During the night, which was as noisy as usual, the Chinese built a new barricade in the Imperial Carriage Park enclosure, close to the high west wall of the Hanlin, and also established a sandbag battery on top of it. Behind this they placed a large black silk flag with the Chinese character for "artillery" inscribed thereon. This battery abutted on to our advanced post in the Hanlin. Mr Mitchell, the American gunner, and Sergeant Preston, of the Marine Guard, in the Hanlin, made a dash for the flag, and jumping up seized it. Instantly a volley of rifle shots went whizzing in all directions: one struck a stone sending the fragments into Sergeant Preston's face; stunned by the blow he let go his hold and fell. Mitchell, however, retained his hold of the flag, and a species of see-saw ensued, with the wall as a fulcrum; several marines and volunteers dashed forward and seized hold of Mitchell. The added weight broke the staff and the flag and part of the staff was triumphantly retained on our side of the wall. This plucky act was the signal for a tremendous outburst of firing from all the enemy's positions which commanded the Hanlin, but our men keeping well under cover no damage was done.

The French garrison the same afternoon made a gallant sortie and captured a large silk flag with scarlet characters on a white ground, setting forth that the flag was presented by the Dowager-Empress to General Ma, commanding the left wing of Yung-lu's army. Dashing forward the French sailors deliberately lassoed the flag and hauled it over to their side of the barricade. A tremendous outburst of rifle-fire was the result, by which, unfortunately, four marines were wounded.

13TH JULY (AND A FRIDAY)

This was the most harassing day for the defence during the whole course of the siege. During the night Tung-fu Hsiang's men had been particularly active in the Hanlin. Shortly after daylight the Fu was heavily shelled by four guns with shrapnel; the defenders could do nothing with such a hail of shot except keep close under cover. The attack became so severe that notwithstanding reinforcements and a most stubborn resistance on the part of the Japanese, Italian, and British, they were compelled to fall back to the last position but one.

Colonel Shiba had originally planned nine lines of defence, one behind the other. The seventh had been held since the 9th instant but had now to be abandoned, as most of its buildings were in flames, and the enemy's Krupp guns were riddling them with common shell and shrapnel shell at a range of 150 yards.

About 4 a tremendous fusillade broke out on all sides. The "general attack" bell sounded, and as many men as could be spared were fallen in ready to reinforce any part of the defences, which were more than usually hard pressed. The firing in the Fu was heavier and more continuous than I have ever heard it before, and accompanied with yells of "Kill, kill," which could be distinctly heard in the Legation; the sound of the firing seemed as if the defenders were being gradually driven back, and I expected every minute to see our people coming out of the Fu gate, crossing the canal, and falling back on to the Legation. I had sent over every man that could be spared, for on all sides we, too, were being attacked.

I wrote to the Russian Legation for reinforcements and very soon ten marines came over at the double. As soon as they had got their breath I sent them over in charge of M. Barbier, a Russian volunteer, who did good service throughout, and who knew the geography of the Fu well. They had hardly disappeared through the gate of the latter when a welcome messenger came from Colonel Shiba to say that he was holding his own and had driven off the enemy, and for the moment required no further men.

I was about to recall the Russians when Herr von Bergen, Second Secretary of the German Legation, came running across the lawn with an urgent written message from the German Chargé d'Affaires, saying that he was very hard pressed and begging for immediate help. The ten Russian marines no longer required at the Fu were at once sent to his aid, and arrived in the nick of time. The enemy, after a smart fusillade, had left their defences and charged into the open with waving banners and loud shouts. They were met by a volley which accounted for six or seven of their number; the rest wavered. The Russians coming up at that moment, the united forces under Lieutenant von Soden charged with fixed bayonets and pursued the enemy capturing one of their standards.

In the meanwhile the French Legation was being vigorously attacked, and shortly after 7 the Chinese exploded two mines underneath the Second Secretary's house and the east side of the Minister's; the explosion completely destroyed these buildings and set fire to those adjacent; two French sailors were killed and buried under the ruins. Captain D'Arcy, the Commandant, was also partially buried and badly cut about the head by falling stones; his wounds were fortunately not serious. The enemy not having properly judged the force of the explosion, suffered severely, and the spy stated that carts next day carried away thirty of their dead from the vicinity of the crater formed by the explosion.

The command of the French detachment for the moment devolved upon Captain Labrousse, an officer of Marine Infantry, a visitor to Peking. When he had satisfied himself that it was impossible to recover the bodies of the buried men, he ordered a retreat to the next line of defence. After the explosion the Chinese, notwithstanding their losses, seemed to be greatly elated at the success of their mining venture and opened a sharp fusillade, but did not leave their defences.

The French and Austrians now occupied a trench which they had prepared, and also the Legation chapel, which was loopholed, and held the enemy at bay. In spite of their severe repulse by the Russian and German detachments, the Chinese attempted another attack along the road leading at the back of the German Legation under the city wall. The Americans were at this moment changing guard at this post; in the half light they detected the attempt, and the double guard opened a withering fire on the advancing enemy, who retired in confusion, leaving twenty dead on the road.

While all this fighting had been going on in the east and north-east, the enemy had also made demonstrations against the Hanlin, but had been kept in check by the fire from the loopholed defences and the upper windows of the students' quarters; just in front of the west corner of the Hanlin defences against the Carriage Park wall there had been a temple; this had been burnt by the enemy on the 23rd June, and only the four walls remained standing. Captain Strouts saw it was important to occupy this enclosure, as the enemy had pushed their attack to within a few yards of it; a hole was made through the wall, and a party under Captain Poole dashed in and occupied the place; a heavy fusillade was opened, but by keeping close to the west wall no one was hit; here two sentry posts were established, so close to the enemy's sand-bag entrenchment on the Carriage Park wall, that amenities in the shape of bricks, stones, and water-melon rinds were freely exchanged between the besiegers and besieged, and our sentries could hear the enemy quarrelling over their rice rations and discussing matters generally.

The net result of this day was that the enemy had undoubtedly lost heavily and had been severely handled, and our defences had been pushed forward in the Hanlin, as shown above, but we had lost ground both in the French Legation and in the Fu; our losses amongst the fast diminishing garrison were very serious, amounting to five killed and about double that number wounded.

That evening, together with Colonel Shiba, I inspected the new position in the Fu, to which we had been driven back; the left of the line was pretty strong, consisting of two buildings defended by a high parapet with a species of small fort built against the wall; the ground in front of this was clear, but the enemy had crept up and made a high barricade, its right resting against the wall some 15 yards from the little fort; the parapet was now extended to the right, but unfortunately it was impossible owing to the nature of the ground, to construct it parallel to the enemy's attack, but it fell back considerably, taking in a little artificial mound whereon a redoubt had been constructed. The fort and buildings above mentioned were held by an Italian guard under M. Caetani, Lieutenant Paolini being still incapacitated by his wound. The little hill redoubt was held by Austrians and Italians.

The line then proceeded east some 30 yards, where a building half in ruins was arrived at; this was held by Japanese sailors and volunteers. Looking through the loopholes one could see the enemy's positions amongst the still smoking ruins some 50 yards off; the parapet was carried south-east again till it met a high wall which divided the Su Wang Fu into two portions, the official buildings being on the right and the private dwelling-houses on the left; the defence line followed this till it came to a hole made by the Japanese;

here it went due east enclosing two buildings east and west of the big centre gateway to the Prince's official residence.

In front of this entrance was a large courtyard with gates east and west; in this courtyard the Christian converts had originally taken refuge, but had been obliged to abandon it owing to shrapnel and rifle fire; this courtyard formed the right of the line of the Fu defences; it was 260 metres south of the fort held by the Italians, and 220 metres east. The two gates of the courtyard were held by the Japanese marines and British marines and volunteers, the advance sentries being posted by Colonel Shiba and myself at loopholes in the two buildings above mentioned. Looking through these loopholes manned by a British and Japanese sentry side by side, the flames from the burning buildings in front actually touched the muzzles of their rifles. Fortunately, what little wind there was came from the south, increasing in strength as the night advanced; it blew the fire back towards the enemy; but for this the buildings must have caught, the main gate would have followed, and the enemy entering here the whole position would have been taken in reverse. When this fire had burnt itself out our position was strengthened, for it had cleared a space in front of the advanced sentries.

During the night it rained heavily, and the enemy, in consequence, kept up a brisk fusillade; the forenoon was quiet. In the afternoon matters livened up somewhat, and an attack was made on the Russian Legation, the Minister's house being shelled, and his study riddled with shrapnel. The Italian gun was sent over, and assisted in repelling the attack. The "International" went to the French Legation, where, under the able direction of the American gunner it did excellent work, bursting a shell in a Chinese barricade and scattering the enemy.

On this day a Chinese convert, late gatekeeper at the Roman Catholic Cathedral, called the Nan Tang, who had volunteered to take a message to Tien-tsin, came with a letter addressed to me, signed "Prince Ching and others". The messenger bore evidence of having been badly beaten, and he told a sad tale of his experiences. He had been caught attempting to leave the Chinese city, and compelled to give up his letter, which the enemy read. After beating him, they took him to Yung Lu, who ordered that his life should be spared, and handed him this letter. The Roman Catholic missionaries gave the man an indifferent character, so he was kept apart from the rest of the converts, and not allowed to roam about the defences. On the following day he quite willingly took back an answer to Yung Lu.

The enemy having been successful with their mining operations in the French Legation, were evidently bent on trying this means of attack at other points. Sounds of picking were distinctly heard by placing one's ear at the back of our foremost barricade in the Hanlin, close to the Carriage Park wall. Mr Wintour, of the Imperial Maritime Customs, obtained leave and commenced a countermine just at the back of the barricade, and worked in the direction of the sound; three of the Chinese converts, who had proved themselves expert diggers, were told off [assigned to this duty] and put under his orders.

15TH JULY

A quiet night. The Chinese, judging by the sound, were very busy in the early morning in the Carriage Park with pick and shovel, though no signs of what they were at, or exactly where they were, could be detected. One of our marines was brought in dangerously wounded from the Fu. During the afternoon the Russians made a successful sortie, and pulled down some houses outside their defences, which had been giving cover to the enemy.

At 6.30, Mr Warren, student interpreter, was brought in from the Fu mortally wounded by a splinter of a shell in the face; he died within a few hours without recovering consciousness; he had only been in Peking a few months, and was much liked by his fellow-students.

Heavy firing in the direction of the Peitang, the celebrated Roman Catholic Mission, presided over by Mgr Favier. We were aware that several thousand refugees, as well as a number of foreign priests and Sisters, were besieged within its walls. When the Legation guards had first come up, a French officer and thirty men, and an Italian officer and eleven men, had been sent to assist in the defence of this important Mission. Though several attempts were made, we never succeeded in establishing communication with this place, which lay only some 4 miles off, but through streets packed with the enemy.

Colonel Shiba reported to me that the men of his detachment, sailors and volunteers, were quite exhausted; they had all been up on duty night and day since the commencement of the siege, and had none of them even changed their clothes since the 20th June, nor had they had more than three or four hours of consecutive sleep during that time; he begged that, if possible, half might be taken off duty for a clear twenty-four hours, and replaced by British marines and volunteers, after which the second half might be relieved in a similar manner. I consulted with Captain Strouts, and it was arranged that, although our people were in the same plight, an effort should be made to carry out Colonel Shiba's wishes. The marines and volunteers responded with alacrity to this call made upon them, for they knew what splendid work the Japanese had done and were doing. It was decided that the Japanese sentries should be relieved by ours at 7 o'clock on the following morning.

16TH JULY

At 7 a.m. Captain Strouts took over the relief party; he was accompanied by Dr Morrison, *The Times* correspondent. After having posted the last sentry, they were returning, and had just left the Italian post, when a shower of bullets came over the barricade, and Captain Strouts fell mortally wounded by a bullet through the groin, which shattered the upper part of the thigh-bone. Dr Morrison was shot almost at the same time by a bullet through the thigh, but which, fortunately, did not strike the bone. Colonel Shiba, who was coming towards them at the time, seeing Captain Strouts and Dr Morrison fall, ran forward to help them; stretchers were procured, and both wounded men were brought into hospital; this was done under heavy fire, a bullet passing through Colonel Shiba's coat.

From the first there was no hope for Captain Strouts, and he died within three hours of his entry into hospital. He was a first-rate officer, cool, calm, and fearless, and his death was a great blow to me and to the entire defence. He was buried at 6 p.m. in the same grave with young Warren, who had been killed the day before. The funeral was attended by all the foreign Representatives, the officers commanding detachments and as many of the garrison as could be spared from their defence duties.

While the mournful procession was proceeding through the Legation grounds to the little cemetery close by the First Secretary's house, the old Chinese messenger who had taken a letter to "Prince Ching and others", bearing a large white flag aloft in one hand, and holding in the other what proved afterwards to be a sufficiently friendly reply to our letter, was marching solemnly along the side of the canal from the North Bridge towards the Legation. The enemy—whether they had in the meantime relented of the friendly tone of the letter he carried, or whether they wished to accelerate his movements—deftly exploded a shell over his head, fortunately without doing him any harm; the next two shells followed in the same line, exploding in the trees just above the funeral party, but the fragments were carried into the ruins of some neighbouring houses, and did no damage.

The document from "Prince Ching and others", which was an answer to my letter of the previous day, practically initiated a species of armed truce. For the first day or two the enemy were embarrassingly demonstrative in their endeavours to be friendly, and came out unarmed from behind their barricades in considerable numbers, and advanced towards ours. They had repeatedly to be warned back, for we were afraid of treachery; neither did we wish them to see how few were the defenders behind barricades which otherwise looked formidable to them.

As time wore on this friendliness became less and less apparent, and by the end of the month matters had become almost normal, and the attacks and counter-attacks were as brisk and determined as ever.

The precious days of comparative peace which followed the 16th were utilized by us in working with increased energy at our defences. At no time, however, after the 20th was it safe to show for one second outside the defences. The slightest exposure was a signal for a hail of bullets. The old Chinese messenger, besides the official despatch from Prince Ching, brought a cypher telegram for Mr Conger from the State Department at Washington. This, the messenger said, he had received from the Tsung-li Yamên.

The arrival of this telegram created great excitement amongst the besieged, as it was the first news we had had from the outside world since the 18th June. There could be no question of the genuineness of the message, as it was in a cypher possessed only by Mr Conger and the State Department. Mr Conger replied in the same cypher. This message was duly forwarded by the Yamên and duly arrived at Washington, but the public were unwilling to credit it, having apparently quite made up their mind that the Legations had been destroyed, and the besieged massacred.

17TH JULY

At the east barricade in the Fu, the Chinese came from behind their defences in considerable numbers and advanced up to Colonel Shiba's post. Six of them were forthwith made prisoners, the rest beat a hasty retreat. Colonel Shiba reported the matter to me and I ordered the men to be released with a message to their commander to the effect that if more than two left their barricades together they would be fired on.

The same afternoon I was on the Tartar city wall, inspecting the defences, together with Mr Squiers, whom I had appointed Chief of the Staff. The Colonel commanding Tung-fu Hsiang's troops in the opposing barricade, some sixty yards off, had shouted a message across for permission to bury his dead which were lying at the foot of our barricade, the result of the sortie of the 3rd instant. This permission, as may be imagined, was readily granted.

The Chinese barricade was swarming with men, at least 250 being crowded on it and the adjacent walls; their arms were all out of sight. They were dressed in a variety of uniforms, scarlet and black of Tung-fu Hsiang's men predominating. Six of the Chinese soldiery descended with spades and large pieces of matting, on which they proceeded to carry away the rotting corpses. Through Mr Splingard, our interpreter, I requested the Colonel to come and have a talk with me. After some demur he consented. I offered him a cigar, which he gladly accepted, and we sat on the outside of our barricade and chatted until our cigars were finished. He told me that he belonged to the Kansu troops, but was at present under the immediate orders of Yung Lu, who was desirous of stopping the fighting. I remarked that the fighting was none of our doing, but we were quite prepared to defend ourselves whenever attacked. I said that, to prevent misunderstandings, it would be better if not more than two men left their barricades at a time. If more than that number did so I should be compelled to open fire. He said he thought it would be a good thing if some such understanding were arrived at, and suggested my writing a letter to Yung Lu to this effect. He assured me that any letter handed to him for Yung Lu would most certainly reach its destination. On my return, whilst standing on the top of our barricade, I could see the enemy's positions stretching away to the north until they disappeared in the direction of the Carriage Park.

There were barricades in the streets below the wall. A large temple was loopholed and put into a state of defence and full of men. More men were amongst the ruins west of the Russian Legation, and a species of mound which commanded this Legation and the Mongol Market was gay with the uniforms of hundreds of Imperial infantry. Following the line west of the Mongol Market the tops of the houses carried nests of these brightcoated soldiery. Altogether from my position I saw some 1,500 to 2,000 men, and many more must have been hidden behind the walls and ruined houses. From where I stood I noticed that the men in the opposing barricade could overlook certain portions of our position on the wall, and would probably remark on the very small garrison we were able to maintain. I therefore requested the American and Russian Commandants to send up as many of their reserve men as could be spared, with orders to show themselves as much as possible on the barricades. This order was promptly and quietly carried out, and very shortly our position was occupied by a goodly number of Russian and American sailors, as well as by some twenty of our marines.

On my return to the Legation I wrote a despatch to Yung Lu, and stated that in view of the negotiations which had commenced with the Tsung-li Yamên the defenders of the Legation would not fire unless they were fired at, but to prevent misunderstandings it would be better if not more than two soldiers left their barricades, and these must be unarmed. Any armed soldier leaving his barricade would at once be fired at. I also added that if the enemy were seen making new barricades in advance of those already existing, fire would be opened on the working parties, even if they were unarmed. This letter was delivered into the hands of my friend the Colonel, who promised to deliver it to Yung Lu.

The Commanders of all portions of the defence reported that the enemy had ceased firing, and showed a friendly disposition and a desire to enter into conversation with the besieged. This was much less the case in the north and west, where they were decidedly treacherous and unfriendly, though they had evidently received the same orders as their comrades. From information picked up by the Japanese at their barricade it was evident that the cause of this sudden change in the demeanour of our assailants was due to the news which the high authorities, whoever they may have been, had received of the capture of the native city of Tien-tsin by the allies, and the rout of the Chinese army. By some friendly soldiers we were warned against mines which were especially to be directed against the British Legation. In addition to the countermine begun by Mr Wintour on the 14th, and which by now had been sunk to a depth of some 9 feet, and then for a short distance carried under the Carriage Park wall, a system of countermines had been organized in the north and west of the Legation, and carried out most efficiently under Mr Gamewell's direction. They consisted of trenches some 11 or 12 feet deep close up against our advanced lines, and it would have been impossible for the enemy to pass these trenches without being immediately detected.

WEEK FIVE (18TH–24TH JULY)

18TH–19TH JULY

On the 18th July a messenger who had been sent out by Colonel Shiba returned from Tien-tsin with a letter from the Japanese head-quarters staff at that place. It contained the news that the native city had been taken by the allies, and that a relief force was being organized consisting of 24,000 Japanese, 4,000 Russians, 2,000 British, 1,500 Americans, and 1,500 French, and would leave on or about the 20th July and advance on Peking. This notice was posted on the Bell Tower. It was the first news we had had from Tien-tsin, and was joyfully welcomed by the besieged, though many were disappointed that the force was not already well on its way. In fact the message was far less hopeful. It mentioned the heavy losses sustained by the allies, and also spoke of the absolute absence of transport. To keep up the spirits of the besieged, however, the message as posted was made as cheerful as possible.

As an instance of the curious state of affairs which existed at this time between the besiegers and besieged, especially on the east side where the Japanese and French were in contact with the enemy, a young Frenchman, by name Pelliot, wandered over to the opposing barricade and entered into conversation with the Chinese soldiery; without thinking he stepped inside their barricade and was instantly made prisoner; he was not roughly treated but taken to a Yamên at some distance where he was brought before some high Mandarins who courteously asked him several questions regarding our strength, losses, etc., all of which he answered in an evasive manner; eventually he was conducted under an escort of Yung Lu's men through streets full of Boxers and soldiery, back to the barricade, and set at liberty.

The Japanese started a small market for eggs which the Chinese soldiers brought over hidden in their capacious sleeves and sold to our people; the eggs were mostly distributed by the Food Supply Committee to the hospital, and amongst the women and children. The weather was very hot and the latter began to feel the want of proper food; six of the younger ones were to die in the Legation.

20TH TO 24TH JULY

On the 20th it was reported to me that the Chinese were heard mining in close proximity to the Hanlin. I went down Mr Wintour's countermine and heard them distinctly at work; they seemed quite close but somewhat above my level; a pick was handed down and at the first few blows the enemy stopped working. From that time a strict watch was kept at this countermine, but the enemy had either abandoned their mine or had changed direction, for the sounds gradually died away and then stopped altogether.

Later the mine was thoroughly examined by the Royal Engineers; it was found to commence in one of the large buildings in the Carriage Park enclosure and to proceed straight for our barricade in the Hanlin. It arrived within a few feet of Mr Wintour's countermine and then suddenly changed direction to the south and followed parallel to the dividing wall for some 40 feet, till it arrived opposite the centre of the building, forming the students' library and mess-room when, instead of turning east under this building, it turned west, described a curve and ended at a point some 30 yards due south of where it started. There is no doubt that Mr Wintour's countermine checked the enemy's advance underground and headed them south, but why, when they got to a convenient striking point, they went away from their objective, it is impossible to say.

During this spell of comparative quiet the enemy were very busy working at their barricades, and besides the one I have mentioned, mines were started by them on the top of the Tartar city wall endeavouring to get under the Russo-American barricade, also in Legation Street working towards the Russian barricade; similar mines were commenced against the French and Japanese defences on the east; we, in the meanwhile, were equally busy working at our defences and countermines.

Later, a letter was found addressed to the General Commanding at the Hata Men, on the subject of mines. The writer had been a teacher at the British Legation in the employ of Her Majesty's Government for four years and was well known to the student interpreters; together with all the other teachers he disappeared about the middle of June. The letter was dated the beginning of July and pointed out that the General's methods of attacking the Legation were faulty and were bound to lead to considerable loss in the future as they had done in the past. The proper method of attack, the writer said, was by mining; to assist the General in his attack he enclosed a correct plan of the British Legation, with which he was well acquainted, and marked on the plan the most suitable place for the mine to be driven. Eager inquiries have been made since the siege was raised for the writer of the letter but as yet he has not been found.

On the 18th July one of Yung Lu's men advanced with a flag of truce along the city wall, and came down to the German defences with a letter for me from Yung Lu, accepting the arrangement suggested with regard to terms of a truce. This man was very intelligent and friendly; he had been specially selected to come, as he had had to deal with foreigners, having been a police-man on the Peking–Tien-tsin Railway. He was recognized by one or two Europeans in the Legation. The same afternoon another soldier came in with his ear partially severed; he had been in the employ of Sir Robert Hart, and was bugler to the regiment at the Hata Gate. He came in, he said, to have his ear seen to, as he knew that foreign surgeons were good and humane men. His officer had wounded him with a blow of his sword for not being sufficiently proficient on his bugle. He informed us, further, that the men were very dis-contented, and were sick of fighting the foreigners. The same story was told by three soldiers who strolled along the wall from the direction of the Hata Gate to the American barricade.

It was very evident throughout the siege that the enemy on the east were much more friendly, and had not the same stomach for fighting as our friends in the north and west; from this direction not a single man ever came in, neither did any of our messengers ever succeed in getting out. My con-versation with the Colonel on the city wall was the only instance of a friendly act on that side.

Even when the truce was at its height, from the 17th to the 20th, it was unsafe to show oneself for an instant at the barricades in the Hanlin. On the 19th some of the enemy held out a water melon at the end of a pole on one of the Hanlin barricades; a volunteer of ours advanced to take it, and was instantly fired at, the bullet passing within an inch of his head.

On the 20th and subsequent days several of our people, mostly Chinese converts, were hit whilst working at the defences; this was, of course, in accordance with the terms of truce, and we returned the compliment.

On the 24th the supply of eggs began to dwindle down, and the men who brought them reported to the Japanese that their officers had threat-ened to execute anybody found bringing in anything to the besieged. On the 23rd two men were beheaded for this reason within sight of the Japanese.

28TH JULY

On the 28th July the boy messenger, who had been sent out on the 4th July, returned from Tien-tsin. His arrival caused great excitement; he brought, sowed in the collar of his coat, the British Consul's letter in answer to mine. The news ran like wildfire through the Legation, and eager crowds surrounded the Bell Tower, waiting to hear what was posted on the notice board. This was the message:

> Yours of the 4th July. 24,000 troops have now landed, and 19,000 here. General Gaselee expected Taku to-morrow. Russians hold Pei Tsan. Tien-tsin city under foreign Government, and Boxer power has exploded. Plenty of troops are on the way if you can hold out with food. Almost all ladies have left Tien-tsin.

This letter caused great disappointment amongst the garrison, as the general opinion was that ample time had elapsed between the 20th June and the 21st July to organize and start a relief expedition.

In justice to Mr Carles, who has been blamed for not sending more information, it is right to state that, had he written the true state of affairs which then existed in Tien-tsin, the effect on the beleaguered garrison would have been crushing; he consequently made the note as cheerful as he could under the circumstances. Had not the arrival of the messenger been witnessed by numbers of people, it is more than probable no notice of the contents of the letter would have been posted on the Bell Tower.

During the early days of the armistice from their barricades on the east of the Fu, the Chinese adopted a novel way of communicating with the Japanese defenders. One day a large dog trotted into the Japanese barricade with a note tied round its neck. This was from the Chinese General commanding in that quarter, pointing out the futility of further defence, and recommending unconditional surrender. A reply, declining the suggestion in somewhat forcible terms, was tied on the dog's neck, with which it trotted back.

This was repeated several times, the advisability of surrender being urged with greater insistence each time. The answers varied only in the strength of their language. Letters demanding and suggesting surrender were also tied to arrows and shot into the Japanese lines. A remarkable instance which took place at this time of filial obedience and good faith on the part of a Chinese soldier, was recounted to me by Colonel Shiba.

Amongst the men who brought eggs for sale was one who belonged to Yung Lu's force, who was distinguished from his fellows by the hard bargains which he drove for his wares. Noticing this, Colonel Shiba thought the man might be induced for a price to carry a letter to Tien-tsin and bring back an answer. He was accordingly approached on the subject, and after considerable discussion about the amount, he agreed to go for the sum of 250 dollars, the money to be paid over on his return with the answer. The man left on the 22nd and returned on the 1st August, bringing with him a reply from the Chief of staff of the Japanese division. It ran as follows:

> Your letter of 22nd received. Departure of troops from Tien-tsin delayed by difficulties of transport, but advance will be made in two or three days. Will write again as soon as estimated date of arrival at Peking is fixed.

The letter was dated the 26th July. The bearer refused to accept the 250 dollars, and no amount of persuasion could induce him to do so. Thinking that perhaps he was unwilling to be discovered in possession of so large a sum, he was offered a letter to the Consul at Tien-tsin in the form of a promissory note, but he declined everything. On being asked why he refused now, when he had been previously so keen to acquire the money, he told Colonel Shiba that on arrival at Tien-tsin, after delivery of the letter and receiving the answer, he went to his own home; his mother did all she could to prevent his returning to Peking, but he said he had promised the foreign officer to return, and return he must. "Then," said she, "you must accept no money, for what you are doing is for the good of your country." He, therefore, in obedience to his mother's wishes, steadfastly refused any money whatever. He offered to take a letter back to Tien-tsin if it was written at once, but he could not, he said, bring back an answer. Seeing that it was impossible to shake the man's resolution, Colonel Shiba wrote another letter which the messenger duly delivered at the Consulate at Tien-tsin, but again refused all offers of money.

29TH–31ST JULY

On the afternoon of the 29th July the Chinese began to throw out heaps of bricks and stones at the corner of some ruined houses at the east end of the north bridge. This bridge was commanded by the north stable picket, and by a caponier which had been constructed in front of the main gate of the Legation, called by the marines "Fort Halliday". The road across it is one of the main arteries of the city from east to west, and to avoid the bridge the Chinese had to make a considerable detour through the Imperial city. It had always been a source of surprise to us that no barricade had been constructed across the bridge, because in addition to allowing passage across, the fire from it, the barricade, would command the whole length of the canal with the roads on either side, and would sweep the south bridge, which was one of our means of communication (the only one for carts), between the east and west defences. During the night-time the bridge was undoubtedly used by the enemy; but in the daylight the fire of our pickets was so deadly, that after losing several men, they gave up all attempts at crossing it.

It soon became evident that the heap of bricks and stones was the commencement of the long-expected barricade; immediately a lively fusillade was opened on the inoffensive-looking heap, and bricks and stones were sent flying, but so soon as they were shot away others appeared in their place. Very shortly wooden cases, evidently filled with bricks and stones, were pushed forward from behind the heap and the barricade stealthily crept forward.

The enemy's sharpshooters in the ruins on the other side of the canal were in the meanwhile very busy, and some very pretty shooting took place. They had the most modern rifle with smokeless powder, and the men in the north stable picket had some very narrow escapes, bullets pattering round their loopholes and in some instances coming through.

The "International" gun was at that time doing good service in the French Legation so could not be used, but the Italian 1-pr. with its solid pewter bullet was hauled up on to a sandbag battery on the roof of the cow-house which formed part of the north stable picket, and opened fire. The enemy were not slow to return the compliment, and the Mauser bullets soon began to knock the sandbags about, at the close range of 60 yards, cutting them into shreds.

The Italian gunner behaved with great coolness. Unfortunately, as he was laying the gun for the third round his hand was smashed by a Mauser bullet, and he was taken to hospital. The sergeant commanding the marine detachment went up and fired the round, but the enemy's fire now became so hot, pieces of silk damask and sand being scattered in every direction by the hail of bullets. It was found impossible to continue the gun in action; it was also impossible to remove it. This was eventually done under cover of darkness.

On the following morning it was found that the enemy had succeeded in building a barricade 6 foot high the whole length of the north bridge, a distance of 30 to 40 yards.

In the correspondence which was at this time proceeding between the Diplomatic Body and the Chinese Government as represented by "Prince Ching and others", expostulations had been made respecting the strengthening of our defences. Attention was, therefore, drawn to the building of this formidable barricade by the Chinese Imperial troops. The reply received was that "we must not be alarmed as the troops of Tung-fu Hsiang were only engaged in mending the road!"

Fire was immediately opened from this barricade, and the road along the canal became very dangerous. To obviate this a large traverse was run across the road at the smaller gate of the Legation and a barricade constructed across the south bridge.

WEEK SEVEN (1ST–7TH AUGUST)

2ND–6TH AUGUST

On the 2nd August the fortifications having been thoroughly strengthened on the north and east, it was determined to improve our western defences. Consequently, a small party of British marines and volunteers of various nationalities, mostly belonging to the Imperial Maritime Customs, under M. von Strauch, an ex-officer of the German army, were directed to cut a hole through the west wall of the stable quarters and occupy some buildings forming the east side of the Mongol Market. The hour chosen was that of the Chinese siesta, shortly before noon. The houses were successfully occupied without the enemy becoming aware of our intentions. They were found to be in a good state of preservation, and a party of Christian converts under Mr Gamewell's orders were at once set to work to loophole the walls and make barricades where necessary. Three Chinese soldiers were found dead in the houses, where they had evidently dragged themselves to die.

In a few days this position, which was one of considerable importance, was greatly strengthened. Thus on the north and west the British Legation defences had been pushed forward in the direction of the enemy. The latter very soon discovered this new occupation, and the whole of the Mongol Market barricades blazed out on our working parties. These, however, kept well under cover, and only a few casualties took place.

For the remaining few days of the siege this position was the scene of constant attack. The enemy, whose barricades by the Carriage Park wall were within stone-throwing distance, kept up a constant fire, also hurling bricks and stones over the ruined walls. One of our marines was badly cut on the head by one of these missiles.

On this day a messenger arrived from Tien-tsin bearing many letters. The following were posted on the Bell Tower:

> From the American consul, Tien-tsin, to American Minister, dated the 28th July.

> Had lost all hope of seeing you again. Prospect now brighter. We had thirty days shelling here, nine days siege, thought that bad enough. Scarcely a house escaped damage. Excitement at home is intense; of course, our prayers and hopes are for your safety and speedy rescue. Advance of troops to-morrow probable.

Another from Lieutenant-Colonel Mallory, United States' Army, dated the 30th July:

> A relief column of 10,000 is on the point of starting for Peking; more to follow. God grant they may be in time.

The one which contained the most news was written by Mr Lowry, of the American Legation, who was in Tien-tsin when the railway was cut. The letter was to his wife, one of the besieged. It was as follows:

> The bearer arrived last Friday with news from Peking. The 9th, 14th United States' Regiments already at Tien-tsin. 6th Cavalry at Taku on its way up. An advance guard of several regiments has already started. There was fighting this morning at Pei Tsang. Everything is quiet here now. Word came today Boxers killing Christians at Tsun Hua and many other places. Tien-tsin full of foreign troops and more coming all the time. Railway open between here and Tangku. Many ladies and children went back to United States on transport "Logan". All property at Pei-tai Hoa destroyed.

This letter was dated the 30th July.

This news greatly cheered the spirits of the garrison.

7TH AUGUST

On the 7th August "Prince Ching and others" sent condolences on the death of the Duke of Saxe-Coburg and Gotha and the firing was heavier than usual. The enemy seemed now to be concentrating their attention on the British Legation, the fire from the Mongol Market being particularly severe; the bullets were also coming lower. Mr Gamewell reported that our fortifications in this quarter were being damaged by rifle fire to an extent which had not before occurred. We ascertained afterwards through spies that a new division of troops had come from Shansi under a Brigadier-General, who had sworn to take the Legation in five days. This division was stationed in the Mongol Market.

Orders were posted on the Bell Tower that women and children were not to walk about the grounds while firing was going on, several very narrow escapes having taken place. To meet the attacks from the west the Nordenfelt was mounted on a platform on the top of the wall at the back of the Chinese Secretary's house and did excellent work. A platform was also made in our new defences in the Mongol Market for the "International" gun, which was still in charge of the indefatigable American gunner, Mitchell.

WEEK EIGHT (8TH–14TH AUGUST)

9TH–10TH AUGUST

On the 9th August the Fu, which had enjoyed a spell of comparative quiet, was again attacked, and fresh flags were planted behind the enemy's barricades. The attack was evidently now closing in. We had, however, worked so hard on the defences that our casualties were very few.

On 10th August, at 3 in the afternoon a tremendous fusillade took place against the Fu and all our defences, Hanlin, Carriage Park, and Mongol Market. The big gun fire had entirely ceased since the commencement of the armistice, but the rifle fire was very heavy, and cut our fortifications about considerably.

On this day a messenger, who had been sent out on the 6th to the advancing forces, returned with the following letter from General Gaselee, dated the 8th August, Tsai Tsung:

> Strong force of allies advancing. Twice defeated enemy. Keep up your spirits.

Colonel Shiba also received a letter from General Fukushima, dated Camp at Chong Chiang, 2 p.m., north of Nan Tsai Tsung, the 8th August:

> Japanese and American troops defeated enemy on 5th instant near Pei-tsang and occupied Yang-tsun. The allied force, consisting of Americans, British, and Russians, left Yang-tsun this morning, and while marching north I received your letter at 8 p.m. at a village called Nan Tsai Tsung. It is very gratifying to know that the foreign community at Peking are holding on, and believe me it is the earnest and unanimous desire of the Lieutenant-General and all of us to arrive at Peking as soon as possible, and relieve you from your perilous position. Unless some

unforeseen event takes place the allied force will be at Ho Si Wu on the 9th, Matou, 10th, Chang Chin-wan, 11th, Tung Chou, 12th, and arrive Peking 13th or 14th.

On the 6th Mr Squiers, my Chief of the staff, had drawn up a plan of the city, showing the sluice gate through the Tartar city wall, and our position on the wall, which was marked by three flags, a Russian on the western extremity, a British flag in the centre, and an American on the east. Directions were given in this letter in English and American cypher as to the best means of entrance. The letter was addressed to the American and English Generals, and was duly delivered to them on the 8th instant.

12TH AUGUST

From the various quarters of the defence reports came in that the enemy were very active, and it became evident that the relief force was nearing. From the Russo-American position on the Tartar city wall numerous bodies of troops were reported leaving the Cheng Meng. From the north stable picket bodies of cavalry were seen to advance up to the bridge, dismount, and lead their horses across under cover of the barricade; their movements were considerably accelerated by our riflemen from that post and the Main Gate caponier; the Krupp gun by the Hata Gate, which had been silent for several days, again opened fire. Nickel-plated bullets, fired at a range of 20 yards, pierced our defences in the Mongol Market and elsewhere. In their eagerness to press forward, the enemy overthrew one of their own barricades. Instantly our sharpshooters opened a deadly fire, and the Nordenfelt was brought to bear. Before they could escape this hail of bullets twenty-seven, including their leader, fell in a riddled heap. The next day "Prince Ching and others" wrote an indignant protest, saying that the "converts" had again opened fire on the Imperial troops, killing an officer and twenty-six men. We subsequently heard that the officer was none other than the General of Division whose rash oath has been recorded.

When the evening closed in the enemy had made no advance in any direction and had lost severely. Our casualties were few, but they included Captain Labrousse, of the French Staff, an officer who had done excellent service both in the French Legation and on the Tartar city wall; in this capacity he came particularly under my notice, his reports being very lucid and of great service to the defence. In him the French army lost a smart and capable officer.

13TH AUGUST

The morning of the 13th commenced with sharp firing in every direction, which lasted with scarcely an interval throughout the day. Towards evening it was reported to me that the enemy were at work in the battery on the Imperial city wall. I immediately, proceeded to the north stable picket, and, in the failing light, through glasses, saw that work of some kind was being carried on. The sergeant of the picket reported that previous to my arrival he had seen what he thought was a modern piece of artillery owing to the light catching on brass mountings. As the enemy had not fired from this battery since the 16th July, I thought that it would be advisable to let sleeping dogs lie and not to draw the fire unnecessarily, especially as the relief force was so close; but, to be on the safe side, before the light died away altogether the Austrian Maxim was brought into the north stable and careful aim taken at the battery. The American gunner in charge of the automatic Colt, in the Main Gate caponier, was instructed also to lay his gun on the embrasure. Both had orders that immediately fire was opened from it the two machine-guns were to return the fire. The ranges were 200 and 350 yards.

Shortly before 8 a tremendous rifle fire opened all round, and instantly the above-mentioned battery joined in. The sergeant had been right in his surmise, for, instead of our old friend the smooth bore, it was a 2-inch quick-firing Krupp which opened on us with segment and common shell. Hardly had the crash of the first exploding shell taken place when the Austrian Maxim and the American Colt rattled out their reply. At the seventh round this gun was silenced, but not before it had done considerable damage; three shots struck Fort Halliday, stunning the inmates, though hurting nobody; one carried away a tall chimney in the Minister's house, another struck a brick pillar in the upstairs balcony of the north-east corner of said house (a post commonly known as Rosamond's Bower), completely demolishing the pillar and part of the balcony, and one pierced the roof and exploded in my dressing-room, creating very considerable havoc; fortunately, not a single casualty resulted from all this cannonade.

14TH AUGUST

Four times between sunset and sunrise the "general attack" bell was sounded, when all reserves turned out and stood ready for emergencies. The enemy seemed particularly active in the Mongol Market; reinforcements were urgently requested from this quarter, and were promptly sent. The Chinese officers were heard inciting the men to charge, laying stress on the fact that they far outnumbered us and the distance was very short. The firing ceased, and an ominous silence followed, as if they were in reality gathering for the attack. It was then that our Commandant sent for reinforcements; before they arrived the enemy had evidently thought better of their intention to attack with the bayonet, and had recommenced firing and throwing bricks. The din of rifle fire, the rattle of bullets on the roofs, and the scream and crash of large ordnance was deafening.

At about 2 a.m. there was a pause, when very distinctly the delighted garrison heard the boom of heavier guns away to the east and the sound of many Maxims evidently outside the city walls. The scene in the Legation was indescribable. Those who, tired out, had fallen asleep were wakened by these unwanted sounds, and there was much cheering and shaking of hands. The enemy, too, had heard it. For a moment there was silence; then the rifle fire broke out more angry and deafening than before, instantly responded to by the rattle of our sharpshooters and the grunt of the five-barrelled Nordenfelt, which, under the able management of the *Orlando's* armourer and Sergeant Murphy of the marines, refused to jam, but hailed volleys of bullets into the Mongol Market barricades.

The "International" was also particularly active, and fired at point blank range into the said barricade until the gallant gunner Mitchell had his arm badly broken by a Mauser bullet, and was taken to hospital. After the siege had ended, the little garrison of the Mongol Market defences found that the "International" was loaded, but owing to the accident to the gunner had not been fired. As it was impossible to draw the charge, the muzzle was elevated, and the last shot fired from this unique gun descended amongst the yellow-tiled pavilions of the Pink or Forbidden City.

With daylight the firing died down, and there was a period of calm. A sharp look-out was kept from all the posts, especially the Tartar city wall, for any possible appearance of the relieving force. Mr Squiers, my energetic Chief of the Staff, reported from the American Legation shortly after daybreak: "On the wall there has been no sign of the approach of our troops beyond the firing of the machine-guns. The direction of the firing seemed to be the Chinese wall just to the right of the part where it joins the Tartar city wall. There is no commotion in the Chinese city or at either of the gates. Your flag-staff was shot away during the night, the flag falling over the wall. Fortunately it was secured, and pulled back before the Chinese had a chance to capture it. If you will send a carpenter I will attend to repairs." The armourer and signalman of the *Orlando* were sent, the staff was mended, and the flag rehoisted.

At 6 a.m. Mr Squiers again reported: "The Chinese have three guns mounted at the Hata Men, which they have been firing in an easterly direction. All the musketry fire seemed to be on the wall between the Hata Men and the tower at the corner. No excitement in the Chinese city. The Chien Men is still open, but few passing in or out." Again, at 7 a.m.: "Heavy firing at the Chi-hua Men; also further machine-gun fire beyond the Hata Men. No movement in the Chinese city." This was the Japanese, Russian, and American attack developing along the east side of the Tartar city. As can be seen, Mr Squiers is careful to report any movement in the Chinese city, for in accordance with the plan sent out it was in this direction the relief was expected. At 9.15 he reports: "For the past half-hour Chinese soldiers have been pouring out of the Chien Men, going in the direction of the south gate; cavalry, infantry, and two pieces of artillery. In the direction of the Hata Men there is heavy cannon fire, and a large shell has just exploded in the roof of the tower in the south-east angle of the Tartar city."

At 11 the report came: "Large numbers of Chinese soldiers are passing through the Chien Men into the Imperial city." The defending troops were evidently being withdrawn from the Chinese city to meet the Japanese attack on the east gate of the Tartar city.

Shortly before 3 p.m. a breathless messenger from the Tartar city wall arrived to say that foreign troops were under the city wall opposite the water gate. I immediately followed him, and arrived in time to receive General Gaselee and his staff as they came through the said gate and stood on the canal road. From there I led them through the Russian Legation to the British, where they were welcomed by the rest of the besieged garrison. The regiment which first entered the Legation quarter was the 7th Rajpoots under Major Vaughan. With them was Major Scott, of the 3rd Sikhs, attached to the 1st Sikhs, with a few men of this regiment. This officer with several men ran along the canal road from the south bridge to the gateway opposite the First Secretary's house, and were the first to enter the British Legation. This portion of the canal road was under the enemy's fire from the north bridge barricade, and three casualties occurred here later in the afternoon.

On arriving in the Legation, which was still being hotly attacked by the enemy form the Hanlin and Mongol Market, a small detachment of the 7th was sent into the Main Gate caponier to assist in repelling the attack. A man of this regiment was almost immediately seriously wounded; one of the ladies of the garrison was also wounded on the lawn. In the meanwhile, Mr Squiers with a small party of Russian and American marines, under Captain Vroubleffsky and Captain Perry Smith, had proceeded along Legation Street to the Chien Gate, which they opened, allowing the 1st Sikhs, under Colonel Pollock and the Hong Kong artillery to enter, the Chinese making a stand here and charging up to the Maxims of the artillery. The American troops under General Chaffey, and Russians under General Linievitch had, with considerable loss, forced the north-east gate of the Chinese city, and proceeding underneath the wall, had entered, some by the water gate and some by the Chien Gate. Two guns of Major Johnson's Battery Royal Artillery had also been got through the water gate and up an improvised ramp on to the canal road. One of these guns was brought on to the south bridge, and effectively shelled the north bridge barricade, and the battery on the Imperial city wall.

The besieged lost no time in taking the offensive. As has been seen, the American and Russian Legations were instrumental in opening the Chien Gate; Lieutenant von Soden with a detachment of his men attacked the enemy and drove them to the Hata Gate, capturing their guns and banners; the Italian and Japanese detachment in the Fu drove the enemy from their positions and reoccupied the entire Fu.

A detachment of British marines and volunteers under Captain Poole cut a hole through the Carriage Park wall and occupied the whole of this enclosure, killing three of the enemy.

Two days later a detachment of French, Russian, and English troops relieved our gallant fellow prisoners in the Pei-tang, whose sufferings had been worse than ours, and the siege of Peking came to an end.

END OF THE SIEGE

During the siege the following number of cases passed through the International Hospital: 126 wounded, all severely, of whom 17 died; 40 cases of sickness, mostly anteric and dysentry, of whom 2 died. Of the 166 cases treated 142 were soldiers or sailors, the rest civilians; 165 were men; 1 woman was wounded. Of the above cases 21 were Germans; Americans, 17; English 55; French, 17; Dutch, 1; Japanese, 14; Italians, 17; Austrians, 6; and Russians, 18.

The slightly wounded are not mentioned in this Return; many of these were treated on the spot by the excellent French and Japanese military surgeons, who remained with their detachments in the French Legation and Fu.

The latter post has frequently been mentioned as the scene of severe fighting. The following Return of the numbers killed and wounded therein will be of interest:

	Killed	Wounded
English	2	11
French	1	2
Russians	0	2
Austrians	1	1
Italians	7	11
Japanese	9	21
Chinese	18	85
Total	38	133

The Chinese were mostly employed working in the defences, though Colonel Shiba had organized a force of some twenty Chinese armed with swords and spears who were very useful in keeping watch.

A Return of the officers killed and wounded of the various marine detachments will be of interest:

	Officers arrived	Killed	Wounded
British	3	1	2
Italians	2	0	2
Russians	2	0	0
Japanese	2	1	1
German	1	0	0
French	3	2	1
Austrians	4	1	2
Americans	2	0	1
Total	19	5	9

The total number of foreigners killed during the siege from the 20th June to the 14th July inclusive, was sixty-six.

From the 20th June to the 13th July the garrisons of the Su Wang Fu and the French Legation were driven back step by step, disputing every inch of the ground, yielding only to superior numbers and having to cope with shell fire, incendiarism, and in the case of the French Legation, subterranean mines, until, after twenty-three days' fighting, three quarters of each of these two positions was in the hands of the enemy. Had the latter pressed on after the 13th July with the same persistence they showed up to that date, and also having an attenuated and worn-out garrison to deal with, they would have captured both positions by the 20th July at latest. Fortunately, on the 14th instant, Tien-tsin was taken by the allies; this produced a marked effect on the besiegers, and the besieged received nearly twenty days' respite, which enabled them to materially strengthen their defences and recuperate generally, so that the final attacks of the enemy were repulsed with ease.

RECOMMENDATIONS BY SIR CLAUDE MACDONALD

Sir C. MacDonald to the Marquess of Lansdowne (received February 2, 1901)

Tokio, December 26, 1900

My Lord,

In my Report dated the 20th September last, I had the honour to recommend certain officers and civilians who performed exceptionally good service during the siege of Peking.

To the names then mentioned, it gives me great pleasure to add the names of the following gentlemen volunteers, members of the Imperial Maritime Customs, whose services have been specially brought to my notice by Captain Poole, who was in charge of volunteers.

CLAUDE M. MACDONALD

Enclosure

List of Members of the Imperial Maritime Customs recommended by
Sir C. MacDonald

Mr Macoun was for some time in charge of the Customs contingent of volunteers, arranged their roster, and was himself unceasingly on duty in either the dangerous Prince Su's Park or West Hanlin. He was an indefatigable worker. He was wounded in the thigh by a bullet in Prince Su's Park on the 12th July, and, though lame from the effects, cheerfully resumed his duties after a week's rest. I understand that he is not even now fully recovered.

Mr de Courcy was also conspicuous by his hard work, and cheerfully resumed his dangerous duty in the park and elsewhere before his health really rendered it advisable for him to do so. After the siege his health completely broke down, and he died at Tien-tsin on the 29th September. He was also slightly wounded in the Legation compound.

Mr Smythe, too ill at the commencement for work, took his duty at the very earliest opportunity, and was always only too eager to supplement his own watches by relieving those who were worn out by the extreme length of the watches towards the end of the siege. His health suffered severely under the strain of his self-denying good nature, resulting in an attack of typhoid after the relief.

Mr Bethell's extreme youth made the work done by him as a volunteer the more specially noticeable. The strain and hardship brought on a sickness which necessitated his going to hospital for a short time during the siege, yet, in spite of this, he resumed his duty at the earliest chance.

Mr Russell's arduous, willing, and self-denying services in the commissariat, where he had charge of and dealt out daily the rations of the plainer foodstuff to foreigners and natives, excited general admiration, and they were always rendered with the greatest cheerfulness. The important and difficult work of milling the grain, in obtaining which he was also largely instrumental, was also entrusted to him.

I cannot conclude this despatch without saying a word of praise respecting the ladies of all nationalities who so ably and devotedly assisted the defence, notwithstanding the terrible shadow which at all times hung over the legation—a shadow which the never-ceasing rattle of musketry and crash of round shot and shell and the diminishing number of defenders rendered ever present. They behaved with infinite patience and cheerfulness, helping personally in the hospital or, in making sandbags and bandages, and in assisting in every possible way the work of defence. Especially commended are two young ladies—Miss Myers and Miss Daisy Brazier—who daily filtered the water for the hospital, in tropical heat, and carried it with bullets whistling and shells bursting in the trees overhead.

The Marquess of Lansdowne to Sir C. MacDonald
Foreign Office, February 10, 1901

Sir,

I have received and laid before the King your despatch of the 24th December, enclosing a report, in continuation of those already received, with accompanying maps, on events at Peking from the 20th June to the 14th August regarded from the military aspect.

As the present report completes your account of the siege and relief of the Legations, I desire to take this opportunity of stating how highly His Majesty's Government value these admirable and exhaustive records of an episode of the deepest historic interest.

The gallantry with which the defence was maintained by all the foreign forces engaged, more especially after the failure of the first relief expedition, and the consequent disappointment to the besieged, coupled with the energy and courage with which the efforts of the regular forces were seconded by the Legation staffs and other civilians, has commanded the admiration of the whole civilized world.

His Majesty's Government desire also to place on record their appreciation of the important part borne by yourself throughout this crisis. On the 22nd June, at the request of your colleagues, you took charge of the defence, a position for which, from your military training, you possessed exceptional qualifications; and from that date you continued to direct the operations of the garrison until the relief took place on the 14th August.

Information has reached His Majesty's Government from various sources that the success of the defence was largely due to your personal efforts, and more particularly to the unity and cohesion which you found means of establishing and maintaining among the forces of so many different nationalities operating over an extended area. Competent eye-witnesses have expressed the opinion that if it can be said that the European community owe their lives to any one man more than to another, where so many distinguished themselves, it is to you they are indebted for their safety.

I cannot conclude this despatch without asking you to convey to Lady MacDonald the thanks of His Majesty's Government for her unceasing and devoted attention to the comfort and welfare of the sick and wounded. Her work, and that of the ladies who assisted her, have earned the lasting gratitude not only of those who benefited by her ministrations, but also of their relatives in Europe who were kept for so many weeks in a condition of the most painful anxiety and suspense.

LANSDOWNE

INDEX

The Siege of Kars

INDEX

The Boer War: Ladysmith and Mafeking

Page references for maps are in italics.

INDEX

The Siege of the Peking Embassy

Page references for maps are in italics.